Barcode in Back

S0-BQY-923

THE ETHICAL TRAVEL GUIDE

'This is tourism with the lightest of touches. It's a new way of travelling for a new age. Book nothing till you've read it – it's the closest you'll get to guilt-free travel.'
Paul Heiney, television reporter and author

'*The Ethical Travel Guide* gives a refreshingly realistic interpretation of the age old quote "Leave only footprints and take only photos", showing how you can leave a positive impact on the places you visit and take away a new depth of experience and wonderful memories – Brilliant!'
Tarka L'Herpiniere and Katie-Jane Cooper, the first people to walk entire 3000-mile length of the Great Wall of China

'As ever, Tourism Concern is at the forefront of efforts to ensure that the benefits of tourism are shared much more equitably.'
Jonathon Porritt, Co-founder of Forum for the Future

'Proves that, rich or poor, we don't have to stay at home to save the planet, and travel needn't necessarily involve excessive consumption and retrospective remorse ... Easy to read and strangely compelling, *The Ethical Travel Guide* is an inspiration.'
New Consumer

'How to travel ethically: read *The Ethical Travel Guide*.'
Evening Standard

'Something to suit every taste and budget. This is the essential resource for responsible global travellers.'
www.hippyshopper.com

'A directory of exciting and inspirational holiday experiences which do not exploit or damage the local community to suit all tastes and budgets.'
The Bookseller

'If you are going to travel the world, *The Ethical Travel Guide* is a great route planner to help you understand the cultures and environments of people, and to contribute the maximum while disturbing the minimum.'
Peter Shield, www.naturalchoices.co.uk

'This travel guide will ... shed a whole new light on travelling and give potential travellers many new and wonderful ideas for alternative vacations.'
www.treehugger.com

'Ethical travel means that everybody wins: visitors get closer to local communities, which receive more for their efforts. This guide takes you straight to the people who matter and is packed with exciting holiday ideas you won't find in the brochures.'
Dr Nick Middleton, travel writer and Fellow in Physical Geography at Oxford University

THE ETHICAL TRAVEL GUIDE

Your passport to exciting alternative holidays

Polly Pattullo and Orely Minelli

with Patrick Hourmant, Paul Smith,
Lee Viesnik and Amica Dall
for **Tourism Concern**

publishing for a sustainable future

London • Sterling, VA

First published by Earthscan in the UK and USA in 2009

ISBN: 978-1-84407-758-8 (hardback)
       978-1-84407-759-5 (paperback)

Typesetting by MapSet Ltd, Gateshead, UK
Cover design by Susanne Harris

For a full list of publications please contact:

Earthscan
Dunstan House
14a St Cross Street
London, EC1N 8XA, UK
Tel: +44 (0)20 7841 1930
Fax: +44 (0)20 7242 1474
Email: earthinfo@earthscan.co.uk
Web: **www.earthscan.co.uk**

22883 Quicksilver Drive, Sterling, VA 20166–2012, USA

Earthscan publishes in association with the International Institute for Environment and
Development

A catalogue record for this book is available from the British Library

Library of Congress Cataloging-in-Publication Data

The ethical travel guide : your passport to alternative holidays / by Polly Pattullo ...
[et al]
    p. cm.
Previous edition cataloged under: Pattullo, Polly, 1946–
Includes index.
ISBN: 978-1-84407-758-8 (hardback) – ISBN: 978-1-84407-759-5 (pbk.) 1.
Tourism—Moral and ethical aspects. 2. Tourism—Social aspects. I. Pattullo, Polly,
1946- II. Pattullo, Polly, 1946- Ethical travel guide
G155.A1E87 2009
910.46—dc22

                                                                    2009006495

At Earthscan we strive to minimize our environmental impacts and carbon footprint
through reducing waste, recycling and offsetting our CO_2 emissions, including those
created through publication of this book. For more details of our environmental policy,
see www.earthscan.co.uk.

This book was printed in the UK by MPG Books,
an ISO 14001 accredited company. The paper used
is FSC certified and the inks are vegetable based.

CONTENTS

────────DIRECTORY────────

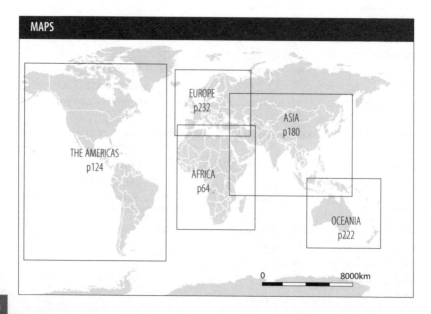

MAPS

EUROPE
p232

ASIA
p180

THE AMERICAS
p124

AFRICA
p64

OCEANIA
p222

0   8000km

FOREWORD

Tricia Barnett

The Ethical Travel Guide is much more than an innovative and stimulating guide to some of the most exciting holiday experiences around. It is an inspirational tool in Tourism Concern's fight to ensure that local people always benefit from tourism.

Thousands of grassroots, low-impact, high-sustainability initiatives all over the world struggle to tell tourists that they exist. Very few of these inspirational initiatives have the resources or skills to market themselves within an industry dominated by multinational companies. *The Ethical Travel Guide* is a challenge to the stranglehold that Western-based companies from the wealthier nations have over the distribution networks of the tourism industry.

This guide provides an opportunity for struggling communities and dedicated local entrepreneurs to tell us about the experiences that they can offer. Entrepreneurs can show how, even at the top end of the market, they can contribute positively to those who share their environment. And the market is lapping it up. The first edition of this guide went to reprint within a month of publication and has already been translated into Dutch and Italian.

The new, updated *Ethical Travel Guide* now includes over 400 places in over 70 countries, many of which will not be found in other guidebooks. Entries include places to stay, organizations, trips, tours and projects, from canoeing the backwaters of the Amazon to luxury breaks in the Indian Ocean. You can stay in very simple local-style accommodation in the rainforest or more sophisticated hotels. But they all have one thing in common. They all support the local economy, bringing much-needed wealth to communities which have struggled to survive. It is a tribute to enterprising people all over the world and a fulfilment of Tourism Concern's commitment to ensure that people in all destinations benefit from tourism.

This ground-breaking book has a hard-hitting introduction by Polly Pattullo, journalist and travel writer, who highlights many of the issues such as displacement of local people, poverty, cultural erosion and environmental degradation that most tourists are unaware of. So, while it provides holiday-makers with fantastic ideas for authentic and guilt-free holidays, it also raises awareness of how this huge business impacts upon the world.

Of course, all good guidebooks get updated. The entries listed in this book must meet our strict criteria – although we are not able to visit them all. They have to fill in an in-depth questionnaire that covers environment, employment policies and community commitment. If they simply tell us that they employ locals, then they're rejected. What: no training scheme? No effort to bring the women into managerial positions? No effort to buy your supplies locally or no commitment to reducing your footprint? Then you won't fit in here. Since our first edition we have gained some amazing new entries. Some are entirely owned by the community, others by businesses working in partnership with the communities, and others are supported by non-governmental organizations. All of them have a great deal to offer – not least with their stories and their enthusiasm.

What is powerful is the number of entrepreneurs who seem to no longer know whether they are a business or a development agency. They have begun to see tourism as a vehicle to help bring development to communities who want it. Many want to help redress the imbalance between the luxury they are offering to visitors and the poverty that surrounds them. This raises difficult issues. Often it is not necessarily about philanthropy, but about opening up opportunities for local people to create add-ons to the hotel: hiring out the horses, opening up cafés and restaurants, laundry services or handicraft businesses.

It has been truly inspiring reading what some groups are up to. Social entrepreneurship abounds with wonderfully creative activities and enjoyable events for all involved. But if you just want to chill out, you have more than enough choice here.

The Ethical Travel Guide is part of an extraordinary movement flourishing all over the world, which involves people in remote places who recognize that they have access to wonderful environments and cultures that others might enjoy. A group in East Timor might not have the least idea of what is happening in Peru. But we in Tourism Concern do, and it is a pleasure to be able to show them off to you. None of them, by the way, has paid to be included in this guide. All of them are places that are keen for you to visit. The warm welcome is genuine.

What is so exciting to know is that if you choose one of these holidays, you'll not only have a great time, but possibly be actively contributing to some wonderful development work. You don't have to be a volunteer to know that the money you are paying for a pleasurable time is contributing to positive change.

Go, have an adventure and enjoy yourself in the best way possible – know that not only do you benefit, but your hosts will too.

Tricia Barnett
Director, Tourism Concern
January, 2009

DISCLAIMER

The enterprises listed in this book are the result of exhausting, but not exhaustive, research. If we have missed anything, please forgive us and let us know about it.

All listings and prices are correct at the time of going to press. We cannot take any responsibility for changes that might occur. We have tried our utmost to ensure that each tour or holiday is beneficial to local people – not just because they're being employed, which we take for granted, but because they actually get something positive in return. It can be the opportunity for workers to gain proper career training; get paid fair wages or ensure that their children will receive an education; that they'll benefit from some health services; or get to share in the profits and decide for themselves where the money is best placed for the community to profit as a whole. We strongly believe that the most authentic, genuine experience comes from people who welcome you because they've been part of the development of the project. They have either some ownership or community investment. But, again, we cannot guarantee that this is the case. Please do tell us if there are issues around community benefits that have concerned you.

Tourism Concern offers a free service to all those enterprises that are listed. No one has paid to be included. But neither do we endorse any of those who are listed here because we do not have the capacity to inspect every one. So there is no Tourism Concern kitemark – just our hope that you will get pleasure from the commitment, passion and energy that is often behind the projects included in this book.

The exciting fact is that the majority of the listings have websites. This is a revolution for many of them that are remote and have no other marketing budgets. They are an invaluable asset and can give you far more information than we are able to, so please use them.

ACKNOWLEDGEMENTS

Tourism Concern has been blessed with the following skilled and supportive contributors. Without them, there would have been no book: Corinne Atwood, Rosalina Babourkova, Benjamin Carey, Stroma Cole, Shirley Eber, Janet Gunter, Nigel Hetherington, Christopher Imbsen, Jonathan Karkut, Neville Linton, Paul Miles, Claire Milne, Oscar Vasquez Monsalve, Louise Norton, Polly Pattullo, Sara Serras Pereira, Victoria Tongue, Monica Vecchi, Mark Walmsley, Tanya Walmsley, Nigel Watt, Elizabeth Williams, Duncan Williamson and Xavier Zapata for writing the informed country introductions; and to Roy de Graff who suggested how we should prepare for our travels.

Other backstage help has come from Roger Diski and Chris McIntyre, who checked Africa out for us, and from Pat Farrington, a stalwart editor, and Emily Walker, an excellent picture editor.

Last, but not least, many thanks, too, to the Tourism Concern members who wrote in about their holiday experiences.

BE PART OF THE MOVEMENT FOR CHANGE

TourismConcern

Fighting Exploitation in Tourism

www.tourismconcern.org.uk

You've bought the guidebook, and hopefully you'll book the holiday. Stay part of this unique movement for change in tourism.

Tourism can be fairly traded and all of us can benefit from it. To find out more about Tourism Concern and to keep up to date with new developments, sign up to our Campaign Action Network via our website, join our Facebook group or contact us at info@tourismconcern.org.uk, telephone +44 (0)20 7133 3800, or turn to the back of the book for details of how to become a member.

UNDER AN ETHICAL SKY

Polly Pattullo

A morality tale

Tourism is no longer a dirty word in Mae Klang Luang, a small village in the Dol Inthanon National Park in northern Thailand and a couple of hours drive from the city of Chiang Mai. In the past, Thailand's tourists – numbering some 13 million a year – had little interest in such places, with their modest clusters of bamboo and thatch homes set on gentle slopes among rice fields. Instead, they piled into the beach resorts of the south, forged to succour the dreams of stressed-out Westerners. Thailand is good at providing such respite (see page 212); but it is not so good at nurturing a tourism that benefits the many Thais who have seen their traditions and communities overrun by hordes of hedonists.

What a handful of Thai villages – and Mae Klang Luang is one of them – are now offering is quite the opposite of mass tourism. Community-based tourism is where visitors stay in local homes, have a glimpse into traditional life, and, most importantly, where management and benefits remain with the community. This means that villagers are properly paid, their culture is respected, and decisions about what the tourists do and see remain with the villagers. No longer, as used to happen in Mae Klang Luang, do tourists arrive unannounced, ask for drugs, show no respect, gawp at the villagers, and depart leaving rubbish but no money. Instead, a radical shift in the balance of power means that tourism now benefits the village, while the visitors glimpse the ways of local people. There is a hike through the forest, learning about the use of plants, a visit to the village organic garden and the fish farm, sipping cups of freshly roasted coffee (fairly traded to the Chiang Mai Starbucks, say the villagers), and, of course, there is plentiful food and the hospitality of a village family for a night's sleep. There is even a small museum full of household equipment and old tools. Even in Mae Klang Luang plastic is replacing terracotta and bamboo, and Som Sak, one of the key villagers behind the tourism initiative, knows that the village must hold on to its heritage.

Indeed, at Mae Klang Luang, tourism has replaced a negative dependency on poppy-growing and the degradation of the forests. As Som Sak said: 'If tourism is one part of our economy, we can save the forest. It is sustainable.' Essentially, tourism has become a tool for development. It is a way for the village's rice-growers, organic flower farmers and foresters to become decision-makers and to continue their lives in a sustainable way.

The same positive reaction to tourism has also been gathering momentum in the often overexploited fishing communities of Thailand's south. In Koh Yao Noi, for example, one villager recognized how tourism could strengthen their culture. 'The sea is normal to us', he said, 'but interesting to tourists. In the past, we didn't see it as important; but taking visitors fishing makes us see things differently. Our tourism is not what you get from a hotel; but our service is from the heart.'

What is happening in Thailand is a completely new approach. But such positive results do not happen by accident. Progress in Mae Klang Luang and Koh Yao Noi was made possible through a radical partnership between tour operators, both local and international, and the communities themselves, initiated by a small Thai non-governmental organization (NGO) called the Community-Based Tourism Initiative (CBTI). Their work creates an important model, and one that provides a power base for the hosts: as Peter Richards, a CBTI worker, said: 'Villages are not products – they are being empowered by the process.' It also nurtures a fruitful relationship for the tour operators – and a fascinating holiday for the tourists. CBTI is also responding to what a small but growing body of holiday-makers want. As one tour operator who works with the CBTI told some community leaders: 'Our guests are looking to discover your way of life, not a prefab additional or one that you think they might want. They could go to a theme park for that.'

An Akha host on one of CBT-I's community-based initiatives in northern Thailand (see page 213)

CBT-I

New role for consumers

Community-based tourism is just one of a number of terms used to describe holidays that benefit both the traveller and the destination. Hard and fast definitions may not exist; but the words 'green', 'responsible', 'fair trade', 'positive' or 'ethical' tourism ('ecotourism' is another term, but is now often associated with greenwash and limited to environmental concerns) are all about treading lightly on people's homes and cultures, about a positive interaction between guests and host countries, and about an awareness of our impact on the well-being of the places where we take our holiday. Essentially, such holidays seek to minimize the negative impacts of tourism and to maximize the benefits to hosts.

Sometimes this might sound sanctimonious or a bit po-faced. Those who use the phrase 'politically correct' to denigrate such experiences like to sneer at the terms 'ethical' or 'responsible' tourism. Critics say that those who promote ethical tourism are snobbish elitists, who are idealizing some pristine age before Tuscany, Barbados or 'that little place in Kerala' had been 'ruined' by 'ordinary people'. The implications are that the holiday-makers who try to be ethical are holier than thou and that their holidays are not really holidays at all, but some sort of wearisome social-work project disguised as pleasure.

This could not be further from the truth. Holidays such as those at Mae Klang Luang are as much fun, and can provide as much excitement and wonder as any other sort of holiday. As it says on the website www.responsibletravel.com: 'If you travel for relaxation, fulfilment, discovery, adventure and to learn – rather than simply to tick off "places and things", then responsible travel is for you.' Responsible tourists can make a difference by getting closer to local cultures and environments and by involving local people.

Travelling to benefit the destination as well as the traveller has become a talking point. The growing crisis of climate change has focused our attention on the environment and the damage we do to our planet and its peoples. It also makes us reflect on what we, as individuals, could and should be doing about it. That's not looking backwards. It represents the cutting edge of thinking. While the travel pages of newspapers have been slow to pick up on this, they no longer ignore the debate. Travel articles about 'green' skiing, about the problematic growth of golf courses or whether it's acceptable to swim with dolphins now crop up more regularly, at least in the 'broadsheet' newspapers. As the *Observer* (26 June 2005) newspaper commented: 'Go on holiday and save the world may sound like a title of a Ben Elton sketch; but the idea seems to be catching on.' Such articles at least sow the seeds of the idea that tourism is a human rights issue.

A brand-new role for consumers in the tourism market has emerged from three trends: first, there is a thirst for different and more 'exciting' holidays; second, there is a growing realization of the negative impacts of tourism – its clod-hopping footprints in other people's homes in the deserts, forests, seashores and mountains of the world; and, third, of course, is climate change. These moods have come together to build a demand for a new type of holiday encapsulated, perhaps, in the 'slow travel' movement, which emphasizes the pleasures of the train over the plane, the reflective moment rather than instant gratification.

However, the ideas behind ethical tourism are also part of something broader – a global consumer movement, which is strengthening as people flex their muscles and make conscious choices about how they spend their holiday money and why. These ideas may be strengthened as economic recession and climate change trigger unprecedented navel-gazing into the choices we have to make for a sustainable future. At the same time, there is also evidence of a change in business practices, evidence that some companies are beginning to embrace a 'social good' element in their policy thinking. These ideas are, too, filtering down to the tourist industry.

The fair-trade movement is a pioneer of this; it is proof that there is a new wave of people power that can provide producers in developing countries with a fair share of the returns from the sale of their produce. Just as more consumers are choosing fairly traded coffee or bananas because they know that such a purchase supports a small coffee grower or banana farmer, rather than a multinational company, so they are beginning to seek a 'fair-trade' type of holiday.

While fair-trade products benefit the producers on the ground, so fair-trade tourism maximizes the benefits to the host countries and their workers. The fact that you can now not only read about 'fair-trade', 'responsible' holidays or 'ethical' holidays, but also go on something approximating one, shows how far tourism is changing for the good.

Meanwhile ... bigger than ever

Nevertheless, holidays like these – like the ones featured in this book – are very special. They do not represent a typical pattern of a holiday, either for the holiday-maker or for the 'tourism providers'. Most tourists remain willing participants in mass tourism, the traditional arm of what has become the world's largest industry – with an annual revenue of almost US$500 billion, according to the World Tourism Organization (WTO) – and the fastest growing.

Nearly 900 million international tourist trips were taken in 2007. This was more than 52 million than in 2006 – which is about the same num-

El Silencio in Costa Rica is a luxury lodge and spa where guests can simply relax, or take yoga classes in the lodge's studio (see page 137)

El Silencio Lodge and Spa

ber as visit Spain each year. In 2020, the WTO tells us that the total will have nearly doubled – to 1.6 billion. Yet, at present, only a tiny percentage of the world goes abroad on holiday: so, despite economic gloom, tourism has virtually only just begun. These figures do not include tourists travelling within their own countries: for example, the extraordinary growth in domestic travel by the Chinese, who, according to the *Economist* magazine, are taking 1.6 billion trips at home every year.

World tourism was expected to generate nearly US$8 trillion in 2008, said the World Travel and Tourism Council, and to provide more than 200 million jobs, with one third of those people working directly in the industry. In fact, one in every ten of the world's workers – from executive managers to chefs, to bellboys, hair braiders and scuba dive instructors – is to be found in travel and tourism. And they are distributed far and wide: in 83 per cent of countries, tourism is one of the top five sources of foreign exchange.

Before the 1960s, travel to places far flung from Western capital cities was an elite pursuit, often an extension of colonial connections. The British upper class, for example, would be seduced by advertisements to 'winter in the West Indies'. Then, as the cost of flying decreased, more and more people could afford a package holiday, first to Spain or Greece, and, later, to further away places, such as Florida, Barbados or Bangkok. The mania for flying now even extends to weekend breaks to Rio de Janeiro or to a South African game park.

Wild China offer tailor-made trips that go off the beaten track, such as this journey to a village in Hunan province (see page 185)

Emma Starks

At the same time as more of us want – and have the money – to travel, the world has become more accessible. Nowadays, you don't have to be a hairy-chested anorak or ascetic travel writer to holiday in a remote part of the globe. 'Ordinary people', who only a generation ago would have spent two weeks enjoying tea and egg sandwiches in their own backyard, are now white-water rafting in the Rockies, bird-watching in the Arctic or trekking in Laos.

Such shifts are reflected in the statistics. In the mid 20th century, Western Europe and North America attracted nearly all of the world's tourists; but by the end of the century, tourists were busy searching out the long-haul destinations. By the mid 1990s, 20 per cent of Europeans and North Americans took their holidays in the developing world (the 'South'), with more than 70 countries (more than one third of the membership of the United Nations) receiving more than 1 million international tourists a year.

In the UK, for example, we took 60 million trips abroad in 2007: 12.5 million to Spain, with France not far behind. But more and more of us went further afield, and growth rates to the Middle East, Asia and the Pacific are particularly high. Until the latest downturns in the global economy, it was estimated that long-haul destinations, in general, were likely to see growth rather than those closer to home. In 2007, for example, the Middle East (the Dubai factor) recorded the highest growth rate (13.4 per cent) of all regions, with Europe showing the lowest at 4.2 per cent, despite Europe's leading position as a tourism destination; France and Spain still trump the USA as the world's most visited countries.

We feel that the world is ours to explore – we have a right to roam. We can go almost anywhere, safely (despite terrorism), in comfort and without having to plan too much for ourselves except the journey to the airport: tour operators, travel agents, ground handlers, tour guides, hotel receptionists do the rest. Yet, this privilege can, in some ways, diminish our enjoyment. So much is now researched, parcelled up, packaged; little is unpredictable or open ended in our travelling patterns.

Why be a host? What's in it for them?

So, what has this new world of travel possibilities done for the South, those corners of the world which are now accessible to anyone with a passport? The answer is that while tourism can create enormous opportunities, it has also plunged the South into debt and dependency, has dissipated cultures, destroyed environments, and caused pain to many. How has this happened?

At first, the idea of earning dollars from tourism appeared to be a terrific idea. The South has, after all, spectacular ready-made natural resources and many magic cultural carpets to sell. As a result, many developing countries turned to tourism as a way out of poverty. A generation ago, tourism became an engine of development. At the same time, international organizations also deemed tourism to be a good thing and preached the message that tourism would attract investment and stimulate the economies of struggling developing world countries. In 1967, for example, the Organisation for Economic Co-operation and Development (OECD) declared that tourism was 'a promising new resource for economic development'. Money poured into mainstream tourism projects. Later, bodies such as the World Bank and the International Monetary Fund expressed their support and provided funds, often linking tourism aid to debt repayment strategies. More recently, the European Union also began to fund tourism projects. In the Caribbean, for example, as the banana industry collapsed in the wake of free trade adjustment, the European Union has poured money into tourism projects – and some would say as offsetting guilt at dumping poor countries into a free-market maelstrom.

The argument is that tourism generates foreign exchange at a time when income from traditional occupations such as agriculture is in decline. So, tourism becomes an attractive option. It provides jobs. It beckons the poor: being a waiter in an air-conditioned restaurant, for example, might seem more desirable than working all day in sun-baked fields.

In a highly interdependent world, poor countries have come to believe that tourism can help them out of their misery. And this philosophy remains on the lips of the tourism establishment. The secretary-general of the UN World Tourism Organization, Francesco Fangialli, has said:

> *Tourism is the major factor in the war on poverty. For most developing countries ... it is their largest single export and major driver of jobs, investment and economic transformation.*

Ban Ki-Moon, secretary-general of the United Nations, also endorses tourism:

> *When approached in a sustainable manner, travel for recreation can also help drive economic growth and alleviate poverty. In fact, tourism has proved one of the leading ways for the least developed countries to increase their participation in the global economy.*

Such claims have made tourism irresistible. In a generation, developing world countries have attracted tourists in their millions: they laid them out on their coral-edged beaches and piled them into their newly built hotels, which looked the same whether in Thailand or, half a world away, in Tobago. But by the mid 1990s, mass tourism had begun to lose some of its appeal for some consumers; it also began to lose its economic edge. In places, the resorts became a bit tacky, the coastline blighted and the entertainment somewhat hackneyed. Even fanatical sun-worshippers were prompted to stir, to rise from their sun beds to peer at more than their footprints in the sand.

And so ecotourism was born ('responsible travel to natural areas that conserves the environment and improves the well-being of local people', according to the Ecotourism Society) – a craze that was pounced on by hosts and tourists alike. By utilizing the hinterlands as well the beaches, ecotourism became an attractive possibility for countries that had never thought they had anything to offer the tourist. Cloud forests and boiling lakes, sizzling deserts and empty tundra regions began to be opened up to tourism. Ecotourism, it was claimed, satisfied the desires of the growing numbers of 'discerning' tourists who wanted a getaway from the holiday hordes.

Madagascar, for example, the fourth largest island in the world and a place of diverse beauty and cultural complexity, had no tourism industry until 1990; now tourism is its second largest source of revenue after coffee (see page 73). It was argued that tourism could help to conserve its natural resources and bring employment. If tourism could generate foreign exchange in Madagascar, one of the world's poorest and least visited countries, it could do so anywhere. The news spread.

In Dominica, for example, an island of rainforest, mountains and rushing rivers in the eastern Caribbean, tourism was slow to develop (see page 126). Then the cruise ships began to arrive – visitors poured off the boats and it was thought that tourism would bring wealth to all corners of the island. For many years, the people of the village of Vieille Case, on the remote north coast, looked forward to receiving tourists; but the tour buses from the cruise ships passed them by. Its people are self-sufficient farmers and fishermen; its community based around the church and local societies and cultural groups. They have been tourists themselves, on holidays or working trips to St Maarten or Antigua, and they believe that their community, too, has something to offer visitors. So, when the man from the tourist board paid a visit and said that tourism would help to sustain the economy and raise foreign exchange, the villagers were enthusiastic. 'We have the people who would make the tourists' time enjoyable, so we can take advantage of tourism', said one villager. Even a few extra dollars would help in times of economic pressure. And although the villagers are still waiting, the expectation remains that tourism will make a difference.

The Nanny Waterfalls in Jamaica, which can be visited during a stay at the Hotel Mocking Bird Hill (see page 131)

Hotel Mocking Bird Hill

Globalization: A new trip

With the world's tourist industry on speed, it appears that the only thing to stop it is an apocalyptic event such as the Boxing Day tsunami that swept across the Indian Ocean in 2004 or the urban devastation of 11 September 2001. A recession may put brakes on it, but it will not kill it.

Such events may keep people at home, but only for a time. Then, it's all go again: back to old places, exploring new places. The extraordinary expansion of tourism did not just happen because of cheap airfares, high-street travel agents and the internet. We now live in an economically interconnected world fanning out from the rich metropolitan centres of Europe and North America, which gives opportunities for investors to find business anywhere in the world.

Globalization is the term used to describe the way in which multinational corporations do business across the boundaries of nation states. And in a climate of free trade, major corporations can run roughshod over the countries and peoples of the poor South. In tourism, thanks to the World Trade Organization, restrictions on foreign ownership, repatriation of profits and the right to hire nationals have made it more difficult for developing countries to control their own tourism industry. But for impoverished governments, investors are like manna from heaven, and few questions are asked.

What is happening in Cambodia, for example, is the latest example of the easy pickings available in poor countries (see page 203). A long and detailed article in the *Guardian Weekend* magazine in April 2008 exposed the scale of the disaster:

> *Arguing that Cambodia could become a tourist magnet to chal-*
> *lenge Thailand, the prime minister began a fire sale of mainland*
> *beaches. By March this year, virtually all Cambodia's accessi-*
> *ble and sandy coast was in private hands, either Cambodian or*
> *foreign. Those who lived or worked there were turfed out – some*
> *jailed, others beaten, virtually all denied meaningful compensa-*
> *tion. The deals went unannounced; no tenders or plans were ever*
> *officially published.*

Dubious Western hedge funds, money launderers, the Cambodian government, British bankers and Russian millionaires all played their part in this carve-up, waiting to maximize their profits for when resorts and casinos replace the placid palms of this once little-known coastline.

Seriously damaging

This economic invasion of vulnerable countries is one aspect of globalization. But as protesters against global capitalism have shown, globalization has also made us aware of our responsibilities as global citizens. Climate change is one pressing example of the 'global village' syndrome in that how we behave affects others living thousands of miles away.

The concept of the global village has triggered an interest in the idea of global citizenship and shared responsibilities. As the *Earth Charter* (March 2000) states, its mission is to 'establish a sound ethical foundation for the emerging global society and to help build a sustainable world based on respect for nature, universal human rights, economic justice and a culture of peace'. Much of this new thinking has come from a growing concern about what the rich North has done to the poor South.

While thoughtful travellers, campaigning NGOs, long-sighted tour operators and radical organizers – in both the North and South – first began to discuss the uncomfortable impacts of tourism in the 1960s, international bodies have taken a lot longer to take action. Recognition of how tourism should be managed was first formally expressed as late as 1991, at the Earth Summit in Rio de Janeiro in its Agenda 21. This stated that 'environmental protection should constitute an integral part of the tourism development process' and that 'tourism development should recognize and support the identity, culture and interests of indigenous people'. Ten years later, the UN World Tourism Organization also adopted a global code of ethics addressing such issues as preventing the

Ecuador has a wide variety of landscape
for the traveller to experience,
including rainforest at Las Tolas
(see pages 49 and 167)

exploitation of women and children. In 2002, what is known as the *Cape Town Declaration* laid down conditions of what it saw as the characteristics of responsible tourism, and in the same year came the International Year of Ecotourism.

More recently, the United Nations Millennium Development Goals put forward a platform for all countries to address poverty and inequality; its goal is to halve the numbers of people living on less than one US dollar a day by 2015, and tourism was identified as a key sector in meeting those goals – in particular, through poverty reduction, gender equality and the protection of the environment. A 'pro-poor tourism' policy has also been adopted by the UK government's Department for International Development. Researchers, however, have discovered that little is really known about the way in which tourism can or does alleviate poverty.

What is clear, however, is that while tourism can be a tool of development, in many instances it is seriously damaging the health of people and places. The potential for good has, in many cases, turned sour.

Smile please, we're tourists

Meanwhile, we continue to book our holidays and delight in hearing that the people of our destination are friendly, smiling and welcoming. But this is not a commodity that anyone gets paid for. It is a human response to a human encounter; it is best when it is unexpected and unsolicited.

The manufactured smile, however, when tourist 'providers' have been trained to smile for the tourists, has a different context. 'Smile: you are a walking tourist attraction' was one slogan used in the Caribbean many years ago. That approach may have disappeared, but the requirement remains and it takes its toll on the workers. In the Dominican Republic, a country which now welcomes more than 3 million tourists a year, one hotel worker said: 'We have to smile to the tourists; but it is not what we are feeling in our souls. We want to work and we want to make your holidays happy. But it is difficult.'

And, then, if the tourists behave like new colonialists trampling over everything you hold dear, the smiles can fade away entirely. As the writer Martin Amis recognized when he visited a village in St Lucia: 'We stop for a can of orange juice and are unsmilingly overcharged. Although you wouldn't call them hostile, they are no more friendly than I would feel, if a stranger drove down my street in a car the size of my house.'

Perhaps, then, we need to ask: why should 'they' smile at 'us'? Have they anything to smile about? Not if they don't benefit from tourism and not if they have no real stake in its future and how it is managed.

Smiling and survival, for example, go hand in hand for the Kayan Padaung women of Burma, who have been refugees in northwest Thailand for a generation. Sometimes known as 'giraffe women', they wear brass rings around their neck, a cultural practice that has turned them into a tourist attraction. Visitors to their especially built 'villages', dubbed by the UN as 'human zoos', take their photographs and can try on the coils. The women see little of the money that the tourists pay to gaze at them. As one Kayan told the *Bangkok Post*: 'The tourists think we are primitive people. The guides say they don't want to see good roads or clean villages or anything modern, so we have to live like this to please the tourists.'

The Kayan are not free to say so; but, just occasionally, from different corners of the world, comes the call: 'Stay away' – don't get out that backpack, don't buy a ticket, don't get on a plane and visit us, however beautiful our home is, however delightful our people, however delicious our food, however spectacular our sunsets. These people are not diseased, crazy or criminal; their demand comes from the recognition that tourists make life worse, not better:

This ecolodge is located on the unspoilt coastline of the Andaman Sea in Thailand (see pages 213–214)

Thailand Koh Ra Ecolodge

> To all the tourists, visitors, travellers or whatever other name you are called: I beg you, please don't come [here]... Tourism is killing us. It is literally sucking the life out of us. We are running out of sweet water. Our lands have been sucked dry. When once there were taro fields and fishponds, today there are golf courses, hotels and urban sprawl.

That call came from Hawaii, one of the most tourist-drenched places in the world, in the mid 1990s (see page 153). Much earlier, during the 1970s, a young Caribbean politician had announced: 'tourism is whorism'.

In Hawaii, the concern was about what millions of visitors had done to its environment and its culture. In the Caribbean, also a region of vulnerable islands, the hostility came from the sense that offering your home up to visitors was a recipe for exploitation and servility, and an echo of slavery. Not much, however, happened to affect the flow of tourists when those appeals were made. Holiday-makers continue to flock to Hawaii, while tourism has become the lifeblood of the Caribbean.

Then, we didn't take much notice of what was being said. However, when, in 1995, the democratically elected opposition leader Daw Aung San Suu Kyi of Burma first asked the world to stop visiting her country until democracy is restored, there was some suggestion that the world, in part, heeded her request. Some tour operators were persuaded to stop taking tourists to Burma, celebrities pledged not to visit and ordinary tourists decided to boycott the military regime. The protest continues, and in 2008, Tourism Concern, Burma Campaign UK, the *New Internationalist* magazine and the Trades Union Congress launched a new campaign to persuade Lonely Planet to withdraw its guidebook to Burma.

So, although we may not be staying at home – although some people are doing that – we are beginning to make informed choices about where to go on holiday and how we might do things differently. Some people are also thinking about whether the numbers climbing Mount Kilimanjaro should be restricted (Peru now limits the daily numbers trekking to Macchu Pichu). Gradually, both environmental and political decisions are becoming part of the equation as more people recognize that there has been no equal opportunities policy in the tourism industry and that our blissful holidays can damage the planet and its people.

Who gets the money?

'Tourism makes some people extremely rich; but most of them live in the places from where the tourists come', the director of Tourism Concern once said. Tourism has not only become big in numbers, but sophisticated in organization. For the most part, the industry is based not in the countries where it operates, but in the great metropolitan centres of the north. In the UK, for example, two companies (TUI and Thomas Cook) control swathes of the UK travel market. These companies are not only tour operators, but also own airlines and hotels. TUI, for example, owns Thomson Holidays, which owns Thomson Flights and the largest UK travel agents, Thomson. Such a process, known as vertical integration, enables one company to service its customers at all points of a holiday. TUI also owns First Choice, which, in turn, also owns an airline; TUI has also bought up smaller tour operators such as Hayes & Jarvis and Exodus. It is now the largest travel company in the world, operating in 180 countries and with 30 million customers. Little escapes its grasp.

The way in which the industry is organized means that, for the most part, consumers spend much of their holiday cash in buying the package – before they leave home. Much of that goes into the pockets of foreign-owned companies in the host countries: not many nationals of poor countries get to own marble-floored hotels, shopping chains or flashy restaurants serving fusion food. Statistics vary; but some people argue that what is known as economic 'leakage' – the extent to which local economies lose (or never receive) the revenue generated by tourism – is as high as four-fifths the cost of a holiday. Even if it's not that high, leakage remains a serious problem for most host countries.

Studies have shown how this works. For example, you decide to go on holiday in Kenya (see page 67), a country famous for its tourism (wildlife safaris, glorious Indian Ocean beaches). Kenya is glad to welcome you for tourism is its biggest foreign exchange earner. You book through your local high-street UK travel agent or through a large tour operator online: all well and good, and certainly very convenient for you, the customer.

Your holiday costs UK£1500. Of that, 40 per cent goes to the airline and 20 per cent to the tour operator. That leaves Kenya with 40 per cent. But that is not the end of the story because a quarter of that 40 per cent goes on imports (essential for keeping the tourists in the manner in which they are accustomed), while nearly one third is used to service Kenya's debt. Your UK£1500 holiday leaves Kenya just UK£225 richer. None of this, however, reaches the Maasai, the pastoralist people who have lived for generations alongside the elephants and lion, wildebeests and antelopes: the animals you have come to see. In fact, many Maasai no longer tend their cattle on the great grasslands. Displaced from their land to create wildlife parks, they live on the margins. The only way in which they can benefit from tourism is to give up their culture and go to work as waiters, dancers or souvenir-makers.

How about an all-inclusive holiday to the Dominican Republic (see page 127) at UK£549 for seven nights in Puerta Plata? On an all-inclusive holiday you pay for everything upfront: flight, hotel, food, drink, entertainments, sports and so on. That's convenient for the customer, but not so good for those bars, restaurants, food stalls and guides outside the hotel premises. Once you have paid for 'everything', you may not want to spend any more money in the local craft shops, the bars, the roadside food stalls. And while all-inclusives – very popular, in particular, in the Caribbean – have been a successful and well-run sector of the industry, the grassroots see things rather differently. By and large, locals feels bitter about the glittering ghettos which have opened in their midst – local businesses only get the crumbs of the crumbs from those all-inclusive customers who have 'left their wallets behind'. 'Like an alien in we own land' is the title of a St Lucian calypso which describes the writer's feelings about tourism, in general, and all-inclusive hotels, in particular.

Pachamama in Peru offer visitors craft workshops, including learning to weave on a traditional loom (see page 178)

Pachamama Tourismo Alternativo

Or, how about the way in which European Union (EU) free trade agreements restrict the income developing countries receive from tourism? In 2000, the EU signed a free trade agreement with Mexico. This meant that Mexico (see page 145) finds it even harder to protect its own tourist industry. As a result, European companies, mainly Spanish and Italian hotel chains, now control some 90 per cent of tourism services on the Maya Riviera on Mexico's Caribbean coast. Tourists may get sun-baked and tequila-sated; but they are basically paying into the European and not the Mexican economy.

But surely, there is what is known as the 'trickle-down' effect: we might expect tourism to generate benefits across the economy. After all, tourists are demanding: they need feeding and watering and entertaining. They need someone to grow the food, make the furniture, bottle the beer and so on. But too often, in poor countries, tourists eat imported food and sleep in rooms where nothing has been made locally. Tourists demand their cornflakes and steaks, their cheeses and crisps – as if they were at home; and they want imported beers rather than local brands. All of this contributes to leakage. As a result, many tourism earnings are either retained by the tourist-sending countries or repatriated to them in some way. Somehow or other, it ends up with our hosts – not us – picking up much of the bill.

The Maldives, for example, is a scattering of more than 1000 islands (of which one quarter are inhabited) in the Indian Ocean. Tourism is the most important industry after fisheries, and more than half of all jobs are in tourism. It regularly features in polls of the world's most desirable destination. Perhaps this is because it was the birthday choice of Sir Philip Green, owner of Top Shop, who spent millions hosting friends on a private island with George Michael and topless dancers for entertainment; or perhaps it's because the One & Only Reethi Rah resort is man-made, shaped like an octopus, and sells US$300 flip-flops.

Many of the Maldives resorts that bask in unimaginable luxury are pinned on to a single island no more than 1m above sea level; and all that the islands themselves contribute to the tourist industry are a gorgeously benign climate and some swaying palm-trees. Nearly everything else that a tourist needs is imported, such as the beef-burgers from Japanese cows on the Reethi Rah menu. There is ample fish in the sea around the Maldives – before tourism, fishing was the main occupation – but no refrigeration. This means that the catch cannot be stored. Hotels need fish as and when they need it – they cannot be dependent on a poor catch day. So, fish has to be imported, as does practically everything else. Meanwhile, its people live in poverty – up to 42 per cent on just over US$1 a day, with more than 30 per cent of children under five suffering from malnutrition, according to the United Nations. Until November 2008, when President Gayoom was defeated in the island's first fair election, much of the income from tourism was pocketed by members of the regime. The Maldives is an example of how tourism is a deceptive benefactor.

One of the great defences of tourism is that it creates jobs. This is true. But what sort of jobs? Joshua, for example, works in a hotel on the Swahili coast in Kenya:

> I work 10- to 12-hour shifts and am paid 219 shillings (UK£1.50) a day; but not if you are sick or have a rest day. We are only meant to work eight hours a day; but if you don't do overtime then there is no point coming back tomorrow. The managers tell the tour operators we are earning a good wage because the operators don't want their clients to have to pay tips... Only the managers eat the food the tourists don't finish. We are charged a full breakfast of 600 shillings. They treat us very badly. They make us show how much we have in our pockets to stop us keeping tips.

Not all tourist workers, of course, suffer such bad pay and conditions. However, the tourist industry is notorious for being unorganized and exploitative. In much of the developing world, jobs in the tourist sector, many of which are casual, as they are in the UK and Europe, are characterized as being seasonal and part time, with a high turnover of staff. In the Maldives, for example, a newly ratified Employment Act (2008) that provides rights and benefits for tourism workers is being ignored. Staff do not have employment contracts and are considered as casual workers; wages have been kept low despite inflation; and local employees find their pay and conditions inferior to the many foreign staff. Campaigners in the Maldives have recently launched the Tourism Employee Association of Maldives; this aims to establish a trade union, a small but important step for beleaguered workers.

Jobs in tourism are also vulnerable to external events, such as hurricanes or terrorism. Tourists do not take risks; they do not travel to what they perceive to be dangerous places; they can always go elsewhere. When the tourists do not arrive, jobs are lost.

This happened in the wake of the political violence in Kenya following its election in December 2008. The effect on the tourist industry was catastrophic. UK charter flights stopped flying there; the Foreign Office warned travellers to stay away. Even hotels on the coast – hundreds of miles away from the violence – were nearly empty. The headmaster of the Gede primary school near Malindi, a prime tourist coastal resort, told the *Travel Trade Gazette* (8 February 2008) that three-quarters of his pupils' parents had been laid off. As a result, the children were not going home at lunchtime. 'It shows me their families have nothing for them to eat', he said.

Beyond those who work within the hotel walls are unknown numbers of workers in the informal economy. These are taxi drivers, shoeshine boys, the vendors, tour guides, prostitutes – all desperate to pick up the odd 'tourist dollar'. Not surprisingly, wages and conditions are hard. Porters, for example, work in some of the harshest tourism conditions in the world, carrying tourists' backpacks. From Macchu Picchu to the Himalayas, Tourism Concern discovered that porters faced poor wages and poor working conditions. In Nepal, the porters are poor farmers from lowland areas, 'as unused to the high altitudes and harsh conditions as Western trekkers'. They wear thin jackets and inadequate footwear. Yet, they are expected to be super strong. The reality is that they suffer four times more accidents and illnesses than Western trekkers.

Cruise-ship tourism is often associated with glamour, even if it has lost its upper-crust ambience. But for the workers on the cruise ships, life has never been cool. In the Caribbean, for example, which is the world's busiest cruise zone, many cruise lines employ European officers, with North American and Western European staff in the business and entertainment jobs, supported by a crew from the poorest parts of the developing world. These workers are often paid low wages and labour in shoddy working conditions. 'Conditions for workers below deck haven't improved in decades', said an inspector with the International Transport

Workers Federation. 'Many are reluctant to come forward and complain. To most people, workers on cruise liners are nonentities. They have an almost invisible existence.'

Losing your home and your job

Jobs also get destroyed by the arrival of tourism. One of the most alarming negative effects of tourism is the displacement of people from their homes and traditional occupations to make way for tourism developments. These are often multimillion dollar projects backed by powerful investors and local governments. Local people have little say in what happens.

Pastoralist groups in East Africa, for example, have been victims of a tourism policy that has promoted safari tourism at the expense of people. The Maasai have been one of the groups worst affected by displacement – thrown off the land that they and their animals have inhabited for centuries. Conservationists defended their policy of creating national parks and evicting people by arguing that nomadic groups such as the Maasai were responsible for over-grazing and the over-hunting of wildlife. The effect has been devastating. The environmentalist George Mombiot has reported that the Maasai have lost 'all but two of their major dry season pastures and drought reserves'. Now they are confined to spaces that cannot support their herds and their growing populations.

In northern Kenya, the Samburu district used to provide fertile grazing during the dry season for its pastoralists. Now, two national reserves have been created and the Samburu are forbidden to enter. Their watering hole, which provided them with the only pure water in the region, is now a turquoise blue swimming pool in the grounds of the Sarova Shaba Hotel. While tourists frolic, the Samburu have to rely on an inadequate water supply from the Uaso River for their cattle, which graze on land bare of grass. 'The plight of the Samburu is desperate... They were always self-sufficient in food; but without access to their dry-land grazing, their cattle are dying. The Samburu are now dependent on food aid to stay alive', wrote Jean Keefe, a writer on displacement in tourism. As one hunter-gatherer from Mau Forest, Kenya, commented: 'When the whites first arrived in this area, they thought we were wild animals and chased us into the forest. Now that they have found out that we are people, they are chasing us out again.'

One of the most notorious examples of how people have been displaced to make way for tourism has been in Burma, where organizations such as Tourism Concern and Amnesty International have condemned the disturbing link between tourism development and human rights abuses. In Burma, this has also involved forced labour. Tourists witnessed thousands of people – including manacled prisoners, women and children – being forced to help clean the Mandalay palace moat so that the military junta could promote the palace for tourists. In another part of Burma, at the ancient capital of Pagan, founded in the ninth century, more than 5000 people, who lived inside its walls, were told to pack their bags ready for removal to Pagan new town, a parched-earth site, some 5km from the old town. Their homes were destroyed to make way for tourism and the resort hotels that promote their charms online.

The tsunami of 2004, which killed many thousands of people in Asia and Africa, also washed away roads and homes. But post-disaster reconstruction has brought more pain to local people. Governments have seen the tsunami as an opportunity to plan for bigger tourism projects. In India, for example, where the tsunami made thousands homeless, the coastal states of Kerala and Tamil Nadu have been earmarked as emerging tourism destinations. When coastal communities were destroyed, villagers had to relocate, away from the sea. This created an opportunity for land developers to move in, buying up the coastline for hotel developments, forcing up land prices, and squeezing the people away from their homes and traditional livelihoods.

Tourism development does not have to be as ruthless as that to cause hardships to local people. The building of land-guzzling golf courses, particularly in Asia, has denied local people their land and their jobs, as investors have gobbled up land for the golf craze, while paying very little in compensation. There have been protests in a stream of countries, Thailand, Malaysia, Indonesia and the Philippines, at the way in which golf courses have invaded protected forest areas, ancestral lands and farmlands. Chee Yoke Ling of the Global Anti-Golf Movement in Malaysia wrote:

> The golf business dramatically widens the gap between the rich and poor. Contrary to the principle of sustainable development, the game, through alliances between politicians and developers, contributes to the conversion of livelihood-sustaining resources of the poor to opulence-sustaining resources for the rich.

The golfing craze has prompted the United Nations Economic and Social Commission for the Asia-Pacific to comment on the practice:

> Golf course construction has created widespread negative social, cultural and environmental impacts, particularly in the developing countries of the region. Typical impacts include forest destruction and air, water and soil pollution caused by the excessive use of chemicals.

Water rations

But golf courses do not just displace people and pollute the land: they consume vast quantities of water. In the welter of statistics, it has been claimed that one golf course in the USA uses enough water annually to provide at least 1200 people with their basic needs for a year. Golf course projects such as a proposed tourism complex at Cavo Sidero, Crete, continue to outrage environmentalists. As Professor Peter Warren, an archaeologist from Bristol University, pointed out in a letter to the *Guardian* (6 March 2008) about the Cretan plans:

> *The complex will impact severely on an unspoilt landscape of wild natural beauty, high botanical interest and full of ancient sites. There will also be a huge demand for non-existent water, met only by major desalination, which in itself has energy costs.*

And, like golf courses, tourists also use more water than the ordinary consumer. Indeed, the water 'footprint' of the Western world, as in our carbon footprint, is very high. There are already serious water shortages worldwide and a prediction of 'water wars'. The United Nations has claimed that 'The average tourist uses as much water in 24 hours as a third world villager would use to produce rice for 100 days.' Tourists need unlimited supplies of water – they are used to it at home and desire copious amounts on holiday: for drinking, baths and showers, swimming pools, overflowing fountains and green manicured lawns. But water, in

A kung fu lesson in Henan Province, China (see pages 184–185)

Emma Starks

developing countries, is often a precious commodity. More than 2 billion people lack access to clean water and sanitation, and 80 per cent of all deaths in the developing world are water related.

Put a hotel near a local community and the pressure on the water supply is acute. A Goan cartoonist, Alexyz, depicted the situation with these words:

> 'Goa has been declared a drought area', says one local. 'Except the areas of tourist hotels, tourist spots and ministers' bungalows', says another.

In Kerala, southern India, an environment famous for its waterways, local people say that the increase in tourists has led to a loss of fish stock and a decline in biodiversity. As the concreted world of tourism creeps over more coastal land, the water table is lowered; and water that once went back into the soil now pours off straight into the sea.

Exploring or exploiting the landscape

When tourists discovered that it was fun to be in the sun, it was coastal areas that became the first landscapes to be exploited. The United Nations has produced a long list of environmental damage caused by coastal tourism. It includes destruction of mangrove swamps (which protect the land and provide nurseries for fish), destruction of coral reefs (other factors are also to blame), erosion of beaches, sand mining, and pollution from water sports.

Another culprit is the gigantic – and very popular – cruise-ship industry. Its waste-dumping practices can create pressure on small countries with limited refuse sites or can contaminate the sea. According to the Bluewater network, now part of Friends of the Earth, a typical one-week cruise generates 50 tonnes of waste and thousands of gallons of grey water (waste from sinks and showers and so on) and sewage. Almost all is dumped: some is treated, some is not. And while the powerful cruise companies claim that they have done much to reduce pollution, the laws are lax, regulations often ignored and the majority of the big companies have convictions for dumping. Environmentalists are also increasingly worried by larger and larger cruise ships visiting such pristine environments as Antarctica and the Galapagos.

Away from the coast, damage to forests and rivers intensifies with the growth in so-called ecotourism. And while ecotourism sounds, like apple pie, as good as it gets, the pitfalls are becoming clear. Setting a hotel in the middle of a forest by a river does not qualify for an ecotourism badge if the sewage from the hotel goes straight into the river, forests get cut down to build the property and water is diverted from local communities.

Cultural loss

Closely linked to the damage that tourism can do to the environment is the damage to the human environment. As we have extended the scope of our holidays into remote places, we now see 'remote people' as part of our holiday landscape. Our interest in other people's cultures is not always sensitive. What are the implications, for example, of tourists photographing tribal peoples who now demand payment in exchange for becoming models in their finery? In a remote part of Ethiopia called South Omo, local tribes people – including the women of the Mursi people who wear lip plates – have begun to express their hostility to the tourist invasion.

Performing for tourists has become an income earner for tribal groups all over the world. But the income comes with a price. In Peru, for example, a representative of the Yagua tribe wrote that one community is made to:

> ... perform dances on no matter what day, which is contrary to our customs, since with us each dance would be performed at a particular time of the year, times which are festivals for us. Our brothers are exhibited to the tourists like animals, and have to be at their disposal so that they can take photos.

Tourists are also shoppers and love to buy souvenirs. Craft markets spring up to serve the tourists. They make money for locals, although sometimes what is sold is not local at all, but made on a different continent (often China) despite the logo on the candlestick, the T-shirt or the basket. What academics call 'authenticity', the true representation of a people's material culture, is subverted by tourism – reality lost through consumer demands for retail therapy.

Sun, sea, sand – and sex

The Dominican Republic, Thailand and the Philippines are where tourists go most readily and most often for sex. Their young girls (and boys) leave villages for the resorts, and the vagaries of a life of prostitution, whether highly organized or casual. The international sex industry flourishes when first-world punters holiday in faraway playgrounds and look for cheap sex – doing what they would not do at home in a fantasy world of moonlit nights on hot beaches. Children are particularly

vulnerable and the international organization ECPAT campaigns to protect children from commercial sexual exploitation.

HIV infection rates are also sometimes attributed to tourism. Tourists
bring infection to remote places; infection rates flourishes alongside sex
tourism. Similarly, the tourist trade provides an infrastructure in which
the drugs trade can flourish. Good communications systems provided by
tourism make life convenient for drug traffickers.

The social impact of tourism goes beyond the crude effects of drugs
and sex. The arrogance of Western tourists who bring their own moral
codes on holiday with them and expect locals to embrace them can create serious dislocation to distant cultures. Just seeing tourists wear inappropriate clothes can make local people feel marginalized.

Does anyone care?

These are all dismal indicators – economic, environmental, social, cultural – of what can go wrong with tourism. It is a chronicle that builds into
an unsustainable world of greedy tourists and helpless hosts, with the
tourists setting the pace in their quest for ever cheaper holidays. But as
the holidays in this book show, it doesn't have to be like that.

Over 20 years ago, tourism guru Jost Krippendorf predicted a change
in the thinking of tourists in his book *The Holiday Makers* (Heinemann,
1987). Once our basic holiday needs – eating, drinking, sleeping – had
been met, he argued, we would become more adventurous. We would
develop what he called social needs, and we would want those to be ful-
filled on holiday. To this end, Krippendorf foresaw 'an independent and
emancipated tourist, a critical consumer not only at home but also when
travelling'.

Krippendorf was right. More tourists want to be more like travellers
engaging in local cultures and places. This is one aspect of the trend away
from ready-made package holidays bought from the big tour operators
and towards do-it-yourself holidays, researched and bought over the
internet.

The marketing men and women in suits have also noticed a new trend
in holiday-making. Echoing Krippendorf, words such as 'lifestyle' and
'personal enhancement' have entered their vocabulary in response to
consumer interest. 'Lifestyle' decisions may or may not incorporate 'ethical' ones; but what is important is that consumer power now features on
the radar. Could ethical holidays become as trendy as boutique hotels?
Can boutique hotels be ethical? Could there be 'etho-chic' holidays?
Indeed, those at the luxury end of the market claim that their customers
are both aware and interested in sustainable tourism.

With Thailand Hilltribe, visitors take part in village daily life, here picking bamboo shoots (see page 216)

Thailand Hilltribe

As more people realize that the traditional profile of tourism has to change, we are beginning to ask questions about our roles and responsibilities as consumers. An 'understanding and knowledge of the perceived inequity of mass tourism', wrote Clare Weeden, a lecturer at the University of Brighton, is 'an important factor in tourist decision-making' (from a paper titled 'Ethical tourism: An exploration of the concept and its meaning for ethical and responsible tourists').

But how far have we come along that road? A focus group, set up by Weeden and recruited through Tourism Concern, discussed how the group had come to understand the impact of tourism upon the destinations they had visited. It was a shock, they said, when they first realized that tourism was not always 'a good thing'. One member of the group, a geography teacher, remembered a holiday in Southeast Asia:

> There was a lady cutting rice with a little implement, so I thought this was a good photograph and I took her photograph. She was very sweet and I gave her some cigarettes for it and I overpaid her and it changed her instantly into a beggar … it really was a shock.

It was this sort of culture shock and the experience of seeing widespread poverty ('I felt quite embarrassed about being there') that triggered awareness in this group, a key stage along the road towards becoming an 'ethical tourist'.

Leo Hickman, who spent a year living the 'good life' for the *Guardian*, described this new awareness as the 'mangetout moment'. He explained it as 'the rush of guilt that tells you that what you're doing – buying, say, a small pack of mangetout that's been air-freighted out of season from a field in Kenya to the supermarket shelf before you – is somehow a negative force on the world.'

Interested in change?

But what are we doing about it all? How interested are we in change? We have certainly become more aware of our power. As long ago as 1999, an early investigation by the *Ethical Consumer* magazine recorded that nearly half of us had a 'I do what I can' attitude when it came to making 'ethical' consumer decisions. While only 5 per cent of us were hard-line 'global watchdogs', 18 per cent were 'conscientious consumers', classified as more affluent than the 'do what I can' group. The least ethically aware were those with the lowest incomes: 22 per cent had an 'I look after my own' attitude. The problem, however, is that while some of us are concerned about ethical issues, far fewer of us actually behave ethically when it comes to our purchases.

A Mintel market research report on holiday lifestyles in January 2007 revealed disparate attitudes. It showed that while nearly one third of its sample tried to learn a bit about local culture before travelling, 36 per cent 'just want to relax and not be bothered with ethical or environmental issues'. That suggests, however, that nearly two-thirds of people at least register the concept. One fifth was concerned about the impact the holiday has on the local environment and 14 per cent would pay more for an environmentally friendly holiday. However, only a tiny proportion (4 per cent) had sought a holiday with an ethical code of practice and even fewer (3 per cent) had changed their holiday plans because of responsible tourism issues.

But different polls tell different stories. A poll in 2008 from the Association of British Travel Agents (ABTA) showed that 83 per cent said it was important that their holiday should not damage the environment, with 36 per cent saying that it was 'very important'. While care for the environment often scores highly in such opinion polls, the social and economic needs of local people are often less well addressed. In the ABTA poll, however, 77 per cent of holiday-makers believe that it is important that local people benefit from tourism, while 83 per cent believe in experiencing local food and culture. At a time of recession, it remains to be seen whether financial constraints bring an increase, or decrease, in ethical thinking.

ABTA did not reveal the demography of its poll participants; but Mintel suggested that the most 'ethical' group in the UK tends to be middle aged, relatively affluent and well educated. Internationalist in outlook, they are interested in how companies operate in developing countries. These activists may be a niche market; but they are also recognized as trendsetters, with money to spend. In 1999, *Ethical Consumer* magazine summed up this group as: 'potentially important as an engaged consumer group, more likely to act on ethical considerations in purchasing and in other relationships with companies ... they become potential advocates of those they consider ethical' and 'potential critics of those companies they perceive to be unethical'.

These consumers have, as it were, seen the ethical light. Not only are they likely to buy a fairly traded banana, but they are also likely to care about their holidays and the implications of how they spend their holiday cash. Educating the wider public into more ethical thinking, however, may be in for a bumpy ride. Whereas the 'concerned tourist' has emerged from its subculture niche into more mainstream thinking, it is not yet clear how far the general public will swing. In 2003, Mintel had declared: it is 'only a matter of time before public awareness of the impacts of tourism increases further'. In 2008, it concluded, however, that 'there may be an element of burn-out since in some cases there had been a decrease in those who followed a green or ethical agenda'.

At the cutting edge of thinking about ethical holidays are, not surprisingly, members of Tourism Concern. For them, the most important ingredients of a fair-trade holiday tend to focus on local consultation and local control; fair wages, good working conditions and employment opportunities; the use of local products and services; and respect for the environment and respectful consumer behaviour. This group also desires high-quality products and services (e.g. expert guiding) and report that tour operators should provide guidelines for responsible behaviour and information about the local culture. And, of course, they want the sort of experiences that everyone wants – excitement, freedom, relaxation, good friends, healthy food, clean water, clean toilets – and 'not too many other tourists (particularly if they are badly behaved)'.

There is growing unease about using other people's homes as a playground without a backward glance at the needs and desires of the host communities. Weeden's study concluded that:

> ... *ethical and responsible tourists are well informed about the issues of big business and market economics, they take an active approach to their holidays – being aware of the inequities of tourism is not enough for them; they want to make a change in their own behaviour and lead change in others.*

Oh, to be an ethical tourist!

However, whether we do what we say we want to do when it comes to choosing our holidays is another matter. We can aspire to do 'the right thing'; but often our aspiration does not quite match the reality. Sometimes it seems to be difficult to know how to do the right thing, or the enthusiasm to go to a particular place overrides our concerns about our impact as a tourist. We feel ethically challenged, but don't know how to make a difference – or even if we can. As Mintel has pointed out in an attempt to explain just why tourists were not becoming more ethically concerned: '[It] is probably a result of consumers feeling confused and helpless rather than truly jaded.'

Even members of that focus group recruited through Tourism Concern, and well aware of the issues around tourism, were confused. Not only did they find the concept of ethical tourism itself confusing, they also admitted to feeling guilty if their behaviour fell short of their good intentions. Ethical tourism is 'a goal, set up in lights, which is difficult to achieve', said one focus group participant.

In his book *A Life Stripped Bare* (Transworld/The Guardian, 2005), Leo Hickman recorded letters from readers who were also trying to live 'ethically'. What these letters show, as does Hickman's own honest assessment of his challenge, are that our actions are not based on a strict list of dos and don'ts, but are shaped by something more abstract: a sense of trying to make the world a better place even though, as one writer noted, 'one sometimes feels that the odds are overwhelmingly against'.

The need to know

One of the problems is that we're not sure how to be ethical. Consumer research shows that those who care are crying out for information about what we are buying. 'Three-quarters of the public agree that their purchasing decisions would be influenced if they had more information on companies' ethical behaviour', stated a 2003 MORI poll on corporate responsibility. And although it is getting easier to source fair-trade coffee or tea in the supermarket, finding a greener holiday is trickier.

We are still left somewhat in the dark when it comes to making ethical decisions about our holidays. This is not, as we have seen, because we are lazy or grouchy, uncaring or sloppy: it is because the tourism industry has – until recently – been happy to leave us ignorant and powerless.

Back in 1993, when ethical tourism was barely a whisper in even the most radical of salons, Tourism Concern, together with the World Wide Fund for Nature, conducted a survey of 69 companies and institutions from all sectors of the UK tourism industry. It found that the industry

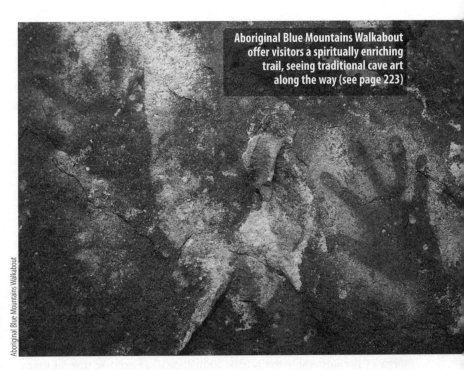

Aboriginal Blue Mountains Walkabout offer visitors a spiritually enriching trail, seeing traditional cave art along the way (see page 223)

Aboriginal Blue Mountains Walkabout

was 'generally aware' that 'long-term environmental and social problems can result from certain types of tourism, and that these can damage the business success of tourism'. In response, sections of the industry had adopted practices such as recycling and waste reduction, educating tourists with tips and advice on sustainable practices, or creating partnerships with local charities and groups. These were positive moves.

However, there were obstacles to further progress: large operators are committed to filling charter flights; this encourages a short-term perspective and allows the market to be dominated by customers who go abroad because it is cheap, rather than from a desire to experience foreign cultures and environments. Since then, cheap overseas holidays for UK tourists have become the norm, with the no-frills airlines leading the way. This has added urgency to one of the fundamental debates for ethical tourists – to fly or not to fly (see pages 42–48).

The survey concluded that sustainable tourism was seen as an 'expensive niche product' and that many companies felt that it was not their responsibility to review their corporate behaviour. The companies put the blame on local governments and consumers. 'It's what the consumer wants' (cheap holidays in Bali) or 'these local governments don't have proper planning regulations (build a resort on the last remaining mangrove swamp) were some of the arguments offered.

Winds of change

Then, in 2001, when the Voluntary Service Overseas (VSO) launched a campaign on UK tour operators' attitudes towards fairer tourism, it found that action was piecemeal, with the smaller operators in the forefront. The VSO concluded that 'an overarching ethical policy addressing a broad range of social-economic issues was rare ... there is still a long way to go before the social, economic and cultural problems raised by tourism are fully addressed'. Indeed, in the same year similar tendencies were reflected by the development agency Tearfund in its report *Tourism: Putting Ethics into Practice*. This showed that only half the companies that responded had any kind of policy regarding responsible tourism, and just one third gave information to their tourists on responsible behaviour.

It has been a slow and reluctant journey. Indeed, a tardy response from the tourism industry is somehow implicit in a comment by Fiona Jeffery, the chair of the World Travel Market, a vast annual jamboree for the industry held in London. In 2008 she wrote: 'The industry is beginning to recognize that it has to behave more responsibly. Many consumers demand it – and we must listen.' And Jonathon Porritt, co-founder of the think-tank Forum for the Future, has warned that, with climate change and other problems coming together to create 'a perfect storm of pressures' for the tourist industry, 'it's worrying that so many tourism businesses still haven't woken up to the daunting environmental, social and economic challenges that are about to engulf them' (quoted on responsibletravel.com).

Now, however, there appears to be a slowly developing head of steam towards a much more proactive agenda, mainly led by some heroic small tour operators, but shifting into the mainstream. Winds of change are in the air. And, as commentators have pointed out, Marks & Spencer and B&Q thrive on socially responsible policies in the retail business. If they can do it, so can the tourist business.

As Ian Reynolds, the former chief executive of ABTA, which represents all the major stakeholders in the British tourism business, told Tourism Concern: 'Initially, it was just specialist tour operators who took an interest in this [responsible tourism] ... now the major tour operators are showing a much greater interest because they see the benefits' (quoted in *Tourism in Focus*, Spring 2004). And it's not, he said, just because of saving costs, but 'because it's a good point to make with consumers who are beginning to appreciate this'. Even the conservative UN World Tourism Organization has recognized that an increasing percentage of people care about the strain that tourism puts on developing countries.

Guests on Pachamama's tours in Peru can try their hand at traditional crafts such as ceramics (see page 178)

Roger Enríquez

Who is doing what?

The pioneers of ethical travel have been those small specialist tour operators, often founded by one person with a passion for a place and desire to share that expertise and experience with others. Often they were practising responsible tourism before the term had been thought of. Now, however, there is a coherent vocabulary to express the philosophy behind ethical tourism, a clearer set of objectives to work towards and a greater will to make it happen. Look on the websites of many specialist tour operators and you will see a clear mission statement – the vision and responsibility of the company – and also the responsibilities of the traveller. The prize-winning Rainbow Tours, for example, which works in Africa, states: 'We aim to turn the rhetoric of "ecotourism" into reality through our code of practice.' That code of practice emphasizes the local: working with local partners, fostering development in marginalized economic communities, promoting less well-known destinations.

Exodus, another adventure tour operator, is bigger and is now owned by TUI; but it too upholds a commitment to responsible tourism. As its website says, it is 'dedicated to responsible travel' and asks its clients to remember that: 'We realize that every destination is someone else's home. We should leave places as we would like to find them. We should ensure that communities benefit from our visit.' Both Rainbow Tours and Exodus are members of the 18-strong Ethical Tour Operators Group, initiated by Tourism Concern to support its members in 'the challenge of running a socially responsible tourism business'.

But, until recently, it was hard to know that any of this was happening in the mainstream industry; the boardrooms seemed to be playing the ethical game close to their chests – if, indeed, they were playing it at all. None of the big companies flagged their social responsibility policies. The silence prevented tourists from making an informed decision about the people who were arranging their holidays and prevented other tourism workers from sharing such good practice. This is still true up to a point, but a raft of recent initiatives is making the task of the caring consumer easier.

Along with the individual policies of the pioneers, tourism organizations are becoming more proactive. The UK's Association of Independent Tour Operators (AITO), which represents many of the specialist companies in the tourism business, now has a set of responsible tourism guidelines for its members. The guidelines govern general good practice and are now a precondition of membership. Its website claims that the AITO is 'the first tourism industry association to incorporate into its business structure a commitment to responsible travel and green tourism'. In 2008, the AITO introduced a new five-star responsible tourism policy for members to work towards. To achieve this, operators have to show that they have implemented – and continue to improve on – their responsible tourism policy. By 2008, 8 of around 150 of its members had achieved five stars, including Explore and Tribes Travel, both members of the Ethical Tour Operators Group.

These small companies – all flag-bearers – can only skim the surface of the travel industry. And, until very recently, the travel giants had not been interested in sustainability. But things seem to be changing even within the multinationals, driven, in part, by the legal requirement since 2006 for public companies to report on social and environmental matters. The thinking, say experts, is that those who avoid addressing their corporate social responsibility (CSR) do so at their peril. As the *Economist* reported in January 2008:

> CSR is booming. Whether through electronic screens, posters or glossy reports, big companies want to tell the world about their good citizenship... Their chief executives queue up to speak at conferences to explain their passion for the community or their new-found commitment to making their company carbon-neutral.

Chris Thompson, responsible tourism coordinator for the Federation of Tour Operators (FTO), whose members sell 70 per cent of UK package holidays, says that 'sustainability is now top of the agenda. It's critical to the core business.' It brings 'huge benefits'. And in 2007, the FTO launched its global Travelife programme, a scheme that hotels can use to measure sustainability. It offers a three-tier award scheme for best practice in hotels, which is being worked on by mainstream operators such as First Choice and Thomas Cook. Auditing started in 2007 and a couple of hundred hotels have already been assessed.

Indeed, First Choice, the largest travel business in the UK, is making a serious attempt to address its own carbon footprint, and its environmental and social responsibilities at its destinations. It is looking internally to change its own culture and is encouraging staff to engage in sustainable tourism projects around the world. It has also initiated the company's World Care Fund that helps fund the charity, the Travel Foundation – with 50p of every sale (customers can choose to opt out) going to the Travel Foundation to support its grassroots projects and 50p to Climate Care, the emissions offsetting scheme.

Thomas Cook, too, is beginning to address sustainability. Its brochures for winter 2009, for example, replicate Tourism Concern's mission statement in a commitment to responsible tourism on the first spread, explaining that the company is a 'strong supporter of ethical and fairly traded tourism and believes that holidays should be as good for the places visited as they are for the people who visit'. That is a ringing statement of intent, but perhaps one that is a little hard to square with the content of its brochures, gleaming with pictures of swimming pools and golf courses surrounded by concrete resorts arising out of the arid landscapes of the Mediterranean. But auditing is taking place – 285 properties have already been assessed, with 42 reaching award status. Thomas Cook says that those who fail the auditing test are assisted to move forward. 'We would not consider pulling out of a hotel due to it not reaching award status; the whole point is to get hoteliers on the path to sustainability', says its sustainability manager. They may have some way to go because, according to Lyndall de Marco of the International Tourism Partnership: 'The vast majority of hotels haven't started to implement sustainability measures. Sustainability is the last thing on the minds of general managers. It is the customer who is making it happen.' So the picture is very mixed.

Yet, Chris Thompson of FTO believes that consumers should, in the future, be able to move beyond the niche operators in their search for a sustainable holiday:

> Sustainability has been associated with ecotourism and people think that if it's not ecotourism you can't have sustainability. This is rubbish – everyone can reduce their impact. Now that there's more information for the consumer, it's about widening your vision.

The mainstream industry donated UK£1 million in 2007 to the Travel Foundation, largely from consumer donation schemes. This allows the Travel Foundation to help change the industry through educational schemes, awareness training for travel agents, and grassroots tourism projects. Such initiatives trickle down to consumers in their search to find information about ethical holidays.

Checking their credentials

But even glowing mission statements and celebratory announcements of good practice are not necessarily proof of the ethical pudding. Claims by tour operators, governments and even NGOs can turn out to be 'greenwash'. They may embrace the concept – recognizing that their customers are beginning to demand it; but, masked by slick marketing, there is sometimes little real evidence of good practice. As the Tearfund report (2000) sternly concluded:

> Simply writing a responsible tourism policy is no longer enough. Clients are becoming increasingly discerning and can see through companies that simply pay lip service to responsibility,

but do little to change the way they operate. Companies will need to show practical examples of where they have made a difference.

But the problem is how do we tell? It's hard to punish the greenwashers by withdrawing our custom if we have no means of measuring one business against another. Some people argue that certification schemes can go some way to expose and shoot down the greenwash cowboys. But what schemes are there to help consumers make a discerning decision?

Numerous accreditation schemes exist, put together by different groups and focusing on different aspects of tourism in different locations. Many operate within Europe, and most are based around beaches or hotels and concentrate on environmental practices. The result is that it is difficult to assess what is on offer; it is rather like comparing apples and pears. More importantly, perhaps, the schemes are rarely independently evaluated.

In 2000, the influential website www.planeta.com carried out the first public global review of ecotourism certification. Ron Mader of planeta.com wrote that while good intentions lay behind the idea, 'most of the programmes contradict one of the main components of ecotourism – local control. If certification programmes are not developed with broad support from various stakeholders, these initiatives jeopardize the goals they intend to support.' Mader claimed that most schemes failed to consult the grassroots, which, in many cases, did not feel that certification was a key to their well-being. It was the consultants seeking endorsement for particular schemes who were in favour. This point is supported in a 2003 report by the Pro-Poor Tourism Research group, which discovered that few of the standards schemes examined the issue of how tourism could be used to fight poverty. Most concentrated on environmental concerns such as water-saving exercises rather than the socio-economic issues that affect poor people.

Green Globe is an international scheme that was launched in 1992 by the World Travel and Tourism Council at the first Earth Summit in Rio de Janeiro. Green Globe did some noteworthy work and promised much. However, its critics have pointed out that anyone can join Green Globe, and that by paying a fee and promising to 'aspire to environmental improvement', any member can use their logo. They also pointed out that Green Globe members include resorts that may have achieved environmental benchmarks but fail, for example, in relation to employees' rights. As Mader also points out, Green Globe, like many international programmes, 'does not provide a message board or forum to discuss specific concerns'.

One of the best-known national accreditation schemes is the Certification in Sustainable Tourism of Costa Rica (see page 132), a country that has made pioneering strides to promote sustainability. Its tourism gurus claimed that tourists are:

> ... demanding a more active, more interactive tourism, with greater respect for the socio-cultural and ecological interests of the local communities, with higher standards of service, and with the ability to protect and regenerate the natural environment as well as to learn about local customs.

Their certification programme, in part, responded to these needs, and is now expanding to cover other countries in the region. It covers 83 properties with grades of one to five; out of these, only three hotels have attained a level five.

What it failed to do, however, was to engage smaller businesses: some people argued that its rigorous and labour-intensive questionnaire alienated the small community-orientated properties. America's Rainforest Alliance has now stepped in to work on expanding the benefits of sustainable tourism certification to smaller enterprises. The alliance is also planning to create a tourism standard throughout the Americas.

On the other side of the world, the Fair Trade in Tourism South Africa (FTTSA) scheme has certified 30 businesses, at both the luxury and budget end of the industry. Elsewhere in Africa, the Ecotourism Society Kenya has given top rating to two safari camps, with 6 businesses gaining silver and 21 bronze. Small specialist tour operators sometimes draw up their own reviews of business partners based on social and environmental performance. Tribes Travel, for example, one of the industry's most dedicated advocates of ethical travel in Africa and South America, has drawn up an 'eco-review' of the accommodation it uses based on social and environmental performance. 'We aim to give our clients plenty of information,' says Tribes Travel, 'thereby giving them the knowledge to allow them to travel with respect and sensitivity. They also become an integral part of our "auditing" process by the feedback they give us after a visit.'

What, then, is the future of certification? There are two potential developments. First, there is the rise of Web 2.0. As Mader says:

> The ease of gathering traveller feedback will be critical in raising standards across the board. Travellers are heading first to sites such as Facebook, Flickr, TripAdvisor and YouTube to learn about the pluses and minuses of individual operations. The next big step will be the consumer demand that national, regional and city government sites inform potential visitors what options are available for those interested in ecotourism, responsible travel and voluntourism.

With Amahoro Tours in Rwanda, guests stay overnight with a family, participating in their daily life, as well as having the opportunity to visit the mountain gorillas (see page 75)

Michael, Amahoro Tours

Second, many people are also looking forward for a Fairtrade label for tourism. This is a massive task and the fair-trade movement, led by Tourism Concern, is getting to grips with research into how such a label could be developed.

Community challenge

In the meantime, the small operators remain the standard-bearers, offering an ethical alternative to the mass rip-offs of host countries by the tourist industry. They have also been in the forefront of establishing partnerships between themselves and workers in the destinations. As Ron Mader has pointed out:

> *Communities are taking the lead… Now the monies are flowing to grassroots efforts, and community-based tourism operations are increasing around the globe. New synergies have arisen that connect localities with regional and international tourism partners.*

This is exactly what is happening in Thailand, where under the Community-Based Tourism Initiative (CBTI), all the players who put together a holiday have come together to discuss their needs and expectations. The village communities say they want help in appropriate marketing and networking, while the tour operators want to learn how things could be done better, and how to listen to local voices and educate their customers.

Similar partnerships are building all over the world. The porters in Nepal, Kenya and Peru whose lives have been blighted by harsh working conditions have come together with UK tour operators, local workers' organizations and NGOs to promote change as part of Tourism Concern's campaigning work. Guidelines have been drawn up to ensure that porters are treated properly: establishing a maximum load, providing shelters and setting up educational programmes. In Peru, the Machu Picchu Porters' Syndicate led a strike in September 2001 demanding regulation on porters' wages. There is now a US$8 a day minimum wage. While some indigenous porters working around Machu Picchu still suffer 'humiliation upon humiliation', others have created alternative trekking routes and tourism campsites. The internet is again taking the lead, with the useful website www.leaplocal.org, based in Peru, providing information on local guides and companies, advocating best practice and organizing training of guides. As the website says, by travellers recommending guides online, the guides who do not have the resources to promote themselves get support and publicity. Some committed tour operators also provide English language classes for porters in the low season. With English skills, they have opportunities to become cooks and guides, and to develop a career in the tourist industry.

Tourists notice such changes, according to Adventure Alternative director Gavin Bate. Having a policy on porters' rights provided:

> ... a strong incentive for clients to book with us... When those same clients come to Africa or Nepal and see firsthand how treating people's/employees' rights has a direct effect on the level of enjoyment, the professionalism, the standard and the success of their expedition or holiday, it makes them feel part of a family.

Human rights organizations are also becoming involved in tourism, supporting indigenous peoples to protect their cultures and to benefit equitably from tourism. The Minority Rights Group, for example, is campaigning with groups in Kenya to support the rights of pastoralists. 'The time has come for all stakeholders to join hands in making the shift towards ethical solutions,' it states, urging that a tourist industry can thrive alongside empowered indigenous communities.

The tourism literature is now full of material describing and analysing the workings of community projects that promote ethical or fair trade, and looking at how different institutions and management structures help or hinder such development. Local ownership and control, often in partnership with Western tour operators, is a growing pattern. The holidays in this book are part of that movement, and are growing fast as local people build on the connections between what their environment and culture can offer, the work of sensitized tour operators, and what the more aware tourist is looking for. As Mader points out, the use of the internet also offers another important development: the possibility for communities to become active players, interacting with partners and using the internet to promote their communities and cultures.

The 2008 winners of the www.responsibletravel.com's annual awards all demonstrate that best practice in tourism is far reaching, and extends beyond what was once understood to constitute tourism – the bubble of plane, hotel and beach. The winner of the poverty reduction award, for example, was Gambia is Good (GIG), an initiative in which both local farmers and tourists benefit. Hoteliers in the Gambia (see page 116) have traditionally imported much of their food while ignoring local farmers whose produce was going to waste. Now, 1000 farmers, most of whom are women, have been helped to supply local hotels. At the same time, the Travel Foundation, one of the funding organizations, and GIG have launched their own farmyard – to demonstrate best practice and to become a tourist attraction on its own merits. Taking tourists to the GIG farmyard, for example, is one way in which they can see how their contribution to sustainability is working.

Such an initiative is about tourism reaching out to create benefits for local communities and to shift relationships between guest and host. It has the ability to empower and transform lives. Liliana Martinez Gonzalez, for example, from the Isla de Chira in Costa Rica (see page 132), found that tourism created a political change among the women of her community:

> When the people saw what we had done, they started to call [our new lodge] the 'ecotourism project of the women of Chira'. They referred to us as 'the women of Chira, the women who work'. The men began to look at us differently. They began to change the way they treated us, not treating us badly anymore. We soon began to realize that we were women and that we had many rights, especially the right to work freely, not pressured by others. We had rights to do what we needed to do for our lives. When we realized all these rights, it felt like a huge liberation.

Another Costa Rican woman, Patricia Chavez, from El Copal in the central valley region, discovered an exchange of benefits from tourism:

> Before [we began the ecotourism project] we never knew the importance of the forest or tourism. We'd say, what's the forest for? Now we see that we can have tourists here and that they get excited about the natural beauty we have. We're thrilled to have something to offer to foreigners and even to Ticos [Costa Ricans]. Now we meet more people and learn from them, and they learn from us, too.

Such examples show how tourism can work to sustain and maintain. Out of this come positive results: children go to school, women are empowered, communities survive, old people retain respect, environments are cherished. And consumers from the rich North get holidays that earlier generations of tourists could never have dreamed of.

Getting it right

Yet, consumers are not going to book an ethical holiday just for the sake of paying the producers fairly or contributing to a village library fund or supporting goat-rearing projects. Research suggests that ethical consumers want high standards and value for money just like any other consumer: they are, in fact, a bit fussier than the average holiday-maker. They don't just want a delightful hideaway using solar heating and recycling of waste; they want that same hideaway to provide high-grade local food (without Thousand Island dressings) and to listen to local music (not wall-to-wall muzak) and an opportunity to get in touch with everyday life. They want everything to be just perfect: a hard act.

At the same time, a new, cool image of ethical tourism, which is far removed from concepts of worthiness and hippy do-gooding, needs to be inclusive. It needs to address entrenched assumptions in customer relations as well as in its relationships with host communities. It's not, for example, just white people who go on holiday. 'Non-white faces in travel brochures are rare except as smiling foreign waiters and exotic entertainers', said Michael Lomotey, who is black British. 'Perhaps it's assumed that black people all travel to visit friends and relatives and have no interest in travelling for leisure like everyone else – a crazy business assumption. Or is it unspoken racism within the tourism industry?'

So, tourism is a tricky business and getting all the relationships to work is complicated. Often, communities anxious to benefit from tourism develop lodges or reserves, treks or facilities, but do not quite know what tourists want or need. One fishing village on the Araya Peninsula in Venezuela, for example, planned some tourist cottages; but they built them with the living accommodation facing inland, away from the sea. Often, such communities also have no expertise in selling their wares, nor do they have access to sophisticated marketing or public relations mechanisms.

Ruaha Hilltop Lodge in Tanzania is typical of the predicament of those tourism businesses without the clout and connections to market themselves. Owned by a Tanzanian businessman who built a small lodge a few miles outside the Ruaha National Park in southern Tanzania, it has everything that a responsible tourist might look for: it is built of traditional materials, the owner is a local man, as are the workers, the food is locally sourced, the owner is well connected to the local community. In total, the lodge 'pushes all the right buttons' for the ethical tourist. But it was not doing as well as the more luxurious and European-owned lodges nearby. The owner had struggled to make contact with tour operators who would bring him the custom he deserves, but he was not part of the international network. At one point, he also wondered whether a European management team would be more effective. A revamped website helped him to gain some business; but other forms of marketing and networking remain a problem. Successful community projects need to be nurtured and mentored by marketing experts.

Roger Diski of Rainbow Tours, a pioneer of community tourism in Southern Africa, says that access to the market is the most difficult and costliest challenge for small businesses. 'For the lucky few, a chance encounter with a tour operator, or links with a proactive NGO, can be the significant factor in success', he says. For example, an encounter with Rainbow Tours brought success to an innovative township tours and homestay business in Cape Town. The owner, Fizal Gangat of Cape Capers, linked up with Rainbow Tours and now employs several guides, has a fleet of vehicles and has moved, says Diski, beyond the township tours to offer mainstream tours along the Garden Route.

When Jeannette Hyde, a *Guardian* journalist, visited the Cape Town townships with Cape Capers in 2004, she said that it changed her life, that it was some kind of 'political awakening'. She wrote:

> The people in the squatter camp and the unemployed in the hostel are part of a world in transition, a jigsaw puzzle that made more sense when I went out to the countryside, whale watching and back to Cape Town, where the only black people seemed to be waiters. (*The Guardian*, 14 March 2004)

Those processes – the opportunities to generate economic wealth at the grassroots and the transformational experience of the guest – are fundamental to ethical tourism. Given the chance – and there are more and more ways to sample such experiences – consumers are recognizing the difference. Because going ethical is about having a better holiday. We, the tourist, can be part of the solution and not part of the problem. So, keep on taking our holidays to their homes. The welcome, the smile, might just be genuine.

CLIMATE CHANGE: TO FLY OR NOT TO FLY?

Tricia Barnett

Given the heightened awareness of the contribution of flying to climate change, how should the ethical traveller best manage their responsibilities to the planet? Holidays can, if carefully managed, generate significant income for impoverished destination countries. As such, tourism is actively promoted by governments and international financial institutions as a means of economic development. So, what would be the consequences for these countries if tourists decided that long-distance travel is no longer an option? As it is, many destination countries are already bearing the brunt of the impacts of climate change, such as the rising sea levels threatening to engulf low-lying island states such as the Maldives, and violent hurricanes that rip through the Caribbean with increasing force and frequency.

These are ethical dilemmas that have not been much in the public arena. Flying has featured heavily in the debate on climate change, as has the fact that poor countries are facing a problem not of their making. However, there has been minimal discussion in the UK about the interplay between tourism, development and global warming and how these should best be managed.

A few facts

Certain facts speak for themselves. First, in the long term, international tourism shows no signs of slowing down, with China, India, Russia and other emerging economies becoming major players. Three-quarters of British outbound tourists travel by air. Since the 1960s, global air passenger traffic has risen by nearly 9 per cent per year. Airfares are around 42 per cent cheaper today than they were ten years ago in real terms.

Air travel is currently responsible for emitting 700 million tonnes of carbon each year, and is growing at a rate of 5 per cent annually. This amounts to about 3 per cent of total global emissions. Long-haul international flights cruising at high altitudes add substantially to the problem. Aircraft pollutants released into the high atmosphere have an enhanced

A sad flycatcher, one of the many species of bird that can be seen in Jamaica (see pages 130–131)

Mike Read

greenhouse effect, and aircraft emissions are thought to be at least twice as damaging as ground-level emissions. Short-haul flights are disproportionately polluting because of the large amount of fuel they burn in order to reach cruising height, followed almost immediately by a descent.

The airlines' claim that they are scapegoats and that aviation represents a mere fraction of the problem. They also claim to be developing new technologies to reduce their impact on the environment. For example, British Airways aims to halve its carbon emissions by 2050. But their reduction plans are largely dependent on emissions-trading schemes, which are themselves problematic.

Taking a position

Hard-line campaigners argue that, with global warming on the increase, flying to take a holiday is no longer an option. At the other extreme are those whose position is often embedded in their business as tour operators, who argue that we should not just focus on flying when there is so much else that we do which results in the emission of greenhouse gases. They are more likely to suggest carbon offsetting flights as a way of managing the problem. This position is supported by the UK government through its aviation and climate change policies. It acknowledges that travel and tourism contribute to climate change, but at the same time supports the expansion of the industry.

Somewhere in the middle are those who would like to travel ethically and who support the rights of people living in developing countries. They recognize that those people are not responsible for global warming and that without alternative livelihoods, their lives will be further embedded in poverty if holiday-makers fail to arrive.

Unsustainable solutions

Carbon offsetting was, for a while, considered to be the way through this dilemma for travellers. However, whether carbon offsetting does anything more than making owners of offsetting companies wealthy and appeasing our own guilt has since been called into question. First, offsetting does not prevent our flights from contributing towards global warming; it also allows travellers to think that they don't need to reduce their emissions at source. Funds raised through offsetting schemes are not necessarily spent in the most meaningful and beneficial manner. The consumer clearly has a role in reducing carbon emissions; but the imperative must also lie with national governments and international bodies to take full responsibility by legislating and regulating industry to effect the required systemic changes.

Our partner organization in India, Equations, speaks for many when it argues that for:

> ... fossil fuel companies and airlines, offsets represent an opportunity to 'greenwash' their activities. Offset schemes tend to lull the customer into falsely believing that human activity that directly exacerbates climate change is effectively 'neutralized', with no impact on the climate. So, airline companies ... oppose aviation taxes and would never advocate that people simply choose not to fly unnecessarily. Instead, through carbon offset companies, they would rather present the section of climate-conscious passengers with the option of flying 'free from concern' over the impact of their emissions. This shift to what is essentially an unregulated and disputed form of eco-taxation away from the company and onto the consumer has gained airline companies an enormous amount of favourable but farcical publicity. (Equations, March 2008).

Carbon trading is also questioned. Airline companies – like other industries and economic sectors – are allocated a limit for carbon emissions each year. If they go over that limit, they will need to buy extra carbon credits from other sectors or companies which will invest that money to improve their own carbon footprint. Known as carbon or emissions trading, this mechanism is thought by some to be the best incentive to finance and implement clean technologies. The response from the South questions this. T. T. Sreekumar from the National University of Singapore and co-founder of Kerala Tourism Watch writes:

It was with great pain and bafflement that the developing world received the news of the European Union's decision to enforce carbon trading. The market argument has been overstretched and it fails to address the issue of social justice in any satisfactory manner. It helps legitimize increased exploitation of Southern energy sources by the North, a strategy that clearly smacks of neo-colonial economic subjugation. (Contours, no 3, October–November 2008)

In addition, biofuels, first welcomed as a possible alternative to fossil fuels, have become a traumatic contributor to the rising costs of food, as land has been turned into massive agri-businesses that feed no one and contribute to the loss of biodiversity. Neither carbon trading nor biofuels are sustainable.

Dependency on tourism

Tourism Concern has always challenged the 'monoculture' approach to tourism growth that leads to a precarious overdependency on what is a highly fickle industry. However, until more balanced ways of bringing in revenue have been established, it's important to hear what people living in the developing world have to say when we make our decision to fly or not to fly.

Guests with Footprint Vietnam work closely with the local population, finding ways to employ traditional handicrafts and agriculture for tourism purposes (see page 217)

Footprint Vietnam Travel

Fei Tevi from the Pacific Conference of Churches in Fiji recognizes the fragility of small islands, particularly low-lying ones. The impacts will be disastrous for the islanders. He is, however, also well aware of the fact that earnings from tourism contribute substantially to gross domestic product (GDP). The tourism industry's World Travel and Tourism Council estimates that by 2018, tourism will be worth 80 per cent of GDP in Antigua and Barbuda, and account for 95 per cent of all jobs. This will be the highest dependency on the planet. The Caribbean is already the most tourism-dependent region in the world, constituting 31 per cent of GDP. The transition to another economic sector that would generate similar income returns to tourism is something that Tevi thinks the bigger countries can consider. A better strategy for the low-lying coral atoll countries is to develop new policies that will lead to reduced emissions in the destinations themselves (Contours, Thailand, October–November 2008).

Felix Finisterre of St Lucia argues that since the removal of preferential trade tariffs for bananas (previously St Lucia's main export crop), his Caribbean island would face mass unemployment without tourism. Although tourism in St Lucia is not typically characterized by fair wages and exemplary working conditions, the consequences, if tourists stopped coming, would be disastrous. Alternative livelihood options are extremely limited. The island is non-competitive in manufacturing and export, even for inter-island and regional trade.

El Silencio is a luxury lodge and spa located on a 500 acre tropical cloud forest reserve in Costa Rica's pristine central volcanic region (see page 137)

El Silencio Lodge and Spa

What are the choices for countries such as St Lucia? Not only does tourism create employment in both the formal and informal economy, but it opens up opportunities for linkages into other sectors, not least the environmental sector. Tourism helps to conserve the environment and opens up new sites and attractions for livelihoods. Tourism is the best guarantee of environmental conservation – loss of the industry would result in overexploitation of St Lucia's natural resources, including forests and fisheries, as people search for alternative means of subsistence.

In particular, the British and European market is critical to St Lucia, providing 30 per cent of annual visitors. On average, European visitors stay longer than their American counterparts, contributing more to the economy. Finisterre argues that their loss to the tourism industry, should British and European visitors decide not to travel so far because of global warming, would result in the loss of vital government taxes and, to put it simply, 'social chaos'.

A suggested way forward

Tourism Concern does not believe that to simply stop flying is the solution, as this would destroy the livelihoods of many people who depend upon tourism for an income. However, we are committed to promoting a responsible and sustainable approach both at home and while visiting other people's countries on our holidays.

Governments should be doing so much more. They must take urgent steps to devise and implement conventions, protocols and resolutions to reduce climate change. International agreements should include fuel taxes for aircraft, and governments must commit to limiting aviation growth while investing in sustainable energy technologies.

The tourism industry lags behind many others in recognizing its responsibilities in relation to climate change and the environment. It has an enormous carbon footprint. It consumes huge quantities of water and energy and fails to manage its waste. It must reduce its climate footprint and seek out and invest in alternative sustainable energy technologies. It has to invest in a sustainable future.

National destination governments must recognize the imperative of legislating to reduce energy and water consumption in tourism establishments. They, too, must look to investing in renewable energy and developing mitigation and adaptation projects.

Every organization involved in tourism has a responsibility to work towards change.

Personal responsibilities

Most of us can do more to cut our own personal emissions – both at home and when we are away.

Tourism Concern supports people in destinations to get a better deal from tourism. We have never suggested that we should not travel. But we do have to do it better: forget weekend trips to New York for shopping or a long weekend to Dubai for the fun of it! When we do go, we should go for as long as we can and we should go less frequently: one big trip a year – maximum if we are flying. Even better, if we want to travel far afield, this would be one long-haul holiday every alternate year – maximum. And, when we get there, we should treat it with respect and ensure that our hosts feel pleased that we have come. We should all do what we can to use public transport where possible, limit water use and switch everything off in our room when we are not in it. We all have the responsibility to do everything we can to balance our presence there on an environmental front – including telling the hotel manager how important the environment is to us and that the little red button maintained permanently on their televisions really ought to be switched off.

TRAVELLERS' TALES

Bob Dall stayed in a home in Las Tolas, a community in the Andean cloud forests of Ecuador (see page 167).

As a frequent business traveller, I am accustomed to staying in good hotels with all modern facilities, so it was with some trepidation that I went to stay in René and Maria's house in a tiny Andean village in Ecuador. The house, built by René from local wood, was luxurious by local standards and boasted a number of bedrooms and a modern bathroom, even though it was outside. Having a bath depended on René carrying water up a steep hill from a communal tap and filling a tank on the roof of the bathroom.

The house was perched on a narrow steep-sided ridge high in the cloud forest. From the back of the house, there were stunning ever-changing views over the valley. One minute there was bright equatorial sunshine illuminating the vibrant colours of the trees, the next minute clouds formed and swirled in the valley below. Frequently, the mountain was wrapped in cool, soft cloud which obscured the view, but provided a welcome relief from the searing power of the sun.

My hosts were extremely friendly and put me to shame with their knowledge of English and their enthusiasm to learn more of the language. I struggled to communicate with them, having no knowledge of Spanish. The other inhabitants of the village were friendly and curious.

My short stay with René and Maria gave me insights into the life of the village and the impact of the modern world on their way of life, which I could not have gained in any other way. Tourism is an opportunity to diversify away from logging and subsistence farming. It also brought me face to face with the conflict between the developed world's desire to preserve environments such as the cloud forest and traditional ways of life and the local population's desire to access the comforts and opportunities of the developed world.

Lucy Eyre went to Ethiopia and found that the country has two underexploited natural resources when it comes to tourism – breathtaking landscape and hospitable people. TESFA Community Tourism (see page 66) makes the most of both of these in this exhilarating travel experience.

The TESFA format is simple; but it's clear that it is the result of careful planning, thorough training and considerable attention to detail. The TESFA tourist is made comfortable, but not spoiled; your basic needs are ably taken care of, leaving you free to revel in the sensation of walk-

Guests and hosts review pictures in
Romania (top; see page 241) and
Nepal (bottom; see page 194)

Bagus Place Retreat

Bagus Place Retreat is a secluded island paradise resort in Malaysia, only accessible by boat (see page 211)

ing through a landscape almost unchanged for thousands of years, far from hotels, 4x4s and other tourists.

The two main features of this trek are the sleeping sites and the walks between them. At each of the 'camps' there is a central building, where meals are cooked and eaten, and houses where the guests sleep. These buildings are solid circular structures made from dark grey stone. Comfortable beds and warm blankets are provided, as it gets chilly after dark at an altitude of over 2700m. There is also a particular winning feature: the long-drop lavatory with a spectacular view.

Each morning, your luggage (soft bags only) is loaded on to donkeys and sometimes (in a rather humiliating display of their superior strength) men and boys. You walk to the next site accompanied by two guides: one from the immediate local area and another English-speaking TESFA employee from the nearby town of Lalibela. En route you encounter wondrous views – the 10,000-foot-high escarpment, eagles and buzzards soaring below your feet, gelada baboons – and glimpses of daily life in the area: yellow-robed priests walking to church, women and girls washing clothes at the pump, farmers ploughing steep rocky fields (using an ox and a steel-tipped stick), children playing (who take the opportunity to ask your name and practice their English).

When you arrive at the next site, your luggage is waiting for you, as are friendly staff with tasty snacks, perhaps chunky pancakes with local thick, white honey and a cup of tea. After a shower – an elevated water-bag with a nozzle and a wooden screen – and a photogenic sunset above the mountain ranges, dinner is served. The meal might consist of pasta and tomato sauce or chicken stew with spinach and rice (this is not what the locals would eat, it is important to note; but the cooks have been trained to provide what tourists like). Sleep beckons after the day's walking; but you can't quite bear to stop looking at the mass of stars in the clear skies above you.

With seven sites (and plans for more), you can make the trek last over a week or do a smaller trip visiting only a couple of sites. Although the walking is at an altitude of between 2700m and 3200m, much of the trekking is flat and gentle. If you wish, you can hire local horses to take the pressure off your legs. Even if you don't wish to ride, it's worth inviting a horse into your party as they come beautifully decorated with red pompoms. On a typical day, you cover around 25km; but there is no need to rush – you can take the whole day to potter between camps. I have done the trek with a 7-year old and a 64-year old. The Ethiopians refused to believe my father was this old – age takes its toll more heavily in these highlands.

What TESFA offers is not just a memorable and well-run experience for the tourist, but also, most importantly, substantial financial support for the community. Many local farmers struggle to grow sufficient food to support their families, and there are very few alternative sources of income. The arrival of tourism seems to have changed nothing about the area beyond supplying much-needed additional income and jobs as cooks, guides, porters and guards (*because it's not safe?*). The landscape alone makes this trek worthwhile, but knowing that you are helping to support a vulnerable community makes it even better.

I lived in Ethiopia for three years and this trek is the first thing that I would recommend to all visitors. I liked it so much, I have done it twice. My words can't do justice to the extraordinary beauty of the landscape and people. I can only urge you to go and experience it for yourselves.

Christine Brissette went to India as an international volunteer to Koormanchal Seva Sansthan/Rural Organization for Social Elevation (KSS/ROSE; see page 191), in the foothills of the Himalayas.

My stay was a brief ten days; but this was time enough to be touched by the depth of ROSE's work and the warmth of this amazing place. The hills around Kanda offer a tranquillity I have found in few places in India. Away from the cars and noise of the nearby tourist hill stations, I found a place to rejuvenate and reconnect with this beautiful country. My first night and day were spent at a puja across the valley where I experienced a goat sacrifice and many holy ceremonies.

With the growing interest of travellers in the area, there is great concern about the potential exploitation of the environment and degradation of local culture. ROSE offers a brilliant alternative providing a system of small-scale (no more than 15 guests at a time) volunteer-based tourism. There are few opportunities for tourists to experience the 'real India' in the way that ROSE offers.

The locals benefit through the work, knowledge and financial contributions of the tourist volunteers. There is also a sense of pride that is cultivated within the community through such interactions. Volunteers participate in farming projects, learning about local organic agricultural methods. Founder Jeevan Lal Verma uses his home to set up pilot projects so that locals can learn about all aspects of environmental management and conservation.

The depth and breadth of the projects organized by ROSE is truly amazing. Amidst the thorns of social injustice, environmental degradation, economic inequality and threatened traditions, it has emerged as a source of hope, aid and happiness for locals and foreigners alike. May it continue to grow in the fertility of perseverance and altruism.

Frances Middleton went to the Andean peaks of Peru along the Minka Fair Trade Trail (see page 178) to experience homestay hospitality.

From Ollantaytambo, the road winds between the mighty peaks of the Andes following the turquoise torrent of the Urubamba River. Nothing is easy in these mountains, and we were already filled with admiration for the communities who make a life here. We were on our way to the village of Cuyo Grande, to visit the artisans who sell their crafts to Minka, a fair-trade NGO in Peru who, in turn, sells to Traidcraft in the UK.

The sun was hot when we arrived, and we stood around Eberto Manatupa's little yard, introducing ourselves. Our hosts did the same, and then threw handfuls of rose petals over us – to say thank you for visiting. We spent an interesting afternoon watching the production of the clay bead jewellery and whistles, and miniature chess sets. We all had a go at making the whistles by pressing clay into moulds. Then it was indoors to watch a demonstration of herbal medicines. After that was a dinner of local produce, including guinea pig for the brave.

Our accommodation was in rooms behind the local shop. The beds were very comfortable, with sheets and warm blankets. The electricity supply is unpredictable, so a good torch is essential, especially when using the loo – down a wooden staircase and across the outside yard. As the sun rose, the cold outside was intense until warmth began to penetrate. Breakfast was in another community house – porridge made with fava beans, cheese and bread, popcorn and mint or coca tea – then it was good-bye to our generous hosts and presents from home to say thank you for their kindness.

We continued to another homestay, speeding over the still waters of Lake Titikaka, for a stay with the Huayllano community on Taquile Island, a beautiful place, with eucalyptus trees and hidden rocky coves –

The Silent Way in Sweden organize unique tours where a small group of travellers mush a team of friendly Alaskan huskies along beautiful wilderness trails (see page 242)

Catrine Anderback

and the houses higgledy piggledy among the rocks. The locals oppose mass tourism and won't allow a hotel to be built. One hopes their resolution stays strong. Tourists stay over in family homes, everyone sharing the hospitality. We were given a magnificent lunch of potato and vegetable soup followed by lake trout and potatoes (this is the home of the potato), and then an introduction to the community and the weaving and knitting they sell to MINKA. We were welcomed profusely and then dispersed with our hosts across the island, some a little distance away up and down the rocky paths. The sun was sinking into the dark sea and streaking the horizon with purples and gold before darkness fell.

The MINKA Fair Trade Trail takes you through ancient Inca ruins, beautiful colonial towns and breathtaking landscapes. Stay in the Peruvian highlands to learn about Peruvian traditions, culture and values. Visit handicraft producers and witness firsthand how products are made through ancestral manufacturing techniques. Support producers in the making of their handicrafts at local workshops. Experience the balance and harmony that Peruvians have with their land to preserve their natural environment and facilitate sustainable production.

The MINKA Fair Trade Trail presents the opportunity to support fair trade by trading directly with local producers and providing them with additional income. It also fosters learning about how fair trade is helping to raise the standards of living for their families and communities.

Helen Jenkinson spent two weeks as a volunteer at the Elephant Nature Park (see page 213), in northern Thailand, looking after and learning about rescued elephants.

My week's stay here (which turned into two weeks!) at the Elephant Nature Park near Chiang Mai in northern Thailand was the most inspirational fortnight of my life. It was set up by a Thai lady called Lek who has used her great passion for elephants to create a safe haven for injured or 'unemployed' elephants, motivated by her dream that one day elephants will be safe in the wild again (and that there will be some wilderness left).

Lek's aim is to change elephant tourism to one where elephants are respected and valued for their natural habits, rather than have them begging in the city, trekking or performing circus acts. Her hope is to educate people to use positive reinforcement as the training method for elephants, as opposed to the cruel *Pajaan* ('breaking the spirit') method that is currently used.

At the time of my visit, there were 27 elephants, around 30 dogs (either rescued or had just appeared!) and 3 cows. Each elephant had a *mahout*, mainly young Karen boys who'd crossed the border to seek employment and escape the brutal Burmese regime.

You can either visit the park for a day or volunteer for the minimum of one week. Volunteers provide extra assistance, such as chopping banana trees and sugar cane as a treat for the elephants, helping to build new shelters or working the land, not to mention the dreaded cleaning of the mudpit! Of course, a fee is paid towards your stay and to contribute towards vet expenses and the huge quantities of food that the elephants consume. The park provides an educational experience, learning about Thai culture and, sadly, the depths of human behaviour towards animals.

You also learn about the history and personalities of each of these gentle giants and help to feed and wash them in the river. A highlight for every visitor is to watch the babies wrestle in the mudpit. Falling asleep each night to the chorus of elephants trumpeting and dogs barking was a unique experience and the joy I felt each morning walking from my hut to the main building, observing my favourite animals wandering around, never wore off.

During the dry season volunteers can take a family of elephants up to the Elephant Haven where they are completely free to roam for the night. The challenge the next morning is to find them and bring them back to the park! We placed monk-blessed robes around trees to protect them from being cut down in an attempt to save the vulnerable forest.

During my visit I was lucky enough to be involved in the rescue of two elephants. The first was an anorexic elderly female from a local trekking agency who had finally been allowed to retire. The second was one of the most challenging experiences of my life and involved an 18-

hour journey each way to Surin Province to collect a beautiful 27-year-old female who'd been brutally blinded in both eyes. She was unsurprisingly very agitated during the journey and my role was to sit up at the top of the van and feed her.

I was on constant alert for the whole journey, watching her trunk move to and fro within inches of my face. The fact that she never once touched me, even though she had the power to kill me, and didn't know I was there to help, brought tears to my eyes. Watching her arrive in her new, safe environment and interact with the other elephants was a very beautiful moment. I was so exhausted that night I fell straight to sleep despite two giant huntsmen spiders on the hut wall staring back at me!

I can't wait to go back to see the elephants.

Tricia Barnett visited Los Campesinos (see page 135), a Costa Rican village, where tourism is helping to regenerate the local economy.

The hanging bridge across the gorge at Los Campesinos was impressive. On the other side was a dramatic waterfall that adventurous travellers could abseil down, equipped with hard hats and harnesses. Just as I had, travellers out for some excitement could drive one and three-quarter hours up a mountain over streams and rocks and gullies in 4x4s to reach the gorge.

Los Campesinos, a tiny settlement of 15 families high in the mountainous rainforest of Costa Rica, was stunning. Almost everyone is involved in the project. We received a warm welcome from Don Miguel who is in charge of this extraordinary initiative. The families had created this settlement 44 years earlier, after they had been forced to move from their land where they had been subsistence farmers.

After 30 years, when their crop of vanilla brought in a good return and the first primary school teacher arrived, they became a totally self-contained community. The men focused on developing the vanilla trees and the women stayed at home with the children. But ten years ago the crop became infected and the trees died. Then there was a hurricane and some of the families left. These crises led to Don Miguel and two other villagers checking out what else they could all do to earn a living.

They discovered tourism, and built the hanging bridge over the deep gorge. Now around 2000 people a year arrive in trucks and have a terrific adventure as they abseil down the waterfall. They then have lunch prepared by the women, who take it in turns to be on duty. For the women, tourism has been a transformative experience. For the first time in their lives, they are earning an income and meeting outsiders. They are happy and confident – but want more people to come so that they can do more work!

What is so wonderful is how the villagers are reinvesting, not only back into their enterprise – which now has attractive accommodation – but also

Guests with Catlins Mohua Park
Eco-accommodation in New Zealand
stay in eco-cottages located on the edge
of a ten-hectare native forest reserve
(see page 228)

into their environment. They are replanting trees, no longer hunt animals and birds, have managed to buy their land and send the older children to school in the nearest town (a 2.5 hour walk). They now have four registered guides, and offer horse riding and walks through the rainforest.

Everywhere I went in Costa Rica, I met farmers and fishermen who were taking control of not just their lives, but also their environment, and were using tourism to support their livelihoods and invest in their forests and seashores.

I wasn't into the abseiling experience, but did go on wonderful guided rainforest walks, stayed overnight in the simple, very peaceful and comfortable accommodation, and learned so much about the richness of life, high in the mountains of Costa Rica.

Sue Wheat visited Kawaza village (see page 113), South Luangwa, Zambia. The villagers work closely with safari operators, particularly Robin Pope Safaris and Expert Africa, who helped them to set up the business and now market it to their clients.

I stood in a thatched rondavel and watched a traditional healer dressed in a white smock with a red cross on it go into a trance and invoke spirits to keep me healthy. It was an utterly surreal experience and one that I would never have had if I hadn't visited Kawaza. Zambia is famous for its spectacular wildlife, and incredible though that was, I remember my time with the villagers of Kawaza far more clearly than the animals I saw on safari.

Kawaza, which lies about 10km outside the South Luangwa National Park, is home to around 40 to 50 people, living a subsistence farming life. The villagers have set up a community-run tourism business, using the income to fund their school and provide water and community facilities.

My village guides were Meya and David, who both spoke good English. They gave me a friendly briefing about what was and wasn't appropriate to do: women should wear a *chitenje* (local sarong) while they are walking around; men and women eat separately; and they ask you not to give money or gifts to children, but to make a donation to the community if you want to.

For 24 hours I experienced everyday Zambian life as realistically as I think it's possible to do while still being a tourist on a short visit. We walked through cotton farms to the connecting villages and watched a blacksmith make a fire with two sticks and then expertly shape a piece of metal. We passed through a family yard and talked to the children plaiting each others' hair while their mother made dinner.

We visited the school where the whole project had started and met the headmaster – a man thoroughly impassioned by the potential of the Kawaza community tourism project to transform the lives of the village's children through the income it generates. Then we returned and I sat and ate *nshima* (ground maize that sets like polenta) with peanut and spinach relish with the local women, while they quizzed me good-humouredly through Meya about my life.

After a warm bath in the privacy of a simple bamboo cubicle for visitors, I went with David to the campfire where people come from surrounding villages to dance and tell stories – Kawaza, it seems, is a local social hub. The energy from their performances was amazing. Then to sleep in a hut identical to those of the other villagers – except they give visitors a bed with a mattress, a mosquito net and more blankets for the cool nights.

The noises here at night were different than in the national park – no throaty serenades by the local hippos on the riverbank, just the occasional murmur of a child waking momentarily from their sleep. Then, around 5.00 am, a rhythmic thump, thump, thump marked the beginning of the new day – sorghum being pounded for the next day's meals. I left itching to see more – I hadn't been fishing in the lagoon, been into the forests to collect honey, made medicinal herbs with the healer or spent enough time with the children. Twenty-four hours at Kawaza had definitely not been enough.

PREPARING FOR YOUR TRIP

Roy Graff

Whether you're setting off on the trip of a lifetime or jetting to an exotic location for your holidays, being conscious of how your actions affect those who live at the other end is always a good start to your travel plans. Being responsible when you travel isn't necessarily just about choosing a community-based holiday or going on an eco-trek. It applies to city breaks, package tours and any other type of domestic or overseas holiday.

This is a general list of simple guidelines and useful tips that can help you to reduce your footprint on the environment, stay safe and frequently also save you money. These are 'dos' rather than 'don'ts' that aim to help you to make the most of your trip, while also making it better for your hosts.

The planning stage: Where to go and how to get there

The entire world is now open to travellers, and although there are no easy answers, it's worth thinking about the implications of your travel to local communities. For example, do your tourist dollars help to support an oppressive regime? Are you planning to visit an area that is being damaged by too much tourism?

Take a guidebook that explains about the history, culture, society and politics of the place, and try to know a little about it before you go. Knowledge is power and can open doors for you. Try to choose a guidebook that engages the ethical dimension of tourism (this one is a good example). Read up on recent local news and pick up tips from other travellers through websites and internet forums.

If you book a package tour, consider that this normally maximizes profit for the tour operator and hotel at the expense of local people and small businesses. With a little bit of research, it is cheaper and more fun to go independently. Look for a travel product that is owned and/or managed by the local community. Many independent tour operators now incorporate responsible travel within their brochures, so it is worth it to shop around. When booking a tour package, why not ask your tour operator how they monitor the treatment and conditions of local staff; do they support local communities and help to preserve the environment; and do they offer 'carbon-neutral' flights (see 'Climate change: To fly or not to fly?', page 42)? Or you could think about slow travel – the pleasures of going by train, bicycle, two feet or donkey.

Stay safe

When planning your trip, it's important to take a look at the UK Foreign and Commonwealth Office (FCO) website travel advisories. The FCO produces travel advisories for over 200 countries and offers a wealth of practical advice on staying safe, secure and healthy, and avoiding problem situations, including piracy! You may also want to look at their Know before You Go campaign, launched in 2001 to promote safer travel.

If you do find yourself in a difficult situation while away, they may be able to help you: www.fco.gov.uk/en/travelling-and-living-overseas.

Packing list: The essentials

Pack the minimum you can, and buy what you need along the way. Leave room for locally produced clothes and souvenirs. This is a short list of recommended items to include that may not appear in other guidebooks:

- *Clothes* – travel trousers with zipped bottoms that turn into shorts are great for hot climates as you get two for the price of one. Look for clothes made from fibres that can be hand washed and that dry quickly. Natural fibres feel better close to the skin if you wear them for a long time.
- *Sun glasses* should cover your eyes well and be of high quality and very durable. Get a hard case for them and always put them in the case when not on you – glasses are the first thing to get lost or broken on a trip.
- *Fairtrade clothes* can be bought in many places now, and are normally of good quality and good value. Buying Fairtrade means the manufacturer gets a fair price for its work.

- *Toothbrush* made from natural rubber, or one with replaceable heads, saves on resources and waste.
- *Soap from natural oils* biodegrades naturally and is gentle on your skin. A gentle liquid soap can be used for the body, face, hair, shaving, washing clothes and disinfecting fruit and vegetables. This means you only need to take one container, saving space and money. Try to use your own products rather than using the disposable packets given at hotels, as hotel toiletries are usually cheap and full of chemicals, not to mention the waste of packaging.
- *Mosquito repellent* – there is no need to get chemical repellents based on DEET. It is harmful to your skin and the environment. There are natural substances (lemon-grass oil extract, citronella or eucalyptus oil) that repel mosquitoes effectively when mixed with a gentle oil such as coconut oil or your body cream. The best way to avoid getting bitten is to stay away from stagnant waterbodies and wear long-sleeved clothes in the evenings.
- *The bottled water industry* is reaping huge rewards by purifying water, putting it in plastic bottles and selling it for high profit. You can purify your own water easily and help to reduce the amount of plastic being thrown each day into landfills. In developing countries, plastic is a huge problem and tourists only make it worse. Aquapure Traveler is a handy bottle with a filter built into the cap. All you do is fill it up from any freshwater source, leave it to stand for 15 minutes and the water comes out clean and pure from the top. The filter contains a physical and chemical barrier to block almost all bacteria and pollutants. One filter cap supplies 350 litres of drinking water.
- Use *a cloth bag for dirty laundry* rather than plastic bags.
- For all *electrical gadgets*, use Ni-Mh rechargeable batteries. You will save money and prevent thousands of batteries in your lifetime from going into landfills and discharging chemicals into the soil. Battery chargers are small and efficient these days, so it's easy to travel with one. You can even get a solar battery charger if you go to a very sunny place.

On the road

When you get to your destination, remember why you are there – local people are what makes that place unique, so get to know them, ask them where to go and what to do instead of relying on outdated guidebooks that encourage a herd mentality:

- Often giving pictures to people can be a great gift, so a Polaroid camera such as the pocket-sized **i-Zone** comes in handy. They are now discontinued but still available online.
- If you buy plastic bottled water, ask if there are recycling bins, and remember to crush the bottle to conserve on space in the landfill.
- If you backpack and stay at guest houses, find out if they provide purified drinking water refills. If not, try suggesting to the owner to start such a service.

Awareness of these issues will help to enhance your experience. Depending upon where you are heading to, there are certain guidelines that you can follow at the destination that are location specific. They address cultural, religious and political issues that should be observed. Please take a look at Tourism Concern's travel code for more information (see box on page 62).

Useful web links:

Guidebooks on your phone: www.xs2theworld.com (mobile city guides)

Aquapure water purifier: www.aquapuretraveller.com

iZone Polaroid camera: www.polaroid.com

Helping communities: www.stuffyourrucksack.com tells you what to take to help local communities in different countries.

Tourism Concern's campaign for fair working conditions for mountain porters raises awareness of the horrific conditions that trekking porters all over the world endure – and we are working to put a stop to these abuses.

Porters often face sub-zero conditions with no protective footwear, clothing or tents:

The wages we receive don't match the physical effort we put in ... [and] the tour operators don't offer us equipment like sleeping bags and waterproofs ... We have to sleep outside. We are contracted as 'beasts of burden' ... and treated as if we weren't human. Peruvian porters' syndicate

Kul Bahadur Rai is a Nepalese porter who was hit by altitude sickness while carrying a heavy load for tourists. An unsympathetic trek leader made him go on, then left him to descend alone. Kul Bahadur slipped into a coma, and woke in hospital to find that his frostbitten feet had to be partially amputated.

Porters earn as little as £2/US$3.50 a day.

How you can make a difference

Tourism Concern believes it's time for tour operators to accept responsibility for improving the harsh conditions in which porters work. As Agha Iqrar Haroon in Pakistan says: 'Tour operators can play a great role in protecting porters' rights. They shouldn't try and keep costs down at the expense of basic human rights.'

Tourism Concern has drawn up guidelines for tour operators on porters' working conditions. But we need your support, to put pressure on tour operators to adopt guidelines – and to make sure they're walking the walk, not just talking the talk.

• If you're thinking of going trekking, ask questions of tour operators:
  – Let them know that it's important to you that your trip doesn't exploit porters.
  – Ask them what policies they have on porters' working conditions – wages; loads; equipment; and what happens if porters have accidents or fall ill.
  If you would like to check which tour operators do have policies on porters, please contact Tourism Concern.
• While you're there, keep your eyes open:
  – What are the porters wearing? Do they have adequate protective clothing?
  – How big are the loads that the porters are carrying?
  – What are the porters eating and where are they sleeping at night?
• When you come back, act on what you saw.
  – If you saw things that worried you about the way porters were treated – speak up.
  – Tell your tour operator – and tell Tourism Concern.
  – And just as important – if the porters were treated fairly, let your tour operator know this was an important factor in an enjoyable trip.
• If you know someone who's going trekking, open their eyes to what's going on. Pass on this information, and get them involved.

If you want to stop human rights abuses in tourism across the board...

Join **Tourism Concern**. We fight exploitation in tourism and campaign to ensure tourism always benefits local communities in the places we visit.

If you'd like to find out more about our porters' campaign or our wider work, visit www.tourismconcern.org.uk, e-mail us at info@tourismconcern.org.uk or telephone +44(0)20 7133 3330

TRAVELLER'S CODE

Anyone can be a responsible tourist and avoid guilt trips. There are big things that you can do and small things that you can do; but they all make a difference to someone's life:

- **Be aware.**
  Start enjoying your travels before you leave. Think about what sort of clothing is appropriate for both men and women. If the locals are covered up, what sort of messages will you be sending out by exposing acres of flesh?

- **Be open.**
  Something may seem bizarre or odd to 'you', but it may be normal and just the way things are done to 'them'. Try not to assume that the Western way is right or best.

- **Our holidays – their homes.**
  Ask before taking pictures of people, even children, and respect their wishes. Talk to local people. What do they think about our lifestyle, clothes and customs? Find out about theirs.

- **'One school pen'.**
  Giving to children encourages begging. A donation to a project, health centre or school is more constructive.

- **Be fair.**
  Try to put money into local hands. If you haggle for the lowest price, your bargain may be at the seller's expense. Even if you pay a little over the odds, does it really matter?

- **Be adventurous.**
  Use your guidebook or hotel as a starting point, not as the only source of information. Find out what's going on by talking to locals, and then have your own adventures.

- **Ask questions.**
  Write a letter to your tour operator about their responsible tourism policy. We will give a FREE copy of our *Good Alternative Travel Guide* to the sender of the best (or worst) operator reply.

- **Think before you fly.**
  Help to repair the damage you do to the environment by flying less. The more and further you fly, the more you contribute to global warming and environmental destruction.

- **Be happy.**
  By taking any, some or all of these actions, you are personally fighting tourism exploitation. Enjoy your guilt-free trip!

Take action and have a better holiday!

A trekking holiday in Bolivia offers opportunities to meet the local people (see page 157)
Artesanias/Tusoco

Trek Apolobamba takes visitors on ancient trails through the Andes, a landscape populated by llamas and condors (see page 160)
Bolivia Trek Apolobamba

Aventures Ashini is wholly owned and run by the Innu community, with whom visitors can learn about traditional camp life in Canada (see page 151)
J. P. Messier

A traditional village welcoming ceremony in Guizhou Province, China (see page 185)
Emma Starks

The Huaorani Eco-lodge in the Amazonian rainforest of Ecuador gives the local Huaorani people the chance to receive an income from tourism while preserving their culture and rainforest territory (see page 169)
Huaorani Ecolodge, Tropic Journeys in Nature

Visitors to Ecuador can see the basin of the Amazon here at the Rio Napo (see page 171)
Amica Dall

A Galapagos crab, one of the many species of wildlife to be seen on a journey to the Galapagos Islands (see pages 167–170)
Galapagos Walking Tours, Tropic Journeys in Nature

Blue-footed boobies, a native species of the Galapagos Islands
Amica Dall

The Santiaguito volcano, which erupts hourly, is the most active in Guatemala and can be seen on a visit to Nueva Alianza (see page 140)
Comunidad Nueva Alianza

Located in the Toubkal National Park, the Kasbah du Toubkal offers traditional Berber hospitality in a mountain setting (see page 91)
Kasbah du Toukbal

A volunteer helps to treat cataracts at a camp run by Socialtreks.com in Nepal (see page 197)
socialtreks.com

With Absolute Carpathian, visitors can see lynxes, bears and beavers in Romania's Piatra Craiului National Park (see page 241)
Absolute Carpathian

A lodge in the rainforest canopy of Sri Lanka, with guided jungle walks on offer (see page 202)
Lars Sorensen

Organic ingredients for a Thai
kitchen grown in Gecko Villa's garden
(see page 214)
Gecko Villa

Footprint Vietnam offer trips to the
north Mekong Delta on foot, by bike
and in junks (see page 217)
Footprint Vietnam Travel

FOR A GREEN HALONGBAY

Princess

DIRECTORY

KEY

ACCOM	accommodation only
AGRI	agritourism or working on local farms
BUDGET	basic accommodation
CENTRE	visitor centre or museum
DAY	full-day or part-day tours
DIS	disabled visitor friendly
HOST	staying with a local family
LUX	upmarket accommodation
ORG	organization supporting community tourism initiatives and offering information about them
RAINFOREST	rainforest, cloud forest tours or wilderness tours and lodges
SAFARI	wildlife tours, lodges
SCHOOL	classes or workshops in language, music, horse riding, etc.
TOUR	tours, usually guided
TOUR OP	tour operator
TREK	multi-day hikes/trekking
VOL	volunteer work placements
WEBSITE	website with useful information

+ This symbol after any of the above indicates that some additional activities are included (eg HOST+ will offer local activities as well as staying with a family).

63

AFRICA

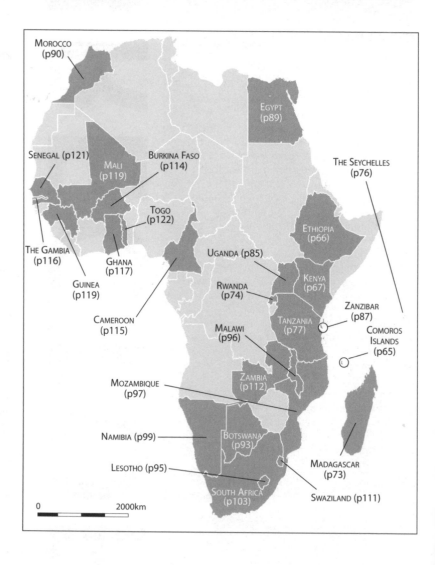

MOROCCO (p90)

EGYPT (p89)

SENEGAL (p121)

MALI (p119)

BURKINA FASO (p114)

THE SEYCHELLES (p76)

TOGO (p122)

ETHIOPIA (p66)

THE GAMBIA (p116)

GHANA (p117)

UGANDA (p85)

KENYA (p67)

GUINEA (p119)

RWANDA (p74)

ZANZIBAR (p87)

CAMEROON (p115)

TANZANIA (p77)

COMOROS ISLANDS (p65)

MALAWI (p96)

MOZAMBIQUE (p97)

ZAMBIA (p112)

NAMIBIA (p99)

BOTSWANA (p93)

MADAGASCAR (p73)

LESOTHO (p95)

SOUTH AFRICA (p103)

SWAZILAND (p111)

0   2000km

64

EAST AFRICA

COMOROS ISLANDS
International dialling code +269

The Comoros consists of four islands in the Indian Ocean between Tanzania and Madagascar. Grande Comore, Mohéli and Anjouan, make up the Union of the Comoros. The fourth, Mayotte, continues to be held by France as an overseas territory; subsidized by France, the people are much better off and no longer want to be reunited with the other islands.

A visit to these islands is unforgettable – mountains on Grande Comore and Anjouan, coral reefs and a local Islamic culture and language very close to that of Zanzibar, Mombasa and Lamu on the East African coast. Visitors arrive at the tiny capital, Moroni, with its mosques and markets, squashed between the sea and the still active volcano, Karthala. The whole of Grande Comore consists of volcanic rock, which breaks down into fertile soil, and here the main crops are the vanilla pod and *ylang ylang*, the basis of many French perfumes. This makes the smell of Comoran agriculture something special! Transport between the islands is possible, but irregular, and such little tourism that there is can be found mainly on Grande Comore.

Politically, the islands have been disastrously unstable since independence in 1975, with over 20 *coups d'état*. The islands of Mohéli and Anjouan unilaterally declared independence in 1997 as a result of which a new constitution was agreed in 2001 in a bid to end the cycle of coups and secession attempts. Each island now gets a semi-autonomous government, parliament and president and there is a rotating presidency for the three islands.

This complex system is too costly for such a desperately poor country and the government is contemplating changes, which may set the conflicts off again. The Comoros have a debt burden of US$297 million – 63 per cent of its gross domestic product (GDP) – and are near the bottom of the United Nations Development Programme's Human Development Index.

ORG/ACCOM/TOUR
UNION DES COMORES, LA MAISON DE L'ECOTOURISME DE MOHÉLI (LAMEM)
'La Maison' is a non-profit organization on the island of Mohéli, which aims to underpin organizationally all facets of ecotourism on the island. On offer are community bungalows, car hire, ecotourism tours and general relaxation on the small islands. Pooling the various accommodation resources gives a total of 50 rooms available for visitors. Any income goes to the local communities – La Maison receives only commissions.

Contact: Habibou Nomane
Tel: +269 7720610 • +269 3327830
Fax: +269 7720610
Email: contact@moheli-tourisme.com • nomane2005@yahoo.fr
Web: www.moheli-tourisme.com
Address: Maison de l'Ecotourisme de Mohéli, Bandar Es Salam, Moheli, Comoros Islands

ETHIOPIA

International dialling code +251

'Thirteen months of sunshine' say the travel posters. This refers to the fact that Ethiopia has never changed its calendar, and this is not the only interesting thing about the country. It is Africa's oldest independent country: apart from a five-year occupation by Mussolini, it has never been colonized, which makes it almost unique in Africa. Until 1974, Ethiopia was ruled by emperors said to be descended from the Queen of Sheba's visit to the bed of King Solomon. The last Emperor, Haile Selassie, is the Ras Tafari worshipped by Rastafarians. It is the second oldest country to become officially Christian, although there has been a considerable Muslim minority since the earliest days of Islam.

In spite of this fascinating history, Ethiopia has been badly affected by a series of droughts and famines, notably the 'biblical' one in 1984, which led to the first Live Aid concert. These problems, caused by overpopulation and deforestation, mainly affect the north and east, so the government has been trying to persuade, and sometimes force, people to move to the more fertile south. It is one of Africa's poorest countries and many of its people still depend upon food aid from abroad. On top of this, it has had a long civil conflict and border war with neighbouring Eritrea.

For those interested in history and art, Ethiopia is well worth a visit, especially to the rock-hewn churches at Lalibela, the painted ceilings of monasteries, the stone columns at Axum (one of which has recently been brought back from Rome, where Mussolini had erected it), the 'theme park' of castles at Gondar, and the ancient city of Harar. There is plenty of good scenery too – Lake Tana and the Blue Nile Falls, lakes in the south, desert in the east and several national parks. The food, music and dance are equally unlike anywhere else in Africa. The people are welcoming but proud, although you can get mildly hassled by kids wanting pen friends, footballs and the like.

ORG/TREK
TOURISM IN ETHIOPIA FOR SUSTAINABLE FUTURE ALTERNATIVES (TESFA)

TESFA is a local NGO which enables local farmers and communities to offer a trekking package including accommodation, food, drink, pack animals and guides. With its help, a network of accommodation and facilities has been established by local communities. The centre is in the ancient city of Lalibela, with its marvellous rock-hewn churches. You will stay in eco-friendly local cottages, simple but clean and nicely equipped, with eco-toilets and solar-heated water in the showers. The food is simple but tasty, three meals a day, and thought is given to the Western palate. The core of the enterprise is the chance to be a guest of the community and watch and learn.

Contact: Hanna Girma or Mark Chapman
Tel: +251 111225024 · +251 111247231
Mobile: +251 911416452 (Mark) · +251 913244480 (Hanna)
Email: chapman@ethionet.et · mark@community-tourism-ethiopia.com · tesfacbt@ethionet.et (bookings)
Web: www.community-tourism-ethiopia.com
Address: TESFA Technical Support, PO Box 3211, Code 1250, Addis Ababa, Ethiopia

KENYA
International dialling code +254

Safari is really just the Kiswahili word for a journey; but in English it has become synonymous with game viewing – and Kenya is where it all started. The colonial carve-up left the British with the drier northern part of East Africa, including the railway line from the coast to Lake Victoria and Uganda. From the hot coastal plain the scenery changes to the high plateau, through the Rift Valley and into the green western provinces on the shore of Lake Victoria. The whole of East Africa was, and still is, incredibly rich in wildlife. Maasai Mara, Tsavo, Amboseli and the Aberdares are among Kenya's well-known national parks. Even without the attractions of the safari, Kenya's coast would be a world-class tourist destination, with golden palm-fringed beaches, coral reefs, the historic city of Mombasa and the idyllic island town of Lamu, Kenya's answer to Zanzibar. Visitors arrive in Nairobi, the busy capital city with its glossy tower blocks, leafy residential areas, crowded back streets and muddy slums. Despite its reputation of being 'Nairobbery', it is a stimulating place. Following the political violence of the 2008 election, peace – and tourism – has returned. Kenya produces good handicrafts, such as Maasai bead work and wood-carvings, which can be purchased from the producers themselves.

SAFARI+
AFRICAN PRO-POOR TOURISM DEVELOPMENT CENTRE (APTDC), KENYA
The APTDC is guided by the mantra: 'Give the local community a fish and you feed them for a day; teach them to fish and you feed them forever.' Rooted in the local community, the APTDC adheres to the principles underpinning fairly traded tourism. Its not-for-profit safaris and ecotours in different Kenyan locations aim to take travellers to places where they can enjoy, admire and study the cultural and natural heritage of Kenya while empowering marginalized communities. Visitors can mingle with local people and better understand their lives. Eighty per cent of the cost (about UK£140/US$250 per day all-inclusive) goes to local communities. There is a clear code of conduct and environmental concerns are paramount.

Contact: Susan Wangwe
Tel: +254 202251766
Mobile: +254 733447108
Fax: +254 202242563
Email: info@propoortourism-kenya.org
Web: www.propoortourism-kenya.org
Address: 2nd Floor, National House, Koinange Street, PO Box 4293, Nairobi 00200, Kenya

LUX+
CAMPI YA KANZI, KENYA
This Italian-owned luxury camp with accommodation for up to 16 people is located between Amboseli and Tsavo national parks. The Maasai of the Kuku Group Ranch receive income from the camp. A fee of US$100 per person per day goes towards wildlife conservation and the community. You can go on game walks and drives with Maasai guides and meet the Maasai landowners to learn about their culture.

Contact: Alice Wairimu
Tel: +254 45622516

Fax: +254 45622516
Email: lucasaf@africaonline.co.ke
Web: www.maasai.com
Address: PO Box 236, Mtito Andei, 90128 Kenya

ACCOM
DIAMOND BEACH VILLAGE

This is an unusual hotel in that the accommodation is in six beach huts or bandas on Manda Island, Kenya. There is also a tree house! The complex makes a good base from which to explore the local scenery and to get to know the Lamu culture and people. Lamu is the oldest town in East Africa. The hotel places itself at the heart of the local community on Manda and local people come to relax on the beach there and chat with the guests. The owners contribute to the local school and all produce is bought locally. Time and mutual goodwill cement the relationship between the hotel and the local community.

Contact: Rachael Holly
Tel: +254 720915001
Email: info@diamondbeachvillage.com
Web: www.diamondbeachvillage.com
Address: PO Box 348, Lamu, 80500 Kenya

HOST
GSE ECOTOURS – VILLAGE HOMESTAYS

The operational side of GSE is in the process of being wedded to a community-based operation called Mukuru Trust. Once merged, it will become a consultancy and the Village Homestays will be handled separately. The visitor stays with a host family for a period of 3 to 14 days. The visitor is a guest rather than a tourist and has the opportunity to take part in everyday activities and tasks. The hosts will also demonstrate elements of their culture (e.g. basketry and traditional medicine), which helps the hosts to value their own culture more. Hosts help to prepare itineraries and dictate the pace at which tours should run. Visitor respect for and absorption of local culture are paralleled by the economic and social benefit to local communities.

Contact: Charlotte Burford (admin@gse-ecotours.com)
Tel: +254 2119945 (Kenya office) • +44 8707669891 (UK office)
Email: enquiries@gse-ecotours.com • admin@gse-ecotours.com
Web: www.gse-ecotours.com
Address: PO Box 2089-00202, Nairobi, Kenya • 75 Scotney Gardens, Maidstone, Kent, ME16 0GR, UK

SAFARI
IL NGWESI LODGE

Located on a rocky outcrop on the north-eastern edge of the Maasai Il Ngwesi Group Ranch, northwest of Mount Kenya, the lodge is considered a role model for community-based tourism in Kenya. Constructed entirely from local materials, it is open plan and organic in character, with timber floors flowing around tree trunks, grass-thatched roofs and six spacious bedrooms. The lodge is 100 per cent owned by the local Maasai who are trained English-speaking hosts and guides. Activities from the lodge include game drives, camel riding, guided bush walks along sand rivers and visiting black and white rhino. Breakfasts and dinners in the bush can be arranged. Guests can also visit a Maasai cultural village to gain an insight into the history and traditions of the Maasai, including livestock keeping, hunting skills and rituals.

Contact: Wanjohi Thairu
Tel: +254 202033122
Email: info@ilngwesi.com
Web: www.ilngwesi.com
Address: PO Box 263, 10406 Timau, Kenya

ACCOM/SAFARI
ILARIAK ECOLODGE
A tented eco-lodge which takes care to look after the environment and ensures that the local community benefits. You can visit a Maasai cultural homestead, enjoy a nature walk, visit a local school, plant trees or assist with a local project. There are also day and night game drives in the famous Maasai Mara Game Reserve to see wild animals in their natural environment.

Contact: Lucy Kenta
Tel: +254 721904434
Fax: +254 202731174
Email: info@ilariak-ecolodge.com • ilariak_osotua@yahoo.com
Web: www.ilariak-ecolodge.com
Address: PO Box 10749, 00400 Nairobi, Kenya

LUX/SAFARI
KAREN BLIXEN CAMP
This luxury camp on the banks of the Mara River in the northern part of the Maasai Mara Reserve aims to employ as many local Maasai guides as possible. The camp also helps the local community by sponsoring the clinic, building boarding facilities at the local school, planting trees and funding a fence around the village to protect it from wildlife. It has a zero waste water system and all vegetable matter is used for compost.

Contact: Carole
Tel: +254 202211496
Fax: +254 302211981
Email: info@karenblixencamp.com
Web: www.karenblixencamp.com
Address: 9913-00100, GPO Nairobi, Kenya

ORG
KENYA COMMUNITY-BASED TOURISM NETWORK (KECOBAT)
The KECOBAT Network can be regarded as a trade association, representing the poorest sections of the tourism sector. By being the central point of contact, KECOBAT forges links between these often inaccessible communities, the government, the private sector, NGOs, donors and training institutions. KECOBAT is in the process of developing a community tourism website to give travellers accurate and comprehensive information, and also intends to develop a tourism map, guidebook and accreditation system to guarantee a high level of service delivery.

Contact: Donald Mombo
Tel: +254 202700646
Mobile: +254 722617998
Fax: +254 204765739
Email: info@kecobat.org • kcbtnet@yahoo.com
Web: www.kecobat.org
Address: KECOBAT Network, Ngong Road, opposite Ngong Hills Hotel, PO Box 10011-00100 Nairobi, Kenya

TOUR OP/SAFARI/HOST
KERETO TOURS AND SAFARIS
On offer is a wide range of safari activities from budget upwards, village stays and educational visits, the core of which is the opportunity to experience Maasai culture, their way of life, ceremonies and rituals. The guiding is done by five experienced Maasai from the community. Income from this company, which is entirely owned and operated by the Maasai in the Maasai Mara, supports projects in and around the Naisoya community area. The mission is to preserve the environment in tandem with improving the health, education and general welfare of the Maasai community, and 50 per cent of the income goes to the community.

Contact: David Ole Kereto
Tel: +254 725787203 · +254 728229820 · +254 5022092
Fax: +254 5022092
Email: davidkereto@hotmail.com
Web: www.keretosafaris.com
Address: PO Box 435-20500, Narok, Kenya

SAFARI
KOIYAKI GUIDING SCHOOL AND WILDERNESS CAMP
This project is Maasai owned and located on the northern edge of the Maasai Mara. The camp is being developed so that its income can sustain the guiding school. Since its inception, the school has produced 76 graduates. The aim is to train professional guides who can seek employment in the tourism industry. The school concentrates on quality rather than quantity. The Wilderness Camp is also a community-initiated project, leased to Basecamp Explorer. The camp aims to secure funding for the school through income-generating activities and to act as a practical training site for students.

Tel: +44 1747831005 (via Tusk Trust) · +254 0735647148 (administrative office) · +254 733586983 (consultant office)
Email: koiyaki@iwayafrica.com
Web: www.koiyaki.com
Address: PO Box 984, Narok-20500, Kenya

SAFARI/LUX
LEWA SAFARIS CAMP
The Lewa Safaris Camp is owned and operated by the Lewa Wildlife Conservancy. All profits are reinvested in their social, environmental, educational and health projects. There is an outstanding range of wildlife, and visitors are more or less guaranteed to see the big five, especially black rhino and Grevy's zebra. Associated with Lewa are Il Ngwesi and Tassia Community Lodges. The luxurious tented camp sleeps 26 in 12 tents, with a pool, hot running water and flush toilets. Visitors learn about the five ecosystems, the community life of the area, and are given the chance to join in the everyday activities of a working conservancy. Possible activities include horse and camel riding, fly fishing, lion tracking, bird-watching, visits to local schools, as well as game drives and walks in the bush. Access is by road and by plane – there are two flights a day from Nairobi landing at the private airstrip.

Contact: Richard Buthe, Clare Moller and Stephen Kasoo
Tel: +254 64 31405 · +254 20 607197
Fax: +254 20 607893
Web: www.bush-and-beyond.com · www.lewa.org
Address: Private bag, Isiolo, Kenya

SAFARI
MAASAI SIMBA CAMP
Completely owned and operated by the Maasai themselves, with no asistance of any kind from government or any other sources, Simba Camp offers the visitor a genuine cross-cultural experience. Activities include daily nature/safari walks, bead-making lessons with women and visits to community-based projects. You can also go on a day excursion to Amboseli National Park. An extra upon request is a 'full-on Maasai warrior experience, camping in the wilderness'. The project has resulted in primary and secondary schools, a health centre and a vocational training school, and has brought clean water to over 4000 people in the Merrueshi area. Over 400 children are in education as a result. This is community tourism at its best.

Contact: Kakuta Ole Maimai
Tel: +254 721761511
Email: info@maasaicamp.com

Web: www.maasaicamp.com
Address: PO Box 231, Emali, Kenya

ACCOM+
MALEWA WILDLIFE LODGES

Malewa is an eco-lodge located in the private 1400ha (3500 acre) Kigio Wildlife Conservancy in the Great Rift Valley between Nakuru and Naivasha. You can enjoy guided nature walks, mountain biking, fishing, game drives and community tours. Evenings are spent by the fireside talking with naturalists and community organizers about the history, culture and environment of the area.

Contact: Beatrice (res@kigio.com)
Tel: +254 203748369
Fax: +254 203742465
Email: conservation@kigio.com
Web: www.kigio.com
Address: PO Box 1690, 00606 Nairobi, Kenya

TOUR OP/VOL
ORIGINS SAFARIS

Origins is based in Nairobi and runs high-end tourist camps as well as organizing cultural and natural history safaris, gorilla trekking and tropical islands exploration throughout East and Central Africa. It also endeavours to give something back to the community. US$20 per client goes to support local community projects, while guests are invited to visit the local ecotourism bandas, try bee-keeping or become involved in activities such as building schools, teaching information technology (IT), English and arithmetic. Visitors can also participate in wildlife and water monitoring in order to better understand the dynamics between humans and wildlife in the community areas near Tsavo National Park, southeast Kenya.

Contact: Samuel Gaturu
Tel: +254 202710171/2/7 • +254 202042695/6/7
Fax: +254 202710178 • +254 202042698
Email: steveturner@originsafaris.info
Web: www.originsafaris.info
Address: Grassroots Logistics, c/o Origins Safaris, LandMark Plaza, 5th Floor, Argwings Kodhek Road, PO Box 48019, 00100 Nairobi, Kenya

SAFARI
RIVERSIDE CAMP (formerly EBENEZER CAMPSITE)

The camp is next to the Talek Gate of the Maasai Mara Park – a feature of the camp is that it has a room where the Maasai women can make and sell their beadwork. Visitors receive an orientation to Maasai culture, and transport to both day and night game drives is provided. Also on offer are trekking safaris with overnight stays in Maasai homes. On a basic level, both half and full board are available. The prime directive is that the community benefits from the income generated from the business. A major aspect is the creation of employment. Income also supports a medical centre, a primary school and other development projects.

Contact: David Ole Kereto
Tel: +254 725787203 • +254 728229820 • +254 5022092
Fax: +254 5022092
Email: davidkereto@hotmail.com
Address: PO Box 435, 20500 Narok, Kenya

ACCOM+
THE MAASAI CONSERVATION AND DEVELOPMENT ORGANISATION

This is a campsite at which the local Maasai are encouraged to play an empowering role in the tourism industry, and so this offers a very different cultural experience from elsewhere. Visitors can go running with the local people, cycling or adventure walking. Cultural activities include traditional Maasai pursuits such as bushcraft, harvesting wild bees, animal tracking, bow and arrow shooting, and spear throwing. Lucky guests will also be invited to participate in ceremonies such as naming, branding of cows, drinking of milk and weddings.

Contact: Resiato Martyn
Tel: +254 790883
Email: olomanaa95@btinternet.com

LUX/ACCOM
TPS SERENA HOTELS

TPS Serena Hotels is an affiliate of the Aga Khan Fund for Economic Development, which promotes tourism by building, or rehabilitating, and managing hotels, safari lodges and luxury resorts. This contributes to economic growth in an environmentally and culturally sensitive manner. They operate not just in Kenya, but also in Tanzania, Uganda, Rwanda and Mozambique, as well as locations in Pakistan, Tajikistan and Afghanistan. There is a genuine commitment to corporate social responsibility. This is high-end tourism with a very real conscience as to the impacts both on the environment and the local community.

Contact: Damaris Agweyu, Rosemary Mugambi and Michael Opondo
Tel: +254 202842000
Fax: +254 202718100/1
Email: dagweyu@serena.co.ke • rmugambi@serena.co.ke • mopondo@serena.co.ke
Web: www.serenahotels.com
Address: Williamson House, 4th Ngong Avenue, PO Box 48690, 00100, Nairobi, Kenya
Note: this chain has representation in many countries.

SAFARI/HOST
TRINITY TOURS AND SAFARIS

Trinity Tours is a Nairobi-based enterprise, which began in 2005 and owns Kichakani Mara Camp. The company has a Christian ministry and aims to organize safaris geared to take care of the spiritual and physical enrichment of the tourists. This is 'not tourism for tourism's sake, but tourism with a purpose'. Visitors share the homes and culture of local people and are advised as to the behaviour and conduct expected of them.

Contact: Moses Mulandi
Denmark **Contact:** Erik Nikolajsen – europe@trinitysafaris.com
US **Contact:** Joshua Nzueni – salesusa@trinitysafaris.com
Tel: +254 206764801
Mobile: +254 711300030
Email: sales@trinitysafaris.com • moses@trinitysafaris.com
Web: www.trinitysafaris.com
Address: PO Box 5533-00200, Nairobi, Kenya

DAY/TOUR
TWIN BUFFALOS SAFARIS

This is a family-run tour operator based in Nairobi. It is a one-stop shop and can organize any travel arrangements, from flights to hotels to volunteer placements at an orphanage. All staff are experienced in the travel industry and will assist in making any visit a memorable experience. They offer urban safaris such as a secure slum safari walk, tours to local charitable projects and a women's craft centre. All of this ties in with its current support of the Daylove Children's Rehabilitation Centre, which aims to rescue street children in Nairobi. Some of the profits also go to other charitable organizations.

Contact: Margaret Ruiyi (Kenya) • David Njane (UK)
Tel: +254 202248976 • +254 202250578
Fax: +254 202250593
Email: info@twinsafaris.com (Kenya) • david@twinsafaris.com (UK)
Web: www.twinsafaris.com
Address: Bruce House, 10th Floor, PO Box 48609, 00100 Nairobi, Kenya

VOL
KENYA VOLUNTARY DEVELOPMENT ASSOCIATION (KVDA)

KVDA has a programme of workcamps throughout the year, as well as longer volunteer placements. It also offers touring possibilities after the workcamp.

Contact: Isaac Oneka Munanairi
Tel: +254 20225379
Fax: +254 20246284
Email: kvdakenya@yahoo.com
Web: www.geocities.com/kvdaonline/aboutus.html
Address: PO Box 48902, Nairobi

MADAGASCAR
International dialling code +261

'La grande île' is an exceptional place, African but with the feel of Southeast Asia. The people of the highlands of the interior are believed to have emigrated from Asia and their customs are very distinct from those of the coastal people. It was an independent kingdom, then a French protectorate from 1896, becoming fully independent in 1960. The country still has strong ties to France.

It is the fourth largest island in the world and, because of its isolation, most of its mammals, half of its birds and most of its plants exist nowhere else on Earth. Some ecologists refer to Madagascar as the 'eighth continent'; but severe poverty and competition for agricultural land have put pressure on the island's magnificent but dwindling forests, removing vital habitats and also affecting the emerging tourist industry, which is based on safaris and ecological tours.

The capital city, Antananarivo, is very attractive, with its colourful market place and steep steps up the hillsides. What remains of the royal palaces are also worth visiting. There are also coastal resorts, but tourism (mostly French) is relatively underdeveloped and so this makes it a good place to visit, apart from tropical cyclones, which can cause torrential flooding.

VOL
BLUE VENTURES EXPEDITIONS/ANDAVADOAKA MARINE CONSERVATION PROJECT

Blue Ventures run marine monitoring and research expeditions for paying volunteers. A community eco-lodge is to be developed in collaboration with the village of Andavadoaka on land donat-

AFRICA

ed by the village. Volunteers have the chance to become really involved in the marine conservation work and in a range of other terrestrial biological research projects. The real commitment is to identify environmental issues vital to the community and to address them with appropriate conservation, education and research plans. An indicator as to the success of the Madagascan project is the plan to replicate it in Fiji.

Contact: Kathleen, Raj or Richard
Tel: +44 2083419819
Email: madagascar@blueventures.org
Web: www.blueventures.org
Address: Unit AS2D, Aberdeen Centre, Highbury Grove, London, N5 2EA, UK

TOUR
TETRAKTYS ORGANIZATION: RAVAKA

In 1994, three French rural/mountain tourism organizations bonded together with a philosophy of developing tourism that is beneficial to the local community. This has resulted in enterprises in Mali, Senegal, Guinea Conakry and, here, in Madagascar. This is integrated, sustainable tourism which assigns 'the whole of the money of the tourist to the local development of the area'. Four mountain lodges offer 10 to 15 places to hikers who can carry out circuit walks, allowing simultaneous immersion in peasant daily life. Please note: participants must be French speakers, not just 'I can get by' speakers.

Contact: Ralitera Mirana Samoela
Tel: +261 4449887
Mobile: 0331128322
Email: ravakarando1@yahoo.fr • miranalitera19@yahoo.fr
Web: www.tetraktys-ong.org
Address: Ravaka, Immeuble Ritz, Rue Ralaimongo, 110 Antsirabe, Madagascar

RWANDA
International dialling code +250

It is Rwanda's misfortune to be famous for a terrible event, the genocide of 1994. But that is no reason not to visit this beautiful little country, the land of *mille collines*: 1000 hills (in fact, they call their villages *collines* even on the rare occasions when they are on the plains). The country is green and fertile, with vistas of ridge upon ridge of hills and, as you ride north from the capital Kigali, on a clear day, the thrilling view of the Virunga: a line of extinct volcanoes. This is the area most visitors come to see because it remains the home of the rare mountain gorillas. Visitors should also visit the excellent national museum at Butare in the south of the country and the various memorials for the genocide. Of course, people are still scarred by what happened in 1994 and bitterness and division exist beneath the surface. However, the visitor will find a very efficient country with regular minibus services, not too much bureaucracy and no visas for British visitors – and a very nice German coffee shop in Kigali. In 2008, it also decided to make English its official language, rather than French, the language of its former colonial master.

TOUR OP/TOUR
AMAHORO TOURS

Amahoro Tours is located about one hour's drive from Kigali in Ruhengeri, northern Rwanda. Guests stay overnight with a family and participate fully in Rwandan daily life. For example, you may visit a women's association to see how banana beer is produced, a traditional healer who demonstrates how to make honey, a home for street kids, or an indigenous Kagano community. Visitor numbers are kept small to ensure an intimate and authentic experience and to guard against impacting negatively upon the local people and their way of life.

Contact: Egide Mukama
Tel: +250 0865523
Email: amahorotours@gmail.com
Web: www.amahoro-tours.com
Address: PO Box 87, Musanze, Rwanda

ACCOM/DAY/HOST
IBY'IWACU CULTURAL VILLAGE

Iby'Iwacu offers visitors the opportunity to stay in a Rwandan village and learn about daily life. You can meet a traditional healer, grind millet and sorghum on the local grinding stone, shoot arrows with the Batwa people, fetch water, help with the potato harvest, visit a replica of a king's house, or enjoy traditional Intore dancing and drumming. There are bicycles available for use. The project is technically and financially supported by Rwanda Ecotours and only employs local people, especially former poachers.

Contact: Twagira Innocent
Tel: +250 500331 • +250 500057
Fax: +250 500057
Email: esabuhoro@rwandaecotours.com • info@rwandaecotours.com
Web: www.rwandaecotours.com
Address: Rue Karisimbi, Capi Shop, PO Box 6292, Kigali, Rwanda

TOUR OP/SAFARI/TOUR/HOST
RWANDA ECO-TOURS

This tour operator offers nature safaris, including gorilla safaris, cultural tours and community-based tourism where visitors can have a really hands-on experience and learn about Rwandan daily life. It has an employment policy of turning former poachers into protectors by giving them seed potatoes and teaching them alternative income-generating activities.

Contact: Edwin Sabuhoro
Tel: +250 500331 • +250 500057
Fax: +250 500057
Email: esabuhoro@rwandaecotours.com • info@rwandaecotours.com
Web: www.rwandaecotours.com
Address: PO Box 6292, Kigali, Rwanda

TOUR OP
WILDLIFE TOURS

This Rwandan-owned tour operator offers are diverse experiences in tourism, wildlife management and conservation. They believe that tourism should be educational, experiential and pro-poor. Their dream is to see all Rwandans benefit from tourism through employment, capacity-building and empowering local communities to improve livelihoods, alleviate poverty and strengthen unity among Rwandans. At the same time, they strive to build strong and lasting relationships with international visitors. Half of the company's profits go towards community development.

Contact: Oliva Mutesi
Tel: +250 8527049 (Rwanda) • +44 7788786147 (UK)

Fax: +250 574490
Email: info@wildlifetours-rwanda.com
Web: www.wildlifetours-rwanda.com
Address: PO Box 601, Kigali, Rwanda

AFRICA

THE SEYCHELLES
International dialling code +248

1000km

o MAHE

More than 150 islands form the Indian Ocean archi-pelago of the Seychelles, 1500km from the coast of Africa. Most of them are granitic: mountaintops poking out from a long-flooded plain. Granite boulders add sculptural elegance to beaches of white sand and turquoise sea. No wonder tourism accounts for 70 per cent of this tiny nation's income. Several small islands, such as North, Cousine and Frégate, are only accessible to those staying at exclusive luxury resorts with private plunge pools.

The beach at Anse Source D'Argent on the island of La Digue is graced with especially picturesque rocks and palm trees. This beach, with its pink sand, is one of the most photographed beaches in the world and is accessible to everyone who visits the island. La Digue, the third largest population centre after Mahé and Praslin, also has some charming locally owned guest houses, bars and restaurants, and is the best destination for travellers wanting to make sure that they contribute to the local economy. It is a laid-back island with few motor vehicles. Most people travel around by foot, bicycle or – if you have heavy luggage – bullock cart.

The Seychelles has an amazing variety of plants and animals, some of them only found on the islands, such as the jellyfish tree, a strange and ancient tree that has resisted all efforts to propagate it. Due to very strict environmental legislation, the Seychelles is a success story in protecting flora and fauna on the islands, with half of its land area under conservation. The island of Cousine, for example, is working hard to conserve and restore ecosystems by reintroducing endangered species. The Seychelles is also a world leader in sustainable tourism because the government realized that more expensive holidays reduce the overall number of visitors.

The islands were a French colony from 1710 until 1811, when the British took over; but they remain emphatically French in many people's opinion. They became independent in 1970 and, after turbulent years featuring invasion by mercenaries and various coups, it is now a stable and prosperous country with unconditional social care for orphans, disabled people and the old.

ACCOM
BIRD ISLAND LODGE

Bird Island offers a unique blend of hospitality, relaxation and simplicity in a natural environment. The lodge consists of 24 simple but comfortable individual chalets nestling among the island's former coconut plantation. Each has a king-sized bed, large shower room and a spacious patio over-looking the gardens to the sea. From May to October, the island is home to over 1 million nesting sooty terns, and with at least 20 other species is a bird-watcher's paradise. Bird Island is also an important nesting site for turtles and boasts the world's largest land tortoise, Esmeralda. It is a private island, with over 5km of pristine white sandy beaches and a reef to explore full of colourful fish.

Contact: Gilles Payet
Tel: +248 224925
Fax: +248 225074
Email: reservations@birdislandseychelles.com • thelodge@birdislandseychelles.com
Web: www.birdislandseychelles.com
Address: PO Box 1419, Seychelles

TANZANIA
International dialling code +255

Tanzania was originally a German colony although, unlike Namibia, the only German remains are a few historic buildings. In 1974, it merged with Zanzibar. It is a huge country with a wide variety of scenery and ecosystems. It is most famous for the wildlife in the Serengeti National Park, the Ngorongoro Crater, Lake Manyara and elsewhere. The main city, Dar es Salaam, is hot and laid back. Away from the city the coastal area is fascinating, less developed than that of Kenya and therefore relatively unspoiled, with the historic town of Bagamoyo, ancient Muslim cemeteries, good fishing, nice beaches, palm groves … and the islands of Kilwa and Mafia, where you can really get away from it all.

In the interior you can sail down Lake Tanganyika to Zambia or visit the hilly area near the border with Malawi. The main scenic attraction, for which you do not have to be a mountaineer, is to climb Mount Kilimanjaro; but you do have to be fit (unhappily, global warming is causing the snow on the summit to melt). It is easy to travel by bus from Nairobi to Arusha, the main centre for the game parks, and Moshi, the base for climbing Kilimanjaro. There are services to Arusha (Kilimanjaro Airport) as well as Dar.

Tanzania has a reputation for peace and stability, having got off to a good start under its popular first president, Julius Nyerere. His policy of 'Pan-African socialism', based on self-reliance, came up against corruption and mismanagement and has, as elsewhere, been replaced by a Western neo-liberal model, which has left the poor poorer and the rich richer; but this is still a country at ease with itself where visitors feel welcome.

VOL/ACCOM/DAY
AGAPE CULTURAL TOURISM
Agape is the brainchild of the Women's Group in Mulala Village near Arusha. The term agape hints at the underlying philosophy of coming together in a spirit of sharing and charity; indeed, they stress aspects such as mutual contribution to the enterprise and equality. The aim is to support an orphanage in the community as well as a primary and secondary school. Available to the visitor are opportunities to join in making cheese, coffee and honey. A walk or low-key trek will reveal fine views, peaceful rivers and Meru Mountain.

Tel: +255 784378951 • +255 767378951 • +255 768888966 • +255 782749006
Email: agapetourism@yahoo.com
Address: PO Box 100, Usa-River, Arusha, Tanzania

SAFARI
DOROBO TOURS AND SAFARIS

Dorobo Tours offers camping and walking in community-owned wilderness accompanied by local guides. It only employs guides from indigenous communities with whom it has tourism agreements. These agreements are with groups who are at the bottom of the social and economic stratum, but who have communal land which is suitable for tourism activities that don't infringe on traditional land use. The agreements last for five years and are re-evaluated every couple of years.

Contact: David Peterson
Tel: +255 272509685
Fax: +255 272508336
Email: dorobo@habari.co.tz
Address: PO Box 2534, Arusha, Tanzania

TOUR/TREK
DUMA EXPLORER

Duma is based in Arusha but operates mostly in national parks. It offers safaris, treks and also Zanzibar-based vacations. The treks include Kilimanjaro and Meru. Staff are recruited locally, well treated and provided with training and educational opportunities. Porters are paid the recommended wages and strict guidelines are followed vis-à-vis their treatment on Kilimanjaro. The company supports a local kindergarten in the Meru community, from whom most of the mountain employees come, and arranges volunteer projects for customers.

Contact: Stacy Readal or Saada Omar
Tel: +255 787079127
Email: info@dumaexplorer.com
Web: www.dumaexplorer.com
Address: PO Box 56, Usa River, Tanzania

TOUR OP/ACCOM+/SAFARI
INTO AFRICA ECO-TRAVEL

This is a locally owned tour firm that is dedicated to upholding the principles of ecotourism. Into Africa is dedicated to showing discerning travellers the real Africa through an African's point of view. Into Africa arranges excursions in Tanzania and Kenya, organizing all the logistics, including air and bus tickets, lodge bookings, vehicle hire and camping equipment. It runs the Boma guest house in Arusha and Boma bandaz campsite, with spectacular views of Lake Manyara. This is a unique opportunity to join in the community project and be, like Wordsworth, 'surprised by joy' – only in this case the 'deeper spirit of African joy'.

Contact: Emmy Richard Moshi
Tel: +254 714049201
Fax: +254 20609610
Email: emmy@intoafrica.co.tz · info@intoafrica.co.tz
Web: www.intoafrica.co.tz
Address: PO Box 19293, Arusha, Tanzania

ACCOM+
KAHAWA SHAMBA, COMMUNITY KILIMANJARO NATIVE CO-OPERATIVE UNION (KNCU)

The accommodation and cultural centre are on a coffee farm. This is a joint venture between the KNCU union and small-scale coffee producers on the slopes of Kilimanjaro, with each party owning 50 per cent of the project. Eight visitors can be housed in four traditional chagga huts, although these have en suite bathrooms with hot showers and Western-style toilets. There are many opportunities to interact with local communities and there is good walking in the area. This community-based project aims at providing additional income to the coffee producers. Kahawa Shamba is 47km from Kilimanjaro International Airport.

Contact: Emilson Malisa
Tel: +255 272750464
Mobile: +255 784517995
Email: kncutourism@kilinet.co.tz
Web: www.kahawashamba.co.tz
Address: PO Box 3032, Moshi, Tanzania

VOL/TOUR
LIVINGSTONE TANZANIA TRUST (LTT)

LTT is a charity whose long-term objective is to tackle poverty in the community by providing meaningful, applicable, sustainable and replicable education facilities. In practical terms, this means building schools. It also has a school farm with crops and livestock, and a cultural tourism programme with hiking opportunities and homestays. LTT's strategy is to provide knowledge, skills and access to funds to a local community so that it can be sustainable, and to then move on when the work is done. It offers employment and training, and education in farming, health and sanitation. Guests participate in construction work or farm work, with training provided. Visitors can also learn Swahili, take dance lessons and go on walks in the community to see other farms, hills and villages. On offer, as well, are a visit to a coffee plantation, mountain climbing and a trip to Lake Babati to enjoy sundowners while listening to the hippos calling.

Contact: Julian Page
Email: info@livingstonetanzaniatrust.com
Web: www.livingstonetanzaniatrust.com
Address: The Cottage, Cupids Way, Great Wakering, Essex SS3 0AX, UK

ORG
KILIMANJARO PORTERS ASSISTANCE PROJECT (KPAP)

KPAP is a Tanzanian NGO working on behalf of porters climbing Mount Kilimanjaro to ensure that they have good working conditions. They provide free clothing for any porter or tour company in need and conduct free classes to empower the porters in subjects such as English, first aid, HIV/AIDS awareness and money management. All the proceeds from these visits benefit the porters' union, women and artists' groups. KPAP also has an important role in educating the public as to porters' working conditions and fair working standards for porters. KPAP monitors tour companies to determine which outfitters adhere to their guidelines for proper porter treatment.

Contact: Karen Valenti
Tel: +255 754817615
Email: info@kiliporters.org
Web: www.kiliporters,org
Address: PO Box 1275, Moshi, Tanzania

TOUR+
MULTI ENVIRONMENTAL SOCIETY (MESO)

The MESO project runs eco-cultural trips, together with safaris in Karafu and the Tanzanian Rift Valley area. The trips begin mostly in Arusha, where the visitor can experience a fantastic range of flora and fauna and also see a multitude of historical and contemporary cultural artefacts, getting an insight into everyday tribal life. The main driver is a desire to combat community poverty and, in parallel, to conserve the social and cultural environment. A community involvement policy aims to maintain wildlife habitat, minimize wildlife/human conflict, foster sustainable and legal use of natural resources, and improve the socio-economic health of the participating local communities.

Contact: Basil Michael or Petro Ahham
Tel: +255 754467472 • +255 272505859

AFRICA

Email: mesotz@hotmail.com • meso@meso-tz.org
Web: www.meso-tz.org
Address: PO Box 229, Arusha, Tanzania

TOUR
PEOPLE TO PEOPLE SAFARIS

This small family business wants to supplement the usual Tanzanian wildlife and scenery tourism with visits to local villages, providing guests with a chance to meet people and find out more about their way of life. People to People design itineraries that integrate cultural, wildlife and activity safaris and provide guided tours to tribal areas and historical sites. Payment for the cultural visits is made directly to the villages. Guests stay in selected lodges and guest houses with occasional options for homestays and camping. People to People also organize artisan tours to craft workshops and connect volunteers with local NGOs and self-help projects.

Contact: Gloria Mlola
Tel: +255 754664569
Email: tatah@p2psafaris.com
Web: www.p2psafaris.com
Address: People to People Tourism Services Ltd, PO Box 11840, Arusha, Tanzania

SAFARI+
RUAHA HILLTOP LODGE

Ruaha Hilltop Lodge is located 110km from Iringa, 5km from Tungamalenga village and near the boundary of Ruaha National Park, one of Tanzania's richest concentrations of animal, bird and plant life. It stands on the slopes of Ideremle Mountain and the panoramic view is breathtaking. Jeeps are available for game drives as well as tours of Iringa. Trips can be arranged to Ruaha National Park and other places of interest such as the Ismila Stone Age site, the Mufindi tea plantations and Lake Nyasa. The lodge also helps local people, providing materials and funding to expand a village school. They actively support a young single mothers' association in Iringa, buying their craft products and helping them with marketing.

Contact: Enelise Mwakalinga
Tel: +255 262701806
Mobile: +255 784726709 • +255 754489375
Fax: +255 262700071
Email: ruahahilltoplodge@yahoo.com
Web: www.ruahahilltoplodge.com
Address: Ruaha Hilltop Lodge, PO Box 2026, Iringa, Tanzania

HOST/TOUR/DAY
RUNGWE TEA & TOURS

Run by the Rungwe Smallholders Tea Growers Association (RSTGA), a collective of 15,000 smallholder tea farmers, the project is located in the southern highlands of Tanzania. It organizes trips to natural attractions in the region, such as volcanoes, crater lakes and waterfalls. Guests can take a tea tour, meeting smallholder tea farmers, and visit a tea factory. You can also go hiking to Matema beach on the shores of Lake Malawi and stay overnight in the villages with the local communities.

Contact: David Limbakisya
Tel: +255 252552489
Mobile: +255 784293042
Email: rungweteatours@yahoo.com
Web: www.rungweteatours.com
Address: Box 734, Tukuyu, Tanzania

ORG

TANZANIAN CULTURAL TOURISM PROGRAMME

The Cultural Tourism Programme was established to diversify Tanzania's tourism products and to provide an opportunity for local communities to improve their livelihoods through offering services to tourists. Visitors are offered a variety of experiences, including nature hikes, cycling tours, farm visits, canoeing, camel safaris and looking after cattle with Maasai herders. Also on offer are visits to development projects, participation in daily activities such as coffee picking, sampling local food and visits to markets.

Tanzania is endowed with a rich cultural heritage of 120 ethnic tribes. The Cultural Tourism Programme provides visitors with authentic cultural experiences that combine nature, scenery, folklore, ceremonies, dances, rituals, tales, art, handicrafts and hospitality that give a unique insight into the people's way of life. These holidays both enrich a travel experience and help contribute to poverty alleviation. With assistance from the Cultural Tourism Programme, local men and women organize tours.

Contact: Mary P. Lwoga
Tel: +255 272050025 · +255 754420258
Fax: +255 272507515
Email: culturaltourism@habari.co.tz
Web: www.tanzaniaculturaltourism.com
Address: Museum Buildings, Boma Road, PO Box 2348, Arusha, Tanzania

BABATI AND HANANG

Home to the Barabaig, charismatic pastoralists who have consciously retained their traditional way of life. Visit the bustling market town of Babati, 170km south of Arusha, or take a local canoe on the lake with its pods of hippo and fine selection of water birds (egrets, pelicans, waders, storks, etc.). Climb the extinct volcano of Mount Hanang, through montane forest and grassland. The summit, at 3418m, offers excellent views over a stretch of the Rift Valley. Visit a Gorowa storyteller with lots of information on rituals.

Tel: +255 784397477
Email: kahembeculture@yahoo.com
Web: www.authenticculture.com

CHILUNGA

195km west of Dar es Salaam, the Morogoro region boasts the Uluguru Mountains, rainforest, waterfalls, historical sites and much more. Visitors have a choice of 10 to 12 different hikes, village visits and scenic tours and can participate in traditional dances.

Tel: +255 754477582 · +255 713663993
Email: chilungamg@yahoo.co.uk
Web: www.chilunga.8m.net

ENGARUKA

Situated below the Rift Valley escarpment about 65km north of Manyara, Engaruka is the Maasai name for the extensive ruins of a mysterious terraced city and irrigation system, constructed at least 500 years ago by a late Iron Age culture in the eastern foothills of Mount Empakaai. A variety of guided walks, hikes and climbs are offered in this area.

Tel: +255 787228653 · +255 754507939
Email: engaruka@yahoo.com

ILKINDING'A

Experience Wa-Arusha culture by visiting a healer and tasting traditional food. Take a guided walk through agricultural systems on the slope of Mount Meru or visit craftsmen who produce stools, knives, jewellery and other traditional objects.

Tel: +255 713520264 · +255 784520264
Email: enmasarie@yahoo.com

AFRICA

ILKUROT

A traditional Maasai village, situated about 20km west of Arusha, Ilkurot embodies the Maasai lifestyle with their '*bomas*', holy trees, beaded handicrafts, traditional healers and, most important-ly, their valued cattle. Experience the Maasai lifestyle and participate in traditional dancing. It is a Maasai belief that God gave all the cattle in the world to the Maasai. A five-day safari with donkeys through beautiful scenery is offered.

Tel: +255 784459296 · +255 713332005
Email: kinyorllomon@yahoo.com

KISANGARA

The Kisangara cultural tourism site is located 62km southeast of Moshi, high in the Pare Mountains amid natural forests. The nearby Nyumba ya Mungu (House of God) Dam boasts rich birdlife and breathtaking scenery, including views of Mount Kilimanjaro and Mount Meru. Enjoy life with a local family, join the local women in their dances and experience walks in the bush.

Tel: +255 272757789 · +255 754487193
Email: msafirigrace@yahoo.com

LONGIDO

This is a walking safari with Maasai warriors that provides an insight into the culture and daily life of the Maasai. Visitors can expect to see a variety of birds (including several colourful finches and barbets), and there is a fair amount of large game left in the area, notably gerenuk, lesser kudu, giraffe, Thomson's gazelle and black-backed jackal. Tours include guided walks on the Maasai Plains and climbs of Longido Mountain (an ascent of approximately 2690m).

Tel: +255 787855185
Email: tourymanl@yahoo.com

MACHAME

Here live the Wachagga people of Kilimanjaro. Tours include visits to Chagga homesteads and typ-ical Chagga coffee and banana subsistence farms, as well as environmental and cultural walks/hikes through forested areas along fast-flowing rivers and streams.

Tel: +255 272756906 · +255 713496207 · +255 784347369
E-mail: fodamachame@elct.org

MAMBA AND MARANGU

The name Marangu derives from the local Chagga word meaning 'spring water' and the village is situated on the lower slopes of Kilimanjaro about 40km from Moshi town. On offer are a variety of half-day trips taking in various natural and cultural sites on the surrounding slopes. Other walks lead to nearby Mamba and Makundi, known for their traditional Chagga blacksmiths and wood-carvers. Walk beside numerous waterfalls, through lush green valleys with stunning views of Mount Kilimanjaro. Visit ancient caves used for hiding during wars.

Tel: +255 754818273 · +255 754390084
Email: marvellouscreation@mailcity.com

MBEYA

An insight is given into tea farming and processing, and the traditional cultures of the area. Visit Ngosi Crater Lake, where legends recount a monster residing under the water; climb Mount Rungwe, which dominates the area; or visit the Mbozi meteorite, weighing 12 tonnes, and the nat-ural stone bridge of Kiwira. Relax at Matema Beach on the shores of Lake Nyasa, with a full view of the Livingstone Mountain Range and Udzunwa National Park. Marvel at the scenic beauty of southern Tanzania.

Tel: +255 754463471 · +255 754087689
Email: sisikwasisitours@hotmail.com

AFRICA

MKURU

The main attractions here are organized camelback trips, which range in duration from a short half-day excursion to a week-long camel safari through the surrounding dry plains that are rich in birdlife and still support a few game animals. There are traditional *bomas* scattered throughout this Maasai-dominated region, and climbs of the pyramid-shaped Ol Donyo Landaree Mountain can be arranged.

Tel: +255 784724498
Email: mkurucamels@yahoo.co.uk

MONDULI JUU

A cluster of four small Maasai villages situated 50km west of Arusha in the Monduli Hills, Monduli Juu offers *boma* visits, escarpment climbs, rainforest tours and visits to local hospital, primary school, dispensary and kindergarten projects, a Maasai herbalist and a women's jewellery factory. Try the traditional nyama choma with Maasai warriors in Orpul where visitors cut the meat themselves.

Tel: +255 787755671 • +255 786505300
Email: mpoyoni@yahoo.com

MTO WA MBU

Mto wa Mbu (River of Mosquitoes) is said locally to be the only place in Tanzania where representatives of 120 Tanzanian tribes are resident. Different walks and hikes are arranged through and around this Rift Valley town, which lies close to the entrance gate of Lake Manyara National Park.

Tel: +255 784606654 • +255 272539303
Email: mtoculturalprogramme@hotmail.com
Web: www.mtoculturalprogramme.tripod.com

MULALA

A village on the footslopes of Mount Meru, Mulala lies at an altitude of 1450m, some 30km from Arusha, in a fertile agricultural area which produces coffee, bananas and other fruits and vegetables. Several short walks can be undertaken in the surrounding hills, including one to the forested Marisha River, home to a variety of birds and primates. Another local place of interest is Mama Anna's Dairy, which supplies cheese to several upmarket hotels in Arusha. A glimpse is given into the daily life of Meru farmers and their surrounding crops and vegetation.

Tel: +255 784378951 • +255 784747433
Email: agapetourism@yahoo.com

NG'IRESI

Set on the slopes of Mount Meru some 7km from Arusha town, this cultural tourism programme based in the traditional Wa-Arusha village of Ng'iresi offers many insights into the local culture and agricultural practices. There are also some delightful walks in the surrounding Mount Meru foothills, to Songota waterfall and across the Themi River to Navuru waterfall.

Tel: +255 754476079 • +255 754476903 • +255 75553367
Email: lotisayero@hotmail.com

NORTHERN PARE MOUNTAINS

Situated 50km southeast of Moshi, the Northern Pare Mountains have at their heart a village called Usangi, a centre of economic activities. The cultural tourism programme here offers a walk through Kindoroko Forest Reserve, climbs to different mountain peaks for splendid views of Kilimanjaro, Lake Jipe and Nyumba ya Mungu, and visits to historical sites and projects concerning irrigation, soil conservation and reforestation.

Tel: +255 272757924/27
Email: nelsonkangero@hotmail.com

OLDONYO SAMBU

Located 36km northwest of Arusha on the main Arusha–Nairobi highway, the major attraction of Oldonyo Sambu is the busy, colourful Maasai market, which is held weekly. Other attractions include walks and hikes in the hills, visits to traditional *bomas*, and horse, camel and donkey rides across Maasai country.

Tel: +255 784663381 • +255 784694790
Email: thomaslaoi@yahoo.co.uk

OSOTWA CULTURAL TOURISM INITIATIVE

The Osotwa initiative provides walks through nine villages on the slopes of Mount Meru; a walk up Sambasha Hill, an old volcano surrounded by Colobus monkeys; a guided tour to a Maasai market on Thursdays or Sundays; and a visit to Kitatuk Hill, Osotwa's indigenous tree planting project, with over 18,000 trees planted so far.

Tel: +255 754090203 • +255 755391439
Email: osotwa_cbco@yahoo.com

PANGANI COAST

A visit to a former slave labour camp and slave market site, a river cruise through vast coconut plantations, a guided walk through historical Pangani town and a fishing experience with local fishermen are all provided. Also to be enjoyed here are white beaches and splendid coral reefs which harbour a great diversity of tropical marine life. Saadani National Park, Tanzania's only beach and wildlife park, is in close proximity to Pangani.

Tel: +255 784489129
Fax: +255 272644316
Email: sekibahaculturetours@yahoo.co.uk

SOUTHERN PARE MOUNTAINS

150km from Moshi Town, this area offers walks along steep slopes, through dense tropical forests and the villages of Pare in the Mbaga Hills deep within the southern Pare Mountains. See and hear the legend of the 'growing rock', visit the villages, the farmers, and listen to the legends of the Pare people.

Tel: +255 754852010
Email: tona_lodge@hotmail.com

TENGERU

Situated on the slopes of Mount Meru, Tengeru is 13km from Arusha along the Arusha to Moshi road. Visit Lake Duluti, a deep caldera lake, River Malala, Shimbumbu Hill and Mangalla waterfalls, or take a three-hour tour of Patandi village and the homes of the villagers. Visit a local herbalist and primary schools (including one for the disabled). Enjoy local singing, dancing, drumming and poetry of the Meru culture around a bonfire at night.

Tel: +255 754960176 • +255 756981602
Email: tengeru_cultural_tourism@yahoo.com

USAMBARA MOUNTAINS

Favoured by the Germans and British during colonial times, the Usambaras are rich in historical buildings from the period. Situated in the north-eastern part of Tanzania, these mountains are known for their pleasant climate, beautiful viewpoints and fertile slopes and tumbling rivers. Take your choice from the many cultural, historical, scenic and bird-watching tours that are on offer here, and visit irrigation and soil conservation projects.

Tel: +255 784 689848 • +255 784 423917
Email: usambaras2005@yahoo.co.uk

AFRICA

TOUR OP/TREK
TANZANIA JOURNEYS

Tanzania Journeys is an ethical and innovative tour operator. It believes that everyone working for the organization should benefit from fair wages and good working conditions. It offers Kilimanjaro and other mountain climbs, with consideration for the porters' welfare, and game drive safaris combined with walks, boats and bikes. It also organizes activity holidays such as trekking, biking, running, team sports and yoga. Cultural and historical tours may include discovering film, music, sculpture and architecture. Tanzania Journeys' community development perspective influences all of the trips it organizes, and it acts responsibly, always considering the social, economic and environmental impacts of its tours.

Contact: Mark Donnelly
Tel: +27 2754293
Mobile: 0787834152
Fax: +27 2754016
Email: info@tanzaniajourneys.com
Web: www.tanzaniajourneys.com
Address: PO Box 1724, Moshi,Tanzania

VOL
UVIKIUTA

A well-run volunteer association managing regular workcamps since 1983.

Contact: Ben Mongi
Tel: +255 754833909
Email: uvikiuta83@yahoo.com
Address: PO Box 71373, Dar es Salaam, Tanzania

UGANDA
International dialling code +256

'The pearl of Africa'. Ugandans are proud of this description, reputedly first coined by the young Winston Churchill. Straddling the Equator and flanked by Mount Elgon in the west and the Ruwenzori Mountain range in the east, landlocked Uganda is, with the exception of the arid north, one of the most fertile places in Africa. In the south of the country the four kingdoms of Buganda, Bunyoro, Ankole and Toro have strong surviving political structures; but there are many other ethnic groups and languages. The common language is English; but Luganda is widely spoken. Some people speak Swahili, although the Baganda people especially prefer not to.

A small country by the continent's standards, Uganda contains great natural diversity: unique plant life on the fabled Mountains of the Moon; big game in the Queen Elizabeth National Park; and mountain gorillas and chimpanzees in the impenetrable forests of Bwindi and Kibale.

Its history has been turbulent: the atrocities of Idi Amin and Milton Obote during the 1970s and 1980s are well known. Many of the 35,000 Ugandan Asians who were expelled by Amin have since regained their property; but they are less visible than they used to be. Uganda has enjoyed stability and growing prosperity since Yoweri Museveni came to power in 1986; but political tensions have increased as

AFRICA

Museveni has tried to hang on to power. The long running war in the north against the Lord's Resistance Army, led by the notorious Joseph Kony, has cost many lives, a great deal of money and traumatized numbers of abducted children.

Uganda has been ravaged by AIDS, which has left close to 1 million children orphaned. However, it faced the problem openly and was the first country to seriously reverse the advance of the pandemic.

Uganda has a lot to offer the visitor and caters for all pockets, and you will not forget local people's hospitality and generosity.

HOST/ACCOM+/VOL
KANAAMA INTERACTIVE
This new enterprise aims to provide a base for volunteers, visitors and researchers. You can choose between a 12-day introductory course, a longer volunteering period, or a study tour enshrining your wishes. You will live in a house, probably sharing a room, and eat communally in the evenings. Food is provided by the village hosts. Immerse yourself in village life. Help to build another future. Activities in the community are too many to list – you would not be bored or idle. And the natural world is on your doorstep.

Contact: Prue Chamberlayne
Tel: +44 2088839297
Email: kiafrica@gmail.com
Web: www.kiafrica.org
Address: 24A Princess Avenue, London N10 3LR, UK

ACCOM
THE LAKE BUNYONI DEVELOPMENT PROJECT
Bushara Island Camp is owned by the Lake Bunyoni Development Company, which is a non-profit enterprise. It is great for bird-watching and marine-based activity, as well as simply relaxing. It's about 6.5 hours from Entebbe Airport by road and then, briefly, motorboat. All of the money earned is used on development projects for those living around the lake. Four orphanages are supported, schools sponsored, widows introduced to new skills such as tie-dyeing and local people taught hospitality skills. In addition, they organize swimming lessons in schools and communities around the lake region, and HIV/AIDS education. Experiments in land management and agroforestry have filtered through and become local practice. A tent costs UK£22/US$28 a night for a double. Recommended by the Uganda Community Tourism Association (UCOTA).

Contact: Edith Bampabwire
Tel: +256 48626110 · +256 77464585
Email: busharaisland@africaonline.co.ug
Web: www.acts.ca/lbdc · www.busharaislandcamp.com/lbdc.htm
Address: Bushara Island Camp, PO Box 794, Kabale, Uganda

ACCOM
RUBONI COMMUNITY CAMP
Ruboni is owned by a group of 50 but benefits the whole community – the profits are assigned to projects at a community general meeting. The camp is located at the main gate to the central circuit of Rwenzori Mountains National Park, with a marvellous view of the Rwenzori Mountains. Other national parks are, respectively, 94km and 45km away. Accommodation is mostly in Bandas or safari tents, but there are some homestays. Visitors have the chance to participate in local development and conservation projects, which Ruboni supports.

Contact: Rumba Ferdinand
Tel: +256 774195859 · +256 752503554 · +256 773650049
Email: ucota@africaonline.co.ug · ruboni.communitytourism@gmail.com

Web: www.rcdctourism.org/ruboni
Address: PO Box 320, Kasese, Uganda

VOL
UGANDA PIONEERS' ASSOCIATION (UPA)
A well-established workcamp association offering workcamps and placements.

Contact: Samuel Waddimba
Tel: +256 77388290 · +256 75504301
Fax: +256 41530765 (attn UPA)
Email: uganda_pioneers22@hotmail.com
Web: www.upa.sphosting.com
Address: PO Box 25973, Kampala

VOL
UGANDA VOLUNTARY DEVELOPMENT ASSOCIATION (UVDA)
Uganda's oldest voluntary workcamp association, which also offers placements.

Contact: Rogers Kamwasi
Tel: +256 782929021 · +256 2645479
Fax: +256 41345580 · +256 41349203
Email: uvda69@yahoo.com
Web: www.uvda-uganda.com
Address: PO Box 22253, Kampala

ZANZIBAR
International dialling code +255 24

Mosques, narrow streets and the smell of cloves – what could be more exotic than Zanzibar, a place with a rich fusion of African, Arab, European and Indian influences? Because the main products are cloves, nutmeg, cinnamon and pepper, they were known as the Spice Islands (a name shared with an island in Indonesia).

More significantly, Zanzibar was a centre of the slave trade when it was an independent state. Slavery was abolished in 1873 and in 1890 the British declared Zanzibar a protectorate. In 1963 it became independent; but this was followed by a leftist revolution against the minority Arab ruling elite. In 1964 Zanzibar decided to join with what was then Tanganika to become the United Republic of Tanzania.

Zanzibar has several small islands and two main ones: Unguja, commonly known as Zanzibar, and Pemba. It is a lovely, relaxing place for a holiday. There are beaches, the beautiful United Nations Educational, Scientific and Cultural Organization (UNESCO) World Heritage Stone Town, good facilities, boat trips, fishing and luscious fruits. Pemba can be visited by boat and, in fact, you can reach Zanzibar by boat from Dar es Salaam as an alternative to flying. It is only 24km to 32km off the coast of Tanzania. Tourism is Zanzibar's newest and biggest industry, with considerable development taking place. The all-inclusive developments sit uncomfortably with the smaller enterprises; but most Zanzibaris have yet to benefit from it as they earn, on average, less than US$1 a day.

AFRICA

ACCOM+
CHUMBE ISLAND CORAL PARK (CHICOP) LTD

This island is a fully managed conservation area, sustained by proceeds from genuine ecotourism. It offers a marine park, forest reserve, guided snorkelling and walks, forest trails and historic monuments. As you lie in your bungalow hammock, your toes will be only seconds away from warm tropical water. All you have to bring is enough time to appreciate what Chumbe has to offer. The best kind of all-inclusive – only the alcohol is extra!

Contact: Prisca David Laizer
Tel/Fax: +255 242231040
Mobile: +255 777413232 · +255 777413582
Email: chumbe@zitec.org · office@chumbeisland.com
Web: www.chumbeisland.com
Address: PO Box 3203, Zanzibar, Tanzania

NORTH AFRICA

EGYPT
International dialling code +20

1000km
CAIRO

Any visit to 'Ancient Egypt' must include the Pyramids; the Egyptian Museum in Cairo with the treasures of Tuthankhamun; a visit to Luxor with its the Valley of the Kings and the Karnak temples; Aswan and the temples of Philae; and, if possible, an excursion to Abu Simbel in the far south. The independent traveller can visit countless other interesting historical sites in this country, which was home to one of the oldest cultures in the world, spanning 3000 years of continuous history.

Unforgettable as these places are, Egypt is not just the land of pyramids, tombs and temples. Arab Egypt, especially old Cairo, is worth a visit on its own and Alexandria still has a certain charm. The fastest-growing tourist area is the Red Sea coast where, in spite of dramatic damage to the environment (mainly the coral reefs), swimming, diving and sunbathing provide a very different Egyptian holiday. What makes any trip to Egypt special is the hospitality of the Egyptian people, so make time for tea and a chat with people where you can.

Egypt has the second biggest economy in the Middle East after Saudi Arabia; but there is a lot of individual poverty in this socially conservative country. Its most famous writer is Naguib Mahfouz, who was the first Arab-language writer to win the Nobel Prize for Literature in 1988. His best-known work is the Cairo Trilogy, *Palace Walk*, *Palace of Desire* and *Sugar Street*, which explores the urban traditional lives of three generations of a Cairo family from World War I to the 1950s. His later work conceals political criticism under allegory and symbolism.

ACCOM
BASATA ECO-LODGE
Basata offers blissfully peaceful accommodation in tents, huts and chalets on the beach. This is a ground-breaking initiative on the Red Sea, and has been running since 1986. The eco-lodge itself has very well-integrated policies on recycling, water conservation and pollution alleviation, and has strong links with the local community, employing several Bedouin workers. The owner of Basata also runs Hemaya, an NGO which has pioneered environmental clean-up campaigns, built windmills for the local population, and set up a van with computers and satellite internet connection to educate local people for free on how to use a computer.

Contact: Sherif El Ghamrawy
Tel: +20 693500480/81
Fax: +20 693502050
Email: basata@basata.com
Web: basata@basata.com
Address: Basata, Nuweiba, South Sinai, Egypt

MOROCCO
International dialling code +212

1000km

RABAT

At the crossroads between Africa and Europe, with influences from the Middle East, Morocco has to be one of the world's most exciting tourist experiences. The greatest attractions are the four great imperial cities – Fez, Meknes, Marrakech and Rabat – and the chance to experience the Sahara Desert in relative comfort. Add to this the two dramatic mountain ranges of the Atlas and the Rif; numerous delightful smaller towns such as Tetuan, Tangier, Chefchaouen, Safi and Essaouira; the Atlantic coast resorts around Agadir, colonized by the package tour industry; and the cosmopolitan city of Casablanca, with its stupendous new Grande Mosque.

Moroccan craftsmanship is legendary, exemplified in traditional architecture, textiles, jewellery and pottery. Shopping for these things in the souk is also part of the fun, provided you can cope with the high-pressure sales talk. Having a meal in the Djemaa el Fna, the big open-air square in Marrakech, is also unforgettable because of the entertainers – and likely to be delicious. Apart from its incredible variety, Morocco is very easy to visit. It is the only African country easily reached by train from Europe – to Algeciras and then by ferry to Tangier. Moroccan railways are modern and efficient and there are good bus services too. Tourism is well developed and it is possible to survive on a small budget.

Morocco managed to stay independent until 1912 when it became a French protectorate (look out for the French influences that remain). The country recovered its independence in 1956 and since then has been a constitutional monarchy, though the king has wide executive powers.

VOL
CHANTIERS JEUNESSE MAROC (CJM)
A well-established workcamp association in a country where voluntary service has a long history.

Contact: Najib Benabdellah
Tel: +212 37722140
Fax: +212 37726658
Email: cjm.volontariat@menara.ma
Web: www.users.mtds.com/~cjm
Address: BP 1351, 10001 Rabat RP

ORG/HOST
CHAOUEN RURAL
This is a non-profit organization that aims to develop rural tourism and create extra income for the rural population in the province of Chefchaouen. Visitors can stay with families for two to four days while going on excursions in the area to learn about Chaoueni rural life, culture and traditions. Worth visiting are the Talassemtane Natural Park and the Bouhachem Reserve.

Contact: Fatima Habte
Tel: +212 39987267 · +212 72743374 · +212 10210146
Fax: +212 39987267
Email: info@chaouenrural.org · reservation@chaouenrural.org
Web: www.chaouenrural.org
Address: Place Makhzine, Chefchaouen, Morocco; or Rue Machichi, Quartier Kharrzine, N7 Bureau 3, Chefchaouen, Morocco

ACCOM+
KASBAH DU TOUBKAL

The Kasbah prefers to call itself a Berber Hospitality Centre rather than a hotel. Located in the mountainous Toubkal National Park, it was transformed by traditional methods from the home of a feudal Caid into an 'unprecedented haven'. Owned by Discover Ltd UK and operated by Moroccan staff, the Kasbah strives to maximize the economic trickle-down by buying locally and using local mule transport for goods. Five per cent of the profits go to the Village Association. The Kasbah is a 90-minute drive from Marrakech followed by a 10-minute walk or mule ride. Tours and trekking are also organized. A more recent development for the more adventurous is the Toubkal Lodge, a sister place to stay, some four hours by foot from the Kasbah, at an altitude of 2500m.

Contact: Kerrie Wrigley
Tel: +212 24485611
Fax: +212 24485636
Email: kasbah@discover.ltd.uk
Web: www.kasbahdutoubkal.com
Address: Imlil, BP 31, Asni (near Marrakech), Morocco

TOUR OP
NATURALLY MOROCCO

A tour operator which promotes responsible tourism, ensuring payment for carbon offsetting on all flights and promoting environmental consciousness in local guest houses. Visitors can go on bespoke tours to local Berber villages, take Arabic lessons and enjoy traditional music and dancing. Also on offer are Moroccan cookery lessons, and guided tours around the national parks, mountains, towns and cities of Morocco given by knowledgeable English speaking guides. Naturally Morocco also supports local charities both directly and by managing donations from its customers.

Contact: Giles Giffin
Tel: +44 1239710814
Fax: 07092379725
Email: giles@naturallymorocco.co.uk
Web: www.naturallymorocco.co.uk
Address: 29 Parc Hafan, Newcastle Emlyn, Carmarthenshire SA38 9AR, UK

TREK/ACCOM
SOCIÉTÉ RENARD BLEU TOUAREG

A tour operator, owned and founded by nomads, which aims to offer an experience that is both out of the ordinary, socially acceptable and environmentally sustainable. They organize trekking tours and camps in the breathtaking landscape of the Moroccan desert, where guests are treated like members of the nomadic family, gaining a real insight into the nomads' rich and ancient culture. There is also a guest house called Le Sauvage Noble, situated at the rim of the Moroccan part of the Sahara Desert. It is a brick earth building restored using traditional techniques, set in the beautiful location of an oasis.

Contact: Abdellah Naji, Morocco • Daniela Vogt, Europe
Tel: +212 61348413
Fax: +212 24846251
Email: info@renard-bleu-touareg.org
Web: www.renard-bleu-touareg.org • www.sauvage-noble.org
Address: Société Renard Bleu Touareg, BP 140, Zagora, Morocco

AFRICA

TOUR OP
TIZI RANDONNEES
This is a travel agency that promotes sustainable and fairly traded tourism. Visitors will experience many sides of Moroccan society, such as local co-operatives and craft workers practising fair trade. They are also involved in several development projects in Morocco, including a centre for street children in Kénitra. A Spanish NGO assists with funding these projects.

Contact: Kais Baraket
Tel: +212 37375354 · +212 37360981
Fax: +212 37374009
Email: info@tizirando.com · tizirando@hotmail.com
Web: www.tizirando.com · www.tazitounte.com
Address: 46 Avenue Moulay Abderrahmane, No 1 Kénitra, Morocco

SOUTHERN AFRICA

BOTSWANA
International dialling code +267

1000km

GABORONE

One of Africa's success stories, Botswana was a haven of peace even while South Africa was still a land of apartheid. Independent since 1966, it is Africa's longest continuous multi-party democracy and is relatively free of corruption. With a high literacy rate (over 80 per cent), it has been called the Hampstead of Africa. However, it has the second highest rate of HIV in the world after Swaziland.

Most of its huge landlocked area consists of the Kalahari Desert, which is inhabited by dwindling numbers of Bushman hunter-gatherers. The desert is worth a visit in itself; but it is the north of the country that mainly attracts tourists. The Chobe National Park on the border with Zambia and Namibia (and handy for a side trip to the Victoria Falls) is one of Africa's greatest game parks and home to more elephants than you can ever imagine. Further west is the amazing Okavango Delta, where a major river splits into a vast swamp and soaks away into the desert, providing refuge for a variety of antelope and a paradise for bird-watchers. Safari-based tourism, tightly controlled and often upmarket, is an important source of income for the country. The populated areas in the east and south of the country are also worth a visit.

The large traditional villages, such as Serowe and Mochudi, are as large as small towns and they are the base from which people take their cattle out to distant 'cattle posts' on the edge of the desert during the (slightly) rainy season. Gaborone, the capital, is modern and expanding fast. It is the home of that famous fictional character, Mma Precious Ramotswe of the *Ladies' No 1 Detective Agency* books by Alexander McCall Smith.

VOL
BOTSWANA WORKCAMP ASSOCIATION (BWA)
An efficient association that organizes international workcamps, some in game reserves.

Tel: +267 5748610
Fax: +267 5748610
Email: bwa@info.bw
Address: PO BOX 1185, Mochudi

LUX/SAFARI
DUBA PLAINS CAMP
This camp can accommodate 12 visitors at any one time and offers an exceptional big game experience – the area is famed for its lions and buffalo. Guests have an opportunity to learn directly from the locals about the environment and to dip into local culture. The camp is wholly owned by the company, which leases the land from the community, in the form of the Okavango

AFRICA

Community Trust. The cost is a fully inclusive UK£565/US$975 per night, and the contribution to the community in the form of rent is approximately 655 pula (UK£48/US$82). Access to the camp is by light aircraft.

Web: www.wilderness-safaris.com

TREK
KAIE TOURS

Kaie Tours organizes treks in rural Botswana. On the village trek, visitors learn about traditional farming techniques while walking through gentle hill country, while the Tswapong Hills trek offers more challenging walking and spectacular views. The Limpopo River trek follows the banks of the river, spotting wildlife and birds along the way. More adventurous travellers can stay in a wilderness camp in the Kalahari Desert, learn how to survive from the Bushmen, and go for a game drive in the Central Kalahari Game Reserve. It only employs local people and operates a traditional Bushman environmental policy, which causes almost no pollution and leaves a very small carbon footprint.

Contact: Mogs
Tel: +267 3973388 · +267 72261585
Fax: +267 3973388
Email: toye@it.bw
Web: www.kaietours.com
Address: PO Box 26053, Game Cit, Botswana

ACCOM +
KALAHARI SUNSET SAFARIS

The offer is an irresistible cultural experience: camping and living with the Bushmen, while staying in traditional huts and being completely immersed in their culture. Your presence and interest will help to convince them that a living can be made from sharing their knowledge with tourists, and this helps to prevent rural–urban migration and potential alcohol abuse. This encourages the Bushmen to preserve their culture by transmitting it to the young.

Contact: Jason
Tel: +267 72155259
Email: ahs@botsnet.bw · kalaharisunset@yahoo.co.uk
Web: www.kalaharisunset.com
Address: PO Box 651, Ghanzi, Botswana

SAFARI
MASSON SAFARIS

The owners, Sallie and Ewan Masson, offer tailor-made itineraries to suit individuals, families and small groups. They emphasize the importance of seeing not just big game, but also the small things in nature and the wide open spaces. Emphasis is placed on the appreciation of local cultures. Traditional food is served on safari – no international cuisine and claret.

Contact: Sallie Masson
Tel: +267 6862442
Email: massonsafaris@dynabyte.bw
Web: www.massonsafaris.co.bw
Address: Private Bag 257, Maun, Botswana

LESOTHO
International dialling code +266

'The Kingdom in the Sky' is the much reduced realm of the Basotho, who held out in this mountain fortress against the attacks of the Boers during the 19th century. It became a British protectorate until its independence in 1966 and is now a constitutional monarchy. The country is completely surrounded by South Africa. It exports water to its neighbour from the huge Oxbow Project; and traditionally manpower was exported to the mines, which had harmful social consequences but did bring in some income.

Most of the country is a high and rugged plateau, linked to the Drakensberg Mountains in Kwazulu Natal. The scenery comprises great high plateaux and huge rocks, and there are some historic rock paintings too, but it can get very cold in winter. It is a great country for horse trekking – traditionally every Basotho had a horse. The population mainly lives in the lowlands in the west of the country. Maseru, the capital, is a laid-back place with reasonable restaurants and plenty of good handicraft products available, such as tapestries, angora wool and the famous traditional straw hats.

Tourism is vital to the economy, as the country has little cultivatable land and few other resources. Poor rainfall in recent years and the closure of several textile factories has worsened the already bad economic situation. The United Nations describes 40 per cent of the population as 'ultra poor', partly caused by the deaths of farmers from AIDS.

VOL
LESOTHO WORKCAMPS ASSOCIATION (LWA)
A well-established workcamp association with projects at different seasons.

Contact: Kory Masitha
Tel: +266 58719760
Fax: +266 1859560 (mobile phone)
Email: masithak@yahoo.co.uk
Address: PO Box 12783, Maseru 100

ACCOM/TREK
MALEALEA LODGE AND PONY TREK CENTRE
Malealea Lodge and the local community are inter-reliant. Visitors are encouraged to mix with local people, learn about development projects and purchase handicrafts. Wherever possible, services are procured locally. Great efforts are being made in the areas of water conservation, waste management and energy conservation. Pony trekking and hiking allow visitors to get right away and sample village life in remote mountain areas. The lodge has a development trust that contributes to the local community's education, infrastructure, health, environment and economic self-sufficiency.

Contact: Di Jones
Tel: +27 513266766
Mobile: 0829257815 · 0825524215
Fax: 0866481815
Email: malealea@mweb.co.za · di.malealea@mweb.co.za
Web: www.malealea.co.ls · www.malealea.com
Address: Malealea Lodge, Adventure and Pony Trek, Lesotho, PO Box 27974, Danhof, Bloemfontein 9310, South Africa

AFRICA

MALAWI
International dialling code +265

'The warm heart of Africa' and 'the land of the lake' are the standard tourist slogans, and they do fit the bill for Malawi. This is an attractive little country which follows the southern end of the Great Rift Valley, most of which consists of the long expanse of Lake Malawi. This lake and Chogoni Rock Art are on the UNESCO World Heritage list.

The scenery is sometimes stunning, ranging from the wooded shores of the lake to the cool Nyika Plateau, a game reserve, Zomba Mountain and Mount Mulanje, approached through green tea gardens. There are pleasant lakeside resorts, such as Salima and Monkey Bay, and historic mission stations at Livingstonia and on Likoma Island in the lake. The main towns are the commercial capital, Blantyre, the new capital at Lilongwe and the rather charming old capital, now the university town, of Zomba. Communications and the climate are good and the people are very friendly.

However, rapid population growth means that the single major national resource, agricultural land, is under pressure. The food supply system is precarious and prone to natural disasters, both droughts and heavy rainfall, so constant food aid is needed. Sensitive tourism can help to offset increasing poverty.

Malawi is among the world's least developed countries with a low life expectancy, partly due to the high rates of HIV/AIDS infection. However, after more than 70 years as a British colony and three decades of totalitarian rule, it is now a democratic multi-party state, and hopefully it can move forward.

VOL
ACTIVE YOUTH INITIATIVE FOR SOCIAL ENHANCEMENT (AYISE-MWAI)
A fairly new, but reliable, workcamp association.

Contact: Christopher Misuku
Tel: +265 1655079/323/265
Fax: +265 1655079
Email: ayise@malawi.net
Web: www.ayisemw.org
Address: PO Box 90588, Bangwe, Blantyre 9, Malawi

ACCOM +
LUWAWA FOREST LODGE
Founded in the same year as Tourism Concern, this is an ecotourism lodge and outdoor adventure centre. A wide range of outdoor activities is offered and visits can be made to a specially established cultural tourism village, which visitors can stay at for 24 hours, with the US$15 special fee staying with the village. An environmental trust helps local people with income-generating activities. Six local primary schools are being helped physically, and visitor sponsorship is supplying additional educational resources.

Contact: George Wardlow
Tel: +265 1342333 · +265 1991106
Email: Luwawa@malawi.net
Web: www.luwawaforestlodge.com
Address: Luwawa Forest Lodge, Private Bag 43, Mzimba, Malawi

MOZAMBIQUE
International dialling code +258

Mozambique is unusual: a welcoming country where tourism is rare. Wracked by civil war until 1992, recovery was set back by the severe flooding of 2000 and 2001 and drought in 2002. Mozambique has suffered greatly; but although there are legacies of this everywhere, it has made big strides since the end of the civil war and has become a magnet for foreign investment. However, poverty remains widespread with more than half of Mozambicans living on less than US$1 a day.

Mozambique is now emerging as a good holiday destination. Bordering both South Africa and Tanzania, its magnificent coast stretches 2500km and saw centuries of trade with Arabia and India; but the Portuguese legacy from nearly 500 years of colonial rule is most evident today. Portuguese is the official language, although English is now widely spoken.

The towns, although often shabby and run down, still have a Mediterranean flavour. Maputo, the capital, has experienced a boom with a lot of South African investment. If you have time, a visit to the Ilha do Moçambique (Mozambique Island) is worth the effort. A UNESCO World Heritage site, it is the oldest European settlement in East Africa. Protected from damage by the civil war, most of Mozambique's coral reefs and marine life are pristine and largely unexplored.

The southern islands of Bazaruto and Benguerra, offshore islands with top diving sites and exclusive beach lodges are emerging as world-class attractions, and are going to great lengths to preserve their environments for the future. This stance is backed by the government; but commercial pressures may threaten this. Along the coast the Quirimbas Archipelago, like much of the country's interior, remains unexplored but offers huge potential for discovery.

VOL
ASSOCIACAO JUVENIL PARA O DESENVOLVIMENTO DO VOLUNTARIADO EM MOCAMBIQUE (AJUDE)

A very effective local association offering workcamps and volunteer placements all around the country.

Contact: Horacio Ernesto Changa
Tel: +258 2132854 · +258 27398770
Fax: +258 21312854
Email: ajude@tvcabo.co.mz
Web: www.ajude.org.mz
Address: Rua da Mesquita 2222, PO Box 117, Maputo

ACCOM
DIVERS ECO OPERATION (DEO)

The lodge (open in October 2009) is called Nuarro and has seafront bungalows, a high-end restaurant, a marine activity centre and a beach bar, all located on the stunning peninsula of Baixo do Pinda, Nampula Province. This is a vehicle for social, cultural and environmental awareness in Mozambique. The organizers are determined that their tourist project will be ecologically and socially sustainable, going well beyond being a source of employment for the local community. The ofroadandsea.com website works as an e-guide for tourists in Mozambique.

Contact: Trienke Lodewijk
Email: moz@ofroadandsea.com · trienke@nuarro.com
Web: www.ofroadandsea.com · www.nuarro.com

LUX+
GULUDO BEACH LODGE

A luxury eco-lodge squeezed between the Indian Ocean and the wild African bush. Nine sea-facing *bandas* stretch along 12km of white sand beach in the Quirimbas National Park, northern Mozambique. Guests can enjoy the incredible wildlife, go bird-watching, diving and snorkelling, or tour the mangroves and the bush in search of elephants. The lodge also organizes island and village tours, and sunset sails on a locally made *dhow*. Evenings can be spent enjoying great locally sourced cuisine and sharing stories over a few drinks. Guludo caters for visitors of all ages, including groups, families, older guests and honeymooners. The lodge was born out of a desire to use tourism to relieve poverty and protect the environment. The owners work in direct partnership with the local community.

Contact: Becky Pelkonen
Tel: +44 2071274727
Email: contact@bespokeexperience.com
Web: www.guludo.com
Address: Bespoke Experience Ltd, St Christophers, Potters Lane, Woking, Surrey GU23 7AL, UK

LUX+
IBO ISLAND LODGE

Located on Ibo Island in the middle of Quirimbas National Park, the lodge consists of three magnificent 100-year-old beautifully furnished mansions with two swimming pools, set in tropical gardens on the waterfront. Visitors can explore the beaches of the Quirimbas Archipelago, enjoy watersports such as kayaking, snorkelling and swimming, or wander around the forts and old buildings of the colonial town. The evenings can be spent appreciating the sunsets and beautiful views of the bay, while sampling meals of freshly caught seafood.

Contact: Jo-Anna Collard
Tel: +27 217020285
Fax: +27 217020692
Email: fiona@iboisland.com and info@iboisland.com
Web: www.iboisland.com
Address: PO Box 30661, Tokai, 7966, Cape Town, South Africa

LUX
NKWICHI LODGE – MANDA WILDERNESS PROJECT

Nkwichi is a privately owned luxury eco-lodge nestled in the unspoilt shoreline of Lake Niassa/Malawi. Blending with nature and the spectacular surroundings, the lodge is invisible from the lake. It offers unique and comfortable accommodation, while endeavouring to be as environmentally friendly as possible. This includes being entirely powered by solar energy, recycling as much as possible (e.g. by cutting glass bottles in half and turning them into tumblers) and using grey water to irrigate the surrounding natural bush. Nkwichi has been a driving force in the creation of the Umoji Association, representing 20,000 local people. Importantly, it has enabled six communities to secure land rights certificates from the government. This is the first and only community in the country to have done this. It is the winner of the responsibletravel.com's best small hotel for 2008.

Contact: Patrick Simkin
Email: mdwo1@bushmail.net · louise@baobabtravel.com
Web: www.mandawilderness.org
Address: Nkwichi Lodge, CP 123 Lichinga, Provincia do Niassa, Mozambique

NAMIBIA
International dialling code +264

Namibia, with its vast areas of wilderness, has an extraordinary variety of unique landscapes and ecosystems. These include the rich wildlife around the Etosha Pan and the Waterberg Plateau and extraordinary scenery, such as the Fish River Canyon, the sand dunes around Walvis Bay, the wild Kakaoveld in the northwest, and miles of colourful, tall dunes in the Namib Desert, which runs north to south.

For visitors interested in prehistory, some of Africa's most stunning rock art can be seen at Twyfelfontein and the Brandberg. The coastal towns of Swakopmund and Lüderitz preserve some of the atmosphere of the Kaiser's Germany as Namibia was a German colony until the end of the World War I. Until recently, you could still find street signs saying Bismarckstrasse and Bahnhofstrasse and there are many people of German descent. It explains why this is the only African country where you can find *Kaffee und Kuchen* all over the place and why Windhoek, the capital, is probably the cleanest city in Africa.

The majority of Namibia's small population is found in little-visited Ovamboland in the north. Smaller ethnic groups include the Damara-Nama, related to the San people, or 'Bushmen', and the remains of the Herero, victims of genocide during German rule, and the biggest landowners, who are white Afrikaners.

Independent from South Africa only since 1990, Namibia has been relatively stable until now; but the resettlement of landless people may lead to struggles and the high rate of HIV/AIDS (an estimated 25 per cent of the population are affected) seriously threatens the well-being of the country. It also has one of the highest rates of income inequality in the world because of an almost cashless rural economy.

Tourism has grown steadily, and this has been handled in a sensitive manner. Namibia is the only country in the world to specifically address habitat conservation and protection of natural resources in its constitution. Communities are able to create their own conservancies that benefit from wildlife on communal land, working with private companies to manage their own tourism market.

SAFARI/LUX
DAMARALAND

Wilderness Safaris operate small, intimate and luxurious camps in pristine wilderness areas. Damaraland was opened after the local community (Torra Conservancy) was approached with a business plan and a proposal. The luxury eco-friendly tented camp, situated in the Huab River Valley, consists of ten large en-suite units with a swimming pool next to the bar. Guests can experience desert-adapted wildlife (e.g. elephant, cheetah, springbok and black rhino), existing side by side with traditional pastoralists and forming a key part of the community economy. Activities include trips to the magnificent rock engravings at Twyfelfontein, nature drives, walks and mountain biking. Evenings can be spent around an open campfire simply stargazing thanks to crystal-clear night skies. All of the staff at the lodge come from the local community.

Tel: +27 118071800
Fax: +27 118072110
Email: ilanas@wilderness.co.za • enquiry@wilderness.co.za
Web: www.wilderness-safaris.com
Address: PO Box 5219, Rivonia 2128, South Africa

AFRICA

SAFARI/LUX
DORO NAWAS CAMP

This intimate camp in a pristine wilderness area was established when the local community approached the company with a proposal for a joint venture. Accessible by road, it offers an opportunity to see desert-adapted wildlife (e.g. elephant, springbok and giraffe), existing alongside traditional pastoral activities. Cultural aspects are omnipresent as the concession overlaps village and farming activity. The ancient rock engravings at Tywelfontein, a World Heritage site, are a glimpse into a long-gone world. The land is leased from the community, which owns 40 per cent of the camp, as do Wilderness Safaris, with 20 per cent owned by a Namibian black empowerment company. It costs 2995 Namibian dollars (UK£167/US$289) per person, fully inclusive. In 2007, Wilderness Safaris and the Doro Nawas Conservancy made history when they signed one of Namibia's first conservancy joint ventures.

Web: www.wilderness-safaris.com

ACCOM+
IRDNC KUNENE CAMPING TRAIL

Namibian conservancies are communal areas of land where the local community has been granted full responsibility for managing the wildlife and natural resources. IRDNC is a Namibian NGO which provides technical support and advice. The Kunene Camping Trail is a group of conservancy-owned campsites around Kaokoland in northwest Kunene. These campsites are working together with the IRDNC to market themselves as a trail that travellers can follow in order to see the best of the region, while ensuring that their visit directly benefits the local community.

Contact: Charoline Bock/Penny George (Kunene Camping Trail)
Tel: +264 61221918 · +264 61250558 · +264 813766804 (Kunene Camping Trail only)
Fax: +264 61222647
Email: office@nacobta.com.na · penny@nacso-cesp.org.na (Kunene Camping Trail only)
Web: www.nacobta.com.na
Address: 2878 Johann Albrecht Street, Windhoek North, Windhoek, PO Box 86099, Windhoek, Namibia

ORG
NAMIBIA COMMUNITY-BASED TOURISM ASSISTANCE TRUST (NACOBTA)

NACOBTA is a non-profit membership organization that supports communities in their efforts to develop and operate tourism enterprises profitably as well as sustainably. Its mission is to create very strong community-based tourism in Namibia, which greatly contributes to poverty reduction, the reduction of income disparity and overall social stability. NACOBTA was started in 1995 by communities who wanted to develop tourism enterprises in the previously neglected rural areas of Namibia. It offers training in tourism, business skills and tour guiding, business advice, marketing, advocacy and assistance with access to funding.

Tel: +264 61250558 · +264 61221918
Fax: +264 61222647
Email: office@nacobta.com.na
Web: www.nacobta.com.na
Address: 2878 Johann Albrecht Street, Windhoek North, Windhoek, PO Box 86099, Windhoek, Namibia

DAY
DAUREB MOUNTAIN GUIDES

Qualified local guides take visitors to the White Lady and other destinations on the mountain, providing insight on the art, flora and fauna. There are both day treks and overnight camping trips. There are many possible tours, including archaeological tours and a three-day trek to Königstein at the top of the highest peak in Namibia.

Web: www.nacobta.com.na

DAY

HATA ANGU CULTURAL TOURS

These township tours are about trying to uplift the lives of the people in Mondesa by bringing tourism directly to them. As many families as possible are included and the income generated goes directly to the community. In this way visitors are not intruding, but contributing to employment and engaging in meaningful interaction.

Web: www.nacobta.com.na

KANAMUB MOUNTAIN CAMP

Located 27km north of Sesfontein, Kanamub is set in a stunning natural rock formation offering amazing views across the plains to the west. Guests can enjoy a beautiful African sunset with a high chance of viewing oryx, ostrich, springbok and zebra. The campsite accommodates up to 12 people and has an open air (but private) hot shower, flush toilet and full kitchen and *braai* areas. Available by advance booking only.

Web: www.nacobta.com.na

DAY

KATUTURA FACE TO FACE TOURS

Katutura, which means 'we will never settle there', is a former township and a melting pot of people of African origin. On a Face to Face tour visitors become part of the energetic hustle and bustle of this sprawling, vibrant suburb. The guides are all local residents and show aspects of Windhoek rarely seen by tourists. The tour lasts three hours and includes shopping at local markets, meeting local residents, a visit to the Penduka craft co-operative and an innovative recycling project.

Web: www.nacobta.com.na

MARBLE CAMPSITE, ONYUVA

This has recently undergone a facelift and has privately screened sites with food preparation areas, sinks and *braai* areas, a large ablution block with separate male and female showers, and deep-freeze facilities. Himba tours are available with local Himba guides.

Web: www.nacobta.com.na

DAY

MONDESA TOWNSHIP TOURS

There is more to Swakopmund than the old-world charm of Jugendstil buildings from German colonial times. A tour through the suburb of Mondesa introduces visitors to local customs in a very informative and informal way. The guide, Charlotte Shigwedha, has firsthand knowledge as she was born and bred in the former township. Ten per cent of the tour fees go into the Youth Activity Project Fund, which strives to open an after-school activity centre for children and teenagers.

Web: www.nacobta.com.na

OKARUHOMBO CAMPSITE, MARIENFLUSS

This has recently been upgraded and has substantially improved facilities. Situated at the far northern end of the beautiful Marienfluss Valley, alongside the Kunene River and the Angolan border, the camp has eight sites with hot water, showers, washbasins, kitchen sinks and deep-freeze facilities.

Web: www.nacobta.com.na

BUDGET

OMAUNI COMMUNITY CAMP

Omauni offers five sheltered camping sites and three double bedrooms. The camp works in close cooperation with the local community. Visitors can take bush rides in a donkey car or go horse riding. There are tours to traditional homesteads and San shelters. The community forest covers an area of 750ha, and products such as rustic furniture are made locally and sold at the centre. The camp is located 70km from Okongo.

Web: www.nacobta.com.na

SESFONTEIN FIGTREE CAMPSITE

Situated close to Sesfontein Conservancy office, Figtree Campsite offers a shady haven under beautiful giant fig trees. There are four camping sites; each tent has its own flush toilet, handbasin and hot shower. A *braai* (barbecue) area and deep-freeze facility are also available.

Web: www.nacobta.com.na

VAN ZYL'S PASS CAMPSITE, OTJIHENDE

This is the perfect stop-off point before tackling the infamous Van Zyl's Pass en route to the Marienfluss. Located at a stunning spot 20km before the pass near the village of Otjihende, it is built alongside a sandy riverbed and offers three large sites with flush toilets, hot showers, wash-basins, and kitchen and *braai* areas.

Web: www.nacobta.com.na

ACCOM+
NHOMA SAFARI CAMP

This is a tented camp in the remote northeast of Namibia, the ancestral land of the Ju/'hoansi Bushmen, offering an intensive and authentic Bushman experience. The accommodation is comfortable and consists of ten safari tents with en-suite bathrooms and hot-water showers. In the mornings guests go hunting with the hunters, looking for springhare and porcupine or foraging for veldt foods if there are no tracks. They will even learn how to make arrow poison and traditional hunting equipment. Afternoons can be spent watching the Ju/'hoansi make their traditional crafts, such as ostrich eggshell jewellery, and playing traditional games. In the evenings there are elephant or giraffe dances, which have been performed by healers to cure the sick and relieve tension within the community for thousands of years. The local community benefits economically from sharing their activities with the guests, and the camp provides them with medicines and transport to a clinic 90km away.

Contact: Estelle Oosthuysen
Tel: +264 812734606
Email: tsumkwel@iway.na
Web: www.tsumkwel.iway.na
Address: PO Box 1899, Tsumeb, Namibia

ACCOM/TOUR
OMAHEKE SAN TRUST/SAA TA KO CAMPSITE

If your penchant is for Claridge's and power showers, don't bother. But if you want a corrective to TV documentaries of your childhood, read on. The campsite is a San project established to benefit the San people (also known as Bushmen – but you knew that), and that is what you get: a campsite, and the chance to gaze at San life and culture through the clear glass of a community welcome. On offer are traditional performances, bush walks and the opportunity to acquire San crafts and, therefore, to preserve them. The essential experience, though, is embodied in just being and seeing.

Contact: Kathryn Blakemore or Joyce
Tel: +264 62564073
Fax: +264 62564737
Email: ost@africaonline.com.na
Web: www.santrust.org
Address: PO Box 1017, Gobabis, Namibia

SOUTH AFRICA
International dialling codes +27

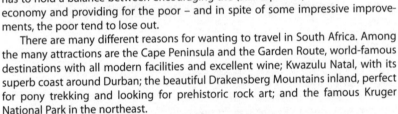

Once boycotted for its apartheid regime, South Africa has changed a lot. For many of its people, however, it has not changed enough. You will still find areas, both rural and urban, of startling poverty close to wealthy suburbs (formerly all white, but now with an increasing number of wealthy black people), modern industries and productive farms. The government has to hold a balance between encouraging the (still capitalist) economy and providing for the poor – and in spite of some impressive improvements, the poor tend to lose out.

There are many different reasons for wanting to travel in South Africa. Among the many attractions are the Cape Peninsula and the Garden Route, world-famous destinations with all modern facilities and excellent wine; Kwazulu Natal, with its superb coast around Durban; the beautiful Drakensberg Mountains inland, perfect for pony trekking and looking for prehistoric rock art; and the famous Kruger National Park in the northeast.

To understand the realities of life and recent history, you can visit Soweto, the museum and Market Theatre in Johannesburg, the District 6 Museum and Robben Island at Cape Town. Politically South Africa is a stable, democratic country, with Jacob Zuma (African National Congress) elected as president in the country's fourth democratic parliament in May 2009.

ACCOM+
ANT'S NEST AND ANT'S HILL

Ant's Hill is a privately owned wildlife reserve in which guests can participate in the running of the reserve. The bush homes are crafted from natural local materials. There are a wide variety of activities on offer, including horse riding, guided walks, game drives and massages for the less energetic. Activities are tailor-made for visitors. The reserves carry a vast variety of game, including sable, nyala, oryx, rhino, brown hyena and buffalo. The horse riding is a specialized operation with over 55 horses catering for all levels, from novice to the advanced. The camp aims to create a home-from-home experience with an intimate atmosphere. The objective is to create sustainable tourism by conserving the environment, enriching the lives of guests and staff, while uplifting the local community by providing skills development.

Contact: Amelia
Tel: +27 147554296 · +27 147553584 · +27 832872885
Fax: +27 865098239
Email: reservations@waterberg.net
Web: www.ridingsouthafrica.com · www.waterberg.net
Address: PO Box 441, Vaalwater 0530, Limpopo Province, South Africa

TOUR
AWOL BICYCLE TOURS

AWOL organizes bicycle tours that offer an opportunity to truly experience the South African countryside. Catering for every level from beginners to hardened cycle tourers, AWOL has a variety of cycle options, depending upon the seasons. A great way to enjoy the varied terrain and picturesque Cape scenery is from the saddle. Examples of the holidays provided include mountain biking in the Karoo Desert, exploring the bizarre rock formations of the Cederberg Mountains, a Garden Route trip, and a whale-watching tour along the southern coastline.

Contact: Sally de Jager
Tel: +27 217881256 · +27 832346428
Email: adventure@withoutlimits.co.za
Web: www.withoutlimits.co.za
Address: PO Box 17, Muizenberg 7950, South Africa

SAFARI/LUX
BUFFALO RIDGE SAFARI LODGE

Like the Thakadu River Camp (below), this is operated by the Madikwe Collection on behalf of the community which owns it. Part of the profits goes to the community to pay off the debt, and the goal is that it will be fully paid for and handed over in about 10 to 15 years. It is a luxury game lodge on the Madikwe Reserve with superb accommodation and food. Morning and evening drives should get you the Big Five. Luxury with a conscience – like Thakadu.

Contact: Victor
Tel: +27 118059995
Fax: +27 118050687
Email: info@madikwecollection.com
Web: www.buffaloridgesafari.com · www.madikwecollection.com
Address: PO Box 4617, Halfway House, 1685, South Africa
Represented in the UK by Luxury Representation Collection:
Petra@luxuryrepcollection.com · Tesna@luxuryrepcollection.com

ACCOM +
BULUNGULA LODGE

This lodge is totally part of the community, being jointly owned by and integrated within the local village. There is every opportunity to experience local culture (cooking, making mud bricks, etc.) and to go horseriding, canoeing up the Xhora River, and utilizing one of the world's most beautiful beaches. There is an affordable restaurant and bar and the whole enterprise is Fair Trade accredited.

Contact: Liesl Benjamin
Tel: +27 475778900
Email: dave@bulungula.com
Web: www.bulungula.com
Address: PO Box 52913, Mthatha, 5099, South Africa

DAY+
CALABASH TOURS

Calabash Tours offers Real City Tours covering both the historical heart of the city of Port Elizabeth, the vibrant black townships and Xhosa culture. Visitors will also enjoy the Shebeen Tour as an opportunity to relax and meet local people, understand social issues, play a game of pool and dance to African rhythms. Calabash Tours is a commercial venture with a strong social agenda. Working closely with the Calabash Trust, it ensures that local, and often disadvantaged, communities benefit from the visits through services provided either by community projects or black-owned township businesses. The trust has many programmes in nearby townships benefiting children and young people.

Certified by Fair Trade in Tourism South Africa (FTTSA).

Contact: Bongie Fesi
Tel: +27 415856162
Fax: +27 415850985
Email: paul@calabashtours.co.za · bongie@calabashtours.co.za
Web: www.calabashtours.co.za · www.calabashtrust.co.za
Address: PO Box 71688, Centrahill, Port Elizabeth 6070, South Africa

TOUR
CAPE CAPERS TOURS

This a wholly black-owned business offering township tours and is firmly rooted in the community. As they say, there is an awareness today that a visit to Cape Town is nothing without a trip to a township on the Cape Flats. Tours stop at community-owned shops, businesses and eating places and also a state-run HIV/AIDS clinic. Cape Capers offers 'a series of tours that educate the public and visitors, and benefit local people at the projects'. They last only a day or half a day, so would make an ideal add-on to a Cape holiday.

Contact: Marie-Line Anelard or Faizal Gangat
Tel: +27 214483117
Fax: +27 214483116
Email: tourcape@mweb.co.za
Web: www.tourcapers.co.za
Address: PO Box 13213, Mowbray 7705, Cape Town, South Africa

SAFARI/LUX
DJUMA GAME RESERVE

At Djuma, guests can go on a safari drive and see the Big Five, while staying at one of three luxury game lodges. As well as offering a breathtaking setting, Djuma has shown a consistent commitment to promoting community development and poverty alleviation. It has developed programmes that champion local socio-economic development, and has supported two local primary schools and a media training centre. It is working with the Djuma and Shangaan communities to realize their shared vision of conserving the land for future generations in a way that benefits the wider community. Hluvukani is the closest town to the Djuma Game Reserve.

Certified by Fair Trade in Tourism South Africa (FTTSA).

Tel: +27 137355118
Fax: +27 137355070
Email: djuma@djuma.co.za
Web: www.djuma.com
Address: PO Box 338, Hluvukani, 1363 South Africa

HOST/TOUR
DREAMCATCHER SOUTH AFRICA

Dreamcatcher (the name signifies the aspirations that they have for visitors) offers accommodation, meals, crafts and lifestyle experience tours to tourists. The founder spent 15 years as a grassroots volunteer in over 20 communities before establishing Dreamcatcher. The cornerstone philosophy is working in communities with local people. With Dreamcatcher there is no bus window between you and reality. Homestays, and short tours, give you contact with a range of cultures. The ultimate aim of Dreamcatcher is to put an end to the concept of 'aid without end' and, on a tourism level, to transplant community-based experiences from niche to mainstream tourism. This is tourism as a 'local economic driver and facilitator of intra-cultural harmony'.

Contact: Margie Carolus
Tel: +27 219769372
Fax: +27 219769372
Email: dreamcatcher@telkomsa.net
Web: www.dreamcatcher.co.za • www.traveldreamcatcher.com
Address: 17 Becks' Place, Gladstone Road, 7550 Durbanville, Cape Town, South Africa

ORG
FAIR TRADE IN TOURISM SOUTH AFRICA (FTTSA)

FTTSA is a non-profit organization that promotes sustainable tourism development. It does this through awareness-raising, research and advocacy, capacity-building and by facilitating the world's first tourism Fair Trade certification programme. The FTTSA certification label is an independent endorsement of fair and responsible tourism practice in South Africa. Certification is based on adherence to specific criteria such as fair wages and working conditions, fair distribution of benefits, ethical business practice, and respect for human rights, culture and the environment.

Contact: Jennifer Seif
Tel: +27 12342 2945/3642
Fax: +27 12342 2946
Email: info@fairtourismsa.co.za
Web: www.fairtourismsa.co.za
Address: Fair Trade in Tourism South Africa (FTTSA), PO Box 12844, Queenswood, Pretoria, 0121 South Africa

ACCOM
HOG HOLLOW COUNTRY LODGE

This four-star lodge is set on the edge of a private nature reserve with panoramic views of the surrounding forests, valleys and mountains. The location used to be an alien wattle plantation in the semi-wilds of a little-known area of the Tsitikamma (Garden Route) known as the Crags. Staff, who come from the local area, are able to assist guests in planning day trips encompassing everything from eco-adventure activities to a local community tour. Hog Hollow is committed to supporting the local economy through procurement and employment.

Certified by Fair Trade in Tourism South Africa (FTTSA).

Tel: +27 445348879
Fax: +27 445348879
Email: info@hog-hollow.com
Web: www.hog-hollow.com
Address: Askop Road, The Crags, PO Box 503, Plettenberg Bay, 6600 South Africa

ACCOM
JAN HARMSGAT COUNTRY HOUSE

Situated about two hours from Cape Town in the Western Cape, this guest house is on a working farm. There is real involvement with the community on both economic and cultural levels. Visitors are given the opportunity to indulge in an authentic country ambience and history. Linked with the enterprise is the Old Gaol coffee shop and restaurant in the nearby town of Swellendam, transformed from the old jail. The mission at the outset was to get the local community involved in tourism through skills training and development. Women from disadvantaged communities were trained and given a stake in the café, where delicacies such as springbok carpaccio and local cheeses are served.

Certified by Fair Trade in Tourism South Africa (FTTSA).

Contact: Gerda
Tel: +27 236163407
Fax: +27 236163201
Email: brinreb@iafrica.com
Web: www.jhghouse.com
Address: PO Box 161, Swellendam 6740, South Africa

AFRICA

DAY
LEBO'S SOWETO BACKPACKERS AND BICYCLE TOUR
This is an ideal way for visitors to explore and experience historical and vibrant Soweto. The business is named after the owner, Lebohang Malepa, who was born and bred in Soweto. Lebo and his team have developed a refreshing approach to township tourism, which enables travellers to experience everyday life in Soweto in a low-impact way. The business also supports community development initiatives targeting youth, as well as a range of businesses, through its operations.

Contact: Lebohang Malepa
Tel: +27 113963444
Email: lebo@sowetobackpackers.com
Web: www.sowetobackpackers.com

LUX/SAFARI
NGALA PRIVATE GAME RESERVE
Ngala is one of the founding lodges of CC Africa, a leading safari company. The lodge has 31 rooms and provides wildlife tours memorable for the quality of the guiding and the local hospitality. Ngala engages with the rural communities of Welverdiend and Hluvakani through Africa Foundation, its community development arm. This brings real benefits to the community, including schools, clinics, water access and income-generating activities. Guests at the lodge are invited to visit the communities with the development officers as part of the safari.

Contact: Alastair Kilpin
Tel: +27 118094440
Email: al.kilpin@ccafrica.com
Web: www.ccafrica.com/reserve-1-id-2-7

SAFARI/LUX
PAFURI CAMP
Another luxurious eco-friendly camp operated by Wilderness Safaris, Pafuri is wholly owned on land leased from the local community. Since 2005, 40 to 50 per cent of net profits have gone to the local community, members of whom approached the company with a joint venture proposal. The accommodation consists of 52 beds at a fully inclusive rate of 2495 South African rand (UK£140/US$240) per person per night. Pafuri is in a unique part of the Kruger National Park, accessible by road, and distinguished by its exceptional biodiversity and big game. Visitors' presence in the Kruger is helping to support both the game and the environment, and that part of the profits from Pafuri is being invested in social infrastructure to benefit the local community.

Web: www.wilderness-safaris.com

HOST/TOUR
PHAPHAMA INITIATIVES – TALK TOURISM
Phaphama organizes township tours of Soweto, as well as tours of Kathorus and Sharpeville, and homestays both in Soweto and the countryside. TALK Tourism also offers visitors the opportunity to go on an African language-learning immersion in a rural or urban area of South Africa. TALK Tourism is part of a broader peace-building programme that aims to bring people together across geographical, social and linguistic barriers. It enables people to build mutual respect and trust as they begin to relate meaningfully and share their lives with one another.

Contact: Judy Connors
Tel: +27 114871950 · +27 118151256 · +27 837981256
Fax: +27 880114871950
Email: judy@phaphama.org
Web: www.phaphama.org
Address: Phaphama Initiatives, PO Box 94144, Yeoville 2143, South Africa

ACCOM/DAY
SHILUVARI LAKESIDE LODGE

Shiluvari is a country-style retreat focusing on community-based tourism, located on the banks of the Albasini Dam in Limpopo Province. It offers accommodation in thatched chalets with an onsite restaurant and bar, a lakeside swimming pool, an *al fresco* terrace and a motorized raft for sunset cruises. Guests can take an arts-and-crafts tour with locally trained guides, a historical skirmishes or footsteps of the ancestors route, or a birding tour as the area is a hot spot for bird-watching.

Contact: Betty Hlungwani
Tel: +27 155563406
Fax: +27 155563413
Email: info@shiluvari.com
Web: www.shiluvari.com
Address: PO Box 560, Louis Trichardt, 0920, Limpopo Province, South Africa

DAY
SOEKERSHOF PRIVATE MAZES AND BOTANICAL GARDENS

Soekershof is an informal, down-to-earth experience. Some visitors may have a 'moment of aware-ness', while others may be inspired by the folklore, or simply enjoy the plants in the garden. It is an experience that seems to differ for each individual visitor. Unlike any other botanical gardens, this has a very different vibrancy. There is humour, storytelling and local folklore next to the 'education-al' finishing touch. Between wine tastings in the Robertson Wine Valley, Western Cape, visitors can taste some flowers at Soekershof Walkabout.

Contact: Herman van Bon
Tel: +27 236264134
Email: info@soekershof.co.za
Web: www.soekershof.com
Address: PO Box 291, Robertson 6705, South Africa

DAY
SOWETO FAIR TOUR

The Soweto Fair Tour is a tour with a difference. Operated by Moratiwa Tours, this is a four-hour bicycle tour for groups of up to 60. Visitors go to popular attractions in Soweto, including the house of President Nelson Mandela. The use of bicycles, rather than a tour vehicle, reduces carbon emissions, which, in turn, impacts positively upon the community and environment. Moratiwa Tours is also engaged in various community upliftment projects.

Certified by Fair Trade in Tourism South Africa (FTTSA).

Contact: Malose Manaka
Tel: +27 118696629
Email: malose@moratiwa.co.za

ACCOM
SOWETO NIGHTS

This is a UK-based one-man band. On offer is guest house accommodation in Soweto, as well as day tours of the township and of Johannesburg. The owner knows the hosts and guides person-ally. The guest houses and guides receive 90 per cent of the payments made by guests. Over five years the significant sum of UK£10,000 has been raised – very large by the host's standards. Guests experience the new South Africa and can talk about the future potential.

Contact: Steve Mendel
Tel: +44 2072544957 · +44 7774851338
Email: steve.mendel@talk21.com
Web: www.sowetonights.com
Address: 7 Palatine Road, London, N16 8XH, UK

ACCOM+
STORMSRIVER ADVENTURES

Stormsriver Adventures is a community-based eco-adventure company situated in the heart of the rural Tsitsikamma on the Eastern Cape, offering 16 varied activities. These range from a tree-tops and canopy tour to a forest tour and hiking trails. Training and development of local staff has been a cornerstone philosophy of the company and a catering company has been established where the staff hold 80 per cent of the equity. Stormsriver Adventures' involvement in community development is diverse and includes environmental education and food provision programmes for local schools. A committed environmental policy is rigidly applied, ensuring the protection of the surrounding sensitive environment.

Certified by Fair Trade in Tourism South Africa (FTTSA).

Tel: +27 422811836
Fax: +27 422811609
Email: adventure@gardenroute.co.za
Web: www.stormsriver.com • www.treetoptour.com
Address: PO Box 116, Storms River Village, Storms River, 6308 Tsitsikamma, Eastern Cape, South Africa

SAFARI/LUX
THAKADU RIVER CAMP

You want the Big Five? And 5-star conditions? And to benefit the local community? This lodge run by the Madikwe Collection is for you. The tents are en suite and air conditioned and are located on the Madikwe Game Reserve: 'a luxury safari getaway with a conscience'. The camp is in the process of acquiring Fair Trade accreditation. The collection operates the lodge on behalf of the community, who own it and to whom it will revert when fully paid for in about 10 to 15 years.

Contact: Claudia
Tel: +27 118059995
Fax: +27 118050687
Email: reservations@thakadurivercamp.com • reservations@madikwecollection.com
Web: www.thakadurivercamp.com • www.madikwecollection.com
Address: PO Box 4617, Halfway House, 1685, Johannesburg, South Africa
Represented in the UK by Luxury Representation Collection:
Petra@luxuryrepcollection.com • Tesna@luxuryrepcollection.com

SAFARI
UMLANI BUSHCAMP

Umlani Bushcamp accommodates up to 16 guests in traditional African reed and thatch huts. Umlani's philosophy of simplistic luxury and getting back to nature is enhanced by the romance of candlelight and oil lamps, which replace electricity. Open-air bush showers complete the experience. There are game drives, guided bush walks and tracking game on foot with experienced Shangaan rangers and trackers in over 10,000ha of Big Five territory. The camp has a staff HIV/AIDS programme, designed by a local expert, and actively supports a Limpopo Department of Labour programme by providing students with an opportunity for onsite experiential training. Umlani Bushcamp prioritizes human development and upliftment by building capacity within its staff complement.

Certified by Fair Trade in Tourism South Africa (FTTSA).

Tel: +27 217855547
Fax: +27 866968518
Email: info@umlani.com
Web: www.umlani.com
Address: PO Box 1435, Sun Valley, 7985, South Africa

AFRICA

ORG/TOUR
UTHANDO (LOVE)

Uthando's aim is to support projects that make a significant, positive and tangible difference to the communities in which they are found. Their field trips (township tours) provide visitors with an authentic introduction to the social problems confronting so many South Africans, while showcasing the innovative and inspirational ways in which these problems are being handled. The tours are interactive experiences where visitors can learn, feel and become inspired, with the assurance that the people at the various projects are not putting on an act but are going about their normal daily activities. Through its fund-raising activities, Uthando hopes to make a significant difference in the lives of the most destitute and marginalized communities living in Southern Africa.

Contact: Gregg Brill
Tel: +27 216838523
Fax: +27 216838520
Email: jamesfernie@uthandosa.org • info@uthandosa.org
Web: www.uthandosa.org
Address: PO Box 16491, Vlaeberg, 8001 Cape Town, South Africa

LUX/SAFARI
WOODBURY LODGE, SAFARI LODGE AND LEEUWENBOSCH COUNTRY HOUSE

These three lodges are situated in the Amakhala Game Reserve, based in Eastern Cape, 75km from Port Elizabeth and near the Addo National Park. The Amakhala Reserve is collectively owned and managed by a number of families who previously farmed the land. Each lodge contributes to a collective fund for education and uplifts their staff through training. The collective focuses strongly on HIV/AIDS by investing time and financial resources to support an orphanage, as well as voluntary counselling and testing. The lodges also support community-based suppliers, including a sewing business and a local laundry.

LEEUWENBOSCH COUNTRY HOUSE

A luxury four-star colonial game lodge with five en-suite bedrooms, including two suites, one family room, one double room and one twin.

Contact: William Fowlds
Tel: +27 422351252
Email: william@amakhala.co.za
Web: www.amakhala.co.za

SAFARI LODGE

A five-star graded romantic thatched lodge with luxury safari huts inspired by African tribal design.

Contact: Mike Weeks
Tel: +27 422351291
Email: mike@amakhala.co.za
Web: www.amakhala.co.za

WOODBURY LODGE

A four-star graded thatched lodge which overlooks the abundant wildlife of the Bushman's River Basin.

Contact: Richard Gush
Tel: +27 422351099
Email: rgush@imaginet.co.za
Web: www.amakhala.co.za

SWAZILAND
International dialling code +268

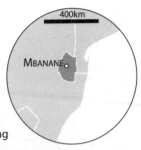

The King of Swaziland is the world's last remaining absolute monarch. He can, for example, still choose a new wife each year from among the young girls at the traditional Reed Dance. Opposition to his power is increasing but ineffective. It has focused on the extravagance of the royal family amid the increasing poverty of the Swazi people.

The country is tiny, the size of Wales, but very green and sce-nic, and has well-developed roads, hotels and shopping. The deep Ezulwini Valley is the tourist heart of the country, with a small game reserve and the 'cuddle puddle' hot springs. The valley links the two main towns, both pleasantly small, Mbabane, the capital, up in the hills and Manzini, the commercial centre, down in the 'middle veld' and close to the airport.

In the days of apartheid in South Africa, Swaziland's tourist trade was based on prostitution and the availability of pornographic and political literature that was banned across the border. This has changed and, with exports of sugar cane and pineapples earning less than they used to, legitimate and sustainable tourism is much needed in this country. Even with recent political and economic changes, Swaziland has the highest rate of HIV in the world.

HOST/DAY/ACCOM/TOUR
WOZA NAWE CULTURAL TOURS

This project is owned by Mxolisi Mdluli-Myxos, who set it up with the aim of benefiting the com-munity of kaPhunga in Swaziland. Here the idea is to experience everyday life on the community farm, about 65km from the nearest town, in the hills of Swaziland. On offer is accommodation in a tented camp for a maximum of 15 people, as well as homestays with families. Guests can try milking and dipping cows, ploughing fields, thatching roofs, and harvesting and shelling maize. This is a chance to really get to know the Swazi people, take language lessons, help the local schoolchildren with English, and learn about traditional healing. There are also opportunities for hiking, mountain biking, an early morning game drive, visiting a local market and simply partici-pating with a family in their daily activities.

Contact: Mxolisi Mdluli-Myxos
Tel: +268 5058363
Mobile: +268 6044102
Email: culturaltour@yahoo.com
Web: www.swazilive/myxo/html
Address: PO Box 2455, Manzini, Swaziland

AFRICA

ZAMBIA
International dialling code +260

Zambia is one of the continent's largest and most sparsely populated countries, shaped like a huge butterfly. Much of the country is an undulating plateau and the most interesting sights are round the edge – the Victoria Falls and Lake Kariba in the south; the Luangwa Valley game reserves in the east; Lake Tanganyika, Kasaba Bay and the Kalambo Falls in the north. There are 70 different ethnic groups and seven main languages, as well as English, which is widely spoken.

Although it is the world's fourth largest supplier of copper (accounting for 75 per cent of its foreign currency), Zambia is a poor country; but after many years of industrial decline the economy has grown in recent years thanks to high prices for copper, cobalt and other exports and to good management, which has led to much of its debt being cancelled as a highly indebted poor country (HIPC). The currency, the kwacha, even appreciated for a time. In one of his last speeches, President Mwanawasa, who died in 2008, regretted that poverty remained as widespread as ever, both in rural areas and urban slums. Two-thirds of the population live on less than US$1 a day and 85 per cent are subsistence farmers.

Zambia has always tried to promote tourism, but it has never taken off in a big way. The country's 19 national parks are being improved and you will not find too many tourists between you and the animals. A speciality in Zambia is walking safaris in the Luangwa Valley. Zambia has the opportunity to learn how to develop tourism from other nations' mistakes and, in a country where there are few tourists, there is a responsibility on the visitor to tread lightly.

BUDGET/VOL
KASANKA CONSERVATION CENTRE

The Kasanka Trust is a charity working to conserve and develop Kasanka National Park in the northern region of Zambia. It is dedicated to reducing poaching in the area by providing sustainable alternatives. The conservation centre is a camp close to the gate of the park which houses an education centre. Local schools are invited to visit the centre and workshops are also organized for the community, together with cultural nights with dancing and drama. The park is well worth visiting and has a rich diversity of animal, plant and bird life, including wattled cranes, blue monkeys and fruit bats, which gather in their millions in November and December. The trust operates two lodges and two campsites in Kasanka, as well as Shoebill Island Camp in the adjacent Bangweulu Wetlands. There are also great opportunities for volunteers to gain research experience or to assist with conservation work.

Contact: Kim Farmer or Inge Akerboom
Tel: +873 762067957
Fax: +873 762067959
Email: wasa@kasanka.com
Web: www.kasanka.com
Address: Kasanka Trust, PO Box 8550073, Serenje, Zambia

AFRICA

SAFARI
KAWAZA VILLAGE

Robin Pope Safaris is the most established and successful safari operator in the South Luangwa National Park, Zambia. Their three camps, Nkwali, Nsefu and the famous Tena Tena offer personalized safaris combining genuine African bush with simple, yet stylish, luxury. Each camp is individual in terms of its atmosphere and location. For 18 years they have supported a school in the Nsefu Village area, which is now seen as a model of how tourism can contribute to a community. Guests who visit the school, and are keen to learn more about local lifestyles, can stay at Kawaza Village for a day or overnight. The Kawaza project is now self-running, overseen by a committee, and the income generated supports the village and also helps to run the school.

Contact: Munyama Mudaala
Tel: +260 216246090/91/92
Fax: +260 216246094
Email: info@robinpopesafaris.net
Web: www.robinpopesafaris.net • www.kawaza.org • www.kawazavillage.co.uk

ACCOM+
NAKAPALAYO TOURISM PROJECT

Community based, owned and managed, Nakapalayo village is well located between Kasanka National Park and the spectacular Bangweulu. It was founded by the community and offers an 'authentic experience in a traditional village'. One quarter of its income goes to community development and conservation projects. Accommodation is in comfortable mud-brick huts; but visitors can choose to camp. A local guide accompanies visitors throughout their stay to introduce them to village life and culture, to dos and don'ts, and to translate. Visitors can try everyday activities such as drawing water, pounding cassava or hoeing the fields. They can go on a bush walk to learn about the traditional use of trees and plants, and in the evenings experience traditional dancing and stories around the fire.

Contact: Kim Farmer or Inge Akerboom
Tel: +873 762067957
Fax: +873 762067959
Email: wasa@kasanka.com
Web: www.kasanka.com
Address: Kasanka Trust, PO Box 850073, Serenje, Zambia

VOL
YOUTH ASSOCIATION OF ZAMBIA (YAZ)

This is not where you go if you want to sip wine under a million stars and dream of the Big Five tomorrow. This is a work and study camp organization that gives volunteers the chance to visit tourist sites during excursions. You will be working mainly on environmental outreach programmes and having an intercultural experience beyond measure. YAZ offer volunteers an orientation workshop on arrival (which you pay for), and it has a wide choice of camps in Zambia, which can be extended worldwide as YAZ is a member of many global camp networks.

Contact: Namatama Mulikelela
Tel: +260 977759444 • +260 955981994 • +260 977464630
Email: yazworkcamps@gmail.com
Address: PO Box 31852, Lusaka, Zambia

WEST AFRICA

BURKINA FASO
International dialling code +226

Most of Burkina Faso is a low plateau ranging from savannah in the south to the semi-desert of the Sahel in the north. It is best known for two things: for the biennial FESPACO film festival – this poor country has produced some of Africa's finest films and the festival is a showcase for African cinema; and for the short presidency of the charismatic Thomas Sankara, who inspired progressive people all over Africa and made profound changes to his country before being overthrown by conservative forces with foreign support. Burkina Faso is a friendly country and those who visit it often come back for more. There are some good museums in the capital, Ouagadougou, and several game reserves. Bobo Dioulasso, the second city, is a fascinating place with examples of Sahelian mud architecture and with a star-shaped street plan laid out by the French colonial government. The scenery is not remarkable, but there are some amazing rock formations in the southwest. There are some excellent markets, notably Goron-Goron in the north, and a big international arts-and-crafts festival each year in October and November.

HOST
TEMPELGA ORGANIZATION

On offer are 15-day immersion stays in a camp on the outskirts of a small village in Burkina Faso. Visitors are invited to participate in many aspects of day-to-day life in the community. Evening discussions focus on intercultural exchange and mutual investigation, and are illuminating for both host and visitor alike. The profits are reinvested in development projects, including regional health centres, and the organization's main campaign to increase adult literacy. Due to the grassroots nature of this project, very good oral French is essential.

Contact: Yann Renou • Roger Theyssandier
Tel: +33 686272823
Email: assotempelga@yahoo.fr
Web: www.tempelga.com
Address: 8 rue Aristide Briand, F-37510 Ballan Mire, France

CAMEROON
International dialling code +237

Sometimes described as 'Africa in miniature', Cameroon is a country of great beauty and diversity. It contains 200 or more ethnic groups and may have been the starting point of the migrations of Bantu-speaking peoples towards the south. The scenery is seldom dull. In the south you will find unspoiled tropical beaches at Kribi and Limbé on the Atlantic shore; Mount Cameroon, the highest peak in West Africa and mainland Africa's only active volcano; hills covered by lush forest; the rolling hills of the 'grassfields' in the northwest; and plantations of coffee, tea and oil palms. In the north you come to dry savannah country and rocky mountains inhabited by people whose traditional beliefs have resisted the advance of Islam and Christianity. There are plenty of things for the visitor to enjoy: a number of national parks, including Lobeke, where lowland gorillas are to be found; the historic town of Foumban, setting of Gerald Durrell's book *The Bafut Beagles*, where you can visit the Fon's palace and museum; and the amazing traditional mountain village of Rhumsiki in the north. The capital, Yaoundé, is a pleasant city. Douala, the commercial capital, is very hot and humid, with the highest rainfall in Africa. Colonized by the Germans, the country was divided between the French and British after World War I and both are now official languages, with Pidgin English as a vernacular in the south. It is strange that such an attractive country with such friendly people has attracted few tourists. Those who do get there do not regret it.

HOST/VOL
RECOSAF

RECOSAF stands for Réseau des Compétences Sans Frontières pour la promotion du tourisme responsable, le commerce équitable et le développement durable, which translates as network of competences without borders for the promotion of a responsible tourism, fair trade and sustainable development. It is an association that wishes to integrate tourism fully into the development process. Tours in the south of the country are organized and the opportunity is there for young people to volunteer in the community and/or immerse themselves in local customs, habits and the general lifestyle of the people. Note: it would be advisable to have good oral French, not just menu French.

Contact: Tchassa Emmanuel
Tel: +237 96951932
Fax: +237 33446381
Email: recosaf@recosaf.org
Web: www.recosaf.org
Address: BP 1172, Bafoussam, Cameroon

THE GAMBIA
International dialling code +220

The Gambia is an accident of history. The British got here first, but the French moved inland and created the colony of Senegal, which surrounds the tiny Gambia, a narrow strip on both sides of the Gambia River. Having few resources other than groundnuts, the country has developed tourism as its main industry. The coastal strip has become a major package holiday destination with cheap charter flights but there has not been much benefit to the majority of the population. Gambians are organizing themselves to insist on a fairer deal.

Being such a small country, it is possible to combine a beach holiday with interesting visits to the nearby Tanbi mangrove swamp, the Makasutu Culture Forest and the small capital city, Banjul. Further up-country you can visit historic Janjanbureh Island; or Juffureh, the village which purports to be the original home of Kunta Kinte, the hero of Alex Haley's novel, *Roots*. The Gambia has a good climate, warm but not unpleasantly hot in winter. Cheap flights are available from the UK.

ORG
ASSET

ASSET (Association of Small-Scale Enterprises in Tourism) is a unique trade association with some 2500 members working in a wide variety of tourism jobs, including guides, fruit juicers, owners of bars, guest houses and hotels, taxi drivers and handicraft vendors. As such it does not provide services directly to the visitor but enables its members to improve their services and products. ASSET also works with tour operators and ground operators so that even mainstream tourism can include ASSET members' services. ASSET supports its members so that formerly marginalized people can play a role in the tourism industry. It has won a major international award for all its work to ensure that tourism alleviates poverty.

Contact: Daouda Niang or Sarah Paget
Tel: +220 4497675 · +220 7017923 · +220 9858942
Fax: +220 4498112
Email: info@asset-gambia.com · asset@qanet.gm
Web: www.asset-gambia.com
Address: ASSET Office and Resource Centre, Off Garba Jumpha Road, Fajara, The Gambia

ACCOM
SAFARI GARDEN HOTEL

A delightful, friendly, small, international award-winning hotel operating in a very green fashion, always working on becoming even more sustainable and environmentally sound. Unusually for The Gambia, food is sourced locally where possible. What is on offer is a quiet, relaxing holiday experience, where guests get a chance to meet interesting people who regularly stay at the hotel, including groups from VSO and Peace Corps. A double room with breakfast costs £43 per night and a single room is £27.50 per night. The hotel frequently hosts courses in responsible tourism and multicultural learning.

Although in an urban residential area, so not located in a community, the hotel has a close relationship with the village of Kartong some 40km away. No direct contribution is made to the local community but the hotel and guests support projects in Kartong.

Contact: Maurice Phillips
Tel: +220 4495887 • +220 4494929
Email: geri@gamspirit.com
Web: www.safarigarden.com • www.gamspirit.com

ACCOM/SCHOOL
SANDELE ECO-RETREAT AND LEARNING CENTRE

A luxury beachside resort offering full- and half-board service in a private, secure and very quiet setting, with excellent cuisine and efficient service. Alongside this is a Learning Centre, available for anyone attracted to the courses, workshops and conferences organized by the Pathways Foundation on a wide range of sustainability issues. The intention is to change the normal dynamic of tourism and put Gambians in the role of teachers and mentors rather than performers and servants. This is run by the same people who own the Safari Garden Hotel with the aim of training and employing all managers from the nearby village of Kartong.

Contact: Maurice Phillips
Tel: +220 7711209
Email: info@sandele.com
Web: www.sandele.com

GHANA
International dialling code +233

Ghana is an exciting place that offers many different and wonderful experiences. The absence of a well-established tourism industry means that this country with its bustling cities, unique cultures and fascinating people retains its own very distinct flavour. Festivals and cultural celebrations are as different in what they celebrate as the number of different languages spoken in the country – more than 100. Ghana also has an infamous legacy in the trade of stolen people manifest in the many well-preserved slaving forts dotted along its sandy coastline. The African Diaspora is drawn towards Ghana, including many African Americans. A strong cultural etiquette exists that is worth checking out before arrival. Music is all pervasive and High Life music and Hip-Life, Ghana youths' original blend of indigenous music and US-style Hip Hop, originated in Ghana.

The country has fantastic Atlantic beaches, rainforest, savannah and the dry, dusty deserts of the north, making it a utopia for lovers of nature – a bird-watchers' paradise. Kakum, Mole and Ankasa national parks are just a few of the places set up to preserve wildlife.

If there is one memorable point that defines Ghana, it is the use of folk sayings most notably seen on the ubiquitous *tro-tros* – the minibuses that make up the bulk of Ghana's transport system. Take a trip on 'I Shall Return', or visit 'It Will Grow Back' hairdressers and eat, if you still have an appetite, at 'Stomach Takes No Holidays' chop bar.

HOST
HOHOE DISTRICT'S COMMUNITY-BASED ECOTOURISM

This is a unique opportunity to directly participate in the daily lives of the people of the Hohoe district of Ghana. Visitors stay in private Ghanaian homes and take part in everyday activities, from preparing local dishes to shopping in the market to working on the land. Guests have many choices of activities, including guided nature walks, bird-watching, participating in palm wine and palm oil production, boat construction and fishing. In the evening guests are invited to take part in dancing and drumming. The income from visitors is held in trust by the communities themselves and used for projects such as water pumps and school fees.

Contact: Dennis Jordor
Tel: +233 21773498 · +233935222 13 (Monday–Friday) · +233 244156309 · +233 244457 (weekends and after hours)
Fax: +233 21256712
Email: tours@mandjtravelghana.com
Web: www.mandjtravelghana.com
Address: PO Box KIA 9732, Accra, Ghana

TOUR/SCHOOL
KASAPA CENTRE

Kasapa is a tourism resort comprised of six guest bungalows, a restaurant, staff and working quarters. It is also the base for a Ghanaian tour operator. Visitors can take part in workshops for traditional drumming and dancing. Excursions are also arranged. In the pipeline are two travelling programmes, one of three weeks to the upper east region bordering on Burkina Faso and a two- to three-week trip round Mole National Park in the northern region. Is it worth it? They have lots of repeat visitors!

Contact: www.schulz-aktiv-reisen.de · www.nature-team.ch
Tel: +233 244617226 (Susanne Stemann-Acheampomg) · +233 244216027 (Kofi B. Acheampong)
Web: www.kasapa.eu
Address: PO Box GP4246, Accra, Ghana

TOUR/HOST/DAY
SAVANNALAND DESTINATION

A community ecotourism initiative which presents a culture and lifestyle to tourists as they are – you bring away with you a vision of a way of life and a sense of what makes the community 'tick'. The proximity of Mole National Park is a real bonus. On offer are a safari, village tours, a canoe safari and a tour along a slave trade route. At the moment, Savannaland activities are concentrated in one part of southwest Ghana, which includes the park and Mognori Eco-Village.

Contact: Marian Thompson (M&J Travel/Tour) or Chelewura Oliver (tourism officer, Mole National Park)
Tel: +233 244514824 (M&J Travel/Tour) · +233 71722041 (Mole National Park)
Email: info@mandjtravelghana.com · molewd@ghana.com
Web: www.mandjtravelghana.com
Address: M&J Travel, PO Box KA9732, Accra, Ghana · Mole, PO Box DM8, Damongo, N/R Ghana

VOL
VOLUNTARY WORKCAMPS ASSOCIATION OF GHANA (VOLU)

Long-established voluntary workcamp association with projects all over the country.

Contact: Emmanuel Agbo
Tel: +233 21663486
Fax: +233 21665960
Email: volu@gppo.africaonline.com.gh
Web: www.voluntaryworkcamps.org
Address: PO Box GP 1540, Accra, Ghana

GUINEA
International dialling code +224

Compared to neighbouring Senegal and Mali, Guinea remains little visited and tourism is very underdeveloped – which can be a welcome relief and an adventure for those who are don't mind few creature comforts. A country of immense cultural and natural riches, it is the source of the three great rivers of West Africa. It is also one of the poorest and least stable countries in West Africa due to an ailing president who has presided over decades of brutality and corruption. The capital Conakry is dirty and dangerous, but has a great music scene, with some of the best musicians in West Africa joining in impromptu jamming sessions. When Conakry gets too much you can escape to the nearby paradise-like Ilse de Los, said to have inspired *Treasure Island*. A mangrove coastline contrasts with a mountainous interior – wonderful for craft, trekking and wildlife – and a dense forest region. Take your pick, be careful and indulge in a DIY adventure.

CAMP/ACCOM
CAMPEMENTS DE SAALA (TETRAKTYS)
In the village of Diari, in the area of Foutah Djallon, popular traditions are not heritage arcania but alive and well. A stay in the tourist camp of Saala, near the falls of that name, immerses the visitor in community values, in daily work and in the very essence of the place. Accommodation is in either the camp (15 places) or in houses. The enterprise is managed collectively and 30 per cent of the profit goes towards local development projects. At 5 Euros a night and 3 Euros for a meal, there is only one caveat: it might be advisable to have some French.

Contact: Abdourahamane Diallo (manager of the camp)
Tel: +224 60607790
Email: administratif@tetraktys-ong.org (via Tetraktys)
Web: www.tetraktys-ong.com (via Tetraktys)

Partner Association: Foutah Trekking Adventure
Contact: Mamadou Cellouba
Tel: +224 60570279
Email: bacellou@gmail.com
Address: PO Box 120 Labé, Republic of Guinea

MALI
International dialling code +223

Yes, Timbuktu really *does* exist – and it's in the wonderful country of Mali. This vast, arid West African country, a bit like the shape of a butterfly's wings, located between Senegal to the west, Algeria to the north and Niger to the east, is a treasure trove waiting to be 'discovered' by English-speaking travellers. Francophone tourists have been visiting for ages, as it was a French colony until 1960 and French remains its official language. It is one of the poorest countries in the world – two-thirds of it affected by drought. The health challenges are related to poverty, malnutrition, inadequate sanitation and supplies of drinking water.

In spite of this, it has an impressively rich cultural heritage, especially seen in the wonderful music, which has been making its mark on the international world music scene. Malian musicians such as Salif Keita, Toumani Diabaté and Basekou Kouyaté

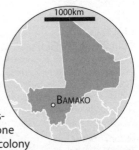

have all won prestigious prizes and play to packed houses in the West. Indeed, one of the main attractions is the annual Festival in the Desert, held in the Sahara north of Timbuktu. Less than a decade old, this festival was originally a meeting ground for the region's nomadic Touareg and today draws thousands of international fans to thrill to the desert sounds and to get a taste of desert living – although nowadays mod cons such as running water for showers are also included.

The ancient and modest town of Timbuktu itself is one of the country's four UNESCO World Heritage sites, and is famous for its religious monuments, such as the Dingarey Bey Mosque. Timbuktu was once the southern terminus of the trans-Saharan trade in gold and salt and capital of the ancient Mali Empire. It became an intellectual and spiritual centre of Islam in the 15th and 16th centuries, with a famous university that, at its peak, had 25,000 students. Important books were written and copied, not only on Islam but also on science and mathematics, which established the city as a centre of significant written tradition in Africa. Today, there are over 700,000 manuscripts in Timbuktu libraries, many dating back to West Africa's Golden Age between the 12th and 16th centuries.

One of the other UNESCO sites is the unmissable mud-baked old town of Djenné and its fabulous Great Mosque. There is also the Dogon Country in the central plateau region, and no visit is complete without spending time in the busy, bustling and dusty capital of Bamako, and experiencing the genuine friendliness and hospitality of the Malian people.

TOUR
DESERT BLEU

The Tuareg offer visitors a unique chance to share in their lifestyle: their music, poetry, tales and their campfires. The profits of the enterprise have helped the schooling of Tuareg children, and have helped to buy drugs and equipment for a new health centre. Support is given to the Tilwat organization, which combats water shortage, desertification, and supports schooling and healthcare. Spoken French is helpful.

Contact: Mossa Ag Attaher
Tel: +223 6051633
Email: moagatt@yahoo.fr
Web: www.desertbleu.net
Address: BP 208, Gao, Mali

TOUR OP
TELLEM VOYAGES

Tellem Voyages is a project still in its relative infancy, but it offers visitors a rare doorway into Dogon culture in its many guises. The progenitors of this enterprise are endeavouring to get a festival up and running built around Dogon culture so that people beyond Mali might acquire knowledge of the culture and way of life. Any income yielded by the enterprise goes to the villages concerned. Most visitors thus far have been Francophone and backpackers – some preparedness for the unexpected might be advisable.

Contact: Amadou A Dolo
Tel: +223 2230319 • +223 6793924
Email: tellemvoyage@yahoo.fr
Web: www.tellemvoyage.com
Address: BP 2509, Avenue de l'OUA Imm, Wally Diawara Badalabougou, collé à l'Institut du Sahel près du Pont des Martyrs, Bamako, Mali

SENEGAL
International dialling code +221

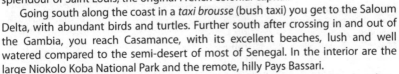

There's a certain glamour to Senegal – baobab trees, tall women in magnificent dresses, handsome colonial architecture, vibrant music and nightlife. Dakar may be too noisy for some, but it is easy to escape. You can take a ferry to the island of Gorée, an atmospheric reminder of the slave trade, but a beautiful spot, especially at sunset. Or you can head north to the faded splendour of Saint Louis, the original French colonial capital.

Going south along the coast in a *taxi brousse* (bush taxi) you get to the Saloum Delta, with abundant birds and turtles. Further south after crossing in and out of the Gambia, you reach Casamance, with its excellent beaches, lush and well watered compared to the semi-desert of most of Senegal. In the interior are the large Niokolo Koba National Park and the remote, hilly Pays Bassari.

Senegal was the first French colony in Africa and it has become the most democratic of the former French countries. It has a rich intellectual and cultural tradition – Senegal's first president was Léopold Sédar Senghor, the poet of *Négritude*, which was a literary and political movement founded in the 1930s in the belief that the shared black heritage of the African Diaspora was the best way to fight French colonialism. The country's best-known writer and film-maker is Ousmane Sembène. Baaba Maal, Youssou N'Dour and Ismael Lô are among the many famous names in Senegalese music.

TOUR/VOL
HELP TRAVEL ASSOCIATION
The HELP travel staff are a cocktail of local people and of people fully integrated into the 'local socio-economic tissue'. On offer is a 'unique blend of discovery, excursions and Community Development Projects'. Ethics drive operations: profound respect for the environment and local people, and observation of the tenets of responsible tourism.

Contact: Luca D'Ottavio
Tel: +221 775160653 · US VOIP #: +1 3609681685
Fax: +39 6233297889
Email: infos@helpassociation.org
Web: www.helptravel.org
Address: HELP Association, BP 1456 Ziguinchor, Senegal

ACCOM
LA CASCADE (TETRAKTYS)
La Cascade, the waterfall, gives the clue. The setting is wonderful: the cascade of Dindefello with its natural swimming pool. This is a place to chill out – though admittedly not physically. Eleven houses can accommodate approximately 35 people on traditional beds with mosquito nets. Another collectively managed enterprise, 30 per cent of the profits go towards local development projects. Overnight stays are €5 a head and a meal €3. Please note: the ability to speak French, not just 'get by', is essential.

Contact: Mr Balla Touré · Mr Ricard
Tel: +221 776588707 · +221 775165875
Email: administratif@tetraktys-ong.org
Web: www.tetraktys-ong.org

HOST/TOUR
VIAGGI SOLIDALI COMMUNITÀ PROMOZIONE SVILUPPO (COMMUNITY DEVELOPMENT PROJECT)

The Italian tour operator Viaggi Solidali works with the NGO CPS to promote responsible travel in Senegal, such as music and dance tours. Visitors stay in family homestays and spend time with the local community. They may go to a dyeing workshop, a palm wine harvest, a local market, or to traditional dance and percussion performances. Guests are accompanied by a local guide and an NGO staff member throughout the holiday. There are several tours available, including a ten day itinerary and a twelve day package that includes two days of visits to rural villages in the Kaffrine region of Senegal.

Contact: Maria Teresa Vecchiattini
Tel: +39 0114379468
Fax: +39 0114379755
Email: info@viaggisolidali.it • africa@viaggisolidali.it • cpsmb@orange.sn
Web: www.viaggisolidali.it
Address: Corso Regina Margherita 205/a, 10144 Torino, Italy

TOGO

1000km

Having been a German colony and a UN Trust Territory under France, Togo gained independence in 1960 but has the unenviable reputation of having had Africa's first ever coup d'état, in 1963, which led to a long period of dictatorship under Gnassingbe Eyadema. Things have improved although the current president is Eyadema's son.

LOMÉ

A long, thin country, stretching from a coastline only 50km long far into the interior, Togo has a variety of scenery and culture. Lomé, the capital, is a laid-back place right on the sea shore and squashed against the Ghana frontier. Going northwest you reach the hilly region of Klouto and the market centre of Atakpamé. Further north is the town of Kara; its fast development is due to its proximity to the home of the president. In the far northeast is Koutammakou, the country of the Batammariba people, which has been declared a UNESCO World Heritage site. These people have preserved their traditions and resisted Islam and Christianity. Their intricate mud clay 'towers' are just one aspect of their culture and are well worth seeing, as is the old colonial town of Aneho on the coast. Togo provides the usual excellent standard of handicrafts found throughout West Africa.

VOL
ASSOCIATION TOGOLAISE DES VOLONTAIRES AU TRAVAIL (ASTOVOT)

One of Africa's first voluntary organizations, with a large programme of workcamps.

Tel: +228 4410715 • +228 9464828
Fax: +228 4410715
Email: sgastovoct@yahoo.fr
Address: Route de Hanyigba BP 97, Kpalime

VOL
FRERES AGRICULTEURS ET ARTISANS POUR LE DEVELOPPEMENT (FAGAD)
A very dynamic association, with workcamps and volunteer placements.

Contact: Kossi Ayeh
Tel: +228 4496015 · +228 9166066
Fax: +228 4496015
Email: fagadtogo@yahoo.fr
Web: www.fagad.org
Address: BP 60, Kpele Adeta (Kloto), Togo

TOUR
PROJECT OF EDUCATION AND SOCIAL ENTERTAINMENT FOR A NEW RELATION WITH AFRICA
This project is in its infancy, with the first group scheduled for early 2009. The plan is for a tour of the country from south to north using the facilities of local communities and including a brief stay in a hotel run by local people. The trip will last 15 days and will give what promises to be a good introduction to the culture. A highlight will be Lome, famous for the Lome Convention, with its Great Market and museum tracing the tragedy of slavery.

Contact: Dario Urselli
Tel: +39 182545674
Fax: +39 182 559463
Email: infokronos@tiscali.it
Address: Coop Kronos – Turismo Sviluppo, Piazza Europa 14, 17031 Albenga (SV), Italy

THE AMERICAS

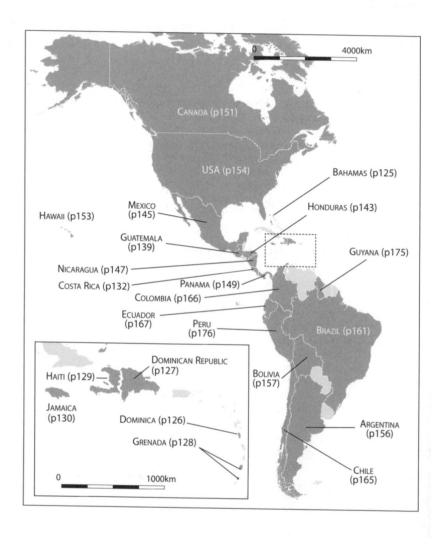

CANADA (p151)

USA (p154)

BAHAMAS (p125)

HAWAII (p153)

MEXICO (p145)

HONDURAS (p143)

GUATEMALA (p139)

GUYANA (p175)

NICARAGUA (p147)

COSTA RICA (p132)

PANAMA (p149)

COLOMBIA (p166)

ECUADOR (p167)

PERU (p176)

BRAZIL (p161)

BOLIVIA (p157)

ARGENTINA (p156)

CHILE (p165)

DOMINICAN REPUBLIC (p127)

HAITI (p129)

JAMAICA (p130)

DOMINICA (p126)

GRENADA (p128)

0   4000km

0   1000km

CARIBBEAN

BAHAMAS
International dialling code +1 242

The Bahamas is an archipelago of 700 hot, flat coral islands (40 are inhabited) lying southeast of Florida and famous for its offshore banks and as the birthplace of Sidney Poitier. Tourism developed there early: Nassau, the capital of New Providence Island, attracted the swanky (and cranky) rich in the 1930s, including the Duke of Windsor, who was sent there as ambassador after his abdication. Another tourism followed in the 1940s when – with concessions and handouts – a landscape of resorts and casinos replaced scrubland and mangroves on the two islands of New Providence and Grand Bahama. Crooks and adventurers abounded, and corruption continued to be part and parcel of tourism dominated by the white merchant class. Modern-day investors include Sol Kerzner, who developed Atlantis, a fantastical resort in Nassau, and the proposed Bimini Bay Resort that is the focus of a Tourism Concern campaign. America seems to dominate the culture, although the great post-Christmas carnival of Junkanoo is a reminder that most Bahamians have an African heritage; then the streets of Nassau rise up in costume, drumming and dance. Otherwise, cruise ships, tacky shopping malls and resort life point to a tired overexploitation.

In contrast, life in the Out Islands barely seems to stir. These strung-out strips of land, from Inagua in the south, famous for its flamingos, to the northern islands of Abacos, settled by UK loyalists fleeing the US revolution, are dotted with communities where doors are never locked and old-fashioned courtesies survive. The sea is everywhere in these paper-thin islands and sailing, diving, snorkelling and fishing are the focus of tourism. You can island hop – at some expense – from one empty white beach and shimmering turquoise horizon to the next. Go to San Salvador, where Columbus is said to have made his first footfall in the New World, or curious Eleuthera, with its pineapple industry and dinky colonial enclaves. Despite the threat to Bimini, the Bahamas has a good record of conservation of its marine environment, and some islands have national parks, both above and below sea level.

ACCOM+
STAFFORD CREEK LODGE
A secluded lodge in an idyllic setting, nestled among the native palms and hugging the banks of the calm, clear waters of Stafford Creek, on the island of Andros. This is a place to discover a new world of bonefish and tarpon, and catch-and-release permit fishing. Experienced guides take guests around this vast fly-fishing wilderness, with numerous creek systems and inland lakes, putting them on the right flats at the right tide. The lodge accommodates up to six anglers; but there are many activities for non-anglers to enjoy, including snorkelling, nature walks, bird-watching, dolphin-watching, a historical tour or simply strolling along white sandy beaches. The lodge's owner, who is local, has a strong commitment to investing back into his community.

Contact: Stacy Smith
Tel: +242 3686050
Fax: +242 3686125
Email: staffordcreeklodge@gmail.com
Web: www.staffordcreeklodge.com
Address: Stafford Creek Lodge, PO Box FC-23302, Fresh Creek, Andros Island, Bahamas

DOMINICA
International dialling code +1 767

400km

ᴿROSEAU

Dominica is the Nature Island of the Caribbean: dazzling greenery, towering mountain ranges, extensive rainforest (including a UNESCO World Heritage site) intersected by rushing rivers, waterfalls, volcanoes, bubbling hot pools (for relaxing) and the second largest Boiling Lake in the world ('I survived the Boiling Lake hike' is a website in itself). So forget the stereotypes of a Caribbean beach holiday.

A former British colony sandwiched between Guadeloupe and Martinique and independent since 1978, Dominica also has a strong Afro-French culture – the Creole language, dance, music (home of *zouk*) and food (where else does the airport café stretch to fresh mandarin juice?). The Caribs (or Kalinagos), the indigenous peoples of the Caribbean who, only on Dominica, survived the arrival of the Europeans, live on the northeast coast: fishermen and farmers, they are also great basket-makers. Roseau, the capital, has some charming French colonial architecture, an excellent museum and a Saturday morning market to die for. Villages are dreamy places, on breezy hillsides or tucked into hidden coves. Tourism is based around locally owned guest houses – small scale, unpretentious, with an emphasis on environmental well-being. Photographers, artists, botanists, gardeners, hikers and divers (it has some of the best diving in the world) go mad in Dominica, seduced by its wildness and natural exuberance. And watch out for glimpses of the island in *Pirates of the Caribbean* (series 2 and 3): it provides a spectacular backdrop to Johnny Depp's antics.

ACCOM+
ROSALIE FOREST ECO-LODGE
The aim is to provide a relaxing and exciting eco-experience in natural surroundings, as well as to protect and preserve the natural world. This eco-lodge works closely with the locals, aiding the development of the community. It is an environment which people on any budget can enjoy. It has a sustainable Living Education Centre; so if you have a green cast of mind, this could be for you.

Contact: Jem Winston or Kemon Cuffy
Tel: +1 767 4461886 or +1 767 2751886
Fax: +1 510 578 6578
Email: info@rosalieforest.com
Web: www.rosalieforest.com
Address: PO Box 1292, Newfoundland Estate, Rosalie, Dominica

DOMINICAN REPUBLIC
International dialling code +1 809

1000km

SANTO
DOMINGO

Tourism, based primarily around all-inclusive resort holidays, has grown strongly in the Spanish-speaking Dominican Republic (often called the DR) since the 1980s, and is playing a significant part in its economic development. Visitors to this substantial island, which it shares with Haiti, are magnetically attracted to strings of idyllic Caribbean beaches – clear blue sea, white sandy shores and palm-tree fringes – and opportunities for water sports (including surfing, windsurfing and diving) and whale-watching.

Venturing beyond the resorts independently, while requiring a bigger budget, is more than worth the effort. To escape the tropical heat of the coast, you can head up to the alpine interior of the Central Highlands, where there are excellent possibilities for hiking – from attractive market-garden towns through sugar and fruit plantations to forested national parks and high mountain peaks (Pico Duarte is the highest in the Caribbean).

If your trip coincides with one of the carnivals or festivals held throughout the year, it will be especially memorable. Non-stop dancing, blasting music (particularly merengue), dazzling costumes and gallons of rum make for a real air of communal extravagance. During quieter periods, you can savour the DR's rich artistic tradition. From ancient Taino rock paintings and brightly hued farmhouses that stretch across the countryside to the great colonial city of Santo Domingo (the first in the new world), you are definitely guaranteed a colourful stay.

ACCOM+
CANO HONDO PARADISE LODGE
The Cano Lodge has 28 rooms in three villas. Wonderful views, natural pools, traditional Creole food, excursions to the national park, Los Haitises, and birding. A slight caveat: it is a long way from other communities. This, of course, could be deemed a virtue.

Contact: Rosanna Selman
Tel: +1 809 2485995 · +1 809 8899454
Email: info@paraisocanohondo.com
Web: www.paraisocanohondo.com
Address: Hotel Paraiso Cano Hondo, Carretera Los Haitises, Sabana de la Mar, Provincia Hato Mayor, Dominican Republic

VOL
THE DOMINICAN REPUBLIC EDUCATION AND MENTORING (DREAM) PROJECT
DREAM is a non-profit organization which runs a community centre and is a partner of several schools. The target is the provision of quality education for children born into rural poverty and small communities of the republic. Tours of the schools and the centre are provided and you can do something useful, such as paint a wall and leave in-kind donations. Side trips of a touristic nature are quite possible.

Contact: Emily MacDowell
Tel: +1 607 2571981
Fax: +1 607 2571937
Email: info@dominicandream.org
Web: www.dominicandream.org
Address: PO Box 4136, Ithaca, NY 14852, USA

TOUR
IGUANA MAMA TOURS

Based in Cabarete on the northern coast, a town famous for windsurfing and kitesurfing, Iguana Mama Tours have been described as 'the leaders in outstanding adventures in the Dominican Republic'. They offer mountain biking, hiking, waterfall adventures and various other ecological tours. It is an entirely different way of getting to know the country; small groups with expert guides avoid the clichéd tourist traps in an environmentally sustainable way while respecting local communities.

Contact: Michael Scates
Tel: +1 809 5710908
Fax: +1 809 5710734
Email: info@iguanamama.com
Address: Calle Principal 74, Cabarete, República Dominicana

GRENADA
International dialling code +1 473

500km

ST
GEORGE'S

Grenada is known as the Spice Island of the Caribbean, famous for its nutmeg. In 1979 it gained international recognition for its socialist revolution, with iconic images of marijuana-smoking dread-locked soldiers holding AK47s. That all ended with the US invasion of 1983. Grenada's culture is based on African and French traditions as well as British – it was a British colony until 1974. Tourism used to be a very low-key affair, with mainly small-scale locally owned resorts, until the devastation of Hurricane Ivan in 2004 led to the selling of national parks and an ill-considered rush towards unregulated foreign developments.

However, Grenada (including its sister isles, Carriacou and Petite Martinique) is still a lure for nature lovers. There's snorkelling and diving off white sand beaches, cooling down in the rainforest around the Grand Etang crater lake, and hiking up waterfalls and hot springs. Such energetic activities can be pursued when not strolling around the pretty capital of St George's, with its 18th-century buildings and forts. There are spice plantations to visit, and the River Antoine rum distillery (whose rum is too strong to be carried on a plane!) and the colourful market square, where Dorothy Dandridge did the limbo in the movie *Island in the Sun*.

Carriacou and Petite Martinique have a closer connection to their African past, with their tombstone feasts and Big Drum Nation Dancing, which perpetuate the dancers' ties to their specific tribal lineages. Boat building, using traditional techniques, and unique wedding rituals particularly define tiny Petite Martinique.

What really makes Grenada special is the geniality of its people. It's still relatively unspoiled, crime free and has a heart-warming sense of community.

HOST/SCHOOL
HOMESTAYS GRENADA

This is an enabling enterprise – the owners place guests with hosts all over the three islands comprising Grenada. The founding aim was to foster non-exploitative tourism among the different island communities. Community tours are also offered. Visitors get involved with what is happening where they are – nothing happens because of their presence. They experience genuine Grenadian culture and lifestyle. Many visitors want to involve themselves further (e.g. in building work, helping on a farm or teaching in a primary school). They are asked to bring school supplies, which are distributed to community libraries and primary schools around the islands.

Contact: Elisabeth and Earl Williams
Tel: +1 4734445845
Fax: +1 4734445845
Email: grenhome@spiceisle.com
Web: www.homestaysgrenada.com
Address: PO Box 810, St George's, Grenada, West Indies

HAITI
International dialling code +509

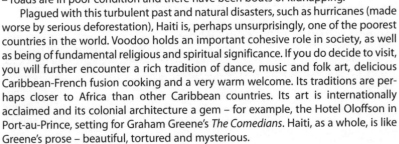

Voodoo and violence are probably the two things most people would associate with Haiti. In many ways, this sums up the conundrum for any prospective tourist: the country's vibrant culture makes it a fascinating place to visit, but only when it is safe to do so. Haiti has a unique but chaotic political history. The world's oldest black-led republic, and the only one established on the back of a successful rebellion by slaves (95 per cent of today's population is of African descent), it has endured colonization by both Spain and France, occupation by the US, and then decades of brutal dictatorship, unstable governance and civil unrest. Even now the general security situation is poor, and at the time of writing the UK Foreign Office advice was for essential travel only. The use of internal flights, however, makes internal travel less hazardous – roads are in poor condition and there have been bouts of kidnapping.

Plagued with this turbulent past and natural disasters, such as hurricanes (made worse by serious deforestation), Haiti is, perhaps unsurprisingly, one of the poorest countries in the world. Voodoo holds an important cohesive role in society, as well as being of fundamental religious and spiritual significance. If you do decide to visit, you will further encounter a rich tradition of dance, music and folk art, delicious Caribbean-French fusion cooking and a very warm welcome. Its traditions are perhaps closer to Africa than other Caribbean countries. Its art is internationally acclaimed and its colonial architecture a gem – for example, the Hotel Oloffson in Port-au-Prince, setting for Graham Greene's *The Comedians*. Haiti, as a whole, is like Greene's prose – beautiful, tortured and mysterious.

HOST
BEYOND BORDERS
A Christian US non-profit organization, which works with a Haitian organization, Limye Lavi (Light for Life) to offer small groups an opportunity to stay for a week with a host family and to experience how Haitians live. The experience is called 'transformational travel' and participants learn that hospitality does not depend upon electricity or running water.

Contact: Jonathan Haggard or David Diggs
Tel: +1 610 2775045
Fax: +1 610 2775045 (call first)
Email: mail@beyondborders.net • dadiggs@gmail.com
Web: www.beyondborders.net
Address: PO Box 2132, Norristown, PA 19404, USA

JAMAICA
International dialling code +1-876

Bigger, brasher, more intoxicating than other Caribbean islands, Jamaica lives on its wits and the talents of its people. It's gorgeous, too, and offers a contrast of landscapes – from the idyllic beaches to the curious limestone Cockpit Country and the glorious Blue Mountains (a great hike to the summit, best climbed at night to meet the dawn). 'Jamaica: We're more than a beach, we're a country' was an apt advertising slogan of the 1970s and one that's still relevant.

Kingston, the capital, has a sadly dangerous reputation (Jamaica has much poverty and infamous ghettos), but it doesn't have to be like that. The Bob Marley museum is in Kingston as is the National Gallery of Art (a fabulous collection which tells the story of the island's art history). Music is at the heart of the culture – Jamaica, of course, is the home of reggae, the great music form with a worldwide reputation, and its sounds are everywhere.

Jamaica has a long tourism tradition; but, latterly, all-inclusives have come to dominate. The north coast, around Montego Bay, and Negril, originally cultivated by hippies, are the main tourist drags. Jamaica, however, is much more than the sum of its resorts. Apart from the cities of Kingston and Montego Bay, Jamaica has wonderful examples of Georgian architecture, such as at Falmouth, great plantation houses, and the former homes of expatriates such as Noel Coward and Ian Fleming, who lived a sybaritic bohemian lifestyle. Jamaicans, too, take their pleasures seriously and open their lives and culture to tourists with great generosity.

ACCOM+
COCKPIT COUNTRY ADVENTURE TOURS
Cockpit Country is noted for its biodiversity and is an important Jamaican wilderness area. The company, based in Albert Town, Trelawny, offers a range of rural experiences, including hiking and bird-watching, and guests stay with local bed-and-breakfast hosts. Goods and services are sourced locally. This gives local people a commitment to the company. Any profits are invested in community projects. This is a low-impact operation aiming to give visitors an environmental and social package that will genuinely educate them about the area and its culture. It's family friendly too.

Contact: Donavan Haughton • Hyacinth Record
Tel: +1 876 6100818
Fax: +1 876 6101676
Email: stea@cwjamaica.com
Web: www.stea.net/ccat.htm
Address: #3 Grants Office Complex, Albert Town, Trelawny, Jamaica, West Indies

ACCOM+
COUNTRYSTYLE COMMUNITY TOURISM NETWORK
This is a village stays and tours project – but that *précis* falls all too short. Countrystyle has pioneered community tourism in Jamaica and represents a network of hotels, homestays, restaurants, visitor centres and so on. The driving vision is the sustainable empowerment and development of communities. Become a Jamaican for a week and join in everything.

Contact: Diana McIntyre-Pike
Tel: +1 876 4887207 • +1 876 9627758
Email: countrystyletourism@yahoo.com • Diana@countrystylejamaica.com
Web: www.countrystylejamaica.com • www.countrystylecommunitytourism.com
Address: Countrystyle International Ltd, Countrystyle Community Tourism Network, The Astra Country Inn, 62 Ward Avenue, PO Box 60, Mandeville, Manchester, Jamaica, West Indies

LUX+/TOUR
HOTEL MOCKING BIRD HILL AND JAMAICA EXPLORATIONS
A boutique hotel which believes in ethical business and sees itself as an engine for social change – fair trading is the watch phrase and the holidays on offer provide economic, ethical and environmental opportunities to develop sustainable tourism. A focus on individuals and small groups ensures minimal impact upon the local culture and resources. This is a green operation. The business is involved in the provision and development of education locally and aims to ensure that its visitors become similarly supportive.

Contact: Kashee Rodney
Tel: +1 876 9937134 • +1 876 9937267
Fax: +1 876 9937133
Email: info@hotelmockingbirdhill.com
Web: www.hotelmockingbirdhill.com
Address: PO Box 254, Port Antonio, Jamaica

THE AMERICAS

CENTRAL AMERICA

COSTA RICA
International dialling code +506

Costa Rica is sometimes called the Switzerland of Central America – it has the region's longest history of political stability, its soundest economy and highest standard of living. During the past decades, it has also become somewhat of a Mecca for ecotourists – with a well-deserved reputation. The country can boast more than a quarter of its territory as protected national park and forest reserve, and is justly proud of its enlightened environmental policy. Most of these conservation areas are easily accessible, and provide some of the continent's best chances of encountering a bewildering array of exotic (and occasionally endangered) plant and animal species. For added variety, you can make trips to active volcanoes and hot springs, and then, of course, there isn't just one 'rich coast' to see (here, decidedly, ends the Swiss comparison). Both Costa Rica's Caribbean and Pacific shores are lined with beautiful beaches (turtle-nesting included).

Costa Rica is rich in local cultures, and you can feel the change as you move around – from the *sabanero* 'cowboy' culture of the northwest to the Afro-Caribbean feel of the east coast. Overwhelmingly, though, you will be impressed by the warmth and friendliness of the Costa Ricans, or *'ticos'*.

ORG
ACTUAR
ACTUAR is the acronym for Asociación Costarricense de Turismo Rural Comunitario, the Costa Rican community-based rural tourism association, and it comprises more than 29 community-based enterprises. Its mission is to promote the environmental, social, cultural and economic sustainability of community-based rural tourism initiatives. Such tourism breaks down the barriers between the visitor and the essence of rural life; with your *campesino* hosts, you meet local traditions and way of life. ACTUAR has its own community-based rural tourism tour operator which offers personalized itineraries that fit your interests, budget and timeframe.

Contact: Kyra Cruz
Tel: +506 22489470
Fax: +506 22489470+1
Email: info@actuarcostarica.com
Web: www.actuarcostarica.com
Address: PO Box 719 –1260, Costa Rica

ACCOM+
AGROTOURISM AT LA AMISTAD, RUN BY ASOPROLA FARMER'S ASSOCIATION
La Amistad is near the entrance to La Amistad National Park. It is the starting point for many unforgettable adventures. This community is famous for its many examples of creative and artistic recy-

cling. Rooms have private bathrooms, and there is a restaurant, meeting room and internet access. On offer are a visit to an organic coffee processing plant, organic farm tours, hiking with guides in La Amistad Park, waterfall tours, horse riding and fishing for tilapia.

Contact: Kyra Cruz
Tel: +506 22489470
Fax: +506 22489470
Email: info@actuarcostarica.com
Web: www.nacientespalmichal.com • www.actuarcostarica.com
Address: Barrio Amón Avenida 9 entre Calle 3 & 5, PO Box 719.1260, Escazú, Costa Rica

RAINFOREST
CASA CALATEAS

This community-based rural tourism lodge is a four-hour drive from San José in the Talamanca Rainforest, only 15 minutes away from Cahuita National Park. It offers walking trails in the forest to see *campesino* life and offers a rich birdlife. It is owned by a local farmers' association dedicated to the protection of the area's biodiversity and the environment.

Contact: Kyra Cruz
Tel: +506 22489470
Fax: +506 22489470
Email: info@actuarcostarica.com
Web: www.nacientespalmichal.com • www.actuarcostarica.com
Address: Barrio Amón Avenida 9 entre Calle 3 & 5, PO Box 719.1260, Escazú, Costa Rica

RAINFOREST+
CERRO BIOLLEY RURAL INN, RUN BY ASOMOBI

This inn is located near the Altamira entrance to La Amistad International Park, which extends from Costa Rica's Talamanca Mountain range into western Panama. La Amistad has one of the most extensive virgin forests in the country, with endemic species such as oaks. Visitors may see the bellbird and spider monkeys among other species, as they explore the area and visit a women's coffee co-operative, who are the owners of the lodge. On offer, too, are a frog and snake tour, a village tour, a tour within La Amistad Park, and hikes to waterfalls and swimming holes. The lodge has four rooms with shared bathrooms, a restaurant and bakery.

Contact: Kyra Cruz
Tel: +506 22489470
Fax: +506 22489470
Email: info@actuarcostarica.com
Web: www.nacientespalmichal.com • www.actuarcostarica.com
Address: Barrio Amón Avenida 9 entre Calle 3 & 5, PO Box 719.1260, Escazú, Costa Rica

RAINFOREST
CERRO ESCONDIDO LODGE

This lodge, in the middle of a private wildlife reserve, is owned by the Ecologist Association of Paquera; it offers guests riding and walking tours with opportunities to swim in natural pools and visit a waterfall. Four cabins with balconies and private bathrooms can accommodate 16 people. The lodge is located in the Karen Mogensen Reserve on the Nicoya Peninsula. All the income from the lodge goes into conservation and environmental education programmes.

Contact: Kyra Cruz
Tel: +506 22489470
Fax: +506 22489470+1
Email: info@actuarcostarica.com
Web: www.nacientespalmichal.com • www.actuarcostarica.com
Address: PO Box 719 –1260, Costa Rica

THE AMERICAS

ACCOM+
EL COPAL

This community-based rural tourism lodge can accommodate up to 20 people in five rooms, with bunk beds and shared bathrooms. This is where biodiversity and agritourism coexist. El Copal was established with the twin aims of conservation and generating alternative income for the farmers involved in the initiative. There is good bird-watching, with 380 species in the area.

Contact: Kyra Cruz
Tel: +506 22489470
Fax: +506 22489470
Email: info@actuarcostarica.com
Web: www.nacientespalmichal.com • www.actuarcostarica.com
Address: Barrio Amón Avenida 9 entre Calle 3 & 5, PO Box 719.1260, Escazú, Costa Rica

ACCOM
EL DESCANSO, RUN BY ASODINT INDIGENOUS ASSOCIATION

The Térraba Indigenous Territories are located in the canton of Buenos Aires in Puntarenas Province, in the Boruca and Pilas districts. El Descanso, in the village of Térraba, just 4km from the Interamerican Highway, offers tranquil surroundings where you can breathe fresh air, relax and get to know the indigenous culture, unique in Costa Rica and in the world. You can savour delicious traditional dishes such as *tamal de arroz*, *chichi* and *picadillos*, and stay in comfortable cabins with traditional designs.

Contact: Kyra Cruz
Tel: +506 22489470
Fax: +506 22489470
Email: info@actuarcostarica.com
Web: www.nacientespalmichal.com • www.actuarcostarica.com
Address: Barrio Amón Avenida 9 entre Calle 3 & 5, PO Box 719.1260, Escazú, Costa Rica

DAY
EL ENCANTO DE LA PIEDRA BLANCA

The Charm of the White Mountain is owned by the Association for the Conservation and Development of Escazu Mountains (CODECE). An unusual experience, this is a rural tour on the urban fringe, near San José. There are half- and full-day tours centred on the Escazu Mountains. Since 1985 the local community of San Antonio has been resisting attempts by the nearby city to acquire its mountains for residential development.

Contact: Kyra Cruz
Tel: +506 22489470
Fax: +506 22489470+1
Email: info@actuarcostarica.com
Web: www.nacientespalmichal.com • www.actuarcostarica.com
Address: PO Box 719 –1260, Costa Rica

ACCOM/TOUR
EL YUE AGRO-ECO FARM AND LODGE

Located in the south Caribbean close to Cahuita NP, El Yue is a women's community-based rural tourism initiative. A distinctive feature is its garden of medicinal plants. El Yue is another example of local people wanting to improve their position by diversifying, but without endangering their environment. You can stay there and take a two-day tour.

Contact: Kyra Cruz
Tel: +506 22489470
Fax: +506 22489470+1
Email: info@actuarcostarica.com
Web: www.nacientespalmichal.com • www.actuarcostarica.com
Address: PO Box 719 –1260, Costa Rica

ACCOM/HOST/VOL
GANDOCA RURAL INN AND TURTLE TOUR
Located about 1.5 hours south of Puerto Viejo, guests can enjoy the beach, search for leatherback turtles laying their eggs at night (from March to June), visit Gandoca lagoon and mangroves, and observe a great variety of native and migratory birds in the Gandoca/Manzanillo Wildlife Refuge. Spend the night at Albergüe El Yolillal, with local families, or in Puerto Viejo or Cahuita.

Contact: Kyra Cruz
Tel: +506 22489470
Fax: +506 22489470
Email: info@actuarcostarica.com
Web: www.nacientespalmichal.com • www.actuarcostarica.com
Address: Barrio Amón Avenida 9 entre Calle 3 & 5, PO Box 719.1260, Escazú, Costa Rica

ACCOM +
ISLA DE CHIRA LODGE
A community-based rural tourism lodge in the Gulf of Nicoya owned by the Association of the Women of Chira Island. It was established in 2000 with the aim of generating alternative income sources for the island's fisherwomen and to foster the conservation and sustainable use of the island's natural resources. Tours of the island – the mangroves are an important resource – are also on offer, and the comfortable lodges (a cabin with two rooms, each with a double and two single beds) also have private bathrooms. There's delicious local food.

Contact: Kyra Cruz
Tel: +506 22489470
Fax: +506 22489470+1
Email: info@actuarcostarica.com
Web: www.nacientespalmichal.com • www.actuarcostarica.com
Address: PO Box 719 –1260, Costa Rica

RAINFOREST+
JUANILAMA RESERVE AND COMMUNITY EXPERIENCE
Located near Caño Negro Wildlife Refuge, toucans, parrots, monkeys and frogs can be found in the Juanilama Reserve, as well as a lovely waterfall pool. This is a great place to experience life in a *campesino* community. You can go fishing, horse riding or learn to make cheese. Especially recommended for families.

Contact: Kyra Cruz
Tel: +506 22489470
Fax: +506 22489470
Email: info@actuarcostarica.com
Web: www.nacientespalmichal.com • www.actuarcostarica.com
Address: Barrio Amón Avenida 9 entre Calle 3 & 5, PO Box 719.1260, Escazú, Costa Rica

RAINFOREST +
LOS CAMPESINOS
This is a rural tourism lodge at the edge of a tiny village, high up in the mountains, offering tours (forest, waterfall and organic farms), horse riding and hiking (you will need a four-wheel drive to access it). Owned by the Asociación Productores de Vainilla (Vanilla Producers Association), it can accommodate six people in two cabins with balconies and private bathrooms. There's also a canopy walkway. Originally the association was producing vanilla essence; but a hurricane and the overexploitation of the forest brought a disease to the vanilla and pushed the community to work together to generate alternative income – through tourism.

Contact: Kyra Cruz
Tel: +506 22489470
Fax: +506 22489470+1

THE AMERICAS

Email: info@actuarcostarica.com
Web: www.nacientespalmichal.com • www.actuarcostarica.com
Address: PO Box 719 –1260, Costa Rica

ACCOM/AGRI
MONTANA VERDE

This enterprise, which is owned by the Asociación Montaba Verde (Green Mountain Association), is a community-based rural tourism lodge. It gives visitors the chance to meet people who live in harmony with their surroundings and, if you wish, to join them in their projects, including organic gardening, research and reforestation.

Contact: Kyra Cruz
Tel: +506 22489470
Fax: +506 22489470+1
Email: info@actuarcostarica.com
Web: www.nacientespalmichal.com • www.actuarcostarica.com
Address: PO Box 719 –1260, Costa Rica

ACCOM +
NACIENTES PALMICHAL RURAL INN RUN BY ADESSARU (ASOCIACIÓN DE DESARROLLO SAN JOSÉ RURAL)

Nacientes Palmichal, located less than one hour's drive from San José, is a community-based rural tourism lodge that has an environmental education centre. There is a sustainable development plan for the area that includes sustainable tourism initiatives. It can accommodate 30 visitors and has eight rooms with private bathrooms. This is an opportunity for guests to learn about green lifestyles and to see one in action.

Contact: Kyra Cruz
Tel: +506 22489470
Fax: +506 22489470+1
Email: info@actuarcostarica.com
Web: www.nacientespalmichal.com • www.actuarcostarica.com
Address: PO Box 719 –1260, Costa Rica

RAINFOREST+
STIBRAWPA CASA DE LAS MUJERES

On the border between Costa Rica and Panama you reach Yorkin with a dug-out canoe, just one hour from Bambu. In 1985, the local women came together to set up Stibrawpa (an association of craftswomen) in order to diversify their means of production and to preserve their culture alongside the creation of alternative income sources. With additional income from tourism, the Bribri people of Yorkin can take their children to school. The women are proud to share their Bribri culture. In the small town a maximum of 20 people can stay in Bribri-style lodgings with shared bathrooms.

Contact: Kyra Cruz
Tel: +506 22489470
Fax: +506 2248 9470+1
Email: info@actuarcostarica.com
Web: www.nacientespalmichal.com • www.actuarcostarica.com
Address: PO Box 719 –1260, Costa Rica

RAINFOREST +
TESORO VERDE

This is a community-based rural tourism lodge on the Osa Peninsula. A few decades ago local people had the dream of increasing their self-sufficiency and yet remaining in harmony with their surroundings – their own reserve and the Corcovado National Park. On offer are accommodation and a three- or four-day tour package visiting Corcovado National Park and Caño Island.

Contact: Kyra Cruz
Tel: +506 22489470
Fax: +506 22489470+1
Email: info@actuarcostarica.com
Web: www.nacientespalmichal.com • www.actuarcostarica.com
Address: PO Box 719 –1260, Costa Rica

LUX/RAINFOREST
EL SILENCIO LODGE AND SPA

This luxury lodge and spa commenced operation in January 2008. Self-described as being 'planet friendly' and offering 'soft adventure and inspired wellness', El Silencio is located on a 200ha tropical cloud forest reserve in Costa Rica's pristine central volcanic region. It is a 'high-end boutique hotel'. Hiring policies prioritize local people, there is a training programme and a promote-from-within mandate. Local culture is respected and the aim is to liaise with local people and businesses to mutual benefit. How much? You know the mantra: if you have to ask the price, you can't afford it.

Contact: Andrey Gomez (general manager)
Tel: +506 27610301
Fax: +506 2761 0302
Email: outreach@elsilenciolodge.com
Web: www.elsilenciolodge.com
Address: El Silencio Lodge and Spa, Bajos del Toro, Alajuela, Costa Rica

RAINFOREST+
ESQUINAS RAINFOREST LODGE

Located next to Piedras National Park in the south of the country, Esquinas is part of a unique project combining conservation, ecotourism, research and development. An Austrian NGO, Rainforest of the Austrians was formed in 1991 with the goal of protecting the Esquinas Forest by purchasing land within the park and donating it to the Costa Rican government. The aim is to provide the local population with alternative sources of income other than exploitation of the rainforest. The organization also pays for two wardens and assists in reintroducing endangered species such as the scarlet macaw, as well as running a research station. The lodge offers rainforest hikes, birdwatching, horseback riding, bike tours and kayak excursions in Golfo Dulce.

Contact: Ana Catalina Torres
Tel: +506 27418001
Fax: +506 27418001
Email: esquinas@racsa.co.cr
Web: www.esquinaslodge.com
Address: La Gamba, Golfito, Provincia de Puntarenas, Costa Rica

AGRI+
JOVENES AGRO ECOLOGISTA DE LA ZONA NORTE (JAZON)

JAZON works with the young people of small farming families in the north region of Costa Rica, offering accommodation with full board and tours. Located in a rural, mountainous national park, the idea of the project is to provide the tourist with an innovative experience of the local culture. The tour provides an insight on agricultural production, and also offers horse riding, trekking and boat tours. The objective of the project is to generate alternatives for young people, in this way stopping migration from the region.

Contact: Christian Vea Solis
Tel: +506 24757494 • +506 83546047
Fax: +506 24757494
Email: christian@costaricaruraltours.com • info@costaricaruraltours.com
Web: www.costaricaruraltours.com
Address: PO Box 130 – 4417, Costa Rica

RAINFOREST
LA LAGUNA DEL LAGARTO LODGE

Located at the northern end of Costa Rica, the Laguna del Lagarto Lodge gives visitors access to 505ha of virgin tropical rainforest. The protected area of forest boasts incredible biodiversity, including 350 different species of birds, making it a haven for bird-watchers and photographers. There is a team of trained local guides who can help visitors explore the area, and keep them informed about local ecological and social complexities. The lodge has commitments to the local community as well as the environment, and, at around UK£25 per night, is good value for very comfortable rainforest accommodation.

Contact: Kurt Schmack
Tel: +506 22898163
Email: info@lagarto-lodge-costa-rica.com
Web: www.lagarto-lodge-costa-rica.com
Address: 995 – 1007 San José, Costa Rica

HOST+/AGRI/VOL
LONGO MAI/FINCA SONADOR

Family life with a host family – the real life of real *campesino* families, plus all the advantages of genuine agro-ecotourism. Full board for a day is not much more than a skinny *latté* and a brownie in Starbucks – about US$16. If you stay longer than two weeks, it reduces to US$14. What's keeping you?

Contact: Christoph Burkard
Tel: +506 83584977 · +506 27714239
Fax: +506 27714239
Email: zsuzsacr@yahoo.co.in · zsp@gmx.net · rolspendling@gmx.net
Web: www.sonador.info
Address: Asociación VIDA NUEVA, Apartado 292-8000, San Isidro PZ, Costa Rica

ORG/HOST
SIMBIOSIS TOURS

Simbiosis is the organizational umbrella for Cooprena Tours, which represents a consortium of 18 small co-operatives and specializes in the promotion of community-based rural and sustainable tourism. There are a range of programmes, including short and long stays, cultural activities, hiking trips and volunteer work. The company can arrange things such as car rental, lodge accommodation and transfers. For the local people involved in the co-operatives, tourism provides a useful socio-economic add-on to their normal income sources such as construction, coffee-picking and guiding.

Contact: Monika Monge (info@turismoruralcr.com) or Mario Ordónez
Tel: +506 22908646
Fax: +506 22908667
Email: mercadeo@turismoruralcr.com
Web: www.turismoruralcr.com
Address: PO Box 6939 – 1000, San José, Costa Rica

GUATEMALA
International dialling code +502

Guatemala has become a popular and inexpensive place to learn Spanish, and many visitors choose to take in a few weeks' homestay study during their travels. Small but geographically diverse, Guatemala's cool mountainous highlands graduate into the tropical jungle lowland north of the Pacific coastline. This spectacular scenery envelops active volcanoes and ancient Mayan ruins, lush rainforest with abundant wildlife and the stunning Lake Atitlán. Guatemala is also rich culturally, with an indigenous population of over 40 per cent, much higher than elsewhere in the region. You can encounter this in numerous native dialects, the fusion of Mayan and Catholic religious practices, and traditional dress and handicrafts, perhaps displayed at a colourful town market or fiesta. Guatemala also has year-round good weather, hence its nickname 'the Land of Eternal Spring', although the dry season is November to April. Almost a decade of civil peace has made it a must-see destination for many travellers; but, unfortunately, it has become less safe to visit recently.

Tourists should take a cautious and vigilant approach to travel as foreigners can be targets for armed robberies and muggings, even in much-visited areas. Travelling at night is inadvisable, and do take great care if travelling unaccompanied or by public bus. Also, always remember to ask permission before photographing local people as this has caused problems in the past. But bring extra film along too, as you will really want to capture this beautiful country.

RAINFOREST
ASSOCIATION AK'TENAMIT

This is an NGO that runs two ecotourism projects 60 minutes by boat from Livingston, in the Río Dulce National Park at the heart of the Guatemalan rainforest, not far from the Caribbean coast. Staying in comfortable guest houses in a Mayan village, there are various things for visitors to enjoy, from guided tours of the rainforest, to traditional dances and music, pre-Colombian religious ceremonies and the opportunity to sample locally made Mayan handicrafts. There are also self-guided trails to take through the jungle along which visitors are free to explore and discover caves, lagoons, waterfalls, rivers and the rich diversity of plants and animals.

Contact: Guillermo Perez
Tel: +502 22541560 • +502 22543346 • +502 79470891
Fax: +502 22541560
Email: gperez@aktenamit.org • oscar.diaz@aktenamit.org
Web: www.aktenamit.org
Address: 11 Avenida 'A' 9-39 zona 2, Guatemala

ACCOM+/HOST
AVENTURA MAYA K'ICHE

Aventura Maya K'Iche is an umbrella organization covering a range of Mayan community groups, from musicians to host families, in San Miguel Totonicapan in the Western Highlands. They 'present visitors with a different experience based on sharing with the host community and its ancestral traditions'. The community is especially noted for handicrafts, music and dance. Visitors stay in a guest house or with local families on a bed-and-breakfast basis, and are spread around the community to ensure that the economic benefits are widespread. Real efforts are made to raise the profile of local women in the tourism context.

Contact: Carlos Molina
Tel: +502 7766 1575 · +502 59988648
Fax: +502 77661575
Email: aventuramayakiche@yahoo.com · kiche78@hotmail.com
Web: www.larutamayaonline.com/aventura
Address: 7a avenida 1-26 zona 1 Totonicapán, Guatemala

VOL/BUDGET
CASA GUATEMALA ORGANIZATION/PROJECT: A HOME FOR CHILDREN COMING FROM EXTREME POVERTY

Casa Guatemala is a home for 250 children and its Backpackers' Hotel has been created to help with the budget of the home. The hotel can accommodate and feed individuals and groups. There are opportunities for working as teachers, helping on the farm or in the clinic, and generally just sharing time with and caring for the children. The aim is to produce citizens of quality for Guatemala.

Contact: Raquel Reyes
Tel: +502 79305480
Fax: +502 23319408
Email: administracion@casa-guatemala.org · hotelbackpackers@casa-guatemala.org
Web: www.casa-guatemala.org · www.hotelbackpackers.com
Address: 14 calle 10-63 zona 1, Guatemala City, Guatemala CA

TOUR OP
CAYAYA BIRDING

This is a specialist bird-watching operator. Tours can start from any main centre and can also include culture, nature and archaeological guiding. For lodging, transport, food and guiding, it cooperates with indigenous communities, conservationist NGOs and other enterprises. A guiding principle is that local people will value the environment more and conserve it if they see it as something that attracts visitors and, therefore, is economically valuable.

Contact: Claudis Avendano or Knut Eisermann
Tel: +502 53085160 · +502 59066479
Fax: +502 24398517
Email: info@cayaya-birding.com
Web: www.cayaya-birding.com
Address: Knut Eisermann, PO Box 98 Periferico, Guatemala

ACCOM+
COMUNIDAD 'NUEVA ALIANZA'

This collective of 40 families owns a fair-trade organic coffee and macadamia nut plantation. In 2005 it opened an eco-lodge which accommodates 25 people and is managed and run by the collective. On offer are tours of the plantation with an opportunity to learn about the work of the growers, and about the medicinal and edible herbs and plants of the tropical forest. Every person has an equal stake in the entire operation and all profits are equally shared. As well as the drive to be fully organic, they are also involved in sustainable energy projects, including a United Nations-funded mini-hydroelectric plant. The area itself has beautiful views of Santiaguito, the most active volcano in Guatemala, which erupts hourly, as well as two waterfalls and a natural swimming hole nearby. Transport is arranged from Cuatro Caminos.

Contact: Rosa Gonzalez
Tel: +502 57299230
Mobile: +502 53622284 (office) · +502 58017849 (Rosa)
Email: comunidadalianza@gmail.com
Web: www.comunidadnuevaalianza.org
Address: El Palmar, Quetzaltenango, Guatemala

ACCOM+
ECO-HOTEL UXLABIL ATITLAN
Perched on the banks of the beautiful Atitlan Lake, the Uxlabil Atitlan is a small, peaceful eco-hotel well off the beaten track. It is run by the local community of Mayan Tzutuhil people, and the hotel's activities are bound up in village life. Guests are invited to meet local painters and craftsmen, visit textile workshops and chat with villagers. There are lots of opportunities to explore the lake and area with local guides on foot, horse or canoe, or the less adventurous can stay in and relax in the garden, sauna or jacuzzi. Prices start at US$20 a night, based on two people sharing.

Contact: Elizabeth Echeverria
Tel: +502 23669555
Fax: +502 23669555 (extension 16)
Email: atitlan@uxabil.com
Web: www.uxlabil.com
Address: 11 calle y 15 Avenida final, 12-53 zona, 10 Oakland CP01010, Guatemala

ORG/TOUR
GATEWAY TO THE MAYAN WORLD
This community-based tourism corridor is situated in the municipality of Chisec and Raxruha. Set in the foothills of the Guatemalan Highlands, Alta Verapaz is an ideal tourist destination offering natural and cultural attractions, as well as sites of archaeological interest. In Sepalau a guided trail leads visitors to the Sepalau lagoons. These crystalline waters are surrounded by karst hills (dramatic landscape created by the effect of water on permeable limestone surfaces) and wildlife-filled rainforest, and are perfect for swimming and kayaking. In Bombil Pek expert guides use specialized mountain-climbing equipment to take visitors up to see pre-Mayan drawings in high-up caves. At Campo Santo and Mucbilha, guided tours, either on foot or by floating inner tube, are available through Central America's largest cave system where subterranean river winds blow through enormous naturally lit caverns. And if this were not enough, on the banks of the Passion River lies Cancuen, excavation site of one of the largest Mayan palaces ever uncovered.

Tel: +502 59781465
Email: info@puertamundomaya.com
Web: www.puertamundomaya.com
Address: Municipality of Chisec, Alta Verapaz, Guatemala

ACCOM
HOTEL DOS LUNAS
A comfortable hotel located less than 1km south of La Aurora International Airport in Guatemala City, in a safe residential area. The hotel is recommended by several travel guides and has various amenities, including free internet access, tourist information, a travel agency and a free airport shuttle. It's very much concerned with the conservation of natural and cultural resources. Its owner, Lorena Artola, coordinated the research and edited *Mosaic of Guatemala* in 2000, the first magazine about ecotourism in Guatemala. In 2001, she was a co-founder of a non-profit organization called Red de Turismo Sostenible de Guatemala. Its aim is to promote and market alternative tourism products of small and micro-enterprises.

Tel: +502 22614248 · +502 22614337
Fax: +502 22614248
Email: info@hoteldoslunas.com · hoteldoslunas@gmail.com
Web: www.hoteldoslunas.com
Address: 21 Calle 10-92 zona 13, Aurora II, Guatemala

ACCOM
LA CASA DE DON DAVID

This hotel, restaurant and tour business is to be found in the village of El Remate, Flores Peten, on a main road about 15 minutes before Tikal National Park. It is privately owned and run and its main thrust comes from a strong belief in sustainability and the need for controlled sustainable tourism, with an emphasis on local education. They have 15 rooms giving 39 beds, and 7 of the rooms are air conditioned. The charges range from US$32 to US$56 for a double with breakfast. There is easy bus access from Flores Airport 28km away.

Contact: Yohana Rodas
Tel: +502 79288469 · +502 53062190
Email: info@lacasadedondavid.com
Web: www.lacasadedondavid.com
Address: Apotada 14 El Remate, Flores Peten, Guatemala

ORG/ACCOM
RICERCA E COOPERAZIONE (RESEARCH AND COOPERATION)

Through campaigns and education, Ricerca e Cooperazione keeps track of the erosion of environmental and cultural heritage, speaks for basic human rights, and increases society's awareness of just which socio-economic phenomena create the disparity between North and South. It also operates a small eco-hotel on the shores of Lake Atitlan. You can canoe and ride, but, best of all, just appreciate the peace and *be*.

Contact: Elizabeth Echeverria
Tel: +502 23669555
Fax: +502 23669555 (extension 116)
Email: Atitlan@uxlabil.com
Web: www.uxlabil.com
Address: 11 calle y 15 Avenida final 12-53 zona 10, Oakland, CP 01010, Guatemala

RAINFOREST/TOUR
TIKAL CONNECTION (formerly ECOMAYA)

This is a project in the Maya Biosphere Reserve in El Peten, the northernmost province of Guatemala. The closest town is Flores City. Tikal Connection offers trekking and horseback expeditions in the jungle to the sites of El Mirador, El Perù-Scarlett Macaw Trail, El Zotz-Tikal and other sites and attractions in Peten. Transportation can also be by 4x4 or motorboat. There is camping in the jungle accompanied by local guides. Among the many tourist attractions in the area is the archaeological site of El Mirador, the largest city in the Mayan world, containing the El Tigre Pyramid. The reserve is also rich in animal and bird life, including crocodiles, bats and the endangered scarlet macaw. Tikal Connection tour operator is an active partner in local community initiatives.

Tel: +502 78675454
Fax: +502 78675454
Mobile: +502 58711169
Email: okanchac@tikalcnx.com
Web: www.tikalcnx.com
Address: Mundo Maya Internacional Airport, Santa Elena, Flores, Peten, 17029, Guatemala

HONDURAS
International dialling code +504

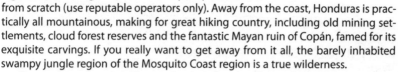

As the legend goes, Columbus named Honduras when finding shelter from sea storms in its calming waters. These days, its Caribbean coastline is one of the main tourist draws, as visitors gravitate to enjoy the laid-back atmosphere of its fishing villages and coconut islands. The Bay Islands, in particular, are great for reef diving and are among the world's cheapest places to learn this from scratch (use reputable operators only). Away from the coast, Honduras is practically all mountainous, making for great hiking country, including old mining settlements, cloud forest reserves and the fantastic Mayan ruin of Copán, famed for its exquisite carvings. If you really want to get away from it all, the barely inhabited swampy jungle region of the Mosquito Coast region is a true wilderness.

On your travels, you will meet landscapes of coffee and banana plantations, crops vital to the Honduran economy. The country cannot escape its legacy as the first 'banana republic', with its more recent economic and political history dominated by foreign fruit interests, to its general detriment. The devastation wreaked by Hurricane Mitch in 1998 is also a painful memory.

Attacks on tourist do sometimes occur, and public buses are prone to hold-ups and accidents. However, if you do take care there is no reason not to follow in Columbus's footsteps: go, explore and find your own calm waters in this beautiful country.

HOST/TOUR
COCO TOURS
Coco Tours is a small multilingual tour operator working to protect the cultural and biological diversity of the Honduran costal area. In partnership with three different indigenous groups, it offers day trips and tours of up to two weeks. Although its trips focus on cultural immersion and include homestays, it offers plenty of opportunities to get adventurous: coral reef snorkelling, treks through lowland humid jungle and visits to Mayan heritage sites. Coco is happy to receive groups and families, and can tailor trips to their needs.

Contact: Miguel Farines
Tel: +504 33354599
Email: tour@hondurascoco.com
Web: www.hondurascoco.com
Address: Barrio el Centro, Triunfo de la Cruz, Tela, Honduras

DAY/VOL
IGUANA RESEARCH AND BREEDING STATION
Located on the island of Utila, the Iguana research station plays a crucial role in the conservation of the island's endemic iguana species *Ctenosaura bakeri*. The iguana is threatened by unsustainable development, as are the environment, the mangroves and the beaches due to pollution and hunting. The station runs an environmental education programme in the schools of Utila, as well as residential opportunities for volunteers and tours for day visitors, led by Iguana experts.

Contact: Jimena Castillo • Sven Zoerner
Tel: +504 4253946
Email: jimena.castillo@utila-iguana.de • sven@utila-iguana.de
Web: www.utila-iguana.de
Address: Iguana Research and Breeding Station, Utila, Islas de la Bahía, Honduras

ACCOM/DAY
PICO BONITO NATIONAL PARK FOUNDATION

Pico Bonito National Park is a spectacular 107,300ha of wet tropical lowland located in the north of the country. The foundation's main activity is regulating the use of the area's natural resources, but it also runs an animal rescue centre and family support. The three communities involved offer day trips (from US$6) and adventure activities, including rafting on rapids, kayaking and mountain climbing. La Pico community also offers accommodation in traditional cabins and camping areas.

Contact: Ing Adonis Hernandez
Tel: +504 4400265 · +504 9827534 · +504 9788868
Fax: +504 4420618
E-mail: turismoelpino@yahoo.es
Web: www.picobonito.org

ORG/TOUR
RIO PLATANO BIOSPHERE RESERVE (RPBR)

This reserve is one of the largest protected areas in Central America and offers a wide range of experiences, from its sandy coastline, host to a sea turtle protection project, to lowland tropical forests, extensive watery networks of inland lagoons and rivers (where travel is by boat or on foot only), grasslands and pine savannahs. The project in its entirety is a partnership between the indigenous Miskito, Pech and Garifuna peoples, and national and international tourism organizations. All tourism-related activities and enterprises associated with the reserve are eco-conscious and locally operated. The prevailing doctrine is best summed up as a marriage of sustainable resources and community development goals. A guidebook to the reserve is available.

Contact: Arden Anderson
Tel: +970 6424454
Fax: +970 6424425
Email: Arden_Anderson@co.blm.gov
Web: www.planeta.com/planeta/97/0597mosquitia.html
Address: BLM – Gunnison Field Office, 216 N Colorado St, Gunnison, CO 81230, USA

ACCOM+/ORG/TOUR
THE GARIFUNA TOURISM GROUP

The Garifuna Tourism group is made up of the leading members of the indigenous Garifuna communities from the peaceful and undeveloped white sandy beaches stretching along the north coast of Honduras. Communities offer grassroots tourism projects, based on cultural exchange and interaction. The central group organizes transportation, lodging, meals and tours. This system ensures that the communities are never oversaturated with tourists, so visitors can expect to feel like invited guests. They can learn all about the Garifuna's traditional fishing culture, their relationship to their environment and their ways of coping with a rapidly developing world. Visitors are also given the chance to share in the vibrant and varied local dance, food and music cultures.

Contact: Arlen Dayanara Bernardez
Tel: +504 9277513 · +504 4480121
Fax: +504 4480605
Email: enkelarmani@myway.com · abg49@hotmail.com
Web: www.geo.ya.com/ENKEL
Address: Barrio Suyapa, Pulp, Francis, Tela, Atlántida, Honduras

MEXICO
International dialling code +52

This vast country can cater for every tourist taste under the sun. While it can take some time to fully explore even just the principal areas of attraction, you will be richly rewarded if you venture off the beaten track. This is made particularly easy by the country's extensive, sophisticated and reliable network of buses (there are different classes depending upon the level of adventure you're after as well!). Wherever you do go, though, you will encounter the fascinating mix of three cultures that seems to define the place: its indigenous heritage – including spectacular ancient ruins and a wealth of native languages and traditions; the legacy of the Spanish colonial period, including beautifully preserved cities and a very strong sense of the Catholic, reflected in ornate church design; and the modern, bustling, industrialized Mexico, home to one of the world's megalopolises, and constantly dealing with its complex social and economic interrelationship with its rich northern neighbour. However, throughout its often turbulent political history, Mexico has maintained a strong tradition in art and crafts, music, literature and, more recently, film. The country's beauty lies truly in its diversity – not just culturally, but also geographically, biologically (where it is ranked top three in the world) and even climatically (although the wet season, where it does occur, is generally in summer). Whatever you are looking for, Mexico can guarantee to deliver it in spades.

ACCOM+
ALBERGUE KENNEDY

Albergue Kennedy is a large and comfortable brick-built lodge and campsite near Contepec in the Michoacán region of Mexico, within the transition zone between the holartic and the neotropical ecosystems. The lodge is geared towards big groups, particularly from colleges and schools; but it also welcomes individual travellers. It runs courses and workshops on the environment, water use, regional development, geography and ecology. It is also a great base for travellers interested in trekking, only 15 minutes away from Cerro de Altamirano hiking base.

Contact: Gerardo Osornio
Tel: +52 5553894764
Fax: +52 55-55348532
Email: gosornio58@yahoo.com
Web: www.turismoaraguro.com
Address: López Mateos No 4 Pueblo Nuevo Contepec, Mich, CP 61020, México

VOL
COCHITLEHUA CENTRO MEXICANO DE INTERCAMBIOS (CEMIAC)

This is the Mexican branch of Service Civil International.

Contact: Ricardo Olvera Flores
Tel: +52 5591160565
Fax: +52 5556393015
Email: cemiac@gmail.com
Address: Anaxágoras 302, col Narvarte, México, DF, Ciudad de México, Distrito Federal, 03320, México

BUDGET/DAY
CORREDOR ECOTURISTICO OCHOVENADO

Eco-Tourism Corridor is based in Tutapec, the largest and most culturally and environmentally diverse region on the Oaxaca coast, as well as the site of its first national park. The ecotourism project is based in two small communities, Jocotepec and Santa Ana, who are supported by the Mexican NGO Ecosta. Visitors sleep in cabins and share meals in family homes. Local people act as guides, giving visitors access to wildlife, spectacular landscapes (including crashing waterfalls), hiking and diverse wildlife. The close contact that visitors have with their hosts means they can learn all about the people's cultures, traditions and heritage.

Contact: Heladio Reyes
Tel: +52 9545438284
Email: ecosta@laneta.apc.org
Web: http://ochovenado.wikispaces.com
Address: Lucio Cabañas #9, Santa Rosa de Lima, Tututepec Oaxaca, CP, 71800, México

LUX+
GRUPO PLAN SA DE CV AND FUNDACION HACIENDAS DEL MUNDO MAYA AC

The boutique hotels which comprise this enterprise represent the modern-day rebirth of haciendas, which were the heart of 19th-century plantation estates. The latter's decline bred local poverty which this well-grounded tourism development aims to reverse by breathing life back into the communities. History is perceived not as artefacts and sites to be viewed, but as a living thing exemplified in the lives of ordinary people. The fundacion was created as a reaction to the damage wrought by Hurricane Isidore in 2002, with the target being micro-regional development in the Yucatan Peninsula, which will improve the lifestyle of the inhabitants.

Contact: Cristina Arroyave or Erika Mendiola
Tel: +52 9999241101 · +52 5552570097
Fax: +52 5552576151
Email: cristina.arroyave@thehaciendas.com · Erika.mendiola@grupoplan.com
Web: www.haciendasmundomaya.com · www.grupoplan.com

ACCOM+/SCHOOL
HOTEL MAR DE JADE

On the Pacific Ocean, about an hour and a half north of Puerto Vallarta, this project has grown from huts in 1983 to today's elegant accommodation (as self-described) for up to 80 guests. You can have the usual kind of beach- and marine-based holiday; but the real speciality of Mar de Jade is its peace and quiet. It is a great place for yoga, meditation and retreats. It's also possible to stay three weeks and learn Spanish. The operation finances and runs a primary care community clinic and a child care programme – and more besides. It's not cheap (US$200/US$250 per night with meals); but you see where the money is going.

Tel: +52 3272194000 (Mexico) · +1 8002570532 (USA)
Email: info@mardejade.com
Web: www.mardejade.com

VOL
NUESTRA TIERRA

Small volunteer association especially interested in projects to conserve sea turtles.

Contact: Juanita Delgado
Tel: +52 3222256940
Fax: +52 32247615
Email: admin@nuestratierra.org.mx
Address: PO Box 2-119, CP, 48350, Pto Vallarta, Jalisco, Mexico

ACCOM/HOST
SIERRA NORTE EXPEDITIONS

Sierra Norte Expeditions is an association of eight communities native to the Sierra Juarez, the mountainous region northeast of Oaxaca. Visitors stay in community-built cabins or homestays, all of which are within the nature reserve. Each community has its own character and traditions; but all of them offer trekking, horse riding and guided nature walks. The communities serve good, hearty traditional food, made with local ingredients. Guests can spend time talking to local people about their history and culture, and can see firsthand the benefits that tourism brings to the community.

Contact: Griselda Santiago Hernandez
Tel: +52 9515148271 · +52 15915143631
Fax: +52 19515148271
Email: sierranorte@oaxaca.com.mx · norte@infosel.net.mx
Web: www.sierranorte.org.mx

VOL
VIVE MEXICO

Large, active association organizing workcamps and volunteer placements.

Contact: Alberto Garcia
Tel: +52 4433245170
Fax: +52 4433245170
Email: international@vivemexico.org
Web: www.vivemexico.org
Address: Bld Garcia de Leon 734-A – Colonia Nueva Chapultepec 58260, Morelia, Michoacan, Mexico

NICARAGUA
International dialling code +505

Geographically the largest country in Central America, Nicaragua has featured far more in the foreign psyche as a bloody war zone than as a potential holiday hot spot. Although both the human and physical damage from its notorious 'civil' conflict during the 1970s and 1980s is still evident today, to think of the country only in this regard is a great injustice, both to Nicaragua and yourself. It is a less well-known tourist destination not because it has little to offer, but because its cultural and natural wealth has been largely ignored. Take another look, and you will be well rewarded.

Nicaragua's tourism infrastructure is far less developed than that of neighbouring Costa Rica, but this heightens the sense of adventure. A word of warning, though: road safety conditions are poor, so keep this in mind when planning each journey. And there are several worth making – across beautiful volcanic landscapes, to colonial cities steeped in history, to sandy beaches with stunning backdrops at sunset, and to the country's jewel, Lake Nicaragua. Amongst the world's largest freshwater lakes, its captivating islets and archipelagos, teeming with wildlife, are just waiting to be explored.

This is an excellent country for walking, particularly around volcanoes; but it is always best to go with a guide – mainly for reasons of safety, but also purely for the chat. Nicaraguans are great conversationalists, guaranteed to bring the country even more to life.

THE AMERICAS

BUDGET/TREK
ALBERGE RURAL NICARAGUA LIBRE

Located inside a large and productive hacienda, the Nicaragua Libre Hotel gives visitors the chance to sample the relaxed pace of rural life. Besides visiting the corn, coffee and watermelon plantations, visitors can ride horses or hike to the nearby Mombacho Volcano. Accommodation in rustic but comfortable shared rooms is US$5 to US$8 a night. Visitors can arrive independently, turning left 60km down the road from Granada to Nandaime onto a dirt track that leads to the community. The hotel is part of the UCA Tierra y Agua Co-operative, and stays can also be booked through them. The UCA Co-operative also works with two local co-operatives offering day trips and hiking in the area. One is at Aguas Argias, where visitors can trek to see the point where the water which forms the river emerges from underground, and the other is at Los Norteños, a co-operative that protects a small area of virgin forest.

Contact: Meylin Nicaragua
Tel: +505 5520238 · +505 8969361 (UCA)
Tel: +505 8411639 (direct)
Email: turismo@ucatierrayagua.org
Web: www.ucatierrayagua.org

BUDGET+
CASA COMUNAL LA GRANADILLA

Only 1km further down the dirt road that leads to Nicaragua Libra Hotel, the Casa Communal La Granadilla has the same rural charm and friendly atmosphere. The Casa Communal also offers visitors the chance to explore the village on guided bicycle tours or by ox carts. Private rooms are available. The Casa Communal is also part of the UCA Tierra y Agua Co-operative, and stays can be booked through them.

Contact: Meylin Nicaragua
Tel: +505 5520238 · +505 8969361 (UCA)
Tel: +505 8411639 (direct)
Email: turismo@ucatierrayagua.org
Web: www.ucatierrayagua.org

ACCOM+
FINCA ESPERANZA VERDE

Visitors to the Finca Esperanza Verde have the option of staying in the beautiful traditionally built lodge, with room for up 26 people, on the campsite, or on a homestay in the town of San Roman. The finca reaches from 1200m above sea level down to 750m, from semi-wet to semi-dry tropical ecosystems. Amongst this natural diversity, the finca boasts bird-watching points, a small wildlife reserve, trails, an organic coffee plantation and a butterfly farm. The income that guests to the lodge and campsite bring is used to improve local education and utilities. Non-Spanish speakers are welcome.

Contact: Gifford Laube or Katiela Rocha
Tel: +505 7725003
Fax: +505 7725003
Email: fincaesperanzaverde@gmail.com · fevmanager@gmail.com
Web: www.fincaesperanzaverde.org
Address: AP 28, Matagalpa, Nicaragua

DAY
GOODLIVE TOURS (formerly LANDCRUISER TOURS)

This two-person company (one incomer, plus one local student of sustainable tourism), based in Granada, offers tours that stress the traditions and culture of Nicaragua with commentaries on history, politics and social issues. It is also developing Foreign Retirement Services, a combination of

THE AMERICAS

tours and presentations for Europeans and Anglo-Americans who are thinking of living in or retiring to Nicaragua. A daily tour costs about UK£27.50/US$49 per person, with a maximum of six people per tour. Most of the income generated is reinvested in the community, which supports local companies and projects that aim to protect the environment.

Contact: Lawrence Goodlive
Tel: +505 8955244 • +505 6455702
Email: legoodlive@att.net
Address: 101 Callejon Central America, Granada, Nicaragua

ACCOM+
SOMOS ECOLOGISTAS EN LUCHA POR LA VIDA Y EL AMBIENTE (SELVA)

SELVA is an environmental NGO working for the development of ecotourism to benefit indigenous people and reforestation. It has built up a collective women's group and organizes radio campaigns to support the rights of local people. The organization can arrange accommodation for visitors in typical 'ranchos' near the Tezoatega Ecological Park for UK£5.50/US$10 per night.

Contact: José Alberto Gutierrez
Tel: +505 8854894 • +505 3440727
Email: selvanic@hotmail.com • infocomp@apcomanejo.com
Address: Parque Ecológico Tezoatega, del Parque Iddentitad Viejana, Nicaragua

PANAMA
International dialling code: +507

The Panama Canal was owned and operated by the USA between its invasion of the country in 1989 and the regaining of its independence in 1999. It is used by thousands of gigantic cargo ships annually and earns the country billions. No visit is complete without at least a short day trip, passing through the enormous Miraflores Locks on a tiny cruise boat. But Panama has far more than just the canal. A small but amazingly diverse country, a traveller can visit not only two different oceans in one day, but also combine in less than a week pristine beaches, untouched rainforest and coffee-growing highlands with a wide range of cultural experiences, including a 300-year-old World Heritage site: Casco Antiguo.

The country's importance as a land bridge between South and North America makes for interesting and abundant wildlife, some of it unique to Panama. Small ecotourism resorts have opened, some owned and run by the local communities. The indigenous Kuna people of Kuna Yala (formerly the San Blas Islands), off the Caribbean coast, rebelled against their Spanish colonial masters. Today, they are semi-autonomous and rely on tourism for an income, either directly through small family-owned island lodges, or indirectly through the sale of handicrafts, especially appliqué work. The Kuna have been able to protect their environment from logging and to insist that any tourism businesses in their areas are at least 50 per cent owned by their own people, which should be a model for indigenous people elsewhere.

Elsewhere in the country, development has not been so well planned. Islands in the Caribbean Bocas del Toro Archipelago have suffered from illegal and inappropriate construction of holiday homes and hotels, as has the coffee-growing area, Boquete, where the world's most expensive coffee grows.

ORG
FUNDACION ALMANAQUE AZUL

This is a foundation devoted to proselytizing the principles of sustainable tourism to any interested parties, from members of the public to local communities with a vested interest. It adheres to a fine line between information provision and concealment (i.e. it does not extol the touristic virtues of locations and communities unready for tourism, which would be ruined by its influx). It follows the guideline of Conservation International: 'Linking communities, tourism and conservation – a tourism assessment process'. A specific focus for its concern is the Panamanian coast.

Contact: Mir Rodriguez
Tel: +507 66449214 · +507 2144377
Email: editor@almanaqueazul.org
Web: www.almanaqueazul.org
Address: Mir Rodriguez, Apartado 0824-00113, Panama, Republic of Panama

NORTH AMERICA

CANADA
International dialling code +1

3500km

Oᴛᴛᴀᴡᴀ

Canada has a lot of geography, as every Canadian schoolchild is taught in the verse: 'A thousand miles of mountain; two thousand miles of plain; a thousand miles of forest; and then the sea again.' From the wild Pacific west coast of Vancouver Island with its rainforests and vast beaches, over the huge wilderness areas of the Rocky Mountains, across the sweep of the prairies, through the lakes and forests of northern Ontario and Quebec, to the rugged cliffs and coves of the Maritime provinces forming the Atlantic coast, Canada invites the visitor to get up close and personal with its geography and to take advantage of the many opportunities to explore it by canoe or kayak, by ski or bike, or on foot.

Canada's history is largely one of a battle between man and nature, of people carving out settlements in an inhospitable wilderness and making their living out of extracting natural resources – fish, furs, lumber and metals – from a supply they didn't know was exhaustible. The best way of appreciating Canada's heritage is to visit one of its reconstructed old towns, such as Upper Canada Village in Ontario, or by spending time in one of the excellent provincial museums where scenes depicting the lives of early Canadians have been carefully recreated to give the visitor a critical awareness of Canada's past. Another important aspect of Canada's culture, that of its First Nations, after decades of being more or less hidden, is now celebrated and made accessible to residents and visitors alike who care to visit native-designed and run Friendship and Culture centres or to attend a public potlatch.

Canada's cities are cosmopolitan and are generally safe and fun places to explore and discover the high quality of eating and performing arts opportunities. Getting around cities is usually easy; but travelling from place to place in Canada, unless you do it by air or car, can be a challenge, although most places can be reached by bus.

Canadians have a deserved reputation for courtesy and hospitality. They want you to have a good experience in their country and will often go out of their way to help you.

TOUR
AVENTURES ASHINI
Aventures is wholly owned and run by members of an Innu family community, with support from both the national government and Quebec. This is First Nations community tourism working in harmony with the code adopted by Aventures Ecotourisme Quebec. If you do not know the Innu, they are also known as the Montagnais. This is your chance to learn who they are, what they stand for, their history, culture and their life today. What you will encounter is termed native wisdom by scholars. The Innu call it 'know-how'.

Contact: Serge Ashini Goupil
Tel: +1 4188429797
Email: info@ashini.com
Web: www.ashini.com
Address: CP 322 Wendake, G0A 4V0, Canada

ACCOM+
CREE VILLAGE ECOLODGE

The Cree Village Ecolodge is a not-for-profit accommodation facility offering a brand of eco-tourism based on the values and principles of the Cree people. You will experience Cree hospitality, and learn about Cree cultural values and history. The lodge works with independent Cree entrepreneurs who offer boat tours describing the history and the regional flora and fauna. Don't pack the bikini though – the lodge is on the edge of the sub-Arctic in north-eastern Canada.

Contact: Greg Williams (eco-lodge manager)
Tel: +1 7056586400
Fax: +1 7056586401
Email: greg.williams@creevillage.com • randyk@mocreebec.com
Web: www.creevillage.com
Address: Cree Village Ecolodge, PO Box 730, Moose Factory, Ontario, P0L 1W0, Canada

ORG
CENTRE NUNAVUT TOURISM

This is a non-profit organization promoting tourism in the territory of Nunavut. Any aspect of tourism which promotes Inuit culture and language is supported. Initiatives backed must be local, sustainable, and ecologically and culturally responsible. As the tourism industry develops in Nunavut, opportunities for the local communities will increase.

Contact: Molly McClure
Tel: +1 8679794636
Tel: +1 866 NUNAVUT (toll free in North America)
Tel: +1 8004917910 (toll free internationally)
Fax: +1 8679791261
Email: info@nunavuttourism.com
Web: www.nunavuttourism.com
Address: Nunavut Tourism Information, PO Box 1450, Iqaluit, Nunavut, X0A 0H0, Canada

RAINFOREST
WASHOW LODGE

This is a wilderness lodge owned and run by the Omushkegowuk, the aboriginal Cree dwellers of the James and Hudson Bay Lowlands. Guests usually come to immerse themselves in Cree culture and experience a traditional lifestyle, enjoying Moose Cree First Nation's northern hospitality. They can ski, snowshoe, canoe and kayak, or simply enjoy the abundance of wildlife, including 160 species of migratory birds, caribou, moose, beaver, bears, muskrats, whales, seals and the occasional walrus.

Contact: Clarence Trapper
Tel: +1 7056584699
Fax: +1 7056584734
Email: tc1@washow.ca
Web: www.washow.ca
Address: Washow Lodge, c/o Moose Cree First Nation, PO Box 190, Moose Factory, Ontario P0L 1W0, Canada

HAWAII

International dialling code: +1 808

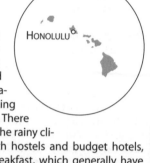

400km

HONOLULU

Although Hawaii is primarily a traditional sun, sea and sand (3-S) holiday paradise, the high-rise beach-front hotel developments are concentrated in a few areas, particularly in Honolulu on Oahu Island and the west coast of Maui. Away from these concentrations are empty landscapes where visitors can go hiking in forests, among volcanic mountains and waterfalls. There are near-deserted beaches on The Big Island, where the rainy climate deters most '3-S' vacationers. As well as youth hostels and budget hotels, there are many private homes offering bed and breakfast, which generally have excellent facilities. Public transportation is almost non-existent apart from on Oahu; but bicycles can be rented easily and fairly inexpensively elsewhere. However, for all but the fittest cyclists, many of the steep mountainous coastal roads are inaccessible except by car. Fortunately, here as elsewhere in the US, car rental is relatively inexpensive (note: under-25s cannot hire cars anywhere in the US). Hawaii is where East meets West, and many independent travellers visit Hawaii to take courses in various New Age therapies and spiritualities, and to experience the native Kahuna culture. As elsewhere in the US, this selling of native culture to visitors is controversial.

DAY/ACCOM
HANA MAUI BOTANICAL GARDENS B&B/VACATION RENTALS

The name says it all: a 4ha garden and two holiday studios for rent – five persons maximum. The botanical stress has always been on the removal of non-native invasive species and the fostering of local ones. The owners are long-established conservationists.

Contact: JoLoyce Kaia
Tel: +1 808 2487725
Email: JoLoyce@aol.com
Web: http://ecoclub.com/hanamaui/
Address: PO Box 404, Hana, Hawaii 96713, USA

ACCOM+/DIS
VOLCANO GUEST HOUSE

This is a family-owned and operated enterprise of bed-and-breakfast housekeeping cottages and apartments located five minutes from the Hawaii Volcanoes National Park. It is both child and wheelchair friendly and encourages a low-impact lifestyle by being a very green operation, including growing its own coffee, tea and breakfast foods.

Contact: Bonnie Goodell or Alan Miller
Tel: +1 808 9677775
Email: innkeeper@volcanoguesthouse.com
Web: www.volcanoguesthouse.com
Address: PO Box 6, Volcano, Hawaii 96785-0006, USA

USA

International dialling code +1

The USA is one of the easiest countries to travel around independently. There is no tourism high season as such – with such a vast area encompassing almost every kind of terrain and climate, it is always the ideal time to visit at least one region. In addition to visiting the great cities and national parks, and obvious attractions such as Disneyland and Universal Studios, visitors can also take tours on Native American Reservations, organized by the residents themselves, with profits staying on the reservations. As well as seeing the spectacular landscapes, particularly Monument Valley on the Navajo Reservation and the mesa-top Hopi pueblos, visitors can participate in ceremonies such as sweat lodges and even vision quests. However, this is the subject of heated controversy among Native Americans, some of whom feel strongly that this is co-modifying and degrading their culture. There are also gambling casinos (alcohol free) on some reservations, which although very profitable is likewise controversial. Some reservations, such as the Apache Reservation in Arizona, have facilities for more traditional outdoor vacation activities such as horse riding and fishing. The rise in the strength of the US dollar in late 2008 means that a US vacation is no longer the great bargain it has been for many years, although it is still good value for money.

TOUR
CHEYENNE TRAILRIDERS

Set in a reservation of 180,000ha of beautiful hills and plains, there is a variety of wildlife, plants and flowers. The hills contain archaeological evidence of people who lived there before. Cheyenne Trailriders offers rides from one hour to a week in the hills, camping in tipis. It teaches the history and culture of the tribe, ethnobotany, how to play native games and how to do native dances. A local flute-maker plays his instruments. There are also car tours of the entire reservation showing how the native people lived then and now, and visits to public buildings such as the Tribal Office and Chief Dull Knife College, to introduce guests to Native Americans who live and work there.

Contact: Sandra Spang
Tel: +1 4067846150
Email: cheyride@rangeweb.net • cheytrider@rangeweb.net
Web: www.cheyennetrailriders.com
Address: PO Box 206, Ashland, MT 59003-0206, USA

TOUR OP
GO NATIVE AMERICA

This operator works on behalf of a group of Plains Indians: the Lakota, Blackfeet, Crow, Ojibwe and Cheyenne. Their *raison d'être* is fair-trade tourism, which they claim to have practised since before the birth of the concept of responsible tourism. All activities have to accord with tribal etiquette. Their guides lead you on a cultural journey into the heart of Native America. On offer is an experience ranging from one day to a month of native experiences and immersion. Take an open mind – and remember that tribal does not mean cheap. The communities need support and what you spend goes to them.

Contact: Sarah Chapman
Tel: +1 8888001876
Fax: +1 8888001876
Email: info@gonativeamerica.com • gonative@nemontel.net
Web: www.gonativeamerica.com
Address: 821 N 27th St, 120 Billings, MT 59101, USA

ACCOM+
LODGEPOLE GALLERY & TIPI VILLAGE
This is a very small enterprise offering a fascinating entrée into the world of Native Americans. It consists of a Blackfeet tipi camp and art gallery – the tipis are pitched in different areas each year to protect the grasses. The visitor receives a Blackfeet cultural experience with an overnight tipi stay, the chance to visit a traditional art workshop, to experience Blackfeet cuisine, and to go horseback riding on a mustang with a Blackfeet guide. Teaching people about Blackfeet culture and history keeps that culture alive. The reservation tour (own vehicle) includes the Museum of the Plains Indian.

Contact: Darrell Norman or Angelika Harden-Norman
Tel: +1 4063382787
Fax: +1 4063382778
Email: tipicamp@3rivers.net
Web: www.blackfeetculturecamp.com
Address: PO Box 1832, Browning, MT 59417, USA

VOL
VOLUNTEERS FOR PEACE (VFP)
Long-established association offering workcamps in socially disadvantaged and ecologically threatened areas.

Contact: Peter Coldwell
Tel: +1 8022592759
Fax: +1 8022592922
Email: vfp@vfp.org
Web: www.vfp.org
Address: 1034, Tiffany Road, Belmont, Vermont 05730, USA

THE AMERICAS

SOUTH AMERICA

ARGENTINA
International dialling code: +54

Vast, magnificent and filled with variety, Argentina's delights were seductively revealed in the film *The Motorcycle Diaries* as the youthful Che Guevara and his mate careered through the country's splendid hinterland. There you will find a landscape for every persuasion – deserts, plains, mountains, lakes and gla-ciers. With a recent history of oppression and military dic-tatorship, Argentina has now returned to democracy (and you can politely mention the Falklands/Malvinas). Buenos Aires is a sophisticated city of boulevards and, of course, tango dancing, and is European (especially Italian – hence the spectacular ice cream) in flavour. Getting to grips with the rest of the country takes time and some organization – the distances are so large; but the pampas (the gaucho cliché lives on), the Andean region bordering on Chile, and the empty wildernesses of Patagonia are full of spectacle and adventure – and fascinat-ing wildlife. Not a great place for vegetarians, Argentina is a feast in waiting for meat eaters, while *maté*, a bitter herbal tea, is a great ritual drink for social occa-sions.

ORG/TOUR/VOL
ID-AS FOUNDATION
The ID-AS (Instituto de Desarrollo Educativo y Accion Social, or institute for educational develop-ment and social action) foundation's work is focused on community development and interven-ing in situations of poverty through fair trade, micro-enterprise and disability support. It offers tours, on which travellers are given the chance to get an insight into its work, as well as learning about the cultural and social history of Argentina and the present-day situation. The tours are fully guided, and include homestays and community visits, and are a really excellent introduction to this fascinating country. The foundation also offers a range of longer-term opportunities for vol-unteers and students, with a 90-day stay costing US$650.

Contact: Hugo Almiron Bassetti
Tel: +54 3514760561
Email: hugo@fundacionideas.org.ar
Web: www.id-as.org.ar
Address: Teodoro Caillet Bois 4312, Barrio Poeta Lugones, Cordoba Capital, Cordoba, CP 5008, Argentina

ORG/DAY/VOL
PLAN21 FOUNDATION, PROTECTED VILLAGES PROGRAMME
Plan21 is an Argentinian NGO promoting responsible tourism in Manzano Amargo, north of Neuquen Province, a rural community of 700. It offers adventure holidays, including trekking, horse riding and rafting. Visitors can also enjoy bird-watching and explore the waterfalls, rivers, lakes and forests of the region. Volunteers can work within the local community.

Contact: Lic Guadelupe Carbó
Tel: +54 2229491708 • +54 9111550206704 • +54 91130046697
Email: gcarbo@plan21.org
Web: www.plan21.org • www.pueblosprotegidos.org.ar
Address: Cochabamba 307 3°D (CP 1150), Buenos Aires, Argentina

BOLIVIA
International dialling code: +591

Despite the warm fertile lowlands that lie in the east of the country, nearly half of the Bolivian population are scattered across the windswept Andean region, where their rich and ancient cultures continue to flourish in harsh environmental conditions. Lake Titicaca, the world's highest navigable body of water in the world, is the focal point of many indigenous peoples' creation myths. Once said to have been the resting place of the Inca Sun Deity, Inti, today it is home to the famous floating islands – giant mobile rafts of reeds that are home to whole villages.

Despite the repeated political upheavals that have dogged the region as a whole, Bolivians have a strong sense of tradition and connection to their landlocked country, the highest and most isolated in the continent. Bolivia has the highest proportion of native language to Spanish speakers in the whole of South America (over two-thirds), and her people display the same natural pride in their music, dress and rituals, which survived and absorbed Catholic Spanish culture from the centuries of colonization with remarkable vigour. In fact, in 2005, when Evo Morales became the first fully indigenous head of state in South America, it marked a real turning point, and he has since been followed by other indigenous leaders.

The salt flats and Atacama Desert are the highlight of many visits: the wind-carved rocks and spectacularly coloured lakes populated by flamingos have become something of a Mecca for backpackers. A traveller can also venture deep below the world's highest city, Potosí, in working tin mines that were originally dug by the Spanish who were in search of silver. Like Peru and Ecuador, Bolivia has a stunning natural variety; a descent down what is reputed to be the world's most dangerous road will lead the adventurous traveller from the Andean Highlands to the northern marsh lands or the most accessible parts of the primary Amazon jungle in just a matter of hours.

ACCOM/TREK/SCHOOL
ARTESANIAS PARA SEGUIR UNIDOS

APSU is a co-operative formed of two communities of Amyara-speaking artisans. Each community has a central lodge, which houses classrooms, craft workshops and visitor accommodation. The surrounding land produces the raw materials for the craftsmen and also belongs to an association of artisans. Visitors are given the chance to learn traditional dances and music, spend time in the workshops, hike the Inca pathways, and eat good local food produced on the community farm.

Contact: Genaro Maraza Quispe
Tel: +591 73830026 • +591 73316767
Email: apsu_bolivia@yahoo.es
Web: www.tusoco.com/es/comunidades/livichuco/index.html

ACCOM+
CAJONES DE ICHILO LODGE

With room for a maximum of eight guests, this remote community-run lodge is situated on the edge of Amboró National Park, a haven not only for travellers but also for wildlife. The lodge is one of the very best places in the world to see the extremely rare horned curassow, known locally as the Cajone de Ichilo. However, not all visitors are lucky enough to get a good sighting, as this bird is on the verge of extinction. The lodge is doing invaluable work in protecting it and its habitat. What is more, the area around the lodge is teeming with other wildlife, three different breeds of monkey, macaws and toucans. The local population has been battling to protect this precious habitat from both hunters and loggers.

Contact: Macario Sardinas (Spanish only)
Tel: +591 76302581 • +591 71089265
Email: ecoichilo@hotmail.com

ACCOM+
LA CHONTA

The Chonta hostel is owned and run by nine families native to a remote rural area at the edge of Amboro National Park. It has two bedrooms with five beds and a camping area. It is a great spot for bird-watching. Nearby is Curichi, a remote and beautiful marshy area that attracts animals. Other possible activities include hiking, animal tracking, horse riding and swimming in the natural pools. For visitors who would like to know more about the life of local people, you can learn to prepare food and make seed jewellery.

Contact: Agustín Salazar
Tel: +591 74620723 • +591 76007785
Email: ecoturismo_lachonta@hotmail.com
Web: www.lasrutasdebuenavista.com

RAINFOREST+
MAPAJO INDIGENOUS TOURISM SRL

Mapajo eco-lodge is a three-hour boat ride from Rurrenabaque, deep inside the Pilon Lajas Reserve. The reserve is a meticulously protected area of primary rainforest, and has been a UNESCO biosphere site since 1977. The lodge is owned and run by three communities of the indigenous Tsimane people, whose culture has continued to flourish under the protection of the reserve. They have retained a remarkable 75 per cent fluency in their native language, and continue to live with relative independence from the outside world. Visitors are taken on forest hikes and night walks by expert local guides and are offered the opportunity to canoe on the river, learn to make indigenous crafts, fish with bows and arrows, and sample traditional food and drink. The project offers a variety of trips: prices start at UK£147 for a minimum three-night/four-day stay.

Contact: Evelin Blanco
Tel: +591 38922317 • +591 71702204
Email: mapajo_eco@yahoo.com
Web: www.mapajo.com

TOUR OP
MICHAEL BLENDINGER NATURE TOURS

The owner, Michael Blendinger, based in Santa Cruz, feels a bit of an ecotourism pioneer. A qualified ecologist, he endeavours to run a green operation and to ensure that his Bolivian, Chilean and Argentinian 'flora and fauna' trips and bird-watching to national parks are in harmony with the environment. Local community-run projects benefit.

Contact: Michael Blendinger
Tel: +591 39446227
Fax: +591 39446227

Email: mblendinger@cotas.com.bo • info@discoveringbolivia.com
Address: Calle Bolivar, frente al Museo Samaipata, Santa Cruz, Bolivia

BUDGET/TREK
PACHA TREK COMMUNITY TOURISM

A four-day trip in which visitors walk to three high-altitude communities accompanied by a local guide. Luggage is carried by llamas and donkeys. During the trek, guests can participate in traditional ceremonies, learn about local agriculture, enjoy the music and dance of the region, and bathe in thermal waters. Throughout the trek visitors interact with the local communities and learn about the differences between Aymara and Quechuan cultures.

Contact: Martha Ajuroro Mamani
Tel: +591 71975397 • +591 73574132
Email: martha_aju@hotmail.com • pacha_trek1@yahoo.es
Web: www.trekapolobamba.com

ACCOM+
PARABA FRENTE ROJA CABINS

The community-owned cabin sits by banks of the River Mizque, across the water from a towering red stone cliff. The cliff face is the favourite spot of the rare red-fronted macaw, or *paraba frente roja*, after whom the cabin is named. The surrounding area is a haven for a wealth of other birds, including two other endemic species. The project was established to support the local communities' efforts to protect the birds' natural habitat. Today, it supports not only conservation, but also a variety of other projects, including local bee-keepers, fruit growers and a healthcare centre in the local village of Petera. Justly famous among bird-watchers, the Cabins has local guides for US$20 a day. The guides have an extraordinarily detailed knowledge about the birds' feeding habits and favourite spots.

Contact: Alejandra Coimbra Cornejo
Tel: +591 33568808
Fax: +591 33568808
Email: armonia@armonia-bo.org
Web: www.armonia-bo.org

ORG/TOUR/HOST/VOL
RED TUSOCO

Tusoco is a network of community tourism organizations in Bolivia. Tusoco supports the indigenous communities involved to use tourism to improve their quality of life, and as a stimulus to preserve their cultural heritage. Tourism is seen as an engine for the improvement of the life of indigenous people in that it helps economically and also supplies impetus for the preservation of cultural heritage. But great care is taken to ensure that local people and tourists do not become caught in a vicious circle of 'memorialization and folklorization'.

The network offers a variety of trips and tours, lasting between one and seven days, and all focus on community visits, often featuring homestays. It also organizes longer trips, from 8 to 20 days for groups, and there are longer-term options for volunteers.

Contact: Julie Forissier
Tel: +591 44588826
Fax: +591 44588827
Email: viajes@tusoco.com
Web: www.tusoco.com
Address: C/ Junin Sur #368, Esq Jordan, Cochabamba, Bolivia

THE AMERICAS

ACCOM+
ECO-TOURISM SAN PEDRO DE SOLA

This is a community tourism project offering accommodation for up to 24 people, including camping. Locally produced organic meals are served, and guests can choose from a variety of activities, including horse riding, guided walks and listening to stories about the history and mythology of the area.

Contact: Anastacio Huanca
Tel: +591 4 6637523 · +591 46665750 · 72983580
Email: sanpedrodesola@hotmail.com

TOUR OP/RAINFOREST
SERERE SANCTUARY/MADIDI TRAVEL

Madidi Travel offers tours to the Serere Sanctuary. It is a protected area of the Amazon, 2.5 hours' journey on the Beni River from Rurrenbaque. Guests can stay in forest-friendly lodges where the owners are working with local people to consolidate their land rights, while promoting the conservation of the area and offering opportunities for the community to benefit from tourism. Employing the expertise of local guides, tours are tailored around the individuals' chosen activities, whether it is walking, swimming, relaxing or viewing the wildlife, which includes reptiles, insects, fish and a great variety of flora.

Tel: +591 22318313
Fax: +591 22318314
Email: info@madidi-travel.com
Web: www.madidi-travel.com
Address: Calle Linares No 968 entre Sagarnaga y Juan XXIII, La Paz, Bolivia

TREK
TREK APOLOBAMBA: LAGUNILLAS TO AGUA BLANCA TREK

Trek Apolobamba is a locally run trekking organization that takes visitors on an ancient pre-Colombian trail through the Andes. The trail, which runs from Lagunillas to Agua Blanca, reaches above 4000m, winding up over five high passes, and down through fantastic mountain landscapes populated by llamas, alpaca, condors, vicuna and viscacha. An independent Spanish NGO financed two hostels at either end of the trek, one at Lagunillas and a second at Agua Blanca. The trek, which can be done in either direction, takes five days, with four nights under canvas. Fully trained local people from the two communities work as guides, and a large chunk of the overall takings is reinvested into community projects. Travellers looking for an alternative to the Inca trail with minimal environmental impact and genuine community-wide benefit need look no further.

Contact: Sam Wilson
Tel: +591 73271710
Email: info@trekapolobamba.com
Web: www.trekapolobamba.com

ACCOM+/TREK
VALLEY OF THE CONDORS

Perched high up in the Andes, the Valley of the Condors mountain refuge shares its home with around 200 pairs of one of the world's rarest and most spectacular birds. The valley is at the very south of Bolivia, and is one of the most important Condor colonies in the world. The refuge offers a variety of treks of up to four days, which are an opportunity to see not only condors, but also hummingbirds, cacti, orchids and llamas. The trekkers sleep in tents and are led by guides indigenous to the area. Visitors staying in the lodge have the opportunity to explore the area on horseback or mountain bike, and can spend time in the community, learning about traditional food or trying Chicha, the nearest Incan equivalent to beer. The project was founded by a Bolivian charity, Educación y Futuro, and most of the profits are reinvested in the community.

Contact: Vincent Danhier
Tel: +591 46660162 • +591 46664973
Email: info@educacionyfuturo.com • vicentedanhier@yahoo.fr
Web: www.educacionyfuturo.com
Address: EDYFU, Casilla – 494, Tarija, Bolivia

BRAZIL
International dialling code: +55

Brazil is a country of mixed colours, flavours, sounds and cultures. More than 500 years after its 'discovery' by the Portuguese, Brazil today is South America's mega-economy and a regional leader. Even though it leans towards the left, unequal income distribution remains a pressing problem. The Brazilian people are known for being friendly, warm and welcoming. Brazil offers an infinite variety of options for tourists (nature, histori-cal, archaeological and modern cities). Brazil has many natural beauties to be seen; but be sure you have sufficient time as Brazil has continental dimensions – it's the fifth largest country in the world.

The north and northeast are the least developed and there's a strong legacy from colonial times, especially in the architecture of the region. Brazil's African her-itage is also best exemplified here. The south and southeast are the wealthiest and most developed, with influences from the migration of Italians and Germans. All of this contrast is what makes this extraordinary country endlessly intriguing.

VOL/DAY/TOUR
ASSOCIACAO IKO PORAN

This association coordinates volunteer programmes and also operates community tours. It works with more than 40 local organizations, and places international volunteers on a basis of volunteer ability/know-how married to organizational need (i.e. round pegs in round holes by preference). There are three programmes in the sustainable tourism field: the volunteer programme; commu-nity tours which show participants how problems are dealt with in low-income settings; and day trips that endeavour to spell out the need for corporate social responsibility by breaking down barriers between high- and low-income groups, and, by implication, showing the former how the latter live.

Contact: Manoela Zangrandi or Priscila Tufani
Tel: +55 2138522916
Fax: +55 2138522917
Email: rj@ikoporan.org (general enquiries) • volunt@ikoporan.org (bookings) • lfmurray@ikoporan.org (general coordinator)
Web: www.ikoporan.org
Address: Rua do Oriente 280/201, Santa Teresa, Rio de Janeiro, RJ, Brazil, CEP 20.2401-30

HOST
CAMA E CAFÉ

Cama e Café was Brazil's first-ever bed-and-breakfast homestay network. Established in 2003, it now has around 50 hosts. Hosts are concentrated in the Santa Teresa district of Rio de Janeiro, a lively area with a rich cultural heritage. There are three categories of host houses available from economy, which would suit a backpacker on a budget, through to superior air-conditioned rooms with a private bathroom. All of the houses are bright, comfortable and welcoming, and the staff at the central office can help match travellers with a host. The network follows the internationally agreed local Agenda 21 and tries to implement sustainable management principles.

Contact: Daniella Greco
Tel: +55 2122217635 · +55 2122254366 · +55 2196017180
Email: camaecafest@hotmail.com
Web: www.camaecafe.com.br
Address: Rua Paschoal Carlos Magno, 136 – Santa Teresa, Rio de Janerio, Brazil

ACCOM/DAY
CASA GRANDE – NOVA OLINDA
Nova Olinda is a village in the Kairiri Valley, Ceará, one of Brazil's poorest states, in the northeast of the country. It is home to the Casa Grande Foundation, working to try to recover the heritage of the local Krui-Kariri people and educate its young. It's regarded as a model of local empowerment, keeping the culture alive through educational projects. A museum, radio and television station have been created as part of the project. Their success brings many visitors to the area. Accommodation is usually within a family home. There are 12 different pousadas, (guest houses) on different sites, all of them offering full board, usually on a four-day package. Visitors usually can participate in workshops and interact with the children and young people, as well as visit archaeological and mythological sites. Part of the income from tourism supports the school. The project is part of TURISOL, a Brazilian network of sustainable and community-based tourism.

Tel: +55 8835461333 · +55 8835218133
Email: casagrande@baydejbc.com.br
Address: Rua Jermias Pereira 444, CEP: 63165-000 Nova Olinda, Ceará, Brazil

ACCOM/DAY
COQUEIRINHO
Coqueirinho organizes hikes and visits to social projects in the region of Aracati. Visitors can go to an MST (Landless Workers' Movement) camp at São Miguel, to understand the movement which fights for agrarian reform and for land redistribution. This is an opportunity to share the difficulties of the workers, and to support them in their struggle for land and human rights.

Contact: Dona Zildene
Tel: +55 8899212810
Email: monicabonadiman@yahoo.it
Web: www.tremembe.it
Address: Assentamento Coqueirinho, Municipio de Fortim, Ceará, Brazil

DAY
ESTRELA COMMUNITY TOURS
Weekly half-day community tours allowing tourists to visit forgotten parts of the city of Salvador, with beautiful natural, historical and cultural attractions. On offer are samba, afro-Brazilian percussion, dance and *capoeira*, with local snacks and fruit juices not easily available to tourists, and the opportunity to learn about local culture and communities by meeting local people and conversing with them directly.

Contact: Julia McNaught da Silva
Tel: +55 7133223854
Email: estrela@atarde.com.br
Web: under construction
Address: Rua do Sodré 444-1°, Centro, CEP 40060-240, Salvador, Bahia, Brazil

THE AMERICAS

DAY
FAVELA TOUR
A tour that reveals a way of life for 20 per cent of Rio's population, changing the common image of *favelas* as no-go areas dominated by criminals. Favela Tour takes visitors to the communities of Vila Canoas and to Rocinha, the largest *favela* in Brazil, with around 60,000 inhabitants. Both are located within the rich neighbourhood of São Conrado. In Vila Canoas, guests take a walking tour through its narrow alleyways and also get a good idea of the social initiatives that are part of many Rio *favelas*. In Rocinha, its huge dimensions, wide variety of commerce and breathtaking views from the summit form are impressive for any visitor.

Contact: Marcello Armstrong
Tel: +55 2133222727
Fax: +55 2133225958
Email: info@favelatour.com.br
Web: www.favelatour.com.br
Address: Estrada das Canoas 722, Apt 125, São Conrado, Rio de Janeiro, CEP: 22610-210, Brazil

ACCOM/TOUR
PONTA GROSSA
This combination of local family investment, charitable donations and NGO assistance has created a network of guest houses, overnight accommodation, restaurants and guide services. It's based in the village of Ponta Grossa, 200km from Fortaleza, capital of Ceará state in northeast Brazil. The main income for the community is from fishing, so tourism income is a very desirable add-on and everyone involved is self-motivated. Visitors can cruise on wooden fishing boats and walk in the dunes and cliffs. The project is part of REDE TUCUM, a Brazilian community-based tourism network.

Contact: Eliabe Crispym
Tel: +55 8834325001
Mobile: +55 8899532209
Email: elicrispym@hotmail.com
Address: Astuma, CEP: 62810-000 Ponta Grossa, Icapuí, Ceará, Brazil

RAINFOREST
POUSADA ALDEIA DOS LAGOS (ASPAC)
This pousada is an experimental ecotourism project, the first in the Amazon region, developed by the Silves Association for the Preservation of the Environment and Culture (ASPAC), on Silves Island, 200km from Manaus, in the Amazon lakes region. The pousada consists of 12 rooms with a private bathroom and balcony, a restaurant, a crafts shop and other facilities such as laundry and recreation areas. It offers 13 different tours. Revenue from the project helps to preserve the lakes and fisheries and improve life in the community. Pousada Aldeia dos Lagos was given technical support by the World Wide Fund for Nature and is part of TURISOL, a Brazilian network of sustainable and community-based tourism.

Tel: +55 9291612920
Email: amazonas@viverde.com.br • aldeiadoslagos@terra.com.br
Web: www.viverde.com.br • www.viverde.com.br/aldeia.html

ACCOM
PRAINHA DO CANTO VERDE
You can relax on the beach in this award-winning, beautiful fishing village in northeast Brazil, knowing that all the economic benefits accrue to the locals. A local co-operative acts as the incoming operator for guest houses and restaurants. Visitors can cruise the sea in wooden fishing boats and can take an ecological path up to the lagoon through the 'moving' dunes. It is very involved in wider community tourism development, especially with other communities in Ceará,

and has a leadership role in promoting the ethos of sustainable community-led tourism. The project is part of REDE TUCUM, a Brazilian network of community-based tourism.

Contact: Antônio Aires
Tel: +55 8596192046 · +55 8599827409 · +55 8533782201
Email: coopercantur@yahoo.com.br
Web: www.prainhadocantoverde.org
Address: Beberibe, Ceará, CEP 62.840-000, Brazil

RAINFOREST/SCHOOL/DAY
RESERVA EL NAGUAL
This is a centre for sustainable living located in the Serra do Mar in the Guanabara Bay area, in the Magé area of Brazil. As well as going on hikes with local guides to see the many rivers and waterfalls of the region, guests can take courses in eco-techniques, handicrafts and guided tours on the environment. The centre aims to be as self-sufficient as possible, using a mini-hydroelectric generator, solar panels, making handicrafts from recycled materials and growing organic vegetables. Guests stay in a six-room inn that can accommodate up to 30 people, or can come for the day to enjoy the centre's natural pools.

Contact: Mariana and Erhard Kalloch
Tel: +55 2126302625 · +55 2199770569 · +55 2198536069
Email: artnagual@hotmail.com
Web: www.artnagual.com.br
Address: Reserva El Nagual, Rua Capitão Antero s/n km 03, 25929 000 Santo Aleixo, Mage, RJ, Brazil

ORG
TERRAMAR
Terramar is a campaigning NGO fighting to promote the integrated development of coastal communities in Ceará, Brazil. Its activities include resisting land-grabbing, building village structures, environmental education and the sustainable use of natural resources. The community tourism activities are overseen by Terramar's coastal management programme, which supports sustainability, local participation and recognition of the value of local cultures.

Tel: +55 8532262476 · +55 8532264154 · +55 88640653
Email: terramar@terramar.org.br · tucum@tucum.org
Web: www.terramar.org.br · www.tucum.org.br
Address: Rua Pinho Pessoa, 86 Joaquim Tavora, CEP: 60135-170, Fortaleza, Ceará, Brazil

AGRI
TREMEMBE
Guests stay in four huts and, as well as hiking through the nature reserves of the area, can gain a unique insight into the agriculture of the region. Visitors are taken to social projects in the region of Aracati, such as an MST (Landless Workers' Movement) camp at São Miguel. There they can learn about the movement which fights for agrarian reform and land redistribution. It is an opportunity to understand and share the difficulties of the workers, and to support them in their struggle for land and human rights.

Contact: Dona Zildene
Tel: +55 8899212810
Email: monicabonadiman@yahoo.it
Web: www.tremembe.it
Address: Assentamento Coqueirinho, Município de Fortim, Ceará, Brazil

CHILE
International dialling code: +56

At a staggering 4300km in length along the Pacific coast of South America, Chile spans an astonishing variety of terrain. From the lunar landscapes of the Atacama Desert to the luscious climes of the Lake District, Chile is full of contrasts. The southern town of Pucon is right next to an active volcano, which towers over Lake Villarica. With a large ski resort nearby, Pucon is the ideal retreat. It was in these fertile valleys that Chile's indigenous ancestors, the Araucanians, first settled.

Closer to the centre of the country lies the metropolitan sprawl of Santiago. The capital is a testament to Chile's relative stability and prosperity, with a wealth of museums, galleries and parks to rival any European hot spot. When you get to the heart of the city, you'll see the presidential palace, La Moneda. Thirty years ago this was the site of one of South America's bloodiest coups. General Pinochet's dictatorship left the country scarred. Now Chile finds itself under the governance of its first woman president, Michelle Bachelet. With her centre-of-left policies, she is reducing the gap between rich and poor, which is among the worst in the world. There has never been a more exciting time to visit Chile.

In the north there are some dizzying landscapes. The Altiplano is the highest part of the Chilean Andes and is filled with glaciers and geysers. Further on you'll find La Tirana, a small desert town that once a year explodes into a frenzy of music, costumes and dance. The religious festival attracts thousands of believers and is a spectacular display of Chilean vitality.

TREK/SCHOOL
CABALGATAS ANTILCO

Can you sit on a horse? The offer is for horseback trail riding for half a day up to 12 days in the valleys around the national parks of Huerquehue and Villarica, and around the Mapuche Indian community at Quelhue. You stay a guest house, a cabin, or on a campsite by the River Liucura. In collaboration with other local people, the organizers also offer hiking, white-water activities, and the chance to climb an active volcano, Villarrica … so check the insurance small print.

Contact: Mathias Boss or Alejandra Curihual
Tel: +56 997139758
Email: mat@antilco.com • ale@antilco.com
Web: www.antilco.com
Address: Antilco, Uruguay 306, 4920000 Pucon, Chile

ACCOM+
ECOCAMP PATAGONIA

Visitors here can explore remote Patagonia with a minimal environmental footprint. There are virgin beech forests, colossal glaciers and towering granite peaks in the Torres del Paine. It is a beautiful place to admire the Southern Cross. The ecocamp offers a perfect compromise between hotel accommodation and camping. There are large dome-shaped tents in the Torres del Paine National Park, tall enough to stand up in, with real beds and good food. Guests avoid the discomforts of camping but are much closer to nature than in a hotel. The English-speaking guides take visitors on wildlife tours and photography safaris to places where it is possible to fully relax away from the pressures of everyday life, surrounded by the natural beauty of Patagonia.

Contact: Daniel Sanhueza
Tel: +56 22329878
Email: daniel@cascada.travel · daniel@ecocamp.travel · info@ecocamp.travel
Web: www.ecocamp.travel

COLOMBIA
International dialling code: +57

Gabriel García Márquez's home country, Colombia, probably does not immediately spring to mind as a place to visit. Frequent reports about murders, kidnappings, narcotics trafficking, drug cartels and endemic corruption are all too familiar. Yet, Colombia deserves its fair share of credit. Located at the northwest tip of South America, Colombia prides itself in its virtually untouched coastlines of more than 3200km on both the Caribbean Sea and Pacific Ocean, with stunning views and pristine beaches. Shielded in the west by three Andes Mountain ranges, plains covered by jungle and savannahs constitute the bulk of the inland before it merges into the vast Amazonian Forest in the east, Colombia's other natural asset. In the centre lies Bogotá, a vibrant urban mix of old and new, of easy-going flow and aggressive bustle. Like its neighbours, Colombia's population is a rich mix of natives, Europeans and Africans, with women enjoying the greatest degree of economic and professional autonomy in Latin America.

Colombia's drug and crime problems are said to have limited its appeal and full potential as a major tourist destination. Once the situation improves, however, this could be a major chance for Colombia to learn from mistakes made by the established tourist destinations in promoting sustainable and community-based tourism.

TOUR OP
SIEMPRE COLOMBIA
Siempre Colombia is an exciting travel company offering trips in several parts of Colombia, including the west coast, tropical lowlands and the Amazon. There is a real focus on cultural interaction, and visitors stay in lodges run by local communities, who are supported not only financially, but also by the numerous educational projects run by the company. Siempre Colombia also offers special trips for students and groups who want to learn more about Colombia and her people.

Contact: Andres Ardila
Tel: +57 16040015 · +57 16044298
Fax: +5716222128
Web: www.siemprecolombia.com
Email: ecoturismo@siemprecolombia.com

ECUADOR
International dialling code +593

Marginally larger in size than the UK, Ecuador is one of the smaller countries in South America and the world's number one supplier of bananas. The Andes Mountain range runs north to south, cutting the country into the hot and humid Amazonian rainforest in the east and the hot and dry Pacific coastal regions in the west. The world-famous Galapagos Islands also form part of Ecuador. High above sea level in the middle of the Andes, Ecuador's capital and main gateway, Quito, is a pleasant and accessible city benefiting from a mild climate throughout the entire year. Once the capital of the mighty Inca Empire, Quito boasts large amounts of Spanish colonial architecture and is now a UNESCO World Heritage site.

The Amazonian rainforest is home to many indigenous Indian tribes, such as the Huaorani and the Siona-Secoya. Logging and recent developments in the oil industry coupled with internal migration all disrupt those people's livelihoods – as well as the fragile environment. Similarly, an ever-increasing number of tourist arrivals threatens the Galapagos Archipelagos – that microcosm of unique and bountiful fauna and flora. In tandem with tourism, local and international initiatives have sprung up in recent years not only to help protect these islands and the rainforest, but also the traditional habitat of the local communities.

RAINFOREST/VOL
BELLAVISTA CLOUD FOREST RESERVE AND LODGE
Bellavista private reserve is located inside the buffer zone of the Mindo-Nambillo protected forest. The lodge, which accommodates a maximum of 40 people, is a peaceful alternative to the tourist hub of Mindo further down the valley. It is a great centre for bird-watching, and it also offers guided treks through the forest. The lodge strives to create minimal environmental impact. Visitors stay in an unusual four-storey geodesic dome with a thatched roof, and the restaurant serves locally sourced food. A budget hostel and campsite are available for the more adventurous and those on a budget. There is also a research centre, and longer-term options are available for volunteers interested in conservation.

Tel: +593 22116232 · +593 22116047
Fax: +593 22903165
Email: info@bellavistacloudforest.com
Web: www.bellavistacloudforest.com
Address: Jorge Washington E7-25 y 6 de Diciembre, Quito, Ecuador

ACCOM+
BLACK SHEEP INN
Perched in the centre of the Andean Highlands, the American-owned Black Sheep Inn offers an affordable and cosy base for travellers looking for rural tranquillity with breathtaking views. It offers access on foot, bike or horseback to some of the natural and cultural highlights of the Cotopaxi region, including indigenous textile markets and Laguna Quilotoa, an emerald volcano crater lake. The inn is an award-winning example of sustainable community development through tourism, offering education, reforestation and healthcare. It is also a pioneer of eco-friendly technology, and alongside the zip-wire, water slide and sauna there are compost toilets, solar panels and an organic garden. Good hearty vegetarian food is served in the restaurant, and the inn welcomes individual travellers as well as families.

Contact: Michelle Kirby · Andres Hammerman
Tel: +593 32814587
Email: info@blacksheepinn.com · blacksheepinn@yahoo.com
Web: www.blacksheepinn.com
Address: PO Box 05-01-240, Chugchilan, Cotopaxi, Ecuador

TOUR OP
EOS ECUADOR

A traditional tour operator in central Quito with an innovative attitude, an unusual past and an exciting future, Eos Ecuador agency offers Galapagos tours, Amazon lodges, coastal tours, hiking, biking, rafting, trekking, hostels and hotels. It was founded to support the work of the Yanapuma Foundation, a development NGO that has been helping communities around Ecuador to tap into the tourism industry in a way that is genuinely sustainable, low impact and culturally and environmentally positive. Eos Ecuador also offers Ecuadorian students the practical work experience that they need to break into this internationally dominated industry at management level. The more mainstream tourism activities that they offer have been chosen with environmental and community impact in mind, and profits made are helping to support Eos's focus on community-based tourism, which they will start to offer in partnership with Yanapuma in the coming year.

Contact: Pablo Cruz or David de la Houssaye
Tel: +593 26013560
Fax: +593 22907259
Email: eos@eosecuador.com · david@eosecuador.com
Web: www.eosecuador.com
Address: Ave Amazonas N23-66 y Joaquin Pinto, Quito, Pichincha, Ecuador

ORG
FOUNDATION INTERNATIONAL SHIWIAR SIN FRONTERAS (FUNSSIF)

This ecotourism initiative by the indigenous Shiwiar people in the remote community (accessible only by air) of Juyuintsa in the Ecuadorian rainforest, near the Peruvian border, offers an unusual experience, but may not be for the faint-hearted. You will have day- and night-guided walks in the rainforest, learn about medicinal plants, see rivers and lakes (and, if you are there in winter, go rafting), and just generally soak in the hospitable waters of the Shiwiar culture. The majority of the income yielded by this sustainable alternative tourism goes towards the education and health of the local people. The Shiwiar are struggling to gain ownership of their land and to protect it from exploitation by oil companies. Tourism can help to generate funds for the struggle, and bring hope and self-respect.

Contact: Pascual Kunchicuy
Tel: +593 2889393 · +593 090168131 · +593 088297677
Fax: +593 2886109
Email: shiwiarfund@hotmail.com · ikiamp21@hotmail.com
Web: www.ikiam.info
Address: PO Box 16-01-703, Puyo, Ecuador

RAINFOREST
FUNDACIÓN PARA LA SOBREVIVENCIA DEL PUEBLO COFÁN (FSC)

The Cofán foundation works in and around Zabalo, a village in the Cuyabeno Rainforest Reserve in north-eastern Ecuador. The area is the heartland of the indigenous Cofán peoples' ancient culture, where they have lived in symbiosis with the forest for centuries. Consequently, Zabalo is surrounded by pristine Amazonian rainforest teaming with wildlife. The foundation only leads a few tours a year; however, it also supports and connects the groups of Cofán who have been receiving tourists for several decades. The enterprise benefits not only the Cofán people who are directly involved, but also aids the sustainable development and preservation of the population as a whole.

Contact: Sadie Siviter or Randy Borman
Tel: +593 22470946
Fax: +593 22470946
Email: sadiesiviter@gmail.com • randy@cofan.org
Web: www.cofan.org
Address: Mariano Cardenal N74-153 y Joaquin Mancheno, Urbanizacion Carcelen Alto, Quito, Casilla 171106089, Ecuador

RAINFOREST/VOL
GOLONDRINAS FOUNDATION

Ecotourism and its companion agritourism represent only one aspect of the work carried out by this not-for-profit organization, which is dedicated to the conservation of natural resources, fighting soil erosion and fostering general environmental education in the Rio Mira area between the provinces of Imbabura and Carchi. A maximum of ten people can be accommodated in a choice of three locations, which gives the visitor the chance to learn about the work being done; it is also possible to contribute in a volunteer capacity. Tours are organized to the cloud forest, jungle or highlands (from one to four days), on foot or on horseback. There are also demonstrations on sustainable agriculture and visits to local schools.

Contact: María Eliza Manteca
Tel: +593 99228440 • +593 82912494 • +593 62648662 • +593 62648679
Email: fgolondrinas@yahoo.com • rnaturaleza@hotmail.com • fgolondrinas.g@gmail.com
Web: www.fgolondrinas.org

ACCOM+
HACIENDA ZUELTA

Located only two hours north of Quito, this family-run Hacienda Zuelta is an ideal first stop for visitors keen to avoid the bustle and crowds of the city. The delightfully dilapidated but elegant colonial homestead is set in expansive grounds, including a working dairy farm, a condor rehabilitation centre and a textile workshop. Excellent traditional meals made with seasonal produce are served in the restaurant or on the open veranda, which looks onto a courtyard visited by Andean hummingbirds. As well as gardens and a museum inside the homestead, visitors are also offered horse riding, mountain biking and guided trips to pre-Incan archaeological sites. The foundation set up by Hacienda Zuelta provides vital support for the education of local people and works to protect their culture as well their environment. The foundation's library is one of the only places in the area where the indigenous language, Kiwchua, is taught.

Contact: Christina Ring or Laura Sánchez
Tel: +593 62662182
Email: info@zuelta.com
Web: www.zuelta.com
Address: Hacienda Zuelta Oficina, Bosmediano 9000 y Sergio Játiva, Quito, Ecuador

RAINFOREST
HUAORANI ECO-LODGE

This eco-lodge opened in 2007 and provides accommodation for ten people in a style harmonious with the surrounding environment and Huaorani culture. It is situated in rainforest an hour's walk from the community of Quehueri'ono in the Ecuadorian Amazon rainforest. Five comfortable palm-thatched cabins are constructed of local wood within which are fitted mosquito nets. All of the cabins have twin beds, a private bathroom with a shower and a flush toilet, a porch and supplies of environmentally friendly soaps and shampoos. Most of the employees are local Huaorani and they were fully involved in the lodge's construction. Solar panels power the lighting, fridge and water pump. The lodge is a way for the Huaorani people to receive an income from tourism while maintaining the integrity of their culture and conserving their rainforest territory.

Contact: Jascivan Carvalho
Tel: +593 22234594 • +593 22225 907
Fax: +593 22560756
Email: info@tropiceco.com
Web: www.tropiceco.com • www.huaorani.com • www.walkingalapagos.com
Address: La niña 327 y Reina Victoria, Quito, Ecuador

RAINFOREST
KAPAWI ECO-LODGE

The privately owned Kapawi Eco-Lodge, on the Peruvian border, was developed with the full cooperation of the Achuar people, who receive monthly rent for the land on which the lodge is situated. In 2008, the Achuar became the owners of the lodge without cost. Thus, the project provides employment and income for education, health and community development. Kapawi is very remote (accessible only by air and then canoe), located in mountainous rainforest. Activities, including hiking, bird-watching, canoeing, camping, fishing and visiting an Achuar community, are geared to visitors' tastes and abilities. The lodge accommodates up to 40 people on a lake and is built in accordance with the Achuar concept of architecture – not a single nail was used!

Contact: Diego Espinel
Tel: +593 26009333 (extension 2017)
Fax: +593 26009334
Email: agent2@kapawi.com
Web: www.kapawi.com

RAINFOREST
LA SELVA JUNGLE LODGE

On offer is what the owners deem a unique rainforest experience. A lot of investment goes into local education and healthcare. The local community is helped with education, health, transportation and gaining qualifications, but without impinging on culture and integrity. La Selva owns 40ha of forest and cares for a further 1200ha of forest surrounding the lodge.

Contact: Veronica Darquea
Tel: +593 22550995 • +593 22545425
Fax: +593 22226840
Email: marketing@laselvajunglelodge.com
Web: www.laselvajunglelodge.com
Address: Mariana de Jesus E7-211 y Pradera, Quito, Ecuador

RAINFOREST
MACQUIPUCANA

The Macquipucana Foundation set up this cloud forest eco-lodge as part of their ecological conservation and restoration project. Visitors get brillant access to the cloud forest's unique ecosystems. The lodge is run by the community who lives within the reserve, and is open to tourists, students and researchers alike. Visitors can enjoy traditional cocoa massages, explore the rivers and waterfalls, or visit bird and wildlife observation huts, the organic farm and the orchid garden.

Contact: Mónica Burbano
Tel: +593 22507198 • +593 2507200
Email: info@maquipucana.org • ecotourism@maquipucana.org
Web: www.maqui.org
Address: Calle Baquerizo Moreno E9-153 y Tamayo, Quito, Ecuador

RAINFOREST/AGRI
MOMOPEHO RAINFOREST HOME

Momopeho offers basic but comfortable accommodation on a farm, with two rooms for up to four people in each. Prices include full board (breakfast, lunch and dinner). There are plenty of different activities all year round, although some depend upon the season, such as bird-watching, walking in the rainforest and farm work, including milking the cows and feeding the guinea pigs. Visitors can learn about the economic, cultural and social life of rural Ecuador, as well as the importance of the rainforest as a supplier of oxygen and fresh water. It is a private enterprise that helps the local community with education and health. It also develops projects for recycling, water conservation and protection of the fauna.

Contact: Alvero Moreno
Tel: +593 98309202
Email: momopeho@yahoo.com
Web: www.momopeho.com

RAINFOREST/TOUR
NUEVO MUNDO EXPEDITIONS/MANATEE AMAZON EXPLORER

This is a 27m-long riverboat that cruises the Napo River in Ecuador. Up to 30 guests stay in comfortable cabins with private bathrooms, running hot water and even internet and satellite TV connections. Tours vary in length from four to ten days and explore the world's largest primeval forest. Guests can see abundant wildlife, guided by multilingual naturalists, including freshwater dolphins, 500 species of birds, half a dozen species of monkeys, caimans, tapirs and butterflies. This is an ideal way of exploring the rainforest without having to camp or even suffer from mosquitos as the ship is surrounded by flowing water and is fully air conditioned. It aims to have only a minimal environmental and social impact by travelling up and down the river, staying as a 'temporary guest' beside the indigenous communities.

Contact: Esthela Luje
Tel: +593 22509431 • +593 99453392
Fax: +593 22565261
Email: ecuador@nuevomundoexpeditions.com • oswaldo@nuevomundoexpeditions.com
Web: www.nuevomundoexpeditions.com
Address: PO Box 1703-402-A, Quito, Ecuador

RAINFOREST
PAVACACHI LODGE

Deep into the Amazon Basin, the remote community of Pavacachi can only be reached by aeroplane, followed by a trip down the river in motorized canoe and a half-hour walk down an open jungle path. The community-run lodge is built from sustainably sourced materials using the traditional methods, and offers single, double and family rooms with private bathrooms. Due to the difficulty of access, the shortest available stay is four days; but this is barely enough time to see and experience everything that this project has to offer. The lodge offers a wide variety of jungle activities, traditional fishing, guided walks, night walks, hiking, bird-watching, animal tracking and canoeing. It hosts talks about local culture and gives visitors the chance to spend time with the local Kuichua and Shiwiar people, learning firsthand about community life. A satellite communication system is available for emergencies, including healthcare, and longer-term options are available for scientists and students.

Contact: Raul Esteban Tapuy Vargas
Tel: +593 32795041 • +593 32889774 • 90410875 • 088044512
Email: tamia212000@yahoo.com
Web: www.earthfoot.org (network)
Address: c/o Código Apartado 16-01-711 Puyo Pastaza, Ave Gonzales Suarez, Cooperativa Jita Yacu Tras el Colegio Pastaza Amazonia, Ecuador

RAINFOREST
PIEDRA BLANCA COMMUNITY TOURISM

Most travellers arrive in the community of Piedra Blanca on horseback, after taking a rickety local bus into the market town of San Luis de Pambil, about half way between Quito and Guayquil. Although it is possible to arrive in a 4x4, Piedra Blanca is well off the beaten track, and the adventure continues after arrival. Visitors can float down a jungle river on a traditionally built raft, visit local farms and explore the jungle at night.

The project was set up by 15 local people who decided to take the fate of their community and what remains of its pristine rainforest environment into their own hands. Tourism has encouraged the community to value the untouched jungle as a resource, and increased their willingness to protect it. Meals are cooked from local recipes using local products. The eco-lodge accommodates up to 20 people. Please advise us in advance of your arrival so that we can arrange for someone to meet you in Luis de Pambil's plaza (we will arrange horses or an inexpensive chartered vehicle, approx. US$10).

Tel: + 593 32656216
Email: community@piedrablanca.org
Web: www.piedrablanca.org
Address: Piedra Blanca, Near San Luis de Pambil, Bolivar Province, Ecuador (no mail service)

VOL
PROYECTO ECOLOGICO CHIRIBOGA

Volunteer association with an ecological bias.

Contact: Virginia Mueses
Tel: +593 22650561
Fax: +593 22650561
Email: ecoproye@andinanet.net
Web: www.ecuador-chiriboga.org.uk
Address: Princesa Toa S9-534 y Canaris – Ciudadela San José, La Magdalena, Quito, Ecuador

HOST+
RUNA TUPARI NATIVE TRAVEL

Runa Tupari was set up by the Union of Organizations of Farmers and Indigenous People of Cotacachi (UNORCAC) in response to discrimination against indigenous people. Visitors stay with local families and partake fully in their lives. Visitors stay in one of twelve comfortable and well-equipped family-run lodges, which are located in four different communities across the area. The homestay, with transport, breakfast and dinner, is around UK£17 per person per night. Community tours and adventure activities, including hiking, camping and trekking, cost extra, from UK£14 to UK£67. Visitors receive a code of conduct before beginning a homestay or taking a tour.

Contact: Christian Garson
Tel: +593 97286756
Fax: +593 6 925 985
Skype: runatupari
Email: nativetravel@runatupari.com • runatupari@hotmail.com
Web: www.runatupari.com
Address: Plaza de los Ponchos Sucre y Quiroga, Otavalo, Ecuador

ACCOM
SALINAS DE GUARANDA

The remote village of Salinas de Guaranda, in the southern Andes, is remarkable in a number of ways. Reorganized many years ago by a couple of Italian priests, the community's economy is thriving in a number of micro-industries. Their activities include cultivating wild mushrooms, weaving traditional alpaca wool jumpers and producing some of the best chocolate to be found anywhere in the country. The village is organized around the central market square, which is bustling with visitors from tiny communities in the area, all with their own traditional dress and with their own produce to sell. The tourist hostel, complete with restaurant and a log fire, is up on the side of the valley above the market and boasts commanding mountain views. The hostel is owned and run by a co-operative, from which all the other co-operatives benefit.

Contact: Groupo de Turismo
Tel: +593 3390020/045/024
Email: viac@accessinter.net
Web: www.salinerito.com

RAINFOREST/VOL
SANTA LUCIA CO-OPERATIVE

Santa Lucia is an environmentally focused lodge located a 1.5-hour hike inside a 730ha cloud forest reserve. The reserve and the lodge are run by a community co-operative of 12 local families, who provide reforestation workshops and environmental education to the rest of the community, as well as supporting small local businesses. The lodge commands stunning views and is a great base for bird-watching. For the more adventurous, it also offers hikes with experienced guides, the opportunity to swim in waterfalls and a traditional sugar-making workshop. Double cabins with private bathrooms are available, and longer-term volunteers who want to get involved with conservation or experience more of community life are welcome.

Contact: Carolyn Halcrow
Tel: +593 2157242
Email: info@santaluciaecuador.com
Web: www.santaluciaecuador.com
Address: Co-operativo Santa Lucia, Apartado 17-07-9414, Quito, Ecuador

HOST/ACCOM+
SARAGURO RIKUY COMMUNITY TOURISM

Saraguro Rikuy is a grassroots network based in the village of Saraguro in the very south of Ecuador, formerly the Incan and colonial heartland. The network, supported by the Kawsay Foundation, brings craftspeople, guides, farmers and host families in a community-wide effort. The village invites guests to share in family and community life, attend dance and musical events, rituals, visit artisan workshops and learn about the area with local guides. Accommodation is also available in the community hostel Achik Wasi, which can hold up to 35 people.

Contact: Laura Guaillas • Polivio Minga
Tel: +593 72200331
Fax: +593 72200331
Email: rikyu@turismosaraguro.com • saraurku@turismosaraguro.com
Web: www.turismosaraguro.com
Address: Fundación Kawsay, Casilla de Correos 11.01.27 Loja, Ecuador

ACCOM+
SUAMOX RANCH

Located 2.5 hours away from Quito, Suamox offers accommodation in rural Ecuador. Activities on offer include bird- and wildlife-watching, walking in the forest and learning about conservation. The ranch sources its food locally and fosters a good relationship with the community. It conserves energy as much as possible, recycles all its waste and has started a CO_2-capturing project. Prices vary from US$16 to US$32 per person per night, with meals at around US$10.

Contact: Martha Ordoñez
Tel: +593 99448741 • +593 99495318
Email: ranchosuamox@hotmail.com • suamoxforest@gmail.com
Web: www.suamoxforest.com
Address: PO Box 1723236, Quito, Ecuador

ACCOM+
TIERRA DEL VOLCÁN

Tierra del Volcán is a warm and welcoming haven high up in the Andes, surrounded by four snow-capped volcanoes, including the active Cotopaxi, whose equatorial position means its peak is the second most distant point from the centre of the Earth. Visitors stay in the central homestead, in cosy canvas-walled rooms in the attic. If it weren't for the constant hot water, visitors could believe that they had been transported back to a bygone age, as elegant colonial styles blend with traditional native hospitality giving a truly unforgettable atmosphere. Visitors are invited to experience the Chagra (highland cowboy) lifestyle and ride around the estate in style. For the more altitude resistant, they also offer trekking, zip-lines, biking and mountain climbing. The most adventurous can go camping, pitching up in small valleys hidden between the folds of the mountain. Wholesome food is served in the traditional candlelit restaurant, and after dinner tea is served in armchairs in front of a roaring log fire.

Contact: Maria Paz Meza
Tel: +593 22231806
Fax: +593 22231806
Email: info@tierradelvolcan.com • ventas@tierradelvolcan.com • info@volcanoland.com
Web: www.tierradelvolcan.com
Address: San Ignacio 1015 y Gonzalez Suarez, Quito, Ecuador

ORG/TREK/TOUR
YACHANA LODGE

This lodge in the Ecuadorian Amazon was established by the non-profit Yachana Foundation. Profits accrued from the running of the lodge help to support the Yachana Technical High School, an innovation in practical education for young people from the Amazon. Yachana is a Quechua word meaning 'a place for learning', which is the central philosophy of the foundation. All of the guides who lead the three- or four-night tours have grown up in the rainforest and learned English in the US. All efforts are made to run a green operation – for example, the lodge runs on solar-powered energy. Access to the lodge is by 30-minute flight from Quito to Coca, followed by a 2.5 hour motorized canoe journey.

Contact: Paola Villalba
Tel: +593 22237133
Fax: +593 22220362
Email: info@yachana.com • paola@yachana.com
Web: www.yachana.com
Address: PO Box 17-17-185, Quito, Ecuador

ORG/BUDGET
YANAPUMA FOUNDATION

Yanapuma is a small organization that supports rural communities across Ecuador. It helps them cope with the increasing economic and environmental strains that globalization and climate change are putting on their traditional way of life. One of the areas they specialize in is sustainable tourism development. The foundation offers travellers the opportunity to go and stay in communities on cultural exchange programmes, giving locals the chance to practise tourism skills and make informed decisions about how or, indeed, whether to develop their tourism projects. Visitors can teach in schools, learn about agricultural practice and the realities of day-to-day life, as well as experience more mainstream tourist activities, such as hiking, bird-watching and eating traditional food. One week stay costs US$150, with additional activities such as hiring horses at small extra cost.

Contact: Stephen Barnes
Tel: +593 22546709
Email: Andy@yanapuma.org

GUYANA
International dialling code +592

Guyana, on the north-eastern shoulder of South America, does not have pretty beaches, unlike its Caribbean neighbours, and so has chosen to use the momentous landscapes of its interior to attract visitors. Tourism is a recent development and trade is still small scale. Away from the coast and its interesting, somewhat crumbling, capital, Georgetown, Guyana has lush forests, stunning waterfalls (Kaieteur is five times bigger than Niagara Falls), cascading rivers and rapids, and dramatic mountains and gorges that have exhausted those looking for El Dorado. Indeed, gold mining is part of the past romance and present reality of Guyana. The remote Mount Roraima was the inspiration for Conan Doyle's *Lost World*. It also has sprawling savannahs, an abundance of wildlife, and over 800 species of birds. Travelling by boat or four-wheel drive into the interior is a great adventure. You can also visit the Iwokrama Reserve – the International Centre for Rainforest Conservation – an imaginative project through which Guyana has offered to the world some 400,000ha of tropical rainforest for sustainable development.

Guyana's population consists mainly of East Indians, Afro-Guyanese and the Amerindians who still live largely in or near their forests and have many forest skills. Their role in developing tourism is to act as guides and porters and to provide indigenous colour – they are not the owners of the tours agencies or the eco-hotels. There are signs, however, that some communities are seeing an opportunity for tourism and are beginning to offer alternative tourism experiences.

RAINFOREST
MORARO

Moraro was primarily started to support the preservation of the traditional forest conservation practices of the local Lokono, Warrau and Carib peoples. Accommodation is modest but comfortable for a group of three or four at any one time, with many outdoor activities including boating and bathing in the creek. Although not a major tourist destination, visitors are welcome to Moraro to find out what life is like for an indigenous community in the interior of Guyana. Guests will be able to see the local wildlife, with a huge variety of birds depending upon the season.

Contact: Claudette De Vieira Fleming
Tel: +44 2085435796
Email: cf003g2296@blueyonder.co.uk
Web: www.forestkeepers.com/artist
Address: 65 Gower House, Chaucer Way, London SW19 1UP, UK

VOL/TOUR
NORTH RUPUNUNI TOURISM PROGRAMME (NRDDB)

The programme is coordinated by a committee representative of the 16 member communities. This is basic ecotourism and all aspects of the project are owned by the various communities. A specific aim is to benefit both young and old and to foster indigenous handicrafts and culture. The various projects differ from village to village. On offer are riding, trekking/hiking, canoeing, wildlife-watching and birding.

Contact: Alphonso Forde
Email: alphonsoforde@yahoo.com
Address: North Rupununi District Development Board, Bina Hill, North Rupununi, Region #9, Guyana

THE AMERICAS

RAINFOREST/SAFARI
RAINBOW RIVER SAFARI

The aim of the enterprise is to entice people of farming stock back from the city to farming, while minimizing the economic risk. Ecotourism helps with their upkeep, so if you fancy trekking along the miles of jungle trails in the nearly 6900ha of unspoiled tropical rainforest, this may be up your alley. The organic farming aims at food self-sufficiency with a hope of exports in the future.

Contact: Edward Sabat
Email: tedsabat@yahoo.com

PERU
International dialling code +51

1250km

LIMA

Three of the most diverse geographic zones on the planet – coast, mountain and jungle – go to make up this huge and diverse country. The flat coastal lands feature harsh deserts and oases as well as the capital, Lima, which is a mind-boggling feat of fairly unsustainable irrigation. The Andes (which stretch from Colombia and Ecuador in the north down through Chile and Argentina in south, and across to Bolivia in the east) are dotted with Inca and pre-Inca ruins. Away from the mountains, in the Inca capital of Cusco, take a bus through the cloud forests and you may be lucky enough to see the scarlet cock-of-the-rock, the Peruvian national bird, before the warm, moist air of the jungle envelops you. Microclimates reign in Peru; check out the weather in the local area in advance to avoid shocks.

Buses and some night buses are excellent, but do go with reputable companies. Most tours will kick off from a town such as Cusco, Lima and Ayacucho, which have shops equal to small-town Europe where you will never be far from a toothbrush, bottled water or a well-stocked chemist. However, once in the jungle it could be days to a hospital. Listen to your guides and give them a generous tip, such as a pair of Wellington boots bought in the local market.

Peru is corrupt and does have a high level of crime, and you will always meet tourists and travellers who have horror stories. However, when these things do happen, it is usually because a traveller has not followed one or more of the golden rules. People are poor, you are rich, and the assumption is you won't really miss your stuff!

RAINFOREST+
AMAZONAS LODGE

This 30-room lodge, which offers all-inclusive packages, is a joint venture between the Native Community of Infierno (NCI) and the Peruvian private ecotourism company, Rainforest Expeditions (RFE), in Tambopota. The lodge is wholly owned by the NCI but operated jointly. The success of the venture has a ripple effect socially and economically, and the community is developing projects that link in to tourism (e.g. handicrafts and fish farms). Tourist activity is controlled in the interests of wildlife. The lodge was built on uninhabited land and the community can be visited only with the permission of the control committee.

Contact: Martin Schmidt
Tel: +51 14218347
Fax: +51 14218183
Email: info@rainforest.com.pe
Web: www.perunature.com
Address: Ave Aramburu 166.2b, Miraflores, Lima, Peru

TREK/TOUR OP
ARACARI TRAVEL CONSULTING
A boutique travel company promoting the natural and cultural heritage of Peru via low-impact high-end tourism. It is deeply involved with the community at Ollantaytambo and supports a local school, basic healthcare and several other projects. It is very aware of the need to consider the welfare of its porters who come from the Ollantaytambo area.

Contact: Cynthia Caceres
Tel: +51 12426673
Fax: +51 12424856
Email: postmaster@aracari.com
Web: www.aracari.com
Address: Avenida Pardo 610 of 802, Miraflores, Lima, Peru

VOL
BRIGADA DE VOLUNTARIOS BOLIVARIANOS DEL PERU
A new and dynamic grassroots association.

Contact: Jorge Galiano
Tel: +51 13285143
Fax: +51 13285143
Email: bolivarianosd@hotmail.com
Web: www.bvbp.tripod.com
Address: Jr Lucanas No 332-A, Lima 01

RAINFOREST/VOL/SCHOOL
CREES EXPEDITIONS (CE)
At the heart of this operation is the Manu Learning Centre in the Manu Biosphere Reserve in Peruvian Amazonia, which aims to promote conservation and sustainability through its work with local communities and the rainforest. On offer are sustainable ecotourism packages, expeditions and field courses. There is also a volunteer programme. The tourism programmes are designed for today's time-poor individuals – a sort of compaction of the rainforest and the Andes that never-theless yields an experience conveying the rich cultures and environment of those areas. The volunteer programme ranges from two weeks to three months after a 15-day induction.

Contact: Quinn Meyer (Peru) or Alexander Stevenson (UK)
Tel: +51 84262433 (Peru) • +44 2075812932 (UK)
Fax: +51 84262433 (Peru) • +44 2075819977 (UK)
Email: info@crees-expeditions.com
Web: www.crees-expeditions.com
Address: Calle San Miguel 250, Cusco, Peru • 5–6 Kendrick Mews, London SW7 3HG, UK

ORG
LEAP LOCAL
The Leap Local website is a free online directory of local guides and services, enabling travellers to get directly in contact with locals offering tourist services, rather than going through an agency. The increased contact between travellers and people whom they are visiting gives a more personal experience to both parties, leading to increased cultural and social understanding. Leap Local encourages tourists to behave in a way that reduces their cultural impact, such as not giving sweets to children and learning phrases in the indigenous language. In return for their sensitivity, travellers are given unparalleled access to some of the most beautiful and culturally distinct locations in the country. The site is focused mainly on Peru, although there are entries from around the world.

Tel: +51 84797162
Email: louise@leaplocal.org
Web: www.leaplocal.org
Address: Lares Calle s-n, Ollantaytambo, Cusco, Peru

ORG/ACCOM
MANO A MANO

Mano a Mano is a charitable foundation based in Lima that uses urban tourism as a tool for community development. It runs some extraordinary projects: alongside traditional education and healthcare efforts, it also trains otherwise marginalized women in construction and repair. Mano a Mano invests much time and energy in ensuring that its visitors are properly prepared and supported. Visitors are offered advice on personal safety in Lima alongside insights into the rich local culture and the difficulties of everyday life. Visitors spend most of their time with local people learning from them firsthand. The foundation can arrange airport pick-ups, and accommodation is US$8 a night. There are cooking facilities and traditionally prepared food is available at a small extra cost. Advance booking is not always required. Visitors are invited to drop into their office, easily accessible from central Lima, on the top floor of 292 Calle Cisnersos.

Contact: Socorro Flores Flores
Tel: +51 15362282
Web: http:/limaman.ifrance.com
Address: Mano a Mano Mz I lote 3 A.H La Merced, La Ensenada de Chillon, Lima 22, Peru

Or in France: **Contact:** Magali Caulier
Tel: +33 233836155
Email: magali.caulier@wanadoo.fr
Address: La Petite Chauviniere, 61400, La Chapelle, Montiligeon, France

TOUR/HOMESTAY
MINKA FAIR TRADE

Minka Fair Trade has been working to combat poverty in Peru for over three decades, and has been a member of the International Fair Trade Association since 1991. It works with artisans across the Andes, helping them to preserve ancient manufacturing techniques and the traditional lifestyle that is so intimately bound up with craft production. On the Minka Fair Trade Trail, travellers visit artisans' workshops, stay in their communities, and learn about day-to-day life in their stunning but challenging environment. Minka Fair Trade guides trekkers from community to community, via beautiful colonial towns and archaeological sites. The routes feature not only remote rural spots, but also the highlights of the Southern Andes, including Machu Picchu and the Nazca Lines.

Contact: Kusi Ruiz
Tel: +51 14427740 • +51 14222132
Fax: +51 1447740
Email: turismo@minkafairtrade.com
Web: www.minkafairtrade.com
Address: Calle Barcelona 115, Lince, Lima, Peru

TOUR OP
PACHAMAMA TURISMO ALTERNATIVO

Pachamama is a responsible tourism company based in Lima but offering trips throughout the country. Originally Pachamama was established as a device to foster craft tourism and to support the production and export of a wide range of Peruvian crafts from different areas. Under its aegis, travellers can now experience true alternative or sustainable tourism as they visit its various programmes. Its mantra could now be 'Craft workshops: a model for alternative tourism'. Notwithstanding this craft focus, it also offers classic tours, adventures and alternative and custom-built tours.

Contact: David Balvín Ramírez • Pamela Ramírez Moreno
Tel: +51 15751851
Fax: +51 1 4847345
Email: pachamama@ciap.org • pachapromo@ciap.org
Web: www.pachamama.ciap.org
Address: Calle Victor Navarro No 339, Urb El Establo Mz, B Lote 13, San Martin de Porres, Lima 31, Peru

ORG/TOUR/HOST
PERUETICO

PeruEtico is a charitable foundation that supports vulnerable people, particularly children and the victims of abuse. It runs three residential homes, and also provides community support in the form of healthcare, fair-trade production and running school buses. Travellers are offered the opportunity to see the day-to-day running of their activities, visit the residential homes and live with families involved in the production of fair-trade goods sold in the UK. Visitors are well supported and given a thorough personal introduction to the tour, including cultural and behavioural advice. Trips cost around 1600 Euros for 20 days, including food, accommodation and guidance.

Contact: Emanuele Riga
Tel: +51 84232069
Email: info@peruetico.com
Web: www.peruetico.com
Address: Calle Matarà 437, Cusco, Peru

TREK/ORG
THE MOUNTAIN INSTITUTE (TMI): PERU INCA NAANI PROJECT

The Mountain Institute (TMI) offers a great opportunity to climb the Inca Trail, combining the trek with a more locally interactive programme. The idea is to involve people from seven different mountain communities who live along the trail path, integrating their knowledge of the land and the touring services that only they can offer with the trek itself. Tents are the only sleeping arrangements available at the moment, although plans are being made within communities to improve services. TMI aims to promote and preserve mountain cultures and environments, encouraging rural families to manage their own development. As with all TMI projects, conservation is the driving force behind development.

Contact: Guido J. van Es
Tel: +51 43423446
Fax: +51 43426610
Email: guidovanes@mountain.org • miriamt@mountain.org
Web: www.mountain.org
Address: PO Box Instituto de Montaña, Casilla 01- Huaraz, Peru or Pasaje Ricardo Palma no 100, Huaraz, Ancash, Peru

ACCOM/TREK/ORG
YACHAQUI WAYI RESPONSIBLE TRAVEL CENTRE/RESPONS

'Yachaqui Wayi' means 'house of learning, of exchanging ideas' and this is a non-profit organization that offers community-based tourism among the Vicos, Humacchuco and Huaripampa communities along the Inca Naani. Vicos and Humacchuco offer homestay experiences: travellers stay in a lodge next to a local family and engage in activities with the family such as hiking and learning about Andean life. Huaripampa offers the chance for visitors to learn how to weave and dye wool with natural ingredients. The Inca Naani is a four- to six-day trek along the Great Inca Road, staying with communities along the way, learning about Inca history and legends, and visiting Inca ruins, with a final destination of the Inca's second largest city.

Contact: Guido Van Es • Pablo Tadeo
Tel: +51 43426538
Email: info@yachaquiwayi.org
Web: www.yachaquiwayi.org
Address: Jr Gabino Uribe 650, Huaraz, Peru

ASIA

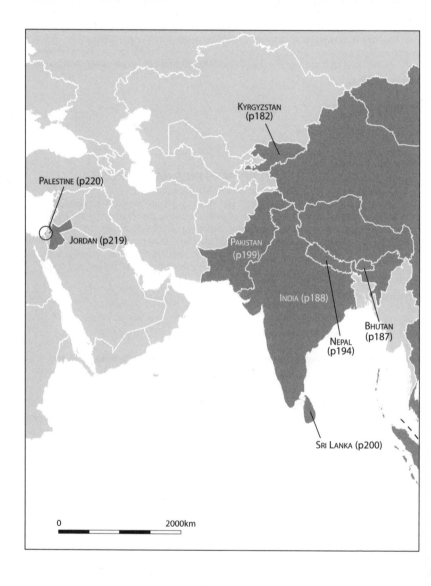

KYRGYZSTAN (p182)

PALESTINE (p220)

JORDAN (p219)

PAKISTAN (p199)

INDIA (p188)

BHUTAN (p187)

NEPAL (p194)

SRI LANKA (p200)

0   2000km

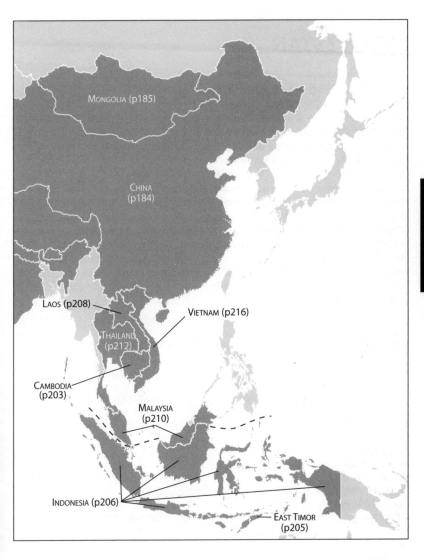

ASIA

CENTRAL ASIA

KYRGYZSTAN
International dialling code +996

Kyrgyzstan is a landlocked and mountainous country at the heart of Central Asia. Some of the highest
mountains in the region, the Tien-Shan and the
Pamir, span over Kyrgyzstan's territory and make the
countryside an adventure to travel through. Outside
the capital city Bishkek, life continues the way it has
done for centuries. Nomadic families move around with
their livestock in a seasonal pattern and are often cut off for
months from the rest of the world. That's why they are particularly fond of travellers
as they bring news from the outside world. Typical Kyrgyz cuisine is very rich and
fatty in order to help the people survive through the long, harsh winter months. An
interesting specialty, somewhat strange to the Western taste, is Kumys, a drink
made from fermented mare's milk. During the hot summer months, the greatest
pleasure is to cool off at the beaches of the largest lake in Kyrgyzstan, the Issyk-Kul.
Locals call it 'hot lake' because it does not freeze in winter, even though it is situated at more than 1500m above sea level.

HOST/TOUR/TREK
KYRGYZ COMMUNITY-BASED TOURISM ASSOCIATION (KCBTA): 'HOSPITALITY KYRGYZSTAN'
KCBTA offers community-based tourism in Kyrgyzstan. Visitors can stay with rural families in village
houses or traditional *yurts* (nomadic tents) in the mountains. They can also enjoy trekking, horseriding tours, local festivals and handicrafts, all of which are organized by, and directly benefit, the
population of rural villages. The association joins together the 17 community-based tourism NGOs
operating in the country, which represent approximately 400 families, all of whom benefit from
tourism activities.

Contact: Asylbek Rajiev
Tel: +996 312540069 • +996 312443331
Fax: +996 312443331
Email: cbt@cbtkyrgyzstan.kg • kcbta@mail.ru • reservation@cbtkyrgyzstan.kg
Web: www.cbtkyrgyzstan.kg
Address: 58 Gor'kiy St (intersection with Matrossov St), Bishkek City, 720031, Kyrgyzstan

TREK
SHEPHERD'S WAY TREKKING
This project was founded by Ishen Obolbekov, his wife Gulmira and his brother Rash. They offer
you horseback-riding treks in the Tian-Shan Mountains along the Shepherd's Way. Trips can be
from 3 to 30 days, with three meals a day at 70 to 90 Euros per day per person. The routes are
geared to riding ability. Sit on carpets in a yurt, sip fermented mare's milk and dream of riding with
the Golden Horde …

Contact: Gulmira Obolbekov
Tel: +996 312434532 • +996 772518315
Email: shepherd@elcat.kg
Web: www.kyrgyztrek.com
Address: Shepherd's Way Trekking, 111 Gogol Street, apt. 150, PO Box 2032, KG-720000 Bishkek, Kyrgyz Republic

Representative in Switzerland:
Contact: Bernard Repond
Mobile: +41 793048404
Address: Buchille 14, CH-1633 Marsens, Switzerland

ASIA

EAST ASIA

CHINA
International dialling code +86

2000km

BEIJING

The impact of the backpacker culture on the development of China's tourism industry cannot be underestimated. Most of the popular tourist attractions now visited by throngs of foreign tour groups, and by millions of Chinese tourists, were until only a few years ago secluded and idyllic backpacker destinations. They provided only basic accommodation in guest houses and simple restaurants selling local food. The inclusion of certain spots in the *Rough Guide* or similar guidebooks brought about interest from package tourists and groups, along with a demand for better accommodation.

Most tours to China take in the various sites in Beijing before moving on to other places. In Beijing, the 'must see' attractions are the Forbidden City, Tiananmen Square, Temple of Heaven, the Lama and Confucius temples, the Summer Palace, the Ming tombs and the Great Wall, accessible in three places within easy reach of Beijing. Recently added sites include the area of the Olympic Green, with such modern landmarks as the Bird's Nest Stadium and the Water Cube.

Outside Beijing, Xian in Shaanxi Province is famous for its stunning army of terracotta soldiers buried in the tombs of Emperor Qin Shi Huangdi from 200BC. Guilin is known for its much-painted landscape of strange rock formations shooting out of the valley floor and the calm appeal of the Li River, as well as the growing popularity of mountain biking and rock climbing. Yunnan Province is possibly the most diverse province, its varied climate ranging from snow-covered mountains in the north to tropical rainforests in the south, and a large number of minority ethnic groups living in traditionally built villages.

Shanghai is China's most modern and fast-moving city. Visiting this 'Paris of the East' is a chance to see how far China has come in its drive for modernization. The Chinese are proud of their accomplishments in this city and routinely put it on tourist itineraries.

There is no agreed definition of ecotourism in China and this label is applied to many attractions and tours that simply have an element of the natural world in them. Hiking is popular in China, and many nature reserves have organized paved hiking routes. In fact, sometimes all paths are paved with stones and concrete, with steps built into the mountain for easier climbing. This evolved from the demand of Buddhist pilgrims climbing up sacred mountains in China.

China is full of history; but sadly much has been destroyed over time and through the zeal of the Red Guard during the Cultural Revolution. However, there are still 31 sites in China on the UNESCO World Heritage List and tourism has an important role to play in protecting these places. If managed badly, it will inevitably destroy the sites it relies on; but if managed well, it will provide sustainable finance for the continued maintenance of these unique sites.

TREK/LUX
WILD CHINA

This is a premium travel company offering distinctive and ecologically sensitive journeys to all corners of China. Exclusive trips are highlighted by superior access to venues and experts. This is authentic off-the-beaten-track travel which eschews the mass market approach of the majority of China tourism. It offers the true diversity of China in culture, landscape, religion, cuisine, ethnicity and environment. Adventure with comfort and sustainability with high service standards go hand in hand – this could be its mission statement.

Tel: +86 1064656602
Fax: +86 1064651793
Email: info@wildchina.com
Web: www.wildchina.com
Address: Room 801, Oriental Place, No 9 East Dongfang Road, North Dongsanhuan Road, Chaoyang District, Beijing 100027, China

MONGOLIA
International dialling code +976

1500km

ULAN
BATOR

ASIA

As one of the most sparsely populated countries on Earth, Mongolia is an ideal getaway from busy urban life in the West. During the 13th century, however, when Genghis Khan united the Mongol tribes and defeated many neighbouring peoples, the Mongolian Empire was at its height.

In the early 1990s, after 70 years of a Soviet-style one-party state, democracy and privatization were introduced; but the economy collapsed after the withdrawal of Soviet support, triggering widespread poverty and unemployment. Despite growth since then, around one third of the population still live below the poverty line.

Landlocked Mongolia is a place of magnificent steppe landscapes, inhabited mainly by herds of wild antelope, donkeys and yaks. For centuries, Mongols have been herding cattle and horses and about one third of the population are still nomadic or semi-nomadic today. Mongols pride themselves on being skilled horsemen, and horse races are a favourite pastime. Nomadic families will travel large distances to attend the biggest games at the annually held Naadam Festival.

Mongolian culture is heavily influenced by Tibetan Buddhism and ancient Shamanist practices, with priceless religious artefacts found in newly reopened monasteries. On a trip to Mongolia, try not to miss the mystical and enthralling throat-singing. A stay in the round and cosy felt tents of the hospitable nomads will be another unforgettable experience, rounded off with a bowl of warm tea and a hearty lamb dish.

ACCOM+
THREE CAMELS LODGE

Three Camels is a wilderness camp that is both luxurious and environmentally conscious. All of the electricity needed comes from solar and wind power. Part of the profits go towards local projects (e.g. they recently planted 1500 trees at a local school), and Nomadic Expeditions, who owns the lodge, also supports local greenhouse projects and schools. All management, staff and guides are from the local area. Listed amongst the top 50 eco-lodges by *National Geographic* in 2008, the camp itself offers a memorable and rewarding stay in Mongolia's Gobi Desert. Guests accompanied by trained guides can visit ancient petroglyphs and sites such as the Flaming Cliffs, the Yol Valley and the Singing Sand Dunes. A stay in a ger, a traditional dome-shaped felt tent, gives the visitor a taste of nomadic culture and lifestyle, yet is still balanced with Western standards of comfort and luxury.

Contact: Undraa Buyannemekh
Tel: + 800 9986634 • +1 609 8609008
Fax: +1 609 8609608
Email: info@threecamellodge.com • info@nomadicexpeditions.com
Web: www.threecamellodge.com • www.nomadicexpeditions.com
Address: Nomadic Expeditions, Inc, 1095 Cranbury-South River Rd, Suite 20 A, Monroe Twp, NJ 08831, USA

SOUTH ASIA

BHUTAN
International dialling code +975

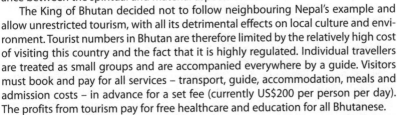

Bhutan is a small, remote and impoverished nation at the eastern end of the Himalayas, known by its people as the 'Land of the Thunder Dragon'. It has breathtaking mountain scenery and a rich culture, which is fiercely guarded under the guiding philosophy of 'gross national happiness', influenced by the dominant religion, Buddhism, which tries to achieve a balance between the spiritual and material aspects of life.

The King of Bhutan decided not to follow neighbouring Nepal's example and allow unrestricted tourism, with all its detrimental effects on local culture and environment. Tourist numbers in Bhutan are therefore limited by the relatively high cost of visiting this country and the fact that it is highly regulated. Individual travellers are treated as small groups and are accompanied everywhere by a guide. Visitors must book and pay for all services – transport, guide, accommodation, meals and admission costs – in advance for a set fee (currently US$200 per person per day). The profits from tourism pay for free healthcare and education for all Bhutanese.

As well as visiting the many Mahayana Buddhist monasteries and picturesque towns with wooden chalet-style houses, trekking in the mountains is increasingly popular. Much of the appeal of Bhutan must lie in the fact that traditional culture has been preserved to an unusual degree. The modern world was kept at bay in Bhutan until the 1970s – the wearing of national dress is mandatory, and television and mobile phones were only introduced in 1999. The national sport of archery is still the most popular male pastime.

The determination to maintain the purity of Bhutanese culture culminated in the 1990s in ethnic Nepalese migrant workers being ordered to adopt Drukpa culture and prove citizenship entitlement based on residency. Large numbers who did not qualify have been in refugee settlements in Nepal since then.

TOUR
SNOW WHITE TREKS AND TOURS
Snow White Treks and Tours is a small company based in Bhutan offering tourists various opportunities to attend festivals, stay in farmhouses with local communities, take cultural tours, trek and go bird-watching. It offers a homely service, and travellers have a memorable experience. State policy imposes a uniform tariff on Bhutan tourism companies and therefore holidays there are not so cheap; but part of the revenue goes towards free healthcare and education.

Contact: Kencho Wangmo Dorjee
Tel: +975 2323028
Fax: + 975 2321696
Email: snowwhite@druknet.bt • kenchod@yahoo.com
Web: www.snowwhitetours.com.bt
Address: Phendey Lam, Post box 1123, Thimphu, Bhutan

INDIA
International dialling code +91

India never fails to astonish: her powerful contrast between old and new, poverty and extravagance, efficiency and chaos guarantee the visitor a roller-coaster ride of adventure. Humanity presents itself in a vibrant and creative diversity of cultures, religions and landscapes. But India's deep cultural roots entwine her people inseparably as one.

India is the world's sixth largest country and with almost 1 billion citizens is the second most populous. It has one of the most ancient civilizations, dating back to 4000BC; yet it is India's modern history that preoccupies most visitors: astonished by the West's – and, moreover, Britain's – detrimental role in shaping the India we see today.

British occupation of India was born out of international trade, the British East India Company giving way to British supremacy in 1852. Mahatma Ghandi is the popular face of Indian independence and his Non-Cooperation Movement exposed colonialism's dependence upon the compliance of ordinary Indians. However, despite India technically winning independence in 1930, it was not the united India that Ghandi had dreamed of: in 1948 the creation of the separate Muslim state of Pakistan resulted in extreme conflict and violence that still persist to this day.

While Indians never tire of paying homage to the British institutions of cricket and the railways, visitors should not be fooled into thinking all is forgiven. Feelings about British imperialism are deep seated and complex and, sadly, are not restricted to the past: today's corporate-led globalization is now widely viewed as neo-colonialism.

Eighty per cent of Indians follow Hinduism and the remainder are Muslims, Christians, Buddhists and Jains. Women visitors should respect the tradition of covering shoulders and legs – this is an Indian, rather than Muslim, tradition; men should refrain from wearing shorts. The handshake is a British tradition, so visitors should greet Indians by placing their hands together in a prayer like gesture – especially women greeting Indian men, as the handshake has become somewhat of a ruse for Indian men, with heavy sexual undertones.

Environmentally, India faces huge challenges. But the banning of plastic bags in various states, including Maharashtra, Goa and Bangalore, highlights India's progressiveness and puts richer nations to shame.

ACCOM+
APANI DHANI ECO-LODGE

On offer are eco-friendly accommodation, meals and activities with local people, and the opportunity to learn about daily life and the traditions of rural India. Although located in Rajasthan, this is a chance not so much to see the architectural marvels of that state as to experience the everyday wonders of India as manifested in its people.

Contact: Ramesh C. Jangid or Krishan Sahal
Tel: +91 1594222239
Email: apanidhani@gmail.com
Web: www.apanidhani.com
Address: Jhunjhunu Road, Nawalgarh 333042, Rajasthan, India

TOUR
BILLION STAR HOTEL CAMEL SAFARIS
This is a splendid opportunity to combine the wonders of Jaisalmer in Rajasthan with insight into the lives of the nomads of the Thar Desert in that state. You are collected by jeep from Jaisalmer and driven into the desert. There you will camel ride and then eat and sleep under the 'billion stars'. The next day will see more camel riding and then you will be returned to the city. Of course, you can stay longer … it takes a long time to count a billion stars.

Contact: Rosie Jardine
Tel: +91 9414660782 (Fatan Khan)
Fax: +91 299251414 (attention: Billion Star Hotel)
Email: rosie@billionstarhotel.com • bookings@billionstarhotel.com
Web: www.billionstarhotel.com

ACCOM/TOUR
COCO HOUSEBOATS KERALA
Coco Planet Tours specializes in backwater tourism in Kerala, southwest India. It offers eco-friendly houseboats featuring well-furnished bedrooms, but leaving the traditional character of the boats intact. The boats are run on solar power, and the crew prepare all of the food in the traditional way, using mud pots. Despite its speciality houseboats, it can also organize package tours with guided service throughout Kerala and to the Maldives Islands. Coco Houseboats provides ten families with employment.

Contact: Switen George
Tel: +91 4772239904
Fax: +91 477223 9903 • +91 9847325026 (24 hrs)
Email: cocoindiagroup@yahoo.com
Web: www.beautifulkerala.com • www.cocohouseboatskerala.com
Address: Kariyil Chira Buildings, Near Nehru Trophy Finishing Point, Thathampally post, Alleppey 688 013, Kerala State, India

TOUR/HOST
ECOSPHERE
Ecosphere is an NGO that organizes various tours in Spiti, offering travellers an insight into this mystical hidden valley in the trans-Himalayas of Himachal Pradesh in India. It ensures that its visits have a minimal impact upon this pristine environment, and that they contribute to local livelihoods and the sustainable development of Spiti. Examples of tours include Buddhist Paths, Rustic Revelations and Trans-Himalayan trails across ancient passes and beside emerald lakes. Ecosphere is also very active in developing energy efficiency and promoting solar energy, and visitors are invited to offset their carbon emissions by contributing to these projects.

Contact: Ishita Khanna
Tel: +91 9899492417 • +91 9418860099 • +91 1906222652
Email: ishita@spitiecosphere.com
Web: www.spitiecosphere.com
Address: Ecosphere, Main Market Kaza, Spiti, Himachal Pradesh, 172114, India

VOL/ORG
FIELD SERVICES AND INTERCULTURAL LEARNING (FSL)
FSL organizes a large programme of volunteer projects in Karnataka and other parts of south India.

Contact: Rakesh Soans
Tel: +91 8057657647 • +91 8025564883
Fax: +91 805914 505
Email: fsl_rakesh@rediffmail.com
Web: www.fslindia.org
Address: # 21, New Bypanahalli Extension, Indiranagar Post, Old Madras Road, 560038 Bangalore, India

ASIA

189

TOUR
GRASS ROUTES PVT LTD
This is a private company offering tours in the Indian state of Orissa. Trips are geared to specific themes (e.g. arts and culture, faith, nature and wildlife, and indigenous communities). Accommodation is, at present, in tented camps; but the company is trying to develop rural home-stays. One result of this would be a feeling of ownership on the villagers' part. Grass Routes is devoted to meaningful interaction between local disadvantaged communities and travellers.

Contact: Claire Prest
Tel: +91 6752250560 · +91 9437029698 · +91 9437022663
Email: info@grassroutesjourneys.com
Web: www.grassroutesjourneys.com
Address: Grass Routes Pvt Ltd, 280 Bank Colony, Talabania, Puri 752002, Orissa, India

HOST
HIMALAYAN HOMESTAYS
Himalayan Homestays is one of the initiatives developed by the Snow Leopard Conservancy (SLC), which promotes community-based stewardship of the snow leopard and its environment. This entails a marriage of conservation and the interests of local people and their domestic livestock. As a visitor you will be offered a comfortable room, traditional meals, clean solar-boiled spring water to drink, a clean, dry composting toilet, and the opportunity to enjoy the rhythm of life in a village where farming and livestock herding has been the way of life for centuries.

Contact: Daya of Maitreya Tours
Tel: +91 17079353851
Email: maitreyatours@rediffmail.com · rinchen@snowleopardindia.org
Web: www.himalayan-homestays.com
Address: Snow Leopard Conservancy India Trust, Shangara House, Main Tukcha Road, Leh-194101, Ladakh, India

TOUR
INSIDER TOURS
Insider Tours offers tailor-made guided tours throughout southern India and Sri Lanka, with wed-dings and honeymoons being a speciality. The entire operation is embedded in the local people and the company's relationship with them. The company prefers to use homestays and lodges, and small locally owned hotels. To this end, the tours are built around regions or projects that ben-efit the community so that visitors can support the local economy, travel less and relax more and absorb the local culture.

Tel: +44 1233811771
Email: info@insider-tours.com
Web: www.insider-tours.com
Address: Insider Tours Ltd, 15 Churchfield Way, Wye, Kent, TN25 5EQ, UK

HOST+
KABANI
Kabani has initiated a community-based tourism project entitled Bamboo Village in Trikkaipatta, Wyanad, in Kerala. Tourism is integrated with other development components such as organic farming and sustainable waste management practices. Kabani offer homestays with farmers in the village, comfortable rooms with attached bathrooms, and local trekking. It has a flexible pro-gramme called Tour MASC, which covers all aspects of village life. Kabani's long-term plan is to connect this project to the other community-based tourism models.

Contact: Sumesh Mangalashery
Tel: +91 9388402948
Email: kabanitour@yahoo.com
Web: www.kabani.org
Address: c/o Sruthi, PO Kottarakunnu, Vellamunda, 670 645, Wayanad, Keralam, India

TOUR OP
KOLAM RESPONSIBLE TOURS AND SOFT TRAVEL

Operating under the banner of 'Small is beautiful, small is powerful, small is bountiful', this travel service promotes a personalized travel culture that attempts to be people orientated, culturally sensitive and politically conscious. It invites the informed and concerned traveller to come and celebrate the living traditional values of India, which it sees as integral to change. With 20 years of experience behind them, this husband and wife team of Ranjith and Rani Henry run fair-trade, small group and customized tours to any part of India, visiting development projects as well as exploring contemporary life, all from the Indian point of view.

Contact: Ranjith Henry
Mobile: +91 9840176656
Fax: +91 4424900939
Email: kolam@vsnl.com
Web: www.kolam.mimemo.net
Address: F1 Kgeyes Iswarya, Plot No 48 Rukmani Road, Kalakshetra Colony, Besant Nagar Chennai 600 090, India

VOL/HOST
KOORMANCHAL SEVA SANSTHAN/RURAL ORGANIZATION FOR SOCIAL ELEVATION (KSS/ROSE)

KSS/ROSE is an award-winning NGO based in the small village of Kanda, situated in the Kumoani Hills of Uttarakhand, India, at the base of the Himalayas. KSS/ROSE encourages responsible volunteer-based tourism. Visitors stay with families and everyone eats together. Visitors can plant seedlings of local oak and pine to help avoid deforestation, or get involved in building construction, English teaching, organic farming, cooking, housekeeping, and assisting in maintaining water filtration and irrigation systems. They will also get to know the people of this region and their fascinating culture, bringing with them their skills and knowledge to help on various rural development projects.

Contact: Jeevan Lal Verma
Tel: +91 5963241081 • +91 9412167186
Email: Jlverma_rosekanda@hotmail.com • jlverma.rosekanda@gmail.com
Web: www.rosekanda.org • http://rosekanda.wordpress.com
Address: Village-Sonargan, PO-Kanda, District-Bageshwar, State-Uttarakhand 263631, India

HOST
PROJECT SWAGATAM

This is sustainable tourism with a twist: you can just lean back into the 'softness of living', take part in activities such as yoga or cooking, or get involved in ayurvedic care. The local people want to develop the latter, with its 1000-year medical tradition, to create more jobs. They also want to create a new type of touristic stay, one with a more spiritual slant. You will stay in your host's home and share daily life. It's not all spiritual or 'new agey'; there are also handicraft workshops, soap manufacture and … elephants.

Contact: Sarva Atma Mithra or Françoise Cruells
Tel: +91 4742061677 • +91 9895334464 (India)
Tel: +33 467012365 • +33 620389395 (France)
Email: contact@swagatam.org
Web: www.swagatam.org
Address: Nedungolam, Kollam District, 691334 Kerala, India
Swagatam MP Cruells, 53 bis rue Sadi Carnot, F-34300 Agde, France

ASIA

TOUR/HOST
PUSHPANJALI/FAIR TOURISM

Pushpanjali is a fair-trade organization working to spread the benefits of trading partnerships based on transparency, respect and greater equity in trade. Since its establishment in 1982, Pushpanjali has been providing marketing and financial support to small and marginalized producers to improve their living and working conditions. It organizes tours that visit villages and centres of craft production, with an option of homestays in the villages. Pushpanjali also provides medical support to poor people living in villages and educational support to female students who are otherwise unable to afford to go to school.

Contact: Mr Ashu
Tel: +91 9897098809 • +91 5622511930
Fax: +91 5622511930
Email: mittalsc@sancharnet.in • pushpanjali@sancharnet.in • pft@pushpanjali.in
Web: www.pushpanjali.in
Address: 35 Hanuman Nagar, Shahganj, Agra 282010, India

RAINFOREST
SUNDERBANS/MANAS JUNGLE CAMPS

A community-based tourism project offering ethnic accommodation, conservation centres, protection camps and a cultural and education centre. Activities are run and controlled by local people in a forest rich in wildlife, including endangered species such as the Bengal tiger and the Asiatic one-horned rhinoceros. Both jungle camps are located in national parks, and host communities and visitors are able to learn from each other. Stress is placed on environmental sensitivity, social responsibility and on the community having ownership of the project.

Contact: Asit Biswas or Raj Basu
Tel: +91 3324550917 • +91 3324854584 • +91 3532433683 • +91 3532535893
Mobile: +91 9831031980 • +91 9733000444
Email: info@helptourism.com • helptourism@sancharnet.in
Web: www.helptourism.com • www.actnowornever.org • www.manas100.com
Address: 67A, Kali Temple Road, Sadananda Kuthi, Kolkata 700 026, West Bengal, India, or PO Box-67, 143, Hill Cart Road, Malati Bhawan, Siliguri 734 401, West Bengal, India, or 122/1, Ganapati Apartments, Flat-6, Toot Sarai, Malviya Nagar, New Delhi 110 017, India

ACCOM
THE GREEN HOTEL

The Chittaranjan Palace, built for Mysore's princesses, has been lovingly restored as a small hotel. Set in extensive gardens, with formal lawns and shaded pergolas, fringed by majestic trees, the hotel is an oasis of calm. It has been renovated and furnished using traditional Indian craftsmanship, offering comfortable surroundings, friendly staff, and a restful, creative atmosphere. Guests have come for a night and stayed for a month! The Green Hotel has been set up as a model of sustainable tourism by a UK charity. All profits are distributed to charitable and environmental projects in India. Mysore provides an excellent base from which to tour south India. The Western Ghats, the coffee plantations of Coorg, the game reserves of the Nilgris and the Ooty Hill Station are all within a few hours' drive.

Tel: +91 8214255000
Fax: +91 8212516139
Email: thegreenhotel@airtelbroadband.in
Web: www.cardaid.co.uk/greenhotel
Address: Chittaranjan Palace, 2270 Vinoba Road, Jayalakshmipuram, Mysore, 570 012, Karnataka, India

DAY/TREK
THENMALA ECOTOURISM
This ecotourism project in and around the Shenduruney Wildlife Sanctuary in Kerala offers trekking and bird-watching trails, as well as cultural activities. The village of Thenmala is a focal point, with small community-led ecotourism developments within a radius of 50km in the foothills of the Western Ghats Mountains. Young local people have been trained to become guides and the trekking programme is being managed by a local group with support from the private sector and the Forestry Department. A local women's group runs the shops selling handicrafts, as well as a cafeteria. Employees are also given frequent training. There has been huge investment from both national and local governments, as well as the local communities, private enterprise and scientific institutions.

Tel: +91 4712470411 · +91 4712400740 · +91 4713102370
Fax: +91 4712337037
Email: info@thenmalaecotourism.com · skjnaf@yahoo.com
Web: www.thenmalaecotourism.com
Address: Thenmala PO Box 691308, Kollam District, Kerala, India

HOST/VOL/TOUR
VILLAGE VOLUNTARY TOURISM, SUNARGOAN KANDA, BAGESHWAR, UTTARAKHAND, INDIA
This project is the Jeevan Paying Guest Unit, which is the brainchild of Jeevan Lal Verma. It is a tourism project aimed at benefiting both locals and locale – neither must be overburdened. On offer are homestays and a community workcamp. Kanda is a hill station surrounded by a mountain landscape, terraced fields and organic tea plantations – was that a sigh, or did we imagine it? The unit is linked to an NGO called ROSE (Rural Organization for Social Elevation) and tourists with eco-interests can get involved with environmental and/or teaching projects. The cost is 5600 rupees per week – which seems a bargain.

Contact: Jeevan Lal Verma
Tel: +91 5963241081 · +91 9412167186
Email: jlverma_rosekanda@hotmail.com · jlverma.rosekanda@gmail.com
Web: www.rosekanda.org
Address: Sunargoan, Kanda, Bageshwar, Uttarakhand, India 263631

TREK
WILD KERALA TOUR COMPANY (WKTC)
WKTC is a group of hard-core conservationists committed to promoting community-based ecotourism with minimum impact upon the environment in the wilderness of Kerala. Ten per cent of the turnover goes towards conservation activities and local communities. Working hand in hand with the state Forest Department, Wild Kerala Tour Company offers trekking and camping programmes in the national parks and wildlife sanctuaries of Kerala. You can experience the different ecosystems in the southern Western Ghats, such as evergreen, semi-evergreen, moist deciduous and dry deciduous forest, with a vast variety of flora and fauna. Guides come from the local indigenous community, and are accompanied by an experienced naturalist who can help to interpret the various sounds of the jungle. WKTC is committed to responsible tourism and minimum impact upon the environment.

Contact: Pramod KG
Tel: +91 4843099520 · +91 484984662157
Fax: +91 4843099520
Email: mail@wildkeralatours.com
Web: www.wildkeralatours.com
Address: VI/480, KVA Buildings, Bazaar road, Mattancherry, Cochin, Kerala, India PIN 682 002

ASIA

NEPAL
International dialling code +977

The Himalayan Kingdom of Nepal is a small nation, wedged between the giants of India and Tibet (now occupied by China). Its geography is dominated by the eastern Himalayas, including the world's highest mountain, the formidable Mount Everest. Many of today's trekking routes are ancient trade routes, which run between India and Tibet. This and the porter skills of the mountain people are the main factors in allowing Westerners access to the highest regions.

500km

KATHMANDU

The harsh, breathtaking environment of rock and ice makes way in the south to some of the most picturesque and enchanting landscapes, the so-called foothills. A subtropical climate produces a colourful spectrum of rainforest, rice fields and tropical fruit trees. The lowlands of the Terai are hot and humid with enough jungle to provide a home to tigers, elephants and rhinoceros, as in the famous Chitwan National Park.

This diverse geography has shaped an equally diverse kaleidoscope of people and cultural expression. The spiritual heritage shaped by Tibetan Buddhism in the higher regions and Hinduism elsewhere gives substance to people's lives throughout Nepal, making them reverent, kind, hospitable and hard-working people.

Since 1996, Nepal has been embroiled in violent political unrest between Maoist insurgents and the king and government. In early 2007, the Maoists joined an interim government. The monarchy has since been abolished and the Maoists are now in office.

ORG/TREK
ANNAPURNA CONSERVATION AREA PROJECT (ACAP)

ACAP is a Nepalese NGO which was launched in 1986 by the National Trust for Nature Conservation and encompasses the entire Annapurna range, an area of 76,629 square kilometres. ACAP participates with the local community to combine environmental protection with sustainable community development. Tourism is integrated within wider poverty alleviation programmes such as agriculture. The region contains some of the world's highest and most beautiful mountains, rhododendron forest, waterfalls, terraced farms, villages and rare species, including snow leopard and musk deer. There are many treks available, from a few hours to a few weeks, and ACAP is supported by a fee of 2000 Nepalese rupees (approximately UK£15/US$27) collected from all visiting trekkers.

Tel: +977 15526571 · +977 15526573
Fax: +977 15526570
Email: info@ntnc.org.np
Web: www.ntnc.org.np

TOUR/TREK
COMMUNITY ACTION TREKS

Founded by the mountaineer Doug Scott, this is the UK arm of the Nepalese Community Action Trek Nepal. Doug's initial aim was to improve labour conditions in the trekking industry. Profits go to improve conditions in the trekking areas. Everything is done in close consultation with local people. The input to the community is best measured by their being judged 'Best in a mountain environment' in the 2008 Virgin Responsible Travel Awards for using tourism to benefit communi-

ASIA

ties, for the provision of health and education services, and for work with porters that has helped the development of the International Porter Protection Group.

Contact: Ann Foulkes
Tel: +44 1768771890
Fax: +44 1768771325
Email: info@catreks.com
Web: www.catreks.com
Address: Unit 7, Sunset Hill, Keswick, Cumbria, CA12 4RN, UK

ORG/HOST/VOL/TOUR
DISCOVER NEPAL

This is a not-for-profit organization which is working to develop community-based tourism in Nepal, and organizes awareness programmes in Nepalese villages. Accommodation is available in homestays and there are jobs teaching English in government schools in the villages of the Kathmandu Valley. Visitors can also go on village tours and purchase local handicrafts and souvenirs. Its sister organization, Dream Nepal, offers activity holidays such as trekking and whitewater rafting.

Contact: Bijaya Pradhan
Tel: +977 14413690 • +977 9851037866
Fax: +977 14255487
Email: stt@mos.com.np • bijayapradhan@hotmail.com
Web: www.discovernepal.org.np • www.dreamnepal.com.np
Address: GPO Box 20209, Kathmandu, Nepal

TREK
GAURI SHANKER ECO-LODGE TREKKING

Gauri Shanker Eco-Lodge Trekking is a unique product of Nepal, the outcome of a development project supported by Eco Himal of Austria, and is now managed by pioneering local tourism development co-operatives. It is located in the unspoiled Gauri Shanker trekking area. The community lodges are committed to running an environmentally and socially responsible tourism operation, appropriate to the needs of both the local population and visitors.

Tel: +977 14721039 • +977 16226951
Fax: +977 14721039
Email: office.ktm@ecohimal.org
Web: www.ecohimal.org
Address: Phinjo Sherpa, Eco Himal, POBox 21966, Maharajgunj, Kathmandu, Nepal

ORG
INTERNATIONAL PORTERS PROTECTION GROUP (IPPG)

The IPPG is a voluntary organization that promotes awareness of porters' needs and vulnerability, and runs training courses for them. It raises money to build porter shelters in remote areas, and supports other porter charities and organizations worldwide. The IPPG employs one Sherpa in Nepal to run the Machermo Porter Shelter and Rescue Post in the Gokyo Valley, while all other workers are volunteers. Consequently, 99 per cent of donations go directly to their projects as there are no offices or other overheads.

Contact: Jim Duff (international director)
Email: jimduff@ippg.net (UK) • info@ippg.net (Bob Cassidy)
Web: www.ippg.net
Address: 37 Redfern Road, Walton, Stone, Staffordshire ST15 0LF, UK

ASIA

ORG/VOL
KATHMANDU ENVIRONMENTAL EDUCATIONAL PROJECT (KEEP)
KEEP is an NGO that promotes responsible tourism practices, along with the ethics of sustainable tourism to visitors. It works to maximize tourism benefits to local communities by training professionals within the communities working in trekking tourism to develop their capacity and skills.

KEEP has been successfully operating the Visitors' Information Centre, providing free, impartial and independent information to trekkers, as well as educating them on the trekking code for minimum impact. Its Environmental Awareness Programme has been effective in generating awareness about mountain safety, conservation, socio-cultural issues and porters' welfare among trekking professionals.

The Community Development Programme provides opportunities for volunteers to support local communities and schools. Volunteers from Australia, Canada, the UK, New Zealand, El Salvador and Germany have undertaken school renovation work at government schools, while others have engaged in teaching, helping in orphanages and working as teacher trainers and office volunteers.

Tel: +977 14216775 • +977 14216776
Fax: +977 14216774
Email: info@keepnepal.org.np
Web: www.keepnepal.org
Address: PO Box 9178, Jyatha, Thamel, Kathmandu, Nepal

TOUR OP
NEPAL TREKKING
Nepal Trekking specializes in small group and individual tailor-made treks and tours to Nepal. Treks can range from a few days to a few weeks, covering all ability levels. The treks are available at any time during the trekking season to suit the customer. Exclusive use of all services and guides is included. Nepal Trekking is aware of the needs of local people and the environment. It is very much involved with the local Sherpa people in Nepal and, as such, supports families and provides employment, investing in small projects such as children's education. Medical equipment, medicines and consumables are collected in the UK and distributed to villages in the mountains. Nepal Trekking is also involved with fair trade in Nepal and the UK. Working together with a Nepalese NGO, it gives hospital, welfare and rehabilitation assistance to people affected by leprosy and polio.

Contact: Denis Gallagher
Tel: +44 1482703135
Fax: +44 1482 216605
Email: info@nepal-trekking.demon.co.uk • info@nepaltrekking.co.uk
Web: www.nepaltrekking.co.uk
Address: 10 Swinburne Street, Hull HU8 8LY, UK

TOUR
RELIANCE TRAVEL AND TOURS (RTT)
This project is run by, and for, local people. The aim is to improve their health and better their education if at all possible. In this context, a primary focus is the women and children, both from the ethnic minority and the indigenous population. What the visitor will get is cultural tours with the Tharu, Magar and Gurung, with a focus on local culture, language and tradition. What you take away will be the memory of a 'wonderful and memorable stay'. The local communities benefit to the tune of 15 per cent of the total net profits and they are the true owners of the project.

Contact: Prabal Thapa
Tel: +977 14424614 • +977 14424615
Email: info@reliancetravels.com.np
Web: www.reliancetravels.com.np
Address: PO Box 8974, CPC 249, Thamel, Kathmandu, Nepal

TOUR
SOCIAL JOURNEYS TRAVEL AND ADVENTURE
Social Journeys is a private organization that applies the principles of responsible tourism. It aims to enable a win–win situation by acting as a bridge between communities and tourists. Its tours are rooted in the communities, and it offers adventure and ecotours. It strays outside Nepal and also runs special interest tours to Tibet, Bhutan and Sikkim. It sees community-based tourism as being at the core of its activity because tourism should always benefit local people. The motto 'Travel with a purpose' is highly appropriate.

Contact: Jyoti Dhital
Tel: +977 14359287 · +977 9841319127
Email: info@socialjourneys.com
Web: www.socialjourneys.com
Address: PO Box 5358, Kathmandu, Nepal

TOUR/TREK
SOCIALTOURS.COM/SOCIALTREKS.COM
You want to visit Nepal, be sustainable and support local people, but you are not too good at roughing it … this is for you. On offer is specialist custom-tailored 'soft adventure'. The tours are environmentally and culturally sensitive, with the main activity being trekking in Nepal; but the company now has a toehold in Tibet, Bhutan and also in Ghana.

Contact: Bipin Maharjan or Raj Gyawali
Tel: +977 14412508
Fax: +977 14417814
Skype: socialtours · socialtreks
Email: info@socialtours.com
Web: www.socialtours.com · www.socialtreks.com
Address: GPO Box 1663, Kathmandu, Nepal

ORG/TREK/VOL
THE NEPAL TRUST
The Nepal Trust is a Scottish charity working mainly in northwest Nepal with projects in areas such as health, education, renewable energy, heritage preservation and ecotourism. It is recognized that the seemingly disparate are interconnected: traditions attract tourists – the resulting income maintains those traditions and makes daily life better for local people in 'little ways' such as clean drinking water. Alongside the volunteer work, classic treks are offered, as are Treks to Build, in which you trek and work with the local community. A caveat: the treks are not cheap. But they are worthwhile.

Contact: Elisabeth Donovan or Ceris Jones
Tel: +44 1343810358 · +44 1312432638
Fax: +44 1343810359
Email: admin@nepaltrust.org · ceris@nepaltrust.org
Web: www.nepaltrust.org
Address: 4 Marina Quay, Lossiemouth, Moray, IV31 6TJ, Scotland, UK

LUX
TIGER MOUNTAIN POKHARA LODGE
This is another high-end enterprise from the Tiger organization. Slough off the stress of ordinary life and rediscover tranquillity. Local-style iconic accommodation and spa facilities: have a massage and gaze at Annapurna. If you want to stir, there are healthy walking options; but don't worry: no trekking. If the crunch has left you credit, what about it?

Contact: Pragya Mani Lama
Tel: +977 14361500

ASIA

Fax: +977 14361600
Email: reservations@tigermountain.com
Web: www.tigermountain.com
Address: GPO Box 242, Gongabu, Kathmandu, Nepal

LUX/SAFARI
TIGER TOPS JUNGLE LODGE AND TENTED CAMP

On offer here is high-end safari tourism that aims to be sustainable and conservation oriented, as is the sister operation, Tharu Lodge. During your stay at this wildlife safari lodge and camp you will have revealed to you the flora and fauna typical of the Indo-Gangetic Plains. The safaris utilize elephants, jeeps, boats … and, yes, your feet. A fair degree of fitness would be advisable – as might a healthy bank balance.

Contact: Pragya Mani Lama
Tel: +977 14361500
Fax: +977 14361600
Email: reservations@tigermountain.com
Web: www.tigermountain.com
Address: GPO Box 242, Gongabu, Kathmandu, Nepal

ACCOM+
TIGER TOPS THARU LODGE

This is a high-end sustainable conservation tourism cultural lodge – but it is built in the traditional longhouse style of the local community: the Tharus. It supplies a 'living diorama' of the environment, its people and their rich culture. A community support partnership helps to fund schools, health clinic camps and environmental education. A local primary school is operated directly by the lodge.

Contact: Pragya Mani Lama
Tel: +977 14361500
Fax: +977 14361600
Email: reservations@tigermountain.com
Web: www.tigermountain.com
Address: GPO Box 242, Gongabu, Kathmandu, Nepal

ORG
TOURISM FOR RURAL POVERTY ALLEVIATION (TRPAP)

TRPAP is a joint undertaking between the Nepalese government, the United Nations Development Programme (UNDP), the UK Department for International Development (DFID) and The Netherlands Department for International Development. TRPAP supports the development of tourism in rural Nepal. Its aim is to encourage tourism which is pro-poor, pro-women, pro-rural communities and in harmony with the environment. It develops these initiatives in isolated, remote, unexplored and unspoiled rural settings.

Tel: +977 14269768
Fax: +977 14269770
Email: info_trpap@ntb.org.
Web: www.welcomenepal.com/trpap
Address: PO Box 107, UNDP, Nepal

PAKISTAN
International dialling code +92

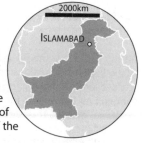

Pakistan is a majority Muslim state in an area that was once home to the ancient Indus civilization, the ruins of which can be seen in places such as Mohenja-daro, Harappa and Taxila. Part of this area belonged to the Persian Empire and later to the Greek Empire of Alexander the Great. From 1858 to 1947 it was part of the British Raj.

The country of Pakistan was created to form a homeland for Indian Muslims at the independence of India in 1947. Originally, it was in two parts; but the eastern wing, now Bangladesh, became independent in 1971. Alternate civilian and military governments in Pakistan have led to political and social instability, with a high risk of terrorism and sectarian violence; but it is now listed as among the 'Next Eleven' economies.

Much like neighbouring India, Pakistan boasts a dizzying variety of natural and cultural wonders, sensational cuisine, a baffling ability to cram more people on public transport than the laws of physics provide for, and an overwhelming bustle of human life. However, for every similarity, there are more differences.

Pakistan receives fewer than 1 million visitors a year, a result of security issues and a low tourism profile. The upside of this is that those who do visit practically get Pakistan to themselves. In accordance with Islamic teachings, guests are considered an expression of God's blessing and are welcomed effusively. Also, with tourism still more or less in its infancy, there are fewer touts, scams and hassles than in many other more established destinations.

Beyond the fast-paced cities, visitors can find tranquillity and breathtaking scenery in the north, with the mighty stretches of the Karakorams, the Himalayas and the Hindu Kush Ranges, marvel at the mangrove forests in the coastal wetlands, or spot crocodiles at the mouth of the Indus River in the south. The variety of landscape includes sandy scrublands with their wild cats and panthers, and the desert in the southwest with its rare Asiatic cheetahs. If adventure is your thing, then take part in trekking, mountaineering (there are several mountains over 7000m, including K2), white-water rafting or camel and yak safaris.

ASIA

TOUR/TREK
CHITRAL ASSOCIATION FOR MOUNTAIN AREA TOURISM (CAMAT)

CAMAT was founded in 1998 by stakeholders in the Chitral district of north Pakistan to help promote ecotourism. Services provided to tourists include guiding, horse riding, festival/cultural information, adventure tours, wildlife-watching and much more. A core aim is to reduce the pressure on agricultural land by trying to create job opportunities for local people in activities rooted in local culture and the environment. Above everything else is the desire to protect the indigenous Kalash culture in Chitral, which is endangered.

Contact: Shams Uddin (manager)
Tel: +92 943413540 • +92 943413708
Fax: +92 943412668
Email: camatchitral@yahoo.com • shamscamat@yahoo.co.uk
Web: www.camat.org.pk
Address: Mountain Inn, Chitral Town, District Chitral, NWF Province, Pakistan

SRI LANKA
International dialling code +94

Sitting just above the equator, Sri Lanka is the pearl
of the Indian Ocean: this small island has everything
a traveller could wish for. Tropical golden palm-
fringed beaches stretch for over 1600km around the
coastline, with the tourism industry gradually recovering after the devastation of the Asian tsunami in 2004.
The cool highland interior features lush green landscapes
of paddy fields and its world-famous tea plantations, along with
scenic waterfalls and mountain passes. The Cultural Triangle is rich in historical
interest, encompassing ancient ruined capitals, rock fortresses, cave temples, giant
Buddhas and the sacred city of Kandy. Then there's the abundant and varied wildlife
– you're practically guaranteed to see a wild elephant (or even a herd) if you know
where to go, and could catch sight of an elusive sloth bear or leopard. And it is an
absolute dream for bird lovers. Throw in the chance to lose your head with adventure and water sports, eat yourself stupid on exotic dishes, experience colourful festivals and indulge in the national obsession – cricket (if that's your cup of tea!) – and
you'll understand why a visit to this country sticks forever in the mind.

But, of course, Sri Lanka also has a protracted and bloody civil war, which sim-
mers under the surface despite the current ceasefire. Tourists should avoid the most
affected parts of the country, although your visit to other areas will be something
to savour.

ACCOM+
HOTEL SIGIRIYA (GREENING INITIATIVES)

This hotel in central Sri Lanka makes active efforts to conserve the environment and reduce its carbon footprint as well as be involved with local people. Guests are taken to a nearby village to participate in people's daily activities at home and at work, as well as to join them in temple ceremonies. The hotel also organizes elephant safaris to Minneriya National Park. As part of its responsibility to the people of the area, volunteer teachers from the Link overseas students exchange
scheme in Scotland are offered accommodation in the hotel and teach English to local schoolchildren.

Contact: Suranjith De Fonseka
Tel: +94 112332155
Fax: +94 112438933
Email: srilal@serendibleisure.lk
Web: www.serindibleisure.com
Address: No 40, AA Building, Sir Mohamed Macan Markar Mawatha, Colombo 0300, Sri Lanka

TOUR/HOST
LAKSARA ECO-HOLIDAYS

Laksara acts on behalf of the local community to organize local tours and also arranges nature and
culture tours around Sri Lanka. It offers visitors an insight into the unvarying rhythms of everyday
life for local fishing communities – and into the centuries of tradition and religious belief practised
and held by the indigenous people of Sri Lanka.

Contact: Sajeewa Emmanuel
Tel: +94 912256621 · +94 777579033
Fax: +94 912256621

ASIA

Email: info@srilankaecotours.com • akroma@sltnet.lk
Web: www.srilankaecotours.com
Address: No 4/11, Patabendimulla, Ambalangoda, Sri Lanka

ACCOM+
RANWELI HOLIDAY VILLAGE

At Ranweli Holiday Village in Waikkal, guests can enjoy bird-watching and nature walks, cycling tours, canoeing, and boating in the marine estuary, where mangrove forests and rivers converge to meet the sea. There are 72 bungalows and it is located on the west coast of the country, which is 18km away from Colombo International Airport. Ranweli aims to promote tourism based on environmental conservation and respect for the welfare of the local community. It is modelled on a traditional Sri Lankan village and built using locally sourced biodegradable materials. There are extensive recycling facilities. Water is heated using solar power and kitchen waste is used to irrigate and fertilize the organic garden. It was recognized by *National Geographic* as one of the top 50 eco-lodges in the world.

Contact: Wimal Dassanayake
Tel: +31 2277359 (Waikkal) • +94 112325284 (Sri Lanka office)
Fax: +31 2277358
Email: ranweligm@sltnet.lk • ranwelihol@sltnet.lk
Web: www.ranweli.com
Address: 50 Hyde Park Corner, Colombo 2, Sri Lanka

VOL
SERVICE CIVIL INTERNATIONAL SRI LANKA

An effective peace-building association that brings Tamils and Sinhalese together.

Tel: +94 812 387188
Fax: +94 812 232343 (attention SCI Sri Lanka)
Email: scisl@sltnet.lk
Web: www.sldoc.be
Address: 18/A/4, Deveni Rajasinghe Mawatha, Kandy, Sri Lanka

ORG/ACCOM+/DAY/TOUR
SEWALANKA FOUNDATION

Sewalanka is a Sri Lankan non-profit that supports community organizations, co-operatives, federations and networks throughout the country, including a network of community-based eco-tourism initiatives. It has published a *Local Alternatives* map that provides information on 170 responsible travel destinations throughout the island. The map can be purchased at Sri Lankan bookshops or directly through Sewalanka. Initiatives include a mangrove lagoon ecotour and a dolphin 'sea safari' guided by local fishermen, homestays in the villages bordering the Sinharaja and Knuckles rainforests, and cultural tours by certified village guides.

Contact: Harshana Hegodagamage
Tel: +94 773863243 • +94 112545362
Fax: +94 112545166
Email: tourism@sewalanka.org • headquarters@sewalanka.org
Web: www.sewalanka.org
Address: No 432A Colombo Road, Boralesgamuwa, Sri Lanka

ASIA

ASIA

HOST/ACCOM/TOUR
SRI LANKA ECOTOURISM FOUNDATION (SLEF) AND SRI LANKA ECO TOURS (SLET)

SLET is a registered travel agency, the tourism business arm of SLEF. It promotes homestays and community-owned eco-lodges in rural Sri Lanka. SLET also promotes camping in protected areas, rainforests and mountainous regions. All of these are focused on ensuring economic benefits and improving the living standards of local communities, many of which had been hit hard by the tsunami. They offer tours from seven to ten days on a half-board basis, 75 per cent of the proceeds going to the local community.

Contact: Palitha Gurusinghe
Tel: + 94 777631334 • + 94 114920344
Fax: + 94 112706433
Email: sleco@sltnet.lk • palithaslef@gmail.com
Web: www.ecotourismsrilanka.net • www.ecotourssrilanka.com • www.ecotourslk.com
Address: 17, Atsumi Holiday Resort, Thuduwa, Madapatha, Sri Lanka

HOST+/TOUR
THE ABODE TRUST

The Abode Trust offers visitors a chance to experience authentic village life in remote communities in Sri Lanka. Guests can live as local people do in harmony with jungle and mountainous environments. This is a chance to get away from the trappings of modern life, enjoy peace and quiet, and learn about the lifestyles, religion and culture of the local people. Visitors can also take overnight walking expeditions into the jungle to see waterfalls, difficult-to-access Buddhist sites and spectacular peaks.

Contact: Sidanthe Elikelwela
Tel: +94 815682256
Mobile: +94 774354430
Email: sue@theabodetrust.com • sid@theabodetrust.com
Web: www.theabodetrust.com
Address: 75 Narendasinghe MW, Kundasale, Sri Lanka

LODGE/SAFARI
TREE TOPS JUNGLE LODGE

The operating premise is that poverty generates environmental destruction and loss of indigenous wildlife, in this case elephants. The only realistic solution is to utilize the environment in the service of ecotourism, as the traditional lifestyle has become unsustainable and destructive. Slash-and-burn land is being regenerated as elephant habitat. Guided jungle walks will show you the slash-and-burn fields, the forest, birdlife, leopard tracks and maybe elephants. Life is difficult since the tsunami and the political conflict involving the Tamil Tigers, and the lodge is temporarily closed. Well worth bearing in mind though.

Contact: Lars Sorensen
Tel: +94 777036554 • +94 715202651
Email: treetopsjunglelodge@gmail.com
Web: www.treetopsjunglelodge.com
Address: Weliara Yala Jungle Road, Buttala, Sri Lanka

SOUTHEAST ASIA

CAMBODIA
International dialling code +855

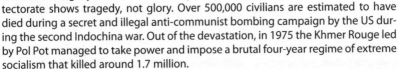

In its heyday, over 600 years ago, the city of Angkor located in the north of modern day Cambodia boasted a civilized population of more than 1 million. At the same time, London was inhabited by less than 35,000. Today, tourists flock to see the remains of the temples, which represent Cambodia's main tourist attraction. Khmer people are incredibly proud of their ancient heritage; yet the recent history of this ex-French protectorate shows tragedy, not glory. Over 500,000 civilians are estimated to have died during a secret and illegal anti-communist bombing campaign by the US during the second Indochina war. Out of the devastation, in 1975 the Khmer Rouge led by Pol Pot managed to take power and impose a brutal four-year regime of extreme socialism that killed around 1.7 million.

During the rule of Pol Pot, the United Nations did not intervene. It was left to Vietnam in 1979 to overthrow the Khmer Rouge. Despite removing such an evil regime, Vietnamese intervention was unacceptable for some countries. In 1992, the UN eventually entered Cambodia and the country has been in the process of recovery since. Human rights remain a huge issue, with many living and working on the streets. The country also remains notorious for child prostitution and sex-worker exploitation from sex tourism, and much of its coastline has been sold to international developers.

Be sure to travel to remote provinces such as Mondulkiri and Ratanakiri, with their ethnic minority inhabitants, or Kratie, where Irriwadi dolphins can be sighted. Learning some Cambodian will almost certainly guarantee smiles from a people who, despite all that they have been through, have a strong national pride and a good sense of keeping daily life light and fun.

ORG
CAMBODIA COMMUNITY-BASED ECOTOURISM NETWORK (CBEN)
The CBEN is a network of organizations involved in community-based ecotourism. The aim is to promote and support this category of tourism to help conserve natural and cultural resources, and to raise the living standards of local communities. Visitors are enabled to get to know local people, their everyday lives, and their culture and environment. This brand of tourism is run by the community for the community in that it aids empowerment and poverty reduction.

Contact: Sok Sophea
Tel: +855 23355272
Fax: +855 12927636
Email: ccben_cam@yahoo.com • info@ccben.org
Web: www.ccben.org
Address: 10A, Street 468 (near Toul Tompong Market), Phnom Penh City, Cambodia

ASIA

TOUR
CARPE DIEM TRAVEL

This is a social enterprise and not-for-profit business offering small group and private trips to Cambodia and emphasizing cultural interaction. It uses local guides and supports local community-based tourism projects. The company's *raison d'être* is the use of 'responsible tourism as a means of helping people in developing countries to lift themselves out of poverty'. Plans are afoot to expand to other countries with the same motivational principles.

Contact: Claire Seager
Tel: +44 8452262198
Fax: +44 8701327589
Email: mail@carpe-diem-travel.com
Web: www.carpe-diem-travel.com
Address: 68 St Peter's Street, London, N1 8JS, UK

VOL/SCHOOL/BUDGET
LE TONLÉ TRAINING CENTRE

This centre is owned by Tourism for Help, which is a Swiss-owned organization dedicated to the promotion of sustainable tourism. Local people have the chance to imbibe theory and practice with half the day in theory class and the remainder operating as waiters, cooks, housekeepers, etc. Guests sleep on site and eat in the restaurant. If they wish they can join in the cookery training and there is also opportunity to play the tourist in the local area and to interact with local people.

Contact: Pen Sokha or Alexandre Aubert
Tel: +855 92674990
Email: alexandre.aubert@tourismforhelp.org • fieldco@tourismforhelp.org
Web: www.tourismforhelp.org

TOUR
SYMBIOSIS EXPEDITION PLANNING (SEP)

SEP is a UK- and Cambodia-based company offering tailor-made holidays and small group expeditions throughout Southeast Asia for travellers concerned about the impact of tourism. Symbiosis will custom design itineraries to suit individual interests, and also runs cycle tours, kayaking, trekking, wildlife watching, cookery and other forms of mostly non-vehicle-based tourism. It encourages the use of local guides, and stays at smaller locally owned hotels and guest houses, which are checked for their environmental policies. It also runs periodical charity fundraising expeditions, such as the Bangkok to Saigon Cycle Challenge. Guests also get the chance to contribute to local well-run charitable organizations and SEP passes these contributions on via its charity bank account.

Contact: Christopher Gow
Tel: +44 8451232844 • +855 23726562
Fax: +44 8451232845 • +855 23993092
Email: enquiry@symbiosis-travel.com
Web: www.symbiosis-travel.com • www.divingsoutheastasia.com
Address: 2 Brambles Enterprise Centre, Waterberry Drive, Waterlooville, PO7 7TH, UK

EAST TIMOR
International dialling code +670

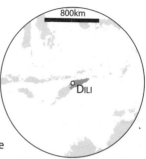

East Timor is a unique 'end of the line' destination for those adventuring in Southeast Asia. At the end of the Nusa Tenggara Archipelago of Indonesia, only recently independent in 2002, this country has a number of appealing qualities for tourists. Its pristine beaches, reefs and marine life will appeal to all from the lazy beachcomber to the avid scuba diver.

East Timor was under Portuguese colonial rule from the 18th century until 1975, giving life a distinct flavour and setting it apart from neighbouring islands. It is, for example, one of only two predominantly Catholic countries in Asia, the other one being the Philippines.

The hard-fought resistance against the subsequent military occupation by Indonesia, as well as the scorched-earth campaign before Indonesia's departure in 1999 have left their marks on the country. At least 100,000 Timorese died as a result of the 24 years of Indonesian occupation. The richness of Timorese traditions and material culture, proudly maintained by a largely rural population, is a testament to the resilience of the Timorese people.

The continued United Nations presence in East Timor means that the capital, Dili, offers Western creature comforts and food for all tastes; yet prices are, consequently, less competitive with neighbouring Indonesia. A handful of quality dive shops and ecotourism operators are carving out a niche from the capital as well.

Outside Dili, the tourist infrastructure is more limited, with a couple of higher-priced originally Portuguese pousadas (guest houses), as well as some more basic ones too. Small-scale community-based tourism projects have sprung up along the beaches and in some scenic mountain locations. Highlights for budget tourists are beach houses in Baucau and Kom, as well as on the tip of the island, Tutuala, which is now part of Konis Santana National Park, the country's first such park.

Timor had just begun to reap the rewards for positive press coverage and attention from the world's best-selling guidebooks when social unrest hit in 2006. Because of the growing pains of independence, there has been slow consolidation of the nation state and consequent violence.

ASIA

ACCOM+
TUA KO'IN ECO-VILLAGE, ATAURO ISLAND

This is a chance to experience a traditional lifestyle in the newest nation in the world. Visitors can go snorkelling and diving on the pristine coral reef surrounding the island. You can also take mountain hikes through eucalyptus and rainforest, or boat trips to visit fishing communities, staying in community-run cabins. Guests can also travel in dug-out canoes, or learn crafts such as wood-carving, weaving and basket-making. This is an opportunity to relax on the remote and unspoiled island of Atauro, listening to the ancient music and experiencing traditional ceremonies. Guests can feel assured that they are participating in a respectful and environmentally friendly holiday that makes a meaningful economic contribution to a poor community.

Contact: Marcelo Belo Soares or Gabrielle Samson
Tel: +670 7236085 (Marcelo) · +61 437527953 (Gabrielle)
Email: tuakoin@yahoo.com · gabrielle_samson@yahoo.com
Web: www.atauroisland.com

ACCOM/TOUR
VILLAGE HOTELS
Village Hotels offer comfortable accommodation in areas of considerable natural beauty. They would like visitors to experience and learn about local culture and history. The 'Village Hotel' model is of a central low-density accommodation base with all amenities. As demand increases, they hope to develop outlying accommodation in huts managed by individual villagers, but with marketing and quality control from the central hotel base. The buildings are constructed from locally available materials and 20 per cent of income from the accommodation goes directly to the local community.

Contact: Anthony Rickard
Tel: +670 3310616 • +670 7396911
Email: enquiries@tvh.tl
Web: www.tvh.tl
Address: Rua Delta Comoro, Dili, East Timor

INDONESIA
International dialling code +62

Indonesia consists of over 17,500 islands, about 6000 of which are inhabited. Located on the edge of a tectonic plate, Indonesia is subject to earthquakes and tsunamis and has 400 volcanoes (130 of which are active – including one with a drive-in crater!). Lying on the boundary between Asia and Australasia, Indonesia has 34,000 miles of coastline with some superb (but endangered) coral reefs and some of the world's best surfing.

Covering an area of more than 2 million square kilometres, Indonesia has an immense variety of natural environments, including tropical rainforests (disappearing at an alarming rate) and mangroves (threatened by prawn farming and other coastal industries), and rare flora and fauna, such as orchids, orang-utans, rhinos, Komodo dragons, tarsiers (a tree-dwelling, nocturnal primate) and birds of paradise.

Following centuries of Dutch colonialism, Indonesia gained its independence after World War II; but since then the country has been turbulent, with challenges posed by corruption, separatism and periods of rapid economic change. Distinctive ethnic, linguistic and religious groups have been brought together under a shared identity defined by a national language and religious pluralism within a majority Muslim population. The national motto is 'Unity in diversity'; but sectarian tensions, especially militant Islamic groups, have led to violent confrontations.

With a population of 232 million from over 350 ethnic groups, the culture is as varied as the environment, ranging from the world's largest Buddhist temple/monument, Borobudur, to Hindu temples and megaliths. A huge range of architectural styles is complemented by flourishing music, art, dance, puppetry, theatre, textiles, wood-carving and so on. Tourism is centred on Bali, parts of which have been spoiled by it.

While over 80 per cent of the population profess to be Muslims, most are not extremists and many are not practising. On some islands, other religions predominate – for example, Hindus on Bali, Catholics on Flores, Protestants on Sumba, etc.

ASIA

Whatever their religious background, in nearly all areas 'conservative dress' is appreciated. Forty-five per cent of Indonesians are employed in agriculture and half live on less than US$2 per day, which should be borne in mind when visiting this country. Nearly all Indonesians (except the very old) speak Indonesian. Learning a little of this very easy language will go a long way in relating to local people out of tourist zones.

VOL
DEJAVATO FOUNDATION INDONESIA
Grassroots volunteer organization.

Contact: Ketut Purwantoro
Tel: +62 2470345516
Email: dejavato@yahoo.com
Web: www.dejavato.com
Address: Jl Borobudur Utara Raya No 35 Manyaran, 50147 Semarang Barat

VOL
INDONESIAN INTERNATIONAL WORKCAMPS ASSOCIATION (IIWC)
This association runs a varied programme of workcamps, including links to the Indonesia Planned Parenthood Association.

Contact: Pujiarti
Tel: +62 247603503 • +62 247609648
Fax: +62 247601989
Email: iiwc1@yahoo.com
Web: www.geocities.com/indonesiainternationalworkcamp/IIWC.html
Address: Jl Jembawan No 8, 50145 Semarang, Central Java, Indonesia

ACCOM+/TOUR
KALIMANTAN TOUR DESTINATIONS
This is self-declared 'tourism with a purpose' in the areas of nature conservation and poverty alleviation. A boat hotel will take you along the rivers not into a Conradian heart of darkness, but into the stress-free experience of the heart of Borneo. You can also take advantage of tailor-made tours including orang-utan and nature tours, longhouse and culture tours, adventure and trekking. This cocktail of comfort and jungle is unusual and one of the better manifestations of ecotourism.

Contact: Henry Fauziah
Tel: +62 811520648
Email: kalimantantours@gmail.com
Web: www.wowborneo.com
Address: Kalimantan Tour Destinations, PO Box 71, Palangkaraya 73112, Central Kalimantan, Indonesia

ACCOM
LSM TANA TAM KRAYAN HULU
This project is located in the subdistrict of Krayan, Nunukan district, East Kalimantan, Borneo. The Krayan Hulu Ecotourism Committee has opened homestay accommodation for tourists. Facilities are modest but adequate, and guests can enjoy a friendly and gentle atmosphere with a host family in Long Layu, Tang Laan and Tanjung Pasir. Visitors can go trekking and take day tours accompanied by local guides.

Contact: Gat Khaleb
Tel: +62 55134010
Email: awing@samarinda.com • tana_tam@yahoo.com
Web: www.borneo-ecotourism.com

LUX+
NIHIWATU RESORT

An upmarket hideaway destination on the island of Sumba in eastern Indonesia. Guests can participate in 46 land- and sea-based activities. On land the focus is on Sumbanese culture and guests are invited to become involved in helping the local community through a foundation. Its philosophy is to be the vehicle of positive change to the community. Staff wear traditional dress, onsite weavers make traditional blankets for the hotel, and local guides take guests on Sumbanese cultural tours.

Contact: Claude Graves
Tel: +62 361757159
Fax: +62 361755259
Email: info@nihiwatu.com
Web: www.nihiwatu.com
Address: Jln Setia Budi, Kuta Poleng Bloc C/2, Kuta – Bali 80361, Indonesia

TREK/ORG
RINJANI TREK ECOTOURISM

Based on the Indonesian island of Lombok, visitors take a guided trek to Mount Rinjani to enjoy the view of the crater lake and panorama from the summit. There are also hot springs and caves in the area. Other journeys that guests can take include a village walk and a hill trek through the rainforest on the other side of Mount Rinjani.

Contact: Ms Liana
Tel: +62 370641124
Fax: +62 370641124
Email: rinjani@indo.net.id • rtmb_lombok@indo.net.id
Web: www.lombokrinjanitrek.org
Address: Rinjani Trek Ecotourism Programme, c/o Lombok Raya Hotel, Jl Panca Usaha No 11, Mataram – NTB, Indonesia

LAOS
International dialling code +856

Dominated by the Mekong and its tributaries, which cut through rugged jungle-covered mountains, Laos, for so long obscured by its more powerful neighbours, is today beginning to assert itself as a must-see destination. Isolated by its terrain and its rudimentary infrastructure, Laos has retained a slow pace of life that affords the visitor a glimpse of a bygone age. In towns such as Luang Prabang, crumbling colonial shop fronts are punctuated with ornate Buddhist temples, outside which sit saffron-robed monks shading from the sun. In a country where 85 per cent of the population are subsistence farmers, life in the countryside has changed little in the last 100 years.

Landlocked and sandwiched between Vietnam and Thailand and with a population comprising over 68 ethnic groups, this diminutive land hides a tragic recent history. Laos has the unfortunate distinction of being, during the Vietnam War, the most heavily bombed nation. In an attempt to destroy North Vietnamese supply routes, the USA waged an illegal and secret war in Laos in which it dropped more bombs than were dropped during the entire World War II, with catastrophic implications for Laos where today unexploded ordnance litters the land.

In 1973, the Pathet Lao came to power, establishing the Laos Peoples' Democratic Republic and sweeping away 600 years of monarchy. Following the collapse of the Soviet Union, upon which Laos was heavily dependent, the country opened its borders in the early 1990s to investors and tourists.

TREK/HOST
EXOTISSIMO TRAVEL LAOS – PROJECT: AKHA EXPERIENCE
The Akha Experience is an authentic ecotourism experience in northern Laos. A joint enterprise of eight villages, it is designed to foster environmental and cultural awareness, as well as contributing to the economic well-being of the villagers involved. Participants travel round the Akha area on a homestay basis and receive genuine insight into the lives of the Akha. It has become clear that the presence of tourists on this basis has not impinged negatively upon villagers or their lifestyle.

Contact: Jean-Yves Paille or Mrs Phetsamone
Tel: +856 21241861 · +856 21241862 · +856 21241863
Fax: +856 21262001
Email: jeanyves@exotissimo.com
Web: www.exotissimo.com
Address: Exotissimo Travel Laos, 44 Pangkham Street, PO Box 4666, Vientiane, Lao PDR

TREK
SAVANNAKHET ECO-GUIDE UNIT
These treks offer visitors the opportunity to explore protected areas in the Savannakhet Province of Laos. There are opportunities to experience daily life in local villages, learn about the customs and traditions of different ethnic groups, and discover the importance of the forest to the local economy. Visitors will find out how the forest provides food, medicine and fuel, and see the wildlife of the forest, including various species of monkey and birds. By participating, travellers have a chance to assist the economic and socio-cultural development of the villages, as well as helping the environment through contributing to the conservation of protected areas.

Contact: Khaisy Vongphoumy
Tel: +856 41214203
Fax: +856 41214203
Email: savannakhetguides2@yahoo.com
Web: www.ecotourismlaos.com
Address: Provincial Tourism Office, Savannakhet, Lao PDR

ACCOM+
THE BOAT LANDING GUEST HOUSE
The owners of this guest house are trying hard to assist the surrounding community of diverse ethnic groups in Luang Namtha by putting guests in touch with tourism service providers, such as boatmen, taxi drivers and guides. Offering varied activities, including bike tours, they also advise other local guest houses and restaurants in areas such as marketing and presentation. They constantly spread the word as to how communities can benefit from tourism, raise money for local projects, and benefit the community by purchasing goods and services in the area.

Contact: Joy Khantisouk
Tel: +856 86312398
Fax: +856 86312239
Email: theboatlanding@yahoo.com
Web: www.theboatlanding.com
Address: PO Box 28, Luang Namtha, Laos

ASIA

DAY
VIENGXAY CAVES VISITOR CENTRE
Viengxay is the location of the 'Hidden City', a network of caves used by the Pathet Lao revolutionary movement to hide from the US, which set out to destroy the revolutionaries in secret bombing raids lasting from 1964 to 1973. More than 20,000 people made the caves their home and they functioned as government ministries, markets, factories, schools, hospitals and even a theatre. Visitors can take a guided tour of the caves and learn about their fascinating history. After exploring the caves, there are several possible activities, including enjoying the leafy, tranquil gardens outside, hiring a bicycle to see the surrounding countryside, or going for a walk around the town of Viengxay.

Contact: Khonephaphane Leuangsychanthong
Tel: +856 64314321
Fax: +856 64314321
Address: Viengxay Town, Houaphanh Province, Lao PDR

ACCOM
WELCOME HOME
Welcome Home offers individual travellers and small groups a chance to share the lives and homes of families in Laos for a few days. During their stay, visitors can learn firsthand about day-to-day life, the country's diverse culture and social heritage. Host families and travellers both sign an ethical charter, which encourages mutual respect and a friendly relationship. There is no fixed schedule or range of activities for homestays; travellers can explore the region with their hosts, and often find they give as much as they take, trading a French lesson for a cooking class, or lending a hand in the kitchen garden in return for the loan of a bicycle. Prices range from 15 to 40 Euros per night and include three meals.

Tel: +33 296326625
Fax: +33 296326638
Email: voyageethique@aol.com
Web: www.welcomehome.fr
Address: Resmarec, F-22170 Lanrodec, France

MALAYSIA
International dialling code +60

Split between the Malay Peninsula and its two Borneo states of Sabah and Sarawak, this historic trading route from Europe to China and India is a cultural melting pot of Malays, Indians and Chinese. These people bring with them a wealth of culture through their Islamic, Buddhist, Taoist and Hindi religions, festivals and varied cuisine. Malaysia boasts a rapidly developing economy, with major cities such as its capital, Kuala Lumpur, hosting modern hotels and shopping malls. Closer investigation into cities such as Georgetown on Penang Island in the north reveals Chinese and Indian cultural districts.

Away from the cities the natural beauty of the country can be explored: from popular, beautiful islands such as Palau Langkawi to the inner regional rainforests and their hidden caves, waterfalls and canopy walkways, offering glimpses of its illusive wildlife and primary rainforest for the determined trekker. Sabah can offer spectacular interactions with nature, including the world's largest flower (*Rafflesia*).

An accessible tourist route assent of the highest peak in Southeast Asia, Mount Kinabalu, presents the opportunity to take in the sun rising across the region. To the east, Sepilok offers an opportunity to experience our close cousins, the orang-utan. Palau Sipadan is a popular dive destination with everything from turtles to sharks. For the more adventurous, Sarawak can offer river rides to interact with local indigenous peoples; however, one should note that tribes such as the Penan in this area are threatened by encroaching development and logging.

ACCOM
BAGUS PLACE RETREAT, TIOMAN ISLAND
Environmentally friendly accommodation in a magical, natural paradise location. The resort is only accessible by boat, ensuring that the location is uniquely available to guests. There are five chalets on site with a maximum of 20 guests and eight staff, small enough to maintain privacy, exclusivity and minimal impact upon the surroundings. The resort is co-owned by two local families and sets out to demonstrate that sustainable development can be achieved by small businesses and still be profitable. Bagus Place is built using local materials such as wood and woven palm leaves in harmony with the environment and avoiding concrete. The food is sourced locally, with lots of freshly caught fish, and most of the staff are from the area.

Contact: Ajay Barai
Tel: +44 7740358020
Email: reservation@bagusplace.com • ajaybarai@totalise.co.uk
Web: www.bagusplace.com

RAINFOREST
BORNEO ADVENTURE/ULU AI PROJECT
Ulu Ai is a traditional longhouse in the Iban heartland, situated in the remote interior of Borneo. A trip to Ulu Ai offers a glimpse into the lifestyles of the local tribes, who for centuries have lived simply, following schedules imposed only by the cycles of nature. The surroundings are idyllic, with clear, clean streams, waterfalls and treks along rainforest trails. Accommodation is at the Borneo Adventure Lodge, which provides simple, clean lodging with Western-style toilets. Visitors can go trekking or travel upriver by longboat and can visit the longhouse and surrounding farms, as well as participate in the daily activities of the Iban people. The enterprise works with and helps the local community by, for example, building a sanitary system to improve health and by setting up a scholarship fund.

A second lodge is located further upriver, Lubok Kasai Lodge, which has been built with the intention of spreading out visitors to the surrounding area. It is even more exclusive compared to the Borneo Adventure Lodge, but offers the same activities.

Contact: Carsten Jensen
Tel: +60 82245175
Fax: +60 82422626
Email: sales@borneoadventure.com
Web: www.borneoadventure.com
Address: No 55 Main Bazaar, 93000, Kuching, Malaysia

DAY/TOUR
BORNEO TOUCH ECOTOURS
This is a family business offering a range of activities such as mountain biking, rafting, climbing, hiking and caving within the national parks. The company has good relations with the indigenous tribes, who benefit from tourist spending and also receive a proportion of the profits and interest-free loans. It hopes to develop an eco-lodge and to organize stays in traditional longhouses.

Contact: Lim Chong Teah
Tel: +60 85211515
Email: walktomulu@yahoo.com.my • borneotouch@yahoo.ca
Web: www.walk2mulu.com
Address: PO Box 10, Limbang, Sarawak, 98700, Malaysia

HOST/TOUR
RED APE ENCOUNTERS AND ADVENTURES
Red Ape offers an educational tour to an orang-utan study site where there is a population of 1000, the largest in Malaysia. The ecotourism company has a scientific research division, and a place for visitors to observe and participate in research work, contributing to the conservation of the orang-utan in the Kinabatangan and the preservation of their natural habitat. Trained research assistants act as nature guides.

Contact: Mohd. Suhailie
Tel: +60 89230268
Fax: +60 89230268
Email: info@redapeencounters.com • suhailie@redapeencounters.com
Web: www.redapeencounters.com
Address: Sdn Bhd (630230-P, KPL/LN: 3981), PO Box 3109, 90734 Sandakan, Sabah, Malaysia

ASIA

THAILAND
International dialling code +66

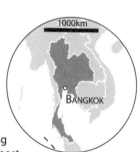

To many people, especially backpackers, the popular image of Thailand is just 'bars and beaches'. To experience the real Thailand requires knowledge and guidance that is rarely featured in holiday brochures or offered by regular travel agents. Yet, there is so much to see and learn in getting to know a fascinating culture so different from our own. It is one of the most strongly Buddhist countries that, among many other things, shows deep respect for the elders both in spiritual practices and everyday life.

Never colonized, the Kingdom of Thailand (or Siam as it used to be known) is a proud country which has adopted many Western ways by choice, but where deep-rooted Asian values endure beneath the glossy veneer of modernity, particularly in rural areas where traditional crafts are very important.

Craft communicates a community's culture without the need for language and helps to build a relationship based on respect for complex, inherited skills. The true value of home-spun and hand-loomed silks, natural dyes, bamboo baskets and intricate silver jewellery, for example, can only be fully appreciated when visiting village communities. Equally important is the context of everyday life around which the crafts are created, which is now being challenged by the intrusions of modern life.

Thailand's reputation as a 'land of smiles', a golden place of mountains, beaches and rice fields with a tradition of hospitality, contrasts with the fact that it is a country that has had military governments on and off between 1947 and 1992 and again between 2006 and 2007. There is political unrest and a high threat of terrorism and, as most people now know, a large-scale sex industry that contributes to a high rate of HIV infection. It is also the country that was hardest hit by the tsunami in 2004.

TOUR
AKHA HILL TRIBE
About 23km from Chiang Rai in the mountains of northern Thailand, at an altitude of 1500m, guests can stay with the Akha people in a project bungalow, knowing that all the profits from their stay are going into the community, and its school and education system. Anyone who does well at school is helped financially to go and study further elsewhere. Akha Hill Tribe offers jungle treks with expert guides, where visitors can catch fish, stay overnight in a banana leaf house, and meet other hill tribes. Please note that tourism is the only source of income since the Thai government banned slash-and-burn farming. There are free daily pick-ups from anywhere within Chiang Rai.

Contact: Jennifer Newton
Tel: +66 0899975505
Fax: +66 053918442
Email: apaehouse@hotmail.com
Web: www.akhahill.com

HOST/VOL/TREK
ANDAMAN DISCOVERIES (AD)
Born out of tsunami relief operations in 2005, this is a grassroots operation offering village-based tours, homestays and volunteer opportunities. The goal is to promote self-sufficiency and auton-omy in the areas of community-based tourism (CBT) and community-led development. CBT is at the heart of AD – the operation connects communities who wish to tap into tourism, and volun-teers who are interested in traditional lifestyles and a pristine ecosystem.

Contact: Mimi Rogers
Tel: +66 879177165
Email: info@andamandiscoveries.com
Web: www.andamandiscoveries.com
Address: 120/2 Sukapiban 3, Kura, Kuraburi, Phang Nga, 82150 Thailand

VOL/TREK/HOST
CBT-I
CBT-I (Thailand Community-Based Tourism Institute) is an NGO working under the umbrella of the Thailand Research Fund, which offers training and consultancy services and also study tours. Its previous incarnation was as Responsible Ecological Social Tours (REST). The CBT programmes are built around those aspects of their lives and culture which local people value highly and wish to share with guests on their own terms. They develop skills and support local projects and the envi-ronment.

Contact: Thiratee Chaijaree (neck_cbtn@yahoo.com) or Potjana Suansri
Tel: +66 53948286
Fax: +66 53807001
Email: info@cbt-i.org • Potjana@cbt-i.org
Web: www.cbt-i.org
Address: PO Box 259, Chiang Mai University Post Office, Chiang Mai 50202, Thailand

DAY/ACCOM/VOL
ELEPHANT NATURE PARK
Do you like elephants playing tricks? Stay away. What you will get if you go will be the chance to interact with domestic elephants both positively and non-exploitatively. This project was devel-oped as a model for sustainable and progressive elephant tourism. You observe natural elephant behaviour and join in basic care for the beasts. Volunteers also visit the neighbouring Thai com-munity to help with English teaching at the local school.

Contact: Saa
Tel: +66 53208246

Fax: +66 53208247
Email: jeff@elephantnaturefoundation.org · booking@elephantnaturefoundation.org
Web: www.elephantnaturefoundation.org
Address: 1 Ratmakka Road, Muang District, Chiang Mai, 50100 Thailand

ACCOM+/AGRI
GECKO VILLA

Constructed by local villagers and with services and goods sourced locally, this is a vacation rental with that little difference. You have a choice: stay in your villa (it is all-inclusive) and lie by the pool or be integrated within local ways of life by the families who run the project. Alternatively, you can get the best of both worlds. Either way you will be off the beaten tourist track and experience the real Thailand.

Contact: Ten
Tel: +66 819180500
Email: info@geckovilla.com
Web: www.geckovilla.com
Address: Baan Um Jaan, A. Prajak Sinlaphakom, Udon Thani, 41110 Thailand

TREK
JORKOE ECOTREK

JorKoe means 'traveller with long vision' in the Karen language. An alternative tour operator based in Mae Hong Son in the upper northwest of Thailand, bordering Burma. It offers community-based sustainable tourism tours and homestays in ethnic minority villages. JorKoe was founded as a fund-raising unit and as a vehicle to share ecotourism projects with visitors, which are implemented by the Thai environmental NGO Project for Recovery of Life and Culture. All accommodation is provided by local families in the communities and has basic facilities.

Tel: +66 53620644
Fax: +66 53620644
Email: prlc@ymail.com
Web: www.huaiheevillage.blogspot.com
Address: JorKoe EcoTrek, 82/1 Khunlum Prapas Rd, Tambon Jongkam, Amphur Muang, Mae Hong Son 58000, Thailand

ACCOM
KOH RA ECOLODGE

The lodge is located on the Andaman sea coast on unspoiled coastline and on the nearest island to Surin National Park. Home to an ecological research programme, it offers many affordable activities such as hiking and diving. Flora and fauna abound. There are 15 bungalow-style rooms with private baths. The central lodge has a restaurant and common area.

Contact: Kim Obermeyer
Tel: +66 871323150
Email: info@thaiecolodge.com
Web: www.thaiecolodge.com
Address: PO Box 10, Kuraburi, Kuta, Phang Nga 82150, Thailand

HOST/SCHOOL/DAY
LAMAI HOMESTAY AND VILLAGE TOURS

A homestay for up to six people in a rural northern Thai village, offering a choice of activities. Most guests opt for a cultural/historical tour of the Khmer ruins at Phimai or Phanom and the archaeological site at Ban Prasat. Visitors can participate in a range of rural craft activities, including a half-day course in spinning or weaving silk, a morning of Isan cookery lessons, an afternoon of raffia mat and basket making, or even rice planting or harvesting, depending upon the season.

ASIA

Contact: Ann Moore
Tel: +66 62585894 (Thailand) · +44 1970871464 (UK)
Fax: +44 1970871995 (UK)
Email: annmoore@northfieldenterprises.co.uk
Web: www.thailandhomestay.com
Address: 23/1 M003, Ban Ko Phet, Bua Yai, Khorat Province, Thailand

HOST
NATURAL FOCUS
Forget Bangkok and Full Moon parties; lift your eyes to the hills of northern Thailand where wisdom comes from. Go and stay with a hill tribe village and learn about traditional culture and how local people use the wisdom of the ages to preserve nature. You will participate in all aspects of life – and share a little of your own background. This makes the management jargon phrase 'a change of experience' almost relevant to real life. This is community-based tourism at its simple best.

Contact: Chookiat Kananusapkul
Tel: +66 53758658
Fax: +66 53758658
Email: Naturalfocus_ecotour@hotmail.com · poo@naturalfocus-cbt.com
Web: www.naturalfocus-cbt.com
Address: 129/1 Moo 4, Soi 4 Pah-Ngiew Road, T. Rob Wiang, Muang, Chiang Rai 57000, Thailand

HOST/TOUR
PDA TOUR
PDA Tour is an agency under the All North Company Limited. The company was created to generate income to support community development in Chiang Rai Province, northern Thailand. The community-based tourism activities in the villages belong to the villagers. Examples of their tours include a day tour of Chiang Rai City, a trip to hill tribe villages, an elephant safari and a tour of the Golden Triangle. Local people are involved in many roles such as porters, guides and hosts of homestays.

Contact: Alberto C. de la Paz
Tel: +66 53740088
Fax: +66 53740088
Email: crpda@hotmail.com · crpdatour@hotmail.com
Web: www.pda.or.th/chiangrai
Address: PDA Tour (All North Co Ltd), 620/25 Thanalai Road, Amphur Muang, Chiang Rai 57000, Thailand

TREK
POOH ECO TREKKING
An environmentally conscious trek in a small group of four to six people in a Pwo Karen hill tribe village in Mae Hong Son Province in northern Thailand. Visitors learn about hill tribe culture, go camping, caving, wade up rivers and learn how to cook naturally and organically in the tradition of the hill tribe people. To minimize the environmental impact, all waste is brought back. Pooh Eco Trekking also helps the local people by providing money for transportation to hospital, and has educated the villagers to recycle waste and run a co-operative shop where the profits are distributed among local families.

Contact: Pooh · Tee
Tel: +66 53208538 · +66 850414971
Fax: +66 53208538
Email: remimin@loxinfo.co.th
Web: www.pooh-ecotrekking.com
Address: 59 Rajchapakinai Rd, Muang, Chiang Mai 50200, Thailand

ASIA

HOST/TOUR
THAILAND HILLTRIBE HOLIDAYS

If you want an insight into a local way of life you could do worse than experience a homestay with a hill tribe family in northern Thailand. The traditional ways of life still hold sway, and this is your chance to experience them ethically and responsibly. You will be with a family in a mountain village inhabited by one of the ethnic minorities such the Lawa or the Karen. The noun 'ecosystem' would assume a new meaning for you at Mae Hong Son.

Contact: Melissa Ah-Sing
Tel: +66 871904469
Email: mja1906@hotmail.com
Web: www.thailandhilltribeholidays.com
Address: 66 mu 12t bankdad, Mae Sariang, Mae Hong Son, 58110, Thailand

VIETNAM
International dialling code +84

1000km

HANOI

It is hard not to let first impressions of Vietnam be characterized by images of the Vietnam War, and yet the country has a lot more to offer than a history of atrocities and bloodshed. This long, thin stretch of land, flanked by Laos and Cambodia on the west and 3000km of coastline on the east, boasts bleached white beaches, paddy fields dotted with the ubiquitous conical hat-clad farmers, heaving head-spinning cities, jungle treks and mist-enfolded pagodas. Despite a decade of war and a legacy of trade embargoes and international isolation, the country is rapidly reinventing itself and is finally beginning to shake off its more damaging communist stereotypes of the past. Today there are few visible reminders of the conflict which saw over 5 million tonnes of bombs dropped, accounting for the loss of 2.2 million hectares of forest. The craters that still pockmark the country are slowly being refilled or used as fish farms or small-scale irrigation systems. Vietnam is a country of growing biodiversity and home to a number of rare and endangered species, including the Javan rhino, thought only to exist in Indonesia, until a recent discovery in 1989, and the previously unknown soala, a species of ox. A trip into the hill country of the north may lead to an invitation into one of the traditional communal longhouses where you can experience unrivalled hospitality and elaborate displays of age-old customs, complete with tribal costumes and rice wine. Alternatively, a foray into Hanoi, Vietnam's Northern capital, or Ho Chi Minh City, the largest city of the South, encourages you to explore the country's cultural heritage at a slightly more frantic pace.

ACCOM/TREK
A LUOI COMMUNITY-BASED ECOTOURISM INITIATIVE

A Luoi district is located in the Thua Thien Hue Province of Vietnam. The area is rich in history and visitors can visit sites from the Vietnam War such as Hamburger Hill and the Hong Bac tunnels, and travel along the Ho Chi Minh Trail. Guests can stay overnight at a Ta Oi communal house, enjoying traditional music and dancing, and observe local production of handicrafts such as Det Zeng textile weaving. Local guides also take visitors into the forest where they may see flying squirrels, gibbons and pheasants, and enjoy a picnic beside a waterfall. The initiative is supported by the Dutch group SNV.

Contact: Tran Quang Hao
Tel: +84 54830117
Fax: +84 54820257
Email: duyenanhpt@snvworld.org
Web: www.snv.org.vn
Address: SNV Vietnam, North Central Office, 14 Nguyen Van Cu St, Hue City, Vietnam

BUDGET/TOUR
DOI VILLAGE TOURISM INITIATIVE – SNVVIETNAM

This community tourism project aims to bring tourism income to one of the poorest but most interesting regions of Vietnam. Visitors can explore and have lunch at the community house, visit the nearby Kazan Waterfall and Forest, and learn about integrated farming techniques at local home gardens. Guests can stay the night at the traditional communal house and see local crafts-people produce textiles and weave bamboo, as well as sample the high-quality locally produced honey. Visitors can also enjoy the traditional ceremonies of the Katu people and learn about their customs and beliefs.

Contact: Pham Thi Duyen Anh
Tel: +84 54830117
Fax: +84 54820257
Email: duyenhpt@snvworld.org
Web: www.snv.org.vn
Address: SNV Vietnam, North Central Office, 14 Nguyen Van Cu St, Hue City, Vietnam

TOUR OP
FOOTPRINT VIETNAM TRAVEL

Footprint is a tour operator owned and run by three Vietnamese guides. It organizes responsible travel packages and community-based tourism in the north and Mekong Delta, designed in agreement and in cooperation with the local people. These include trekking and cycling trips and small group travel in junks. It also has an education programme to teach children to prevent disease from water and daily activities. By cooperating with the local population, it is able to train them to manage and operate their own projects and support them as they develop ways to harness traditional handicrafts and agriculture for tourism purposes. In this way the local community directly participates and benefits from tourism rather than feels that it is imposed upon them.

Contact: Mr Thanh
Tel: +84 49332844
Fax: +84 49332855
Email: info@footprint.vn
Web: www.footprint.vn
Address: 6 Le Thanh Tong, Hanoi, Vietnam

LUX/DAY
HUETOURIST COMPANY

A community ecotourism project that takes visitors to Tam Giang Lagoon. At over 70km it is the largest in Southeast Asia, and has a rich biodiversity of flora and fauna. Guests can experience daily life in the town of Thuan An, go fishing, plant trees, or observe local crafts such as weaving fishing nets and bamboo mats. Visitors can also explore the mangrove forest, a wetland environment that is home to marine plants and a variety of wildlife, or simply enjoy the spectacular views overlooking the lagoon and have a picnic at Thuan An Beach. Guests can stay overnight at the luxury Abalone resort and spa and Hue Anamandara.

Contact: Tran Quang Hao
Tel: +84 54856967 · 0913458464
Fax: +84 054866033
Email: huetourist@vnn.vn · info@huetouristvietnam.com
Web: www.huetouristvietnam.com

ASIA

217

VOL
SOLIDARITÉS JEUNESSES VIETNAM
A young but extremely dynamic youth association running short- and long-term volunteering programmes mainly around social issues.

Contact: Phuc Do Ti
Tel: +84 4215 4993
Fax: +84 4719 5080
Email: info@sjvietnam.org
Web: www.sjvietnam.org
Address: Office 306, Bldg C6, Block 1, My Dinh 1, Hanoi, Vietnam

ORG/HOST/TOUR
SUPPORT TO SUSTAINABLE TOURISM DEVELOPMENT IN SA PA DISTRICT, LAO CAI PROVINCE
A community-based tourism project that offers homestays in the four ethnic minority villages of Sa Pa in northern Vietnam. Local guides take visitors to see traditional handicrafts being made, folk games and traditional dancing. Trekking and adventure tours are also available as well as agro-tourism tours. The project's aim is to assist the local ethnic minority population in acquiring the necessary knowledge and skills to participate in sustainable community-based tourism. There is also a visitor centre with a museum, craft shop, café and bookshop.

Contact: Nguyen Van Manh
Tel: +84 20871976 • +84 983247519
Fax: +84 20871976
Email: sapatipc@gmail.com • cuong@snv.org.vn
Web: www.snv.org.vn • www.sapa-hotels.com
Address: Nguyen Van Manh, The Sa Pa Tourism Information and Promotion Center, 02 Xuan Vien Street, Sa Pa District, Lao Cai Province, Vietnam

ACCOM/ECO
TOPAS ECO-LODGE
Topas operates this eco-lodge in the hills of North Vietnam. Neighbouring valleys house the minority peoples, the Tay and Red Dao. There are 25 individual lodges in a circle around the hills and each has its own toilet and shower facilities. You can be active and trek or cycle … or just lean back into the peace and quiet and relax. About 75 per cent of the staff are local and from the ethnic minorities in the surrounding villages.

Contact: Tran Ngoc Quan
Tel: +84 437151005
Fax: +84 437151007
Email: info@topas-eco-lodge.com
Web: www.topas-eco-lodge.com
Address: 52 To Ngoc Van, Tay Ho, Hanoi, Vietnam

TREK
TOPAS TRAVEL
Topas is an enabling organization – a tour operator rather than a destination or holiday type *per se*. Originally limited to North Vietnam, it now ranges over the whole country and is able to arrange trips to Laos and Cambodia as well. The specific focus is individual or small group travel and every attempt is made to respect the environment and indigenous culture and lifestyle.

Contact: Mai Xuan Truong
Tel: +84 437151005
Fax: +84 437151007
Email: info@topastravel.vn
Web: www.topastravel.vn
Address: 52 To Ngoc Van, Tay Ho, Hanoi, Vietnam

MIDDLE EAST

JORDAN
International dialling code +962

Don't be surprised when you get to Jordan and a Bedouin invites you to his tent for a cup of sweet tea. The hospitality and warmth of the Jordanian people is just one of the many surprises you'll experience in the Hashemite Kingdom.

400km

AMMAN

From north to south, Jordan's landscape is full of beautiful surprises, with archaeological riches from Neolithic man and relics from many of the world's great civilizations. In the north, you'll stand on hills covered with olive and pine trees that overlook the historic Sea of Galilee. Heading south, you'll come to the lowest place on Earth, the Dead Sea with its healing mineral-laden waters. The salty sea is located in the subtropical Jordan Valley where bananas, tomatoes and watermelon grow year round. Further south is Petra, a registered UNESCO World Heritage site and Jordan's most popular tourist destination. With good reason: the amazing workmanship of the Nabateans and Romans feature amphitheatres and temples, tombs and elaborate buildings cut out of solid rock. Just south lies Wadi Rum, where *Lawrence of Arabia* was filmed, with its majestic mountains and vast desert. The southern tip of the country lies on the Red Sea where Aqaba offers a dream location for avid scuba divers.

The tourism industry has been affected by regional instability in the past several years. Despite these difficulties, Jordan is committed to developing a sustainable tourism industry and is implementing a national tourism strategy. The strategy aims to celebrate Jordan's amazing landscape and tourist sites while showing the rest of the world what hospitality really means.

ASIA

ACCOM+
AMMARIN BEDOUIN CAMP
This is almost the apotheosis of local community-based sustainable tourism. You live with the Bedouin and share their life, art and culture. And as you are within the Petra archaeological reserve, you see the rose-red city into the bargain. This is Bedouin heritage preservation which generates income for the local community.

Contact: Shireen Hijazi
Tel: +962 799755551/2
Fax: +962 65936359
Email: info@bedouincamp.net
Web: www.bedouincamp.net
Address: PO Box 1492, Amman 11118, Jordan

ORG/ACCOM
ROYAL SOCIETY FOR THE CONSERVATION OF NATURE (RSCN)

The Royal Society for the Conservation of Nature (RSCN) is an independent non-profit organization devoted to the conservation of Jordan's natural resources. Its aim is to preserve the biodiversity of Jordan and integrate its conservation programmes with socio-economic development. At the same time, it campaigns for wider public support and action for the protection of the natural environment within Jordan and neighbouring countries. Currently, the RSCN is managing six reserves and will establish more at the beginning of 2009. The RSCN supports local communities by providing work opportunities such as ecotourism and handicraft production, which are entirely managed by the local communities living in and around the reserves. There are many spectacular places to visit at the RSCN reserves, eco-lodges and camps to stay in, and plentiful hiking trails.

Tel: +962 64616523
Fax: +962 64633657
Email: tourism@rcn.org.jo
Web: www.rscn.org.jo
Address: PO Box 1215, Jubaiha 11941, Jordan

PALESTINE

Although Palestine does not yet exist as an independent country, it is generally accepted that its heartland lies in the West Bank, covering 6000 square kilometres west of the Jordan River. The Israeli occupation is tangible in some 120 illegal Jewish settlements, military outposts and checkpoints, and the wall separating the West Bank from Israel, and in the numerous Palestinian refugee camps that bear witness to the unresolved conflicts. Yet the area also attracts tourists and pilgrims since it resonates with ancient and biblical sites.

Among the best known in the arid southern hills of Judea, the town of Bethlehem is the birthplace of Jesus; while Hebron contains the Tomb of the Patriarchs, the burial place of Abraham, revered by both Muslims and Jews; and the palm-fringed city of Jericho, the oldest and lowest town on Earth, includes the spectacular remains of Hisham's summer palace. The northern greener area of ancient Samaria is home to Nablus, with its fascinating Old City, and the summer retreat of Ramallah. However, it is Jerusalem which lies at the political and cultural centre, with the Palestinian eastern side and the Old City containing the most interesting – and contested – sites, including the Church of the Holy Sepulchre, the site of the crucifixion, the Dome of the Rock, and the Western (Wailing) Wall.

Palestine also includes the Gaza Strip, on the Mediterranean coast between Israel and the Egyptian Sinai, from which Israeli settlements and military have recently withdrawn. As 'home' to some 900,000 Palestinian refugees, it is one of most densely populated areas on Earth, and its tourist sites and facilities are yet to be developed.

ORG/HOST/TOUR
ALTERNATIVE TOURISM GROUP (ATG)

The ATG was founded out of a belief that tourism to the area was excessively pilgrim oriented and gave no voice to contemporary Palestinian culture or political realities. Tours relate to present-day issues and can be geared to the specific needs of individuals and groups. Local development benefits – for example, 30 rooms in homes in and around Bethlehem have been restored for local families with whom one can stay on a bed-and-breakfast basis. Tourists are encouraged to stay within Palestinian areas so that their spending will foster revenue streams by the use of local tourist infrastructure such as hotels and restaurants. There is a genuine desire to foster contact between visitors and Palestinians and, therefore, to create a better understanding of the prevailing situation.

Contact: Rami Kassis
Tel: +972 22772151
Fax: +972 22772211
Email: info@atg.ps
Web: www.atg.ps
Address: PO Box 173, Beit Sahour, Palestine

TOUR+
INTERNATIONAL CENTRE OF BETHLEHEM/DIYAR CONSORTIUM
The centre, a member of the Diyar Consortium, developed an Authentic Tourism Programme guided by the strictures of a new theology of pilgrimage. This is a marriage of Christian pilgrimage and exposure to the contemporary situation – a holistic approach offering socially responsible travel and an opportunity for immersion in the local cultures and context.

Contact: Naim Odeh
Tel: +972 22770047
Fax: +972 22770048
Email: nodeh@annadwa.org
Web: www.annadwa.org
Address: Paul VI Street 109, PO Box 162, Bethlehem, Palestine

VOL
INTERNATIONAL PALESTINIAN YOUTH LEAGUE (IPYL)
A very active youth and volunteer organization which welcomes foreign volunteers and takes maximum care of their security.

Contact: Adli Daana
Tel: +972 222291 31
Fax: +972 22215586
Email: info@ipyl.org
Web: www.ipyl.org
Address: 5th Floor, Al-Isra Building, Jaffa Street, PO Box 618, Hebron, West Bank

TOUR+
OLIVE CO-OPERATIVE
Founded in 2003, the co-operative is British and completely worker owned. The *raison d'être* is to run small group tours of generally four to nine people to Palestine and Israel. It is hoped that the tours will promote peace and justice and economic viability in this troubled part of the world. Participants encounter people involved in a host of projects whose common denominator is benefit to the community. Two of the opportunities offered by Olive sum things up: to travel, laugh and exchange experiences; and to return informed and motivated to strive for just and lasting peace. Each tour is built around a theme or topic; but a seeming focus on the contemporary situation still includes visits to the holy places.

Contact: Leonie or Xen
Tel: +44 1612731970
Email: info@olivecoop.com
Web: www.olivecoop.com
Address: Olive Co-operative, 22a Beswick Street, Manchester, M15 5FH, UK

ASIA

OCEANIA

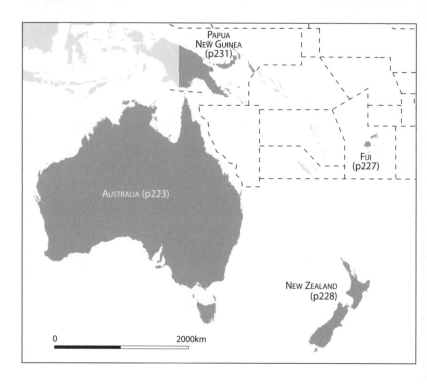

Papua New Guinea (p231)

Fiji (p227)

Australia (p223)

New Zealand (p228)

0   2000km

AUSTRALIA
International dialling code +61

Australia is a sunburned country, there's no doubt about it. The vast 5.2 million square kilometres of 'Outback' is inhospitably dry most of the time and as climate change gathers pace, water shortages cause increasing problems. The majority of Australians hug the coastline, facing the rolling sea. But there's more than surfing dudes and Outback Aboriginals to this beautiful island continent. There are snowy mountains, ancient rainforest, the largest coral reef in the world and spectacular geological phenomena. Combine this with a laid-back city life, where time on the beach or at outdoor cafés is as important as that in the office, and you have, possibly, the perfect destination. No wonder Australia often tops the polls of places to visit. From expensive tropical island hideaways to backpackers' lodges in bohemian seaside towns, there is something for every budget.

You can't leave Australia without learning about its first people. There are an increasing number of Aboriginal experiences. In Queensland's Daintree Rainforest – the oldest rainforest in the world – you can take a tour with clans that have been the traditional owners for millennia. At Uluru, an interpretive centre explains the religious significance of the world's largest monolith, which its traditional owners would prefer you not to climb. Even in Sydney's harbourside botanical gardens, there are guided walks explaining traditional medicinal uses of the plantlife.

DAY
ABORIGINAL BLUE MOUNTAINS WALKABOUT
On offer is a 'holistic Aboriginal cultural experience' – welcome to the dreamtime! This is a non-touristy traditional 8km walkabout along a songline – and accessible by a one-hour train ride from Sydney. This one-man operation aims to connect you to the sacred land. You learn by following the songline. Your senses will be stimulated and your spirit enriched, and you will be amazed at what one day can open up for you.

Contact: Evan Yanna Muru
Tel: +61 408443822
Email: walkaboutguide@yahoo.com
Web: www.BlueMountainsWalkabout.com
Address: PO Box 519, Springwood, NSW 2777, Australia

DAY/TOUR
ABORIGINAL CULTURAL TOURS
Aboriginal Cultural Tours will take you to rarely seen areas of Adjahdura Land (Yorke Peninsula, South Australia). This is an opportunity to walk in the countryside with direct descendants of the original owners of the land, to live with, talk with and experience firsthand their rich culture. Tours vary from one to five days.

Tel: 0429367121
Email: info@diversetravel.com.au • tours@adjahdura.com.au
Web: www.diversetravel.com.au • www.aboriginalaustraliatravel.com

OCEANIA

TOUR
BOOKABEE TOURS

With Aboriginal-owned and Adelaide-based Bookabee Tours you can travel both locally and also escape to the Flinders Ranges north of the city, which house the homeland of one of the two owners. On offer is relaxation plus a unique Aboriginal cultural experience. Listen to creation stories at traditional sites, see ancient paintings and engravings, learn about language and culture, and interact with the local community. Choices range from a two-hour guided museum tour in Adelaide to a five-day trip in the Flinders Ranges.

Contact: Lele Sanderson
Tel: +61 882359954
Fax: +61 882359954
Email: tours@bookabee.com.au
Web: www.bookabee.com.au
Address: PO Box 2134, Henley Beach, South Australia 5022, Australia

TOUR
BUNGOOLEE TOURS

The Bunuba people are the Aboriginal owners of Windjana Gorge, one of the Kimberleys' natural wonders, formed where the Lennard River cut through the old reef system at Tunnel Creek, Western Australia's oldest cave system. This area was the scene of bloody conflict in the late 19th century when local Aboriginal people put up fierce resistance to the inland movement of the European settlers. Tourism provides an opportunity to introduce visitors to historical and contemporary issues affecting the Aboriginal lifestyle, providing an Aboriginal perspective on the landscape and past of the people.

Tel: +61 8 83033418
Fax: +61 883034363
Email: info@diversetravel.com.au
Web: www.diversetravel.com.au • www.aboriginalaustraliatravel.com
Address: 35-37 Stirling Street, Thebarton, SA 5031, Australia

ACCOM+
COORONG WILDERNESS LODGE

The Ngarrindjeri people from Southeast Australia welcome guests to the Coorong. This haunting landscape of wild, untamed beaches, sheltered bays and inlets, and towering dunes plays host to an amazing array of migratory birds. The Ngarrindjeri people look forward to sharing the magic of the Coorong and their culture during the three-day tour. Included is a guided bush walk where visitors can experience the wonders of the Coorong's flora and fauna, and an opportunity to kayak along the beautiful waterways to the sand dunes and small islands. There is considerable birdlife to watch from the lodge. Luxury eco-cabins or basic en suite accommodation are available, as well as camping spaces with or without electricity.

Tel: +61 8 8575 6001
Fax: +61 8 8575 6041
Email: info@diversetravel.com.au
Web: www.diversetravel.com.au • www.aboriginalaustraliatravel.com
Address: Section 14 Hundred of Glyde, Princess Highway, Meningie, SA 5264, Australia

TOUR OP
DIVERSE TRAVEL AUSTRALIA (DTA)

Diverse Travel Australia (DTA) has been operating for 11 years, specializing in developing and promoting authentic Aboriginal tourism experiences both domestically and internationally. It has created close alliances with Aboriginal people and communities across Australia, and has been

OCEANIA

involved in assisting many of them with developing and growing their businesses. Most indige-nous tour businesses are specialized niche market operations and the mainstream travel industry has very limited ongoing knowledge, understanding or contact with the diverse spread of indige-nous experiences available. Diverse Travel is the only tour operator dedicated to developing and promoting indigenous tourism. People can find it difficult to access national Aboriginal experi-ences and often come to Diverse Travel for help in developing innovative and memorable itiner-aries that incorporate Aboriginal experiences with mainstream activities. It offers a very personal service and tailors any experience to suit your needs and budget.

Tel: +61 883033418
Fax: +61 883034363
Email: info@diversetravel.com.au
Web: www.diversetravel.com.au • www.aboriginalaustraliatravel.com
Address: 35-37 Stirling Street, Thebarton, SA 5031, Australia

TOUR
DREAMTIME CULTURAL CENTRE
The key words here are cultural centre: what is offered are guided tours of Aboriginal and Torres Strait Island culture. Among the phenomena included are boomerang throwing and didgeridoo playing. The conference centre can cater for a maximum of 90 persons. Rates are reasonable – this is not a luxury product, just a genuine experience.

Contact: Debra Pearce
Tel: +61 749361655
Fax: +61 749361671
Email: dtime1@iinet.net.au
Web: www.dreamtimecentre.com.au
Address: PO Box 6182, Central QLD Mail Centre, Rockhampton, QLD 4701, Australia

TOUR+
GUURRBI TOURS QUEENSLAND
This tour includes a visit to three rock art sites, including the Great Emu Cave, and provides a fas-cinating introduction to Aboriginal culture and society, as well as the traditional survival tech-niques of the Nugal-warra people.

Tel: +61 740696259
Email: info@diversetravel.com.au
Web: www.diversetravel.com.au • www.aboriginalaustraliatravel.com

TOUR
IGA WARTA
Iga Warta in the northern Flinders Ranges offers visitors an opportunity to experience Adnyamathanha culture and to share the bush with the indigenous people. Visitors have the opportunity to become part of the environment and to learn firsthand the importance of this area to the Adnyamathanha people. Tour options include artefact-making, visiting painting sites, becoming immersed in one of the world's oldest cultures, and learning about social history. Accommodation is available in safari tents, cabins or swag camping.

Tel: +61 886483737
Fax: +61 886483794
Email: enquiries@igawarta.com
Web: www.igawarta.com

OCEANIA

ACCOM+
KOOLJAMAN AT CAPE LEVEQUE
This wilderness camp is located 220km from Broome in Western Australia. It is entirely owned and run by the Bardi people, who try to ensure that their visitors enjoy themselves but also learn about the indigenous customs, culture and traditions of the land and ocean. Seven types of accommodation cater for all budgets, and what guests pay either goes into improving facilities or directly back to the communities. This holiday provides an aboriginal experience and superb beaches. Booking is essential and four-wheel drive is required.

Contact: Julie Blackburn
Tel: +61 891924970
Fax: +61 891924978
Email: leveque@bigpond.com
Web: www.kooljaman.com.au
Address: PMB 8, Cape Leveque, Via Broome, WA 6725, Australia

DAY
RAINBOW SERPENT TOUR – QUEENSLAND
This walk will take you through a dramatic landscape to six rock art sites, including an ancestral Birth Cave and the Reconciliation Cave, where you will hear the stories behind the paintings and why this art is so important to present and future generations of Nugal-warra people.

Tel: +61 740696259
Email: info@diversetravel.com.au
Web: www.diversetravel.com.au • www.aboriginalaustraliatravel.com

DAY/DIS
VALLEY OF THE GIANTS TREE TOP WALK
Based in Western Australia, the Tree Top Walk is an ambitiously designed elevated walkway that lifts visitors 40m above the forest floor through the forest canopy. Designed to preserve the forest of 400-year-old giant red tingle trees, which were under threat from the pressure of visitors, this award-winning project gives visitors a unique perspective as they watch birds fly below them. The project has full community involvement and is wheelchair accessible.

Contact: Julie Ross
Tel: +61 898408263
Fax: +61 898408132
Email: ttw@calm.wa.gov.au
Web: www.dec.wa.gov.au
Address: Department of CALM, South West Highway, Walpole, WA, 6398, Australia

DAY
WARDAN ABORIGINAL CULTURAL CENTRE
The Wardan Aboriginal Cultural Centre is an indigenous tourism project that was 12 years in the making. It is owned and operated by the Bibelmen Mia Aboriginal Corporation and Bill Webb is general manager and Elder. The region, bordered by the south-western Australia coastline to the Capel River in the southwest, was home to the Wardandi people. Bill and his sister Nina, who is head guide, tell childhood stories passed on from grandmothers and they have excellent knowledge of the plant and animals of their cultural heritage gained from frequent bush walks with their grandfather and father.

Tel: +61 897566566
Email: wardan@westnet.com.au
Web: www.wardan.com.au
Address: Injidup Springs Rd, PO Box 30, Yallingup, WA 6282, Australia

OCEANIA

FIJI
International dialling code +679

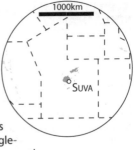

Fijians are some of the friendliest people on the planet. When you see their heavenly country, you understand why. This South Pacific nation consists of several hundred volcanic and coral land masses scattered across turquoise seas. It is an increasingly popular playground for Australians and New Zealanders, with hotels for every budget. From tiny sandy atolls to jagged jungle-covered mountains, there's more than enough to do for a month.

If it's the tropical island experience you want, then head for the Mamanuca or Yasawa island groups, or, if you have more time, to the outlying flat atolls of the Lau group. On the main island of Viti Levu, you can hike to the top of Mount Batilamu in Koroyanitu National Park or go white-water rafting. On Taveuni – 'the garden island' – you can hike into the rainforest to search for one of the world's rarest flowers – the tagimaucia. On Kadavu, people grow the best kava – a root made into a narcotic peppery brew and drunk as a welcome ceremony.

But it is the people whom you will remember most from a visit to Fiji: their cheery 'Bula' greeting, wide smiles and infectious laughter. A highlight of any visit should be some time with a family in a simple thatched *bure* homestay or in a village-run guest house. It may not be the smoothest operation, but relaxing to the rhythm of island life is life-changing.

HOST
FIJIAN VILLAGE HOMESTAYS

Visitors can experience a truly traditional village homestay. When they arrive they are adopted into the community and can participate in traditional village life. This may include ceremonies, daily activities and sharing traditional Fijian foods caught by the villagers. Children especially have an unforgettable time as they are instantly absorbed into the large group of youngsters who live there. Scott Balson, who personally meets the village Elders and arranges the homestay with them, runs the project. A large percentage of the income is placed in a village fund, which has resulted in the development of community halls and building of guest houses.

Contact: Scott Balson
Tel: +61 738927333
Fax: +61 738925333
Email: info@villagehomestays.com
Web: www.fijibure.com • www.villagehomestays.com
Address: PO Box 91, Wellers Hill, QLD 4121, Australia

OCEANIA

NEW ZEALAND
International dialling code +64

Ancient Maori myths place volcanoes at the very core of New Zealand's identity and are as much a part of the uniquely New Zealand way of life as they are a fiery force in its landscape. New Zealanders' innate sense of environmental sustainability and inner spirituality is manifested in the numerous towns making claim to zero waste and their pride in their 'greenness' awards. If it is a love of nature that is drawing you to New Zealand you will be delighted by the myriad of opportunities that present themselves. But while it is easy to feel that you are really at one with nature – for example, by experiencing the wilderness along the 130km Heaphy track in the South Island's northwest corner – tourist hot spots such as the South Island's glacial region have been ravaged by tourists and their insatiable desire for new experiences. The constant whirring of helicopters and small planes, giving visitors an aerial view of Fox Glacier, doesn't let you forget this.

Protest seems ingrained in the Kiwi psyche, which is perhaps due to their earlier victory against the nuclear industry. While visiting New Zealand you are bound to stumble across at least one inspiring local struggle.

In contrast to its Aussie neighbours, white New Zealanders hold a considerably more respectful attitude towards the indigenous Maori culture: many government signs are bilingual and Maori language is widely taught in schools.

DAY

BUSH AND BEYOND GUIDED WALKS

This is a conservation-based guided walking company working in New Zealand's Kahurangi National Park. It is determined to do nothing to compromise the park's wilderness qualities, which includes limiting its own growth as a business to what is sustainable. The walks have an emphasis on New Zealand's flora, fauna, geology and history. Their aim is to educate people on the very fragile ecology, and what we have to do to save the flora and fauna that we have left.

Contact: Maryann Ewers
Tel: +64 3528 9054
Email: info@bushandbeyond.co.nz
Web: www.bushandbeyond.co.nz
Address: PO Box 376, Motueka 7143, New Zealand

RAINFOREST+

CATLINS MOHUA PARK ECO-ACCOMMODATION

Catlins offers eco-cottages located on the edge of a 10ha native forest reserve at Mohua Park, Tawanui. Each cottage is self-contained, comfortable and private, with lovely views and as small an ecological footprint as possible, with solar water heating, extra insulation and an energy-efficient design. The area is ideal for walking, bird-watching, mountain biking and river fishing, and is a short drive to the Catlins waterfalls, coastal beaches and locations for evening dining.

Contact: Mary Sutherland
Tel: +64 34158613
Fax: +64 34158613
Email: info@catlinsmohuapark.co.nz
Web: www.catlinsmohuapark.co.nz
Address: 5 Mirren Street, Papatowai RD 2, Owaka, South Otago 9586, New Zealand

OCEANIA

TOUR
FOOTPRINTS WAIPOUA

Footprints Waipoua conducts guided walks and provides visitors with an opportunity to view, learn about and connect with the oldest and largest kauri trees in the world. It offers several day and night programmes: the signature tour is a four-hour night walk, Twilight Encounter. Experienced local Maori guides share their stories and songs and play musical instruments to enhance the natural sights and sounds of this tranquil and spiritual location. They also run a boat cruise on Hokianga harbour. Crossings Hokianga is a historical and cultural tour visiting the home of both New Zealand's first discoverer 1000 years ago, and of the early European settlers.

Contact: Nikki Stil
Tel: +64 94058207
Fax: +64 94058207
Email: info@footprintswaipoua.co.nz
Web: www.footprintswaipoua.co.nz
Address: PO Box 43, Opononi, Hokianga, Northland, New Zealand

ACCOM+
FRENCH PASS SEA SAFARIS AND BEACHFRONT VILLAS

Located at the end of a spectacular two-hour drive from Nelson, this 16-year-old operation offers accommodation and tours of marine interest – watching (and maybe swimming with) dolphins, seals and whales. The owners have been working for years to bring back native birdlife and to establish marine reserves by eradicating alien pest predators. French Pass itself is a small seaport on the Western Marlborough Sound. The accommodation is self-contained and is priced from $140 to $168 per couple.

Contact: Danny or Lyn Boulton
Tel: +64 35765204
Email: adventure@seasafaris.co.nz
Web: www.seasafaris.co.nz
Address: RD3 French Pass, Marlborough Sounds 7193, New Zealand

ACCOM/DAY
KAPITI ISLAND ALIVE

Kapiti Island has been cleared of all introduced pests and predators, allowing unsurpassed growth in many of New Zealand's rare and endangered native species. Visitors are taken on guided walks with flora and fauna interpretation, and learn about conserving the environment. Overnight guests at the nature lodge can go on guided night walks to find the little spotted kiwi, which only lives on the island. The guides and staff are local Maori belonging to the tribe of the area, and give guests an authentic insight into Maori history and culture.

Contact: Minnie Clark
Tel: +64 63626606
Fax: +64 63645028
Email: john@kapitiislandalive.co.nz • minnie@kapitiislandalive.co.nz
Web: www.kapitiislandalive.co.nz
Address: PO Box 28, Otaki, New Zealand

LUX
KNAPDALE ECO-LODGE

This eco-lodge was opened in 2004 and offers unequalled tranquillity, home and farm-based hospitality and dining. It endeavours to live off the land and to leave as small an ecological footprint as possible. It works with the local Maori community to give the visitor a unique and authentic cultural experience. There are two Maori historical sites on the property and visits to them are mediated by the Maori people. The setting is rural, but being only a ten-minute drive from Gisborne,

OCEANIA

offers both rural tranquillity and the convenience of a regional city with breathtaking beaches. At the moment there are only two rooms priced at NZ$363 (UK£115/US$205) and NZ$303 (UK£97/US$170), respectively, per night for luxurious accommodation and breakfast. Dinner is an additional NZ$75 per person.

Contact: Kees Weytmans
Tel: +64 68625444
Fax: +64 68625006
Email: kees@knapdale.co.nz
Web: www.knapdale.co.nz
Address: 114 Snowsill Road, Waihirere, Gisborne, New Zealand

DAY
TIRITIRI MATANGI ISLAND, DEPARTMENT OF CONSERVATION WILDLIFE RESERVE

This is an ecological restoration project creating a forest and habitat for New Zealand wildlife from bare farming paddocks. Visitors have the opportunity to view up close 11 endangered species, see the results of the community in action, and enjoy beautiful views of the Hauraki Gulf of Auckland. This is one of the top attractions in Auckland and offers an educational experience for people of all ages. A ferry company provides a regular service to the island.

Tel: +64 94245510 · 0800 888 006 (freephone)
Fax: +64 94245510
Email: info@kawaukat.co.nz
Web: www.360discovery.co.nz · www.tiritiri-matangi.htm

DAY
WHITE ISLAND TOURS

This tour takes passengers by boat to White Island, a live marine volcano. It is a one-hour drive from Rotorua or Tauranga. Visitors travel out in a purpose-built 60-foot (18m) launch for 80 minutes. Experienced and knowledgeable guides give a two-hour tour of New Zealand's only live marine volcano. Lunch is served on the boat before the return trip. There are plenty of opportunities to experience bird and marine life, especially dolphins and whales, and time is spent with these mammals whenever possible.

Contact: Dougal Stewart
Tel: +64 73089588
Fax: +64 73080303
Email: info@whiteisland.co.nz
Web: www.whiteisland.co.nz
Address: 15 The Strand East, Whakatane, New Zealand

OCEANIA

PAPUA NEW GUINEA
International dialling code +675

Papua New Guinea may well be the most linguistically and culturally diverse nation in the world. It is also one of the least explored, partly because of the rugged terrain with its steep mountain valleys and consequent difficulties in travelling about. About 80 per cent of the population live in rural areas in traditional societies, having little contact with each other, let alone the outside world. As a result, there are over 700 indigenous languages and myriads of different cultures.

Melanesian villages are full of ancient customs and rituals unchanged for centuries. Many still live a subsistence-based lifestyle – hunting, fishing and growing crops of taro and cassava while living in homes made of materials from the forest. There are coming-of-age ceremonies that involve painful body scarring and others that involve nothing more than fancy hairdressing.

Christian missionaries have tried to eradicate the animistic religions of remote tribes; but many traditional beliefs still hold sway. In recent decades, wealth from mining and logging has caused social divisions and violence. Unfortunately, law and order remains poor or very poor in many parts of the country.

Small-scale village tourism offers a more environmentally and socially friendly way to earn income for the essentials of modern life, such as outboard engines and fees for the local school. Among scuba divers, Papua New Guinea is famed for its marine biodiversity and many claim that its seas have the best diving in the world.

On the tallest snow-capped island on the planet, life is as varied as the landscape: from the cool, wet highland interior where birds of paradise display their plumes, down to the rainforest-clad banks of the mighty Sepik River, full of crocodiles, to low coral-fringed islands. Many undiscovered species of plants and animals are thought to exist in the interior.

RAINFOREST
KUMUL LODGE
This lodge began operations in 1998 and gives visitors a chance to enjoy activities such as birdwatching, orchid farming, trekking and mountain climbing.

Guests have the opportunity to interact with local villagers, participate in traditional cultural events, and purchase handicrafts. They would much prefer you to be in direct contact with nature and the people instead of viewing this from a bus! As well as being locally owned, Kumul Lodge serves as a rural development initiative that works in cooperation with the local village societies.

Contact: Kim Aru
Tel: +675 5421615 · +675 5422162
Radio telephone: +675 5474042 (lodge site)
Fax: +675 5421615
Email: kumul-lodge@global.net.pg
Web: www.kumullodge.com.pg
Address: Kumul Lodge Limited, PO Box 989, Mt Hagen WHP, Papua New Guinea

EUROPE

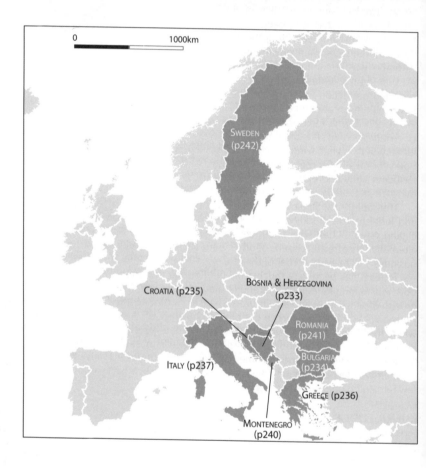

0   1000km

SWEDEN
(p242)

BOSNIA & HERZEGOVINA
(p233)

CROATIA (p235)

ROMANIA
(p241)

BULGARIA
(p234)

ITALY (p237)

GREECE (p236)

MONTENEGRO
(p240)

BOSNIA & HERZEGOVINA
International dialling code +387

300km

SARAJEVO

Situated in the heart of the Balkan peninsular, Bosnia and Herzegovina has long been a cultural junction between West and East. It is here that eastern Byzantine and Ottoman powers met and mingled with the Western influences of Rome, Venice and Austria. The thick forests and deep gorges have always provided protection for the waves of ancient tribes that have one time or another called Bosnia and Herzegovina home.

In 1992 Bosnia and Herzegovina became, for the first time since the 15th century, an independent state once again. In many ways this new country struggles for an identity of its own, having been embraced by its larger and more powerful neighbours for over half a millennium. Covering just over 51,000 square kilometres and including a tiny 22km slice of the Adriatic coast, its diverse cultures and traditions are mirrored in the amazing spread of Alpine and Mediterranean flora and fauna.

The capital city, Sarajevo, epitomizes this sacred mélange of Islam, Christianity and Judaism. This quickly changing city has been reborn into one of the most fascinating cultural bastions in Southeast Europe. The Sarajevo Film Festival, jazz fest, alternative theatre and dozens of other cultural manifestations have attracted curious guests from every corner of the globe.

Tourism has been very much a building bridge in Bosnia and Herzegovina in both rekindling old regional ties and forging new wider links, particularly with the growth of ecotourism and adventure tourism niches. While travelling in Bosnia and Herzegovina, make an effort to get off the beaten path. Visit the ancient villages where man and nature still live in harmony and where guests are treated like members of the family. Local foods are organically grown in most villages and the hospitality will have you wanting to come back for more. Bosnia and Herzegovina is an inexpensive, new and exciting destination right in Europe's backyard – one of the few remaining unexplored corners of the continent.

HOST/TOUR
GREEN VISIONS

Green Visions is a tour operator dedicated to promoting and preserving the cultural and natural heritage of Bosnia and Herzegovina. It sees ecotourism as a way to protect the highland communities of the Central Dinaric Alps. It follows a low-trace, no-impact policy organizing small group mountain tours to the 'old world European villages' throughout Bosnia and Herzegovina. Green Visions provides accommodation, transport, guides, meals and activities. These can vary from hiking, walking, biking, rafting, insightful cultural trips, youth camps, wildlife observation and medicinal herb-picking to skiing or snowshoeing. Visitors stay in rustic but cosy homestays or huts in the mountain villages, enjoying traditional organic food with a real chance to mingle with the local population. Guests leave with a true understanding of the environment that they have experienced, having connected with the social issues, cultures and traditions of the host community.

Contact: Dzenita Delibasic
Tel: +387 33717290 · +387 33717291
Skype: greenvisions
Email: Sarajevo@greenvision.ba
Web: www.greenvisions.ba
Address: Radnicka bb, Sarajevo 71000, Bosnia and Herzegovina

EUROPE

BULGARIA
International dialling code +359

Situated strategically in the very heart of the Balkans, Bulgaria's history and culture are a mesh of Slavic, Mediterranean and Central Asian influences. Having survived 500 years of Ottoman yoke and nearly 50 years of communist rule, Bulgarians are now rediscovering their country's historic and natural treasures. The discovery of ancient archaeological sites, such as the Rock City of Perperikon and the millennia-old tombs of Thracian kings, has made Bulgaria an interesting site for history buffs. Nature lovers won't be disappointed either. If you stay away from the overdeveloped Black Sea Coast, a countryside rich in wildlife and natural attractions is yours to explore. From river wetlands to Alpine heights, there are numerous opportunities for bird-watching, hiking, mountain biking, caving, rafting and other adventures. Visiting Bulgaria in the early summer, you must spend some time in the famous Rose Valley where roses are grown and distilled for Bulgaria's most famous product – rose oil. Real party folk, Bulgarians are very fond of music and dance. Local bands will play folk songs in the pubs using typical instruments such as the accordion, the clarinet, the tambura, the *gaida* and the *tupan* drums. For a real challenge, try following the irregular rhythms of the different types of *horo*, or line dance. Bulgarians enjoy and value their own cuisine and readily ignore McDonald's if *banitsa* (a feta-cheese filled pastry) and *kebapcheta* (grilled mince sausages) are being sold around the corner. The fresh fruit and vegetables are arguably Europe's best and *Shopska* salad is a must with every meal.

TREK
BALKAN TREK
Balkan Trek is a leading specialist adventure, ecotour and nature tour operator in Bulgaria. It prides itself on designing and operating a wide range of walking, wildlife and cultural holidays. Visitors can walk through stunning landscapes, seek out Bulgaria's flora and fauna, or discover its rich history and culture. Examples of the tours include an eight-day adventure in the stunning landscapes of the Rodope Mountains, and a tour taking in the mysteries of ancient Thrace in the land of Orpheus. Balkan Trek is committed to the principles of responsible tourism and supports a range of conservation organizations to help protect Bulgaria's outstanding biodiversity.

Contact: Siya Cholakova or Julian Perry
Tel: +359 29733595
Fax: +359 29733595
Email: office@balkantrek.com
Web: www.balkantrek.com
Address: ul Nikolai Kopernik, bl 152, et 2, Sofia 1113, Bulgaria

TOUR OP
INTECO TRAVEL
This two-person company arranges holidays using small family-run hotels and thus likes to maintain friendly relations with local partners. Adventurous trips offer individuals and groups a wide range of outdoor activities, plus the chance to meet local people and learn about their culture and lifestyle. If you like museums and churches – look elsewhere.

Contact: Ivan Slavchev
Tel: +359 29831832
Fax: +359 29831832
Email: info@intecotravel.com
Web: www.intecotravel.com
Address: 38 Budapeshta Str, Sofia, BG-1202 Bulgaria

TOUR
NEOPHRON TOURS
Neophron offers specialist bird-watching tours – the project is owned by the Bulgarian Society for the Protection of Birds (BSPB)/Bird Life Bulgaria. The society has made significant contributions to the conservation of Bulgarian nature generally. Neophron manages two visitor and nature conservation centres for the BSPB. Wildlife holidays have contributed to the creation and preservation of many natural areas. Locally owned and run hotels and restaurants are used so that local people see the benefit of conserving the wildlife in their area.

Contact: Dimiter Georgiev • Marina Georgieva
Tel: +359 5265230 • +359 888420159
Fax: +359 52650230
Email: info@neophron.com • inquiries@neophron.com • office@neophron.com
Web: www.neophron.com
Address: PO Box 492, BG-9000 Varna, Bulgaria

CROATIA
International dialling code +385

Croatia borders on the Adriatic Sea – a part of the Mediterranean with good seawater quality, clean beaches and rich coastal flora and fauna. The International Blue Flag certificate for exceptional quality of the environment has been awarded to 22 of Croatia's beaches and marinas. The coastline is varied, with hundreds of uninhabited or abandoned islands to see and discover. If you prefer the plains and limestone mountains, you can try a bike tour on the numerous bike routes stretching throughout the country. Horseback riding, rafting, canoeing, kayaking or balloon trips are all adventure tours on offer in the Croatian countryside. Other places of interest include the 900-year-old capital city Zagreb and the old coastal city of Dubrovnik with the small authentic villages surrounding it. Dubrovnik or the 'Jewel of the Adriatic' as it is also called, was built in the 13th century and has remained virtually unchanged until now although it suffered badly during the seven-month siege in 1991 when the Serbs shelled the city from the surrounding mountain tops. A former independent merchant republic, Dubrovnik has lost nothing of its bustling and jovial flair.

DAY/TOUR
ADRIA ADVENTURE
Founded in 2003 by two self-confessed addicts of all things marine, Adria offers one-day and multi-day sea kayaking excursions. It can accommodate up to 30 people and guests stay in local accommodation. Trips explore the Dalmatian coast and the green wooded Elaphite Islands, celebrating the region's natural beauty with minimal negative environmental impact. Adria is very keen to keep the Adriatic clean – if you see plastic floating en route, you take it for recycling.

EUROPE

Contact: Ivana Grzetic
Tel: +385 20332567
Fax: +385 20331573
Email: info@adriatic-sea-kayak.com
Web: www.adriatic-sea-kayak.com
Address: Gorica sv Vlaha 159, 20000 Dubrovnik, Croatia

GREECE
International dialling code +30

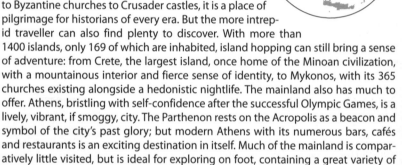

500km

ATHENS

Greece has, for many years, been a favourite package holiday destination. With warm weather from April to October, sandy beaches and turquoise seas in abundance, it is easy to see why it continues to be so popular. With its endless past, from ancient temples to Byzantine churches to Crusader castles, it is a place of pilgrimage for historians of every era. But the more intrepid traveller can also find plenty to discover. With more than 1400 islands, only 169 of which are inhabited, island hopping can still bring a sense of adventure: from Crete, the largest island, once home of the Minoan civilization, with a mountainous interior and fierce sense of identity, to Mykonos, with its 365 churches existing alongside a hedonistic nightlife. The mainland also has much to offer. Athens, bristling with self-confidence after the successful Olympic Games, is a lively, vibrant, if smoggy, city. The Parthenon rests on the Acropolis as a beacon and symbol of the city's past glory; but modern Athens with its numerous bars, cafés and restaurants is an exciting destination in itself. Much of the mainland is comparatively little visited, but is ideal for exploring on foot, containing a great variety of landscape, from the extraordinary monasteries precariously built on rocks at Meteora, to Mount Olympus, home of the gods and still a place to inspire awe.

ACCOM+
CRETE'S CULINARY SANCTUARIES (CCS)

CCS organizes cultural and culinary courses for small groups. Their local network of organic farmers, chefs, historians, mountaineers and other experts share their knowledge of Crete's culture and nature. Visitors go on guided hikes in the countryside and visit historic sites, organic farms, tranquil villages and rural lodges. Journeys change with the seasons to include organic olive oil, wine, cheese, honey and bread production. The seminars offer the opportunity to discover the heart of Crete in the company of local specialists and to learn about sustainable living practices. CCS is run by Nikki Rose, a Greek American chef and food writer.

Contact: Nikki Rose
Tel: +1 415 8359923
Email: info@cookingincrete.com
Web: www.cookingincrete.com

ACCOM
LEVENDIS ESTATE

Are you tempted by lotus eating overlooking the wine-dark sea surrounding Homeric Ithaca, and by the prospect of informal luxury in family friendly accommodation? Then this is for you. Everything Levendis does is geared to the health of an environmentally fragile island. It aims to ensure that it operates only with renewable energy by the end of 2010, and it recycles grey water so that it has had self-sufficiency in water for 12 years. Your spending on the island will benefit local families and businesses. The project has quality and hospitality as its hallmarks.

Contact: Marilyn Raftopulos
Tel: +30 6944169770
Fax: +30 2674031648
Email: levendis@otenet.gr
Web: www.levendisestate.com
Address: PO Box 23, Vathy 28300, Ithaca, Greece

ACCOM/SCHOOL
MILIA MOUNTAIN RETREAT
Milia offers rural accommodation on the island of Crete. Guests who enjoy staying off the beaten track can enjoy peace and quiet, great hospitality and food, and there are endless possibilities for hiking. Milia also organizes courses in cookery and recognizing flora and fauna – a very good place to stay for nature lovers and bird-watchers.

Contact: Tassos Gourgouras
Tel: +30 2821046774 · +30 6945753743
Fax: +30 2821046774 · +30 2822051569
Email: info@milia.gr
Web: www.milia.gr
Address: Milia, Vlatos, Kissamos 73012, Hania, Crete, Greece

ITALY
International dialling code +39

From Julius Caesar to the Pope, from Leonardo da Vinci to Mussolini – Italy's history is peppered with the famous and infamous. Rich in artistic tradition, steeped in culture and awash with stunning architecture, from Mediterranean coastline to Alpine mountains, this country has something to offer everyone. Italy did not become a unified country until 1861; consequently, more cultural identity is attached to the nine regions of the country than to the nation as a whole. This is expressed through very distinct dialects, culinary habits and different standards of living. There is a strong north–south divide, the north being a rapidly growing industrialized society, while the south suffers from low literacy rates, economic and social depression and still operates under a pseudo-feudal system. However, it is the central regions that perhaps characterize the essence of the best of Italy. The rolling landscape of Tuscany not only offers great opportunities for trekking, but also boasts more classified historical monuments than any other country in the world. A visit to Venice can satisfy all your romantic yearnings with its shady canals, hidden alleyways and echoing churches. The middle of the day is siesta time, an age-old tradition of the Mediterranean, followed by the obligatory passeggiata, the evening stroll enjoyed by young and old alike. The Italians are known for their enjoyment of the dolce vita, and no visit would be complete without indulging in fine wine, fine food and fine fashion.

EUROPE

ACCOM/DAY
ARCI TURISMO BY ARCI SICILIA
Arci Sicilia is a social promotion association and Arci Turismo is the committee promoting ethical tourism through the Palermo Branch. Arci is rooted in Sicilian communities and all the projects have been born of local communities. On offer are short walking tours and cultural tours. Longer are the 'legality' tours, which will give you an insight into the more seamy property ownership/Mafia underbelly of life.

Contact: Elisa or Rossana Messina
Tel: +39 0916101000
Fax: +39 0916169798
Email: arciturismo@arcisicilia.it
Web: www.arcisicilia.it/arciturismo
Address: Via Carlo Rao 16, 90133 Palermo, Sicily, Italy

ACCOM+
BIOAGRITURISMO TIRTHA CENTRO CULTURALE
Based near Verona, Bioagriturismo offers a bed-and-breakfast service, and lunch and dinner for groups who come for residential workshops. There are guided tours of the area. The Cultural Centre offers courses in yoga, Pilates, core energy and Zen meditation, as well as concerts, exhibitions, workshops and conferences. There are four rooms with accommodation for 12 people, 45 Euros for a single, and 70 Euros for a double room.

Contact: Anna Bianchedi
Tel: +39 0457150513 · +39 3479264505
Fax: +39 0456770010
Email: info@tirtha.it
Web: www.tirtha.it · www.bioagriturismo.verona.it
Address: Bioagriturismo TIRTHA Centro Culturale, via Tremolè 18/a, 37026 Pescantina (Verona), Italy

ACCOM+
ECO-VILLAGE TORRI SUPERIORE
Situated in the foothills of the Ligurian Alps a few kilometres from the French border and the Mediterranean, medieval Torri Superiore dates from the 13th century and consists of eight levels of stone-built structures. There are three main buildings separated by partly covered alleys; in all the complex has about 160 rooms that are linked by a maze of stairways, terraces and alleys. The complicated and fascinating structure has been compared to a labyrinth or fortress on the side of a mountain. During the 1990s a group of people set out to save this amazing place from a slow death, and it is now fully restored. Guests can stay in single, double or group rooms. This is ideal for visitors interested in learning about eco-village living, with workshops run by the village, or simply for those who wish to enjoy a short break in beautiful surroundings. The restaurant offers locally produced organic cuisine in a self-service buffet, with guests sharing the company of residents at communal tables.

Contact: Lucilla Borio
Tel: +39 184215504
Fax: +39 184215914
Email: info@torri-superiore.org
Web: www.torri-superiore.org
Address: Via Torri Superiore 5, 18039 Ventimiglia IM, Italy

EUROPE

AGRI/ORG
INSTITUTO PER LA CERTIFICAZIONE ETICA E AMBIENTALE (INSTITUTE FOR ETHICAL AND ENVIRONMENTAL CERTIFICATION) (ICEA)

The ICEA operates in many areas, including sustainable tourism, as manifested in bio-agritourism. The theory 'made physical' is a network of holiday farms operated by families and people committed to an organic, environmentally friendly approach. Agriculture is seen as not just food production, but also the provision of rural hospitality and caring for the environment and landscape.

Contact: Roberta Bartoletti or Manuela Cacciato
Tel: +39 051272986
Fax: +39 051232011
Email: Ecoturismo@icea.info
Web: www.icea.info · www.bioagriturismi.it
Address: ICEA, Strada Maggiore 29, 40125 Bologna, Italy

ACCOM/SAFARI/AGRI
LA CERQUA E LA BALUCCA

This is an organic teaching farm inside the Pietralunga Forest in the Carpina Valley, Upper Umbria, not far from Gubbio and Città di Castello. Guests stay in one of three houses. The Oak is a recently restored 14th-century farmhouse, once believed to be a monastery, with six rooms, two suites and an acorn-shaped swimming pool. The Marble Gall is a typical old Umbrian farmhouse with nine rooms, a small football field and two open-air workshops. The Old Barn is a traditional red brick house with two small apartments and a garden, ideal for self-catering. There are also two small farm restaurants which serve organic, locally produced seasonal dishes. Guests can take guided nature walks along the farm paths and go leaf-peeping (admiring the varied colours of leaves).

Contact: Gino Martinelli
Tel: +39 0759460283
Fax: +39 0759462033
Email: info@cerqua.it
Web: www.cerqua.it
Address: La Cerqua, via S. Salvatore 27, 06026 Pietralunga, Italy

BUDGET
OSPITALE DELLE RIFIORENZE

This is a social co-operative in the centre of Florence that offers budget accommodation, as well as organizing events, guided tours and school trips with social relevance. The beautiful Sala della Tacca space can be hired out for free for holding courses. Income from guests goes towards a project to provide homeless people in winter with free food and beds. Accommodation is 19 Euros per night in a four-bedroom, while single and double rooms are also available.

Contact: Mara Butera
Tel: +39 055216798 (April–October) · +39 339720006 (October–April)
Mobile: +39 3397082530
Fax: +39 055720128
Email: info@firenzeospitale.it
Web: www.firenzeospitale.it · www.florencehospitality.org
Address: Via Della Pieve 43-b, Scandicci, Florence, Italy (postal address)

TOUR OP
VIAGGIEMIRAGGI SOCIETA COOPERATIVA SOCIALE ONLUS PER IL TURISMO RESPONSABILE

This social co-operative not-for-profit body offers truly responsible tours in 12 areas of Italy and in more than 20 countries around the globe. The *raison d'être* is to promote responsible tourism in order to reduce the injustices and negative impact of traditional tourism. Local communities

EUROPE

239

receive between 25 and 35 per cent of the proceeds and participants also pay an amount on the spot into a *cassa commune*, or common fund, and they can see where it goes.

Contact: Paola, Irene or Luisa
Tel: +39 0498751997
Fax: +39 049659525
Email: Viaggi@viaggiemiraggi.org
Web: www.viaggiemiraggi.org
Address: Riviera Tito Livio 46, 35123 Padova, Italy

MONTENEGRO
International dialling code +382

This ecological mountain country is said to be the oldest 'state' in the western Balkans. It is here that mountains meet the sea in what most certainly must be one of Southeast Europe's most stunning nature destinations. The seaside resorts and tourist towns are well known to tourists for their crystal-clear Adriatic seawater with breathtaking mountain views towering just behind. The resorts of Sveti Stephan, Herceg Novi, the Bay of Kotor, Bar and Budva are amongst the Adriatic's best. Peel away just one layer of mountain, though, and a magical wilderness world opens up. Lake Shkoeder is a gorgeous bird reserve and a great place for boat rides and fishing. The ancient capital of Montenegro, Cetine, is still the cultural backbone of the country.

Durmitor National Park gets a high rating for its vast wilderness. Perhaps the most exciting experience in Montenegro is the three-day white-water rafting adventure on the Tara River, Europe's deepest river canyon. The northern pocket around Plav has an interesting ethnic mix of orthodox, Slavic Muslims and Albanians. This area is rather poor and underdeveloped, but equally beautiful and worth spending your tourism money.

TOUR
UNITED NATIONS DEVELOPMENT PROGRAMME (UNDP) LO PODGORICA
This UNDP project is implementing a sustainable tourism initiative called Wilderness Biking and Hiking Montenegro. The project represents a partnership between the Ministry of Tourism, the national parks, the local community, local entrepreneurs and NGOs. The aim is to promote and upgrade sustainable tourism services for biking and hiking, which take place throughout the country, and there is a strong infrastructure in terms of available trails.

Tel: +382 81231251
Fax: +382 81231644
Email: sanja@undp.org · bojanic@undp.org · tomica.paovic@undp.org
Web: www.undp.org.me · www.destination-durmitor.org
Address: Beogradska 24b, 81000 Podgorica, Montenegro

EUROPE

ROMANIA
International dialling code +40

Recovering quickly from its socialist past and state-developed generic tourist resorts along the Black Sea, Romania is busy promoting its numerous countryside attractions. Dracula's medieval castle in Transylvania comes to mind; but Romania has plenty of other magnificent fortified churches and castles, a remnant of the Saxon influence during the 13th and 18th centuries. Many of them are now designated UNESCO World Heritage sites. Centuries-old villages and beautiful monasteries complete the cultural landscape. With one quarter of the country covered in forests, wildlife such as bear, lynx, deer and wolf can still roam freely. In the southeast, the Danube Delta Biosphere Reserve boasts the largest biodiversity in Europe and is a haven for bird-watchers. Romania's numerous mineral and thermal springs are the perfect place to enjoy a relaxing treatment, and its wineries offer some exceptional wines for every taste, not be found outside the country's borders.

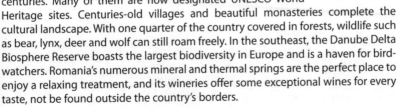

TOUR
ABSOLUTE CARPATHIAN
Wildlife-watching and tracking tours in Piatra Craiului National Park with a focus on lynx, bear, beaver, marmots, deer and birds – a wonderful window onto the natural world is available in what is still quite a wild part of Europe. It will organize an all-included tour for you or merely facilitate access to guest houses, guides and transport. Note: it only operates only from March to September.

Contact: Simona Munteanu
Tel: +40 788578796
Fax: +40 368815453
Email: book@absolute-nature.ro
Web: www.absolute-nature.ro
Address: Zorilor 2/B/7, 505800 – Zarnesti, Brasov County, Romania

TOUR
MY ROMANIA
On offer are individual tailor-made tours that allow participants to stay and eat with local people, walking in easy stages from village to village and really getting a feeling for (and of) Romania and its people. A useful spin-off is that when local people see their culture and its artefacts meet with the esteem of foreign visitors, they value them more themselves – an antidote after the Ceausescu years when national heritage was derided.

Contact: Ramona Cazacu
Tel: +40 723191755
Fax: +40 234324287
Email: office@myromania.com.ro
Web: www.myromania.com.ro
Address: Sat Heltiu 120, Com. Caiuti, Jud. Bacau, Romania

EUROPE

SWEDEN
International dialling code +46

This country in the north of Europe is a heaven for responsible travellers. Swedes care much about the natural environment and are some of the most ecologically responsible people on the planet. Sweden is a mountainous country situated on the Scandinavian Peninsula between Norway and Finland. To the south it is connected to mainland Europe via the ultra-modern Oresund Bridge. In Sweden's most northern town, Kiruna, located 250km beyond the Arctic Circle and a 16-hour train ride away from Stockholm, the Northern Lights can be observed and admired. The north of the country is populated by the Saami people, who at the beginning of the 21st century still manage to preserve their own language, centuries-old customs and their belief in pagan gods. The diverse accommodation base ranges from residing in romantic castles, wild camping sites and inexpensive hostels through to sleeping in a tree-house, in an ice hotel or in a 19th-century converted prison. If you happen to visit Sweden in the month of August, definitely take part in the loud, jovial and silly crayfish parties.

TREK
THE SILENT WAY

A unique tour where a small group of travellers mush a team of friendly Alaskan huskies along beautiful wilderness trails. Each day they travel from lodge to lodge, seeing dense forests, mountain birch, bare white mountains and clear lakes along the way. Evenings are spent enjoying great Lapland meals in the cosy lodges. Travellers will learn about the customs, wildlife and history of the area, and may even see the Northern Lights. Free cold-weather clothing and boots are provided, while the sledges are handmade by Kenneth, the lead musher. The dogs themselves are very sociable and love to be patted as much as they enjoy pulling travellers to beautiful and remote parts of Lapland.

Contact: Catrine Anderback
Tel: +46 95152043 · +46 732771640
Email: info@silent-way.com
Web: www.dogsledding-adventures.com · www.snowmobile-adventure-lapland.com
Address: Umnäs 143, 92397 Slussfors, Lapland, Sweden

TOUR OPERATORS

This list of tour operators and travel agencies is challenging the dominance of mainstream operators. All of them are committed to supporting local communities. Often they are small businesses and are specialists, passionate about the destinations they go to and wanting to ensure that both you (the guest) and those acting as hosts have a good time and benefit from the experience. Thus you should expect a quality, personal service.

All of these operators offer journeys to more than one country. Those that are country specific are identified in the country listings.

Many of the hotels and tours listed in this guide can be booked through these operators.

UK OPERATORS

ADVENTURE ALTERNATIVE

A tour operator that organizes ethical adventures around the world, including expeditions, treks, safaris and gap years. Adventure Alternative began with the specific principle of promoting income from tourism for the host countries rather than a Western bank account. Medical doctor Gavin Bate provided start-up investment for local companies who operate as subsidiaries to his parent company. Profits were ploughed back into staff development, training and resources. The company also underwrites a charity established by Gavin called Moving Mountains. The company is inextricably linked with the charity and its beneficiaries – for example Africampers, a Kenyan project, has 44 staff, all of whom are ex-street children who were educated by the charity and now have stable well-paid jobs with the company. Started in 1991, Adventure Alternative is seeing the fruits of many years of effort investing in the people of Tanzania, Nepal and Kenya, so there is little need to advertise: word of mouth encourages a large proportion of repeat business. Gavin makes frequent visits to the homes of his staff in Tanzania and Nepal, ensuring that salaries properly reflect the increase in living costs.

Contact: Gavin Bate
Tel: +44 2870831258
Email: office@adventurealternative.com
Web: www.adventurealternative.com
Address: PO Box 14, Portstewart, Northern Ireland, BT55 7WS

BAOBAB TRAVEL

Baobab Travel is a UK-based specialist tour operator, born out of a love of Africa and travel, and a desire to actively work with and support local communities in the developing world. Baobab holidays are designed to show visitors the real places, nature and culture in Africa, avoiding resorts that have been 'manufactured' for tourists.

Contact: Louise de Waal
Tel: +44 1213146011
Fax: +44 121316012
Email: info@baobabtravel.com
Web: www.baobabtravel.com
Address: Old Fallings Hall, Old Fallings Lane, Wolverhampton WV10 8BL, UK

BEES ABROAD

Bees Abroad is a charity that organizes bee-keeping projects in Nepal, Cameroon, Nigeria, Malawi and Kenya. These projects employ local people, with an emphasis on the inclusion of women, minority groups and disabled people wherever possible. Bee-keeping offers a means of poverty alleviation through the sales of honey and beeswax products. The bees themselves also provide a very valuable pollination service, which helps to increase crop yields. Bees Abroad holidays offer visitors a chance to visit the countries involved, to see bee-keeping and learn about bee-keeping traditions. A typical 14-day trip includes mainstream tourism activities as well as the chance to visit bee-keepers and their local communities. The holidays are mostly organized by volunteers to enable the maximum contribution possible to be given to the charity for project funding.

Contact: Veronica Brown
Tel: +44 1172300231
Email: veronica@marketingadmin.co.uk
Web: www.beesabroad.org.uk
Address: PO Box 2065, Bristol BS35 9AP, UK

DISCOVERY INITIATIVES

Discovery Initiatives was founded in 1997 as a travel company dedicated to supporting nature, wildlife and conservation through responsible wildlife tourism. As internationally recognized and award winning pioneers in this field, they have set up and run hundreds of small group tours, safaris and expeditions, led by experts in their field to some of the world's greatest wildernesses. They give privileged insight and access to areas and expertise unavailable to conventional tourism, with a network of contacts and experts in wildlife agencies across the globe. By joining their tours, visitors can provide the economic, ethical and environmental incentives to conserve such areas for future generations.

Tel: +44 1285643333 • +44 1285880936
Web: www.discoveryinitiatives.com
Address: 51 Castle Street, Cirencester, Gloucestershire GL7 1QD, UK

DRAGOMAN OVERLAND

Dragoman offers overland travel in Africa, South America, the Far East and China. One of the leading adventure overland companies, Dragoman continues to expand. It now offers a greater range of trips, from short adventure travel journeys to its infamous epics, as well as family trips, volunteer projects and small group travel without trucks. Whether you have 2 weeks or 42, Dragoman will have the adventure you are looking for.

Tel: +44 1728861133
Fax: +44 1728861127
Email: info@dragoman.co.uk
Web: www.dragoman.com
Address: Camp Green, Debenham, Suffolk IP14 6LA, UK

TOUR OPERATORS

EQUATORIAL TRAVEL

Equatorial Travel is a small specialist travel agency set up in conjunction with two fair-trade shops in the UK. Tours go to the Moroccan Sahara, Ecuador and Rajasthan in India. It frequently operates in areas untouched by other tour operators, with expertise in cultural and walking tours for adults and families. The bulk of its holidays are tailor made; but there are some group itineraries advertised via the website. All tours run on fair-trade principles.

Tel: +44 1335348770
Fax: +44 1335300485
Email: tours@equatorialtravel.co.uk
Web: www.EqTravel.co.uk
Address: 3 Victoria Square, Ashbourne, Derbyshire DE6 1GG, UK

EXODUS TRAVELS

Exodus Travels have over 34 years' experience in small group adventure travel. They have always believed that by only operating small groups, they retain a certain amount of control over their social and environmental impacts, both positive and negative. They work very closely with local partners to engrain responsible tourism practices within their everyday product development, finding the most efficient and sustainable ways to maximize potential benefits and to minimize negative impacts. Exodus Travels try to work with NGOs and charities where possible, and use their knowledge and understanding as a guide to appropriate practices and destinations. They also run environmental, educational and community development projects in different destinations to improve the livelihood of the communities affected by their trips.

Tel: +44 2086755550
Email: sales@exodus.co.uk • info@exodus.co.uk
Web: www.exodus.co.uk
Address: Grange Mills, Weir Road, London SW12 0NE, UK

EXPERT AFRICA

Expert Africa (part of the Sunvil Group), specializes in tailor-made trips to Southern and East Africa and the Seychelles, offering value for money with unrivalled expertise. Its trips are individual and highly flexible, catering for free-spirited and discerning travellers. By offering quality trips that support small establishments and local guides, it also tries to minimize any environmental damage and to help the communities whom it visits.

Tel: +44 2082329777
Fax: +44 2087584718
Email: info@expertafrica.com
Web: www.expertafrica.com
Address: 10–11 Upper Square, Old Isleworth, Middlesex, TW7 7BJ, UK

GO DIFFERENTLY

Go Differently offers tailor-made ethical holidays, voluntourism tours and volunteering adventures based on an appreciation and respect for the local environment and people. It is UK based, but operates in South and Southeast Asia. Go Differently supports projects such as volunteering with elephants in southern Thailand, a monkey conservation centre, English teaching and various other community-based tourism initiatives. Usually at least 80 per cent of the price paid for the holiday goes direct to local communities.

Contact: Nikki Bond
Tel: +44 1799521950
Email: info@godifferently.com
Web: www.godifferently.com
Address: 19 West Road, Saffron Walden, Essex CB11 3DS, UK

TOUR OPERATORS

HANDS UP HOLIDAYS

Hands Up specializes in holidays that combine eco-sightseeing with a meaningful taste of volun-teering. For example, a trip may start by spending a few days with a guide exploring the destina-tion while learning something of the local language, culture and etiquette. The next part of the holiday will give the visitor a taste of volunteering: this could be as a reading partner, helping at an orphanage, building a house, conserving the environment or assisting with repairs and reno-vations. The last part of the trip could involve reflecting on the volunteer experience, relaxing, group bonding and continuing to explore with a local guide. Accommodation is usually 4 or 5 stars; but trips are tailor made to suit all budgets. An ideal trip for travellers who value meaningful interaction with other cultures and want to give something back to the local community.

Contact: Audrey Hill
Tel: +44 2088710341
Email: chris@handsupholidays.com
Web: www.handsupholidays.com
Address: 5 Kendal Place, London SW15 2QZ, UK

INTOAFRICA

This is a small (and happy to be so) company specializing in fairly traded treks in Kenya and Tanzania. Its fundamental principle is to benefit local communities, and this is backed up by fair trading practice and direct donations. The operational foci are cultural tourism, wildlife safaris and mountain trekking. It offers neither luxury lodges nor run-of-the-mill adventure safaris. It aims to combine the wildlife and the scenery with genuine insight into local people's lifestyles and envi-ronments. Local communities benefit to the tune of 20 per cent of a holiday's cost as payment for their services.

Contact: Chris Morris
Tel: +44 1142555610
Fax: +44 1142555610
Email: info@intoafrica.co.uk
Web: www.intoafrica.co.uk
Address: IntoAfrica Uk Ltd, 40 Huntingdon Crescent, Sheffield S11 8AX, UK

JOURNEY LATIN AMERICA

Journey Latin America is the UK's number one specialist for Central and South America, offering the widest range of flexible holiday options, including tailor-made travel and small group tours. With a 5-star Association of Independent Tour Operators (AITO) responsible tourism award, its large team of specialists truly understands the ecological and social issues particular to the region. Simply tell them your travel plans and let them show you the Latin America they know and love.

Tel: +44 2087478315
Fax: +44 2089957710
Email: tours@journeylatinamerica.co.uk
Web: www.journeylatinamerica.co.uk
Address: 12/13 Heathfield Terrace, London W4 4JE, UK

LAST FRONTIERS

Last Frontiers is a small tour operator specializing in tailor-made holidays to Latin America, and most of its staff have lived and worked in the region. It recognizes its responsibility to ensure the long-term sustainability of its operations and continually monitors environmental and cultural issues. Last Frontiers is a founder of the Latin American Travel Association (LATA) Foundation.

Tel: +44 1296653000
Email: info@lastfrontiers.com
Web: www.lastfrontiers.com
Address: Fleet Marston Farm, Aylesbury, Buckinghamshire HP18 0QT, UK

MUIR'S TOURS

Muir's Tours is a UK-based tour operator who specializes in Nepal, and a hand-picked selection of wild places for adventure holidays. For example, it goes dog sledding in Lapland and polar bear viewing in Canada. Holidays can vary from trekking in the Himalayas, Peru and Chile, to horse riding in Mongolia and wildlife-watching in Tanzania and Canada. The Nepal Kingdom Foundation, a UK-based charity, is the major beneficiary from Muir's Tours' activities. In Nepal, local people are employed on their terms: they are asked how much they need and so far have been given what they asked for. Muir's Tours continues to pay them even if there is no work to do.

Contact: Maurice Adshead
Tel: +44 1189502281
Email: info@nkf-mt.org.uk
Web: www.nkf-mt.org.uk • www.tibetantraders.org.uk
Address: Nepal House, 97a Swansea Road, Reading, Berkshire RG1 8HA, UK

NORTH SOUTH TRAVEL

North South Travel is a unique travel agency offering global discount fares with excellent personal service. The owner of North South Travel is the NST Development Trust (registered charity 1040656), and all profits from the sale of tickets are donated to grassroots charities worldwide.

Contact: Brenda Skinner
Tel: +44 1245608291
Fax: +44 1245608291
Email: reservations@northsouthtravel.co.uk • brenda@northsouthtravel.co.uk
Web: www.northsouthtravel.co.uk
Address: Moulsham Mill Centre, Parkway, Chelmsford CM2 7PX, UK

OASIS OVERLAND

A tour operator that offers overland adventure tours in Africa, the Middle East, South America and Asia. It usually camps either in designated campsites or on the edge of villages, and over the years has built up good relationships with the villagers, supporting them through buying handicrafts and locally produced food. It also supports other projects, such as providing education and health services to communities in Egypt, Peru, Uganda and Zimbabwe.

Contact: Lin • Jeff • Andy
Tel: +44 1963363400
Fax: +44 1963363200
Email: info@oasisoverland.co.uk
Web: www.oasisoverland.co.uk
Address: Oasis Overland, The Marsh, Henstridge, Somerset BA8 0TF, UK

RAINBOW TOURS

An Africa and Indian Ocean specialist offering some tours, but mostly tailor-made, upmarket itineraries to Southern and East Africa, as well as a comprehensive programme to Madagascar. Rainbow Tours includes many community partnership lodges and bed and breakfasts. Voted 'Best Tour Operator' in the *Guardian/Observer* Travel Awards, 2004, 2005 and 2006. Both Air Travel Organisers' Licensing (ATOL) bonded and an AITO member.

Tel: +44 2072261004
Email: info@rainbowtours.co.uk
Web: www.rainbowtours.co.uk
Address: 305 Upper Street, London N1 2TU, UK

TOUR OPERATORS

SADDLE SKEDADDLE

This UK tour operator offers tours in a joint venture with Traidcraft. On these tours, travellers can meet the people behind fair-trade products, see the impacts of fair trade, the benefits of Traidcraft's work and how this fights poverty. Visitors will learn something of different cultures, visit development projects and meet a wide variety of people, including Traidcraft producers, often having their ideas of developing countries challenged. Travel is in small groups, with a maximum of 14 like-minded individuals. Destinations include Cuba, Peru, India, Vietnam, Bangladesh, the Philippines, South Africa and Malawi. The tours don't include flight costs. All aspects of the tour are organized so as to maximize the economic, social and environmental benefits and to reduce the negative impacts in the destination.

Contact: Lizzie White
Tel: +44 1912651110
Fax: +44 1912651110
Email: info@skedaddle.co.uk
Web: www.traidcraft-tours.com
Address: Saddle Skedaddle, Ouseburn Building, Albion Row, Newcastle upon Tyne NE6 1LL, UK

TELL TALE TRAVEL

Tell Tale Travel offers private soft adventure tours in Thailand and Sri Lanka, with plans to expand to other countries. Its itineraries range from eco-holidays and family adventures to cooking holidays and cultural homestays.

Contact: Chris Bland
Tel: 08000112571
Email: contact@telltaletravel.co.uk
Web: www.telltaletravel.co.uk
Address: 25a Kensington Church Street, London W8 4LL, UK

TRIBES

Tribes, the Fair-Trade Travel™ company, is an award-winning independent travel company, and globally recognized pioneer of responsible travel. Tribes arranges quality tailor-made holidays in Africa, South America, Asia and the Middle East. It has a high client satisfaction rating, and you can expect excellent impartial advice from its friendly expert consultants.

Tel: +44 1728685971
Email: info@tribes.co.uk
Web: www.tribes.co.uk
Address: 12 The Business Centre, Earl Soham, Woodbridge, Suffolk IP13 7SA, UK

WILDERNESS JOURNEYS

Wilderness Journeys offers community-based and environmentally friendly holidays across the world. As an adventure and ecotourism company, it can cater for individuals, small groups and families. It is committed to sustainable tourism and to sharing with others the magic of the world's last wild places. It aims to be a low-impact operation and ensures that its partners share its philosophy and ethos. The company has a genuine commitment to the communities and environments in which it operates.

Contact: Neil Birnie
Tel: +44 1316256635
Fax: +44 1316256636
Email: info@wildernessjourneys.com
Web: www.wildernessjourneys.com
Address: 3a St Vincent Street, Edinburgh EH3 6SW, Scotland, UK

US OPERATORS

CROOKED TRAILS

Crooked Trails is a non-profit, community-based travel organization helping people to broaden their understanding of the planet and its diverse cultures through education, community development and responsible travel. It was founded by two women from Seattle on the premise that tourism does not have to threaten the cultures and environments of popular destinations and fragile regions. As an educational non-profit organization, it creates true cultural exchanges that make positive contributions to host communities and have lasting effects on travellers. Crooked Trails participants return home having learned ways to incorporate lessons from these exchanges into their own lives and communities. It only works with communities who have invited them. With each passing year, the trust and friendship between Crooked Trails staff, programme participants and the local people continue to deepen. In cooperation with other NGOs, it operates travel programmes in support of indigenous peoples in Peru, Thailand, Nepal, India, Ecuador and Kenya, among other destinations. Crooked Trails believes that all of us can improve cultural, ecological and economic conditions around the world by changing the way in which we travel.

Contact: Chris Mackay • Tammy Leland
Tel: +1 2063839828
Fax: +1 2063200505
Email: info@crookedtrails.com
Web: www.crookedtrails.com
Address: PO Box 94034, Seattle, WA 98124, USA

INTERNATIONAL BICYCLE FUND/IBIKE TOURS

Ibike run affordable rural-based bicycle tours in small groups. Participants discover a fascinating world at a personal level. They explore little-visited rural areas, enjoying leisurely interactions with the people they come across during visits to homes, schools and markets, often being awed by the hospitality shown. This kind of travel helps to break down the usual barriers between tourists and the local people, and is a great way to explore the complexity and diversity of a world that is rarely seen in mainstream tourism.

Contact: David Mozer
Tel: +1 2067670848
Email: ibike@ibike.org
Web: www.ibike.org
Address: 4887 Columbia Dr S, Seattle, WA 98108-1919, USA

REALITY TOURS AND GLOBAL EXCHANGE

Global Exchange is a non-profit human rights organization working for global political, environmental and social justice. Its Reality Tours educate the public about international issues through socially responsible travel. They travel to over 35 destinations throughout Africa, Latin America, the Middle East, Central and Southeast Asia, Europe and the USA. Global Exchange has been promoting socially responsible tourism for over 20 years.

Tel: +1 415 2557296
Fax: +1 415 2557498
Email: realitytours@globalexchange.org
Web: www.globalexchange.org • www.realitytours.org
Address: 2017 Mission St, 2nd Floor, San Francisco, CA 94110, USA

TOUR
OPERATORS

TERRA INCOGNITA ECOTOURS

This company pledges to engage in 'responsible travel to natural areas that conserves the environment and improves the well-being of local people'. At each destination, it cooperates with a different conservation partner and part of the cost of a tour goes to that partner – normally 10 per cent. Local communities benefit to the tune of about 70 per cent of the cost. Destinations include Rwanda, Madagascar, Borneo, China, Belize, Costa Rica, Peru and Nicaragua.

Contact: Gerard 'Ged' Caddick
Tel: +1 813 2891049
Fax: +1 813 2891049
Email: ged@ecotours.com
Web: www.ecotours.com
Address: 4016 West Inman Avenue, Tampa, FL 33609, USA

NON-UK/US OPERATORS

BRIDGE-IT

Bridge-It organizes small group journeys to little-explored corners of Asia. Travellers enjoy intimate contact with the local population, experience local food, traditional means of transport, and listen to music and stories from the area. Expeditions go to remote national parks, seeing rare wildlife, and give the feeling of discovering an unseen corner of the Earth. Bridge-It is a partnership between NGOs of four countries, so visitors can be assured that the profits will be delivered to the local population, making their holiday both memorable and sustainable.

Contact: Nadia
Tel: +39 0550113472
Fax: +39 0556802511
Email: nadia@local-global.it
Web: www.local-global.it/project/bridge-it
Address: Local Global SaS, Via di Ricorboli 1, 50126 Firenze, Italy

CROQ'NATURE

Croq'Nature is a French fair-trade organization that began in 1986. It organizes trips to the Sahara with the aim of cultural exchange and development, with the assistance of local families and village communities. It has programmes in Morocco, Algeria, Mali, Niger and Mauritania. The projects that it has have funded include digging wells, founding schools and financing the building of guest houses.

Contact: Jean Luc Gantheil
Tel: +33 562970100
Fax: +33 562979583
Email: croqnature@wanadoo.fr
Web: www.croqnature.com
Address: 9 rue du Marechal Foch, F-65200 Bagneres de Bigorre, France

EXPLORE AND HELP GMBH

This company offers tour groups a chance to experience a country in a different way and to meet local people. Relaxation is allowed – after all, they are tourists. The opportunity is also there to become involved with selected projects as a volunteer. This is concerned travel with a German angle as it is very much wedded to a concept of fund-raising travel: the company works with charities, etc. and arranges trips for their donors in order that the latter might see the fruits of their giving.

Contact: Silke Wehling or Silke Matz
Tel: +49 4036976070
Fax: +49 4036976080
Email: info@exploreandhelp.de
Web: www.exploreandhelp.de
Address: Explore and Help GmbH, Bernstorffstrasse 118, 22767 Hamburg, Germany

ISMALAR RUTAS

Ismalar Rutas is a Malaga-based tour agency that offers trips not only in Spain, but also in Mali, Morocco, Mauritania, Senegal, Syria and Jordan. The trips vary greatly, from trekking through the Atlas Mountains to riding camels across the Sahara. All of the tours focus on giving travellers a broad understanding of the country that they are visiting, its ecology, its people and its cultural and political heritage. All trips are made in small groups and Ismalar Rutas takes care to work with its destinations in a sustainable manner, never over-saturating them or letting tourism make a serious impact upon the local way of life.

Contact: Cristina González
Tel: +34 952217076
Fax: +34 4952217322
Email: info@ismalar.org
Web: www.ismalar.org
Address: Pza Poeta Alfonso Canales, 4, 29001, Málaga

LE MAT – DEVELOPMENT AGENCY FOR SOCIAL ENTREPRENEURS IN TOURISM

Le Mat is a consortium of co-operatives forming an entrepreneurial network. It offers community-based responsible tourism. The small co-ops are based in local communities and are working to develop a sustainable way of living. Guests can stay with the community and get a real insight into how people live and how the co-op operates. Le Mat is becoming a trademark of quality, a community of practitioners of sustainable tourism in harmony with local development who can form common policies.

Contact: Renate Goergen
Tel: +39 3357780682
Email: info@lemat.it
Web: www.lemat.it
Address: Via Foligno 10, I-00182 Roma, Italy

ORIGINS SAFARIS

Origins is based in Nairobi and runs high-end tourist camps, as well as organizing cultural and natural history safaris, gorilla trekking and tropical islands exploration throughout East and Central Africa. It also endeavours to give something back to the community. US$20 per client goes to support local community projects, while guests are invited to visit the local ecotourism bandas, try bee-keeping or become involved in activities such as building schools and teaching IT, English and arithmetic. Visitors can also participate in wildlife and water monitoring in order to better understand the dynamics between humans and wildlife in the community areas near Tsavo National Park, southeast Kenya.

Contact: Samuel Gaturu
Tel: +254 202710171/2/7 · +254 202042695/6/7
Fax: +254 202710178 · +254 202042698
Email: steveturner@originsafaris.info
Web: www.originsafaris.info
Address: Grassroots Logistics, c/o Origins Safaris, LandMark Plaza, 5th Floor, Argwings Kodhek Road, PO Box 48019, 00100 Nairobi, Kenya

PLANET VIAGGI RESPONSABILI

This is a small private travel company with a special focus on tourism to, and in, developing countries and built on cooperation with local communities. It is a vehicle through which such communities can promote themselves and their culture, taking ownership of the tourism projects. Local partners are drawn from mainly South America, Asia, the North African littoral and South Africa.

Contact: Sara Ballarin or Genny Losurdo
Tel: +39 045594061
Fax: +39 0458047932
Email: info@planetviaggi.it • viaggiresponsibili@planetviaggi.it
Web: www.planetviaggi.it
Address: Lungadige Porta Vittoria 21, 37129 Verona, Italy

RAM VIAGGI INCONTRO

RAM is a small company specializing in fair-trade and responsible tourism within Italy and to India, Tibet, Nepal and Southeast Asia. Stress is placed on meeting local people and on the wealth or depth of the experience – if time is short, aim to see less with more concentration.

Contact: Marta Di Cesare
Tel: +39 0185799087
Fax: +39 0185799214
Email: orzonero@hotmail.com • info@ramviaggi.it
Web: www.ramviaggi.it
Address: Via Molino Nuovo 8, 16030 Avegno (Genova), Italy

RENCONTRES AU BOUT DU MONDE

This non-profit organization specializes in ethical and sustainable tourism, especially in Central Asia and the Indian subcontinent. This is a marriage of discovery travel with respect for the environment and for the people who live in it. Fair-trade principles apply, income accrues to the village communities which host the travellers, and a sense of equality between guest and host is nurtured. Groups are numerically small – this is genuine immersion tourism for participants.

Contact: Patrick Wasserman
Tel: +33 442964289
Email: contact@boutdumonde.eu
Web: www.boutdumonde.eu
Address: 1013 Chemin Mouret, 13100 Aix en Provence, France

VISION DU MONDE

Vision du Monde operates mainly in Morocco, Mali, Bulgaria, Peru and Mauritania, and to a lesser extent in Cambodia, Laos, Armenia and Brazil. The holidays offered are characterized by sharing local lifestyles and staying in the community. Groups are 12 maximum. Vision du Monde interests itself principally in projects linked with health, education and access to water. Each year it holds a reunion weekend when new and old clients can exchange memories and discuss what they have seen and done.

Contact: Laurent Besson
Tel: +33 474439182
Fax: +33 474934803
Email: contact@visiondumonde.org
Web: www.visiondumonde.org
Address: 3 route de Chambery, 38300 Bourgoin-Jallieu, France

TOUR OPERATORS

INTERNATIONAL VOLUNTEERING

The popularity of international volunteering, often referred to as the 'gap year', is extraordinary. Tourism Concern's research has identified 75 companies, both profit and non-profit, which are more than happy to help organize our trip. Our research was probably out of date as soon as we had finished it – such is the growth of this new industry.

Whatever our motivations for taking time away to help others, it's really important to ensure that the work that we will be doing has real value for those with whom we will be working and for. The last thing we want to do is take someone else's job and do it for free, pretend we can teach when we've never been trained – just because we can speak English – or do work that no one really wants or needs.

It is therefore very important, indeed, to check out the credentials of any company that you choose to go with. Tourism Concern has developed a code of practice for companies because our research uncovered the uncomfortable fact that too many companies don't interview the people they send or check them out if they're going to be working with children or vulnerable people. Many companies also fail to give training or induction or provide support in-country. It is also important to find a company that is open and transparent and prepared to let you know where your money will be going.

Please do ensure that your money is going to an appropriate home and that your chosen company is going to provide you with what you think you will need to feel comfortable and happy and productive.

Do ask lots of questions. Get a job description at the very least! You can find out more from the Ethical Volunteering Guide, which highlights seven questions to help you pick an ethical international volunteering placement: see the website www.ethicalvolunteering.org.

The volunteer groups listed have (as have all the listings in this guide) answered a detailed questionnaire about themselves.

VOL

CAMPS INTERNATIONAL

Camps International has an uncompromising commitment to social development and environmental protection in both Africa and Asia, and offers responsible travel experiences to adults, gap-year students and groups. International award winner, its business model has been created to maximize the benefits to the destination countries by committing year round to the projects, regardless of volunteer participation. With offices and fully staffed camps running in Kenya, Tanzania and Borneo, projects are run in cooperation with the indigenous communities and in harmony with the wildlife. Activities range from constructing school classrooms to supplying drinking water, assisting anti-poaching patrols, environmental education and marine workshops. In 2007, approximately 30 per cent of Camps International's gross turnover was spent in ways that benefit the planet. This figure exceeds annual net profits for every operating year to date.

Tel: +44 8448001127 · +254 403202946/7/8
Fax: +44 1425485398
Email: info@campsinternational.com
Web: www.campsinternational.com
Address: Unit 1, Kingfisher Park, Headlands Business Park, Salisbury Road, Blashford, Ringwood, Hampshire BH24 3NX, UK, or PO Box 2, Ukanda, Kwale, Kenya

TOUR OPERATORS

VOL
ECHOWAY

This French organization has been working since 2003 to promote tourism which respects both the environment and people. Its website provides information on all the projects they have embraced that conform to their criteria of ethical, ecological and fairly traded tourism. They specialize in Mexico and Central America, but they encompass the world in their search for good tourism practice.

Tel: +33 143735187
Email: info@echoway.org
Web: www.echoway.org
Address: Lionel Parra, 77 rue de Bagnolet, F-75020 Paris, France

VOL
GLOBAL VISION INTERNATIONAL

This volunteer organization sources volunteers to take part in sustainable conservation and community projects around the world. It also sets up, staffs and runs ten research expeditions globally. Volunteers fill a 'critical void' in the fields of environmental research, conservation, education and community development. The vast majority of volunteer money is spent in the field.

Contact: Karina Berg
Tel: +44 1727250250 · +353 1850885880
Fax: +44 1727840666
Email: info@gvi.co.uk · info@gvi-ireland.com
Web: www.gvi.co.uk
Address: 3 High Street, St. Albans, Hertfordshire AL3 4ED, UK

VOL
PEOPLE AND PLACES

The company's role is to recruit volunteers and match them to existing local projects in Africa and Asia. Community needs are paramount. The ECPAT (End Child Prostitution, Child Pornography and Trafficking of Children for Sexual Purposes) code is being adopted and all volunteers are checked by Criminal Records Bureau (CRB) or equivalent. Placements are individually priced and shown in each project's details. People and Places represents a new concept in responsible volunteering and has been recognized after just one year by the World Travel Market Responsible Tourism awards.

Contact: Kate Stefanko
Tel: +44 1795535718
Email: kate@travel-peopleandplaces.co.uk
Web: www.travel-peopleandplaces.co.uk
Address: 1 Naboths Nursery, Canterbury Road, Faversham, Kent ME13 8AX, UK

VOL
THE DIFFERENT TRAVEL COMPANY

This is a specialist volunteer and challenge tour operator who offers people opportunities to combine exciting travel opportunities with volunteering on overseas projects. It works with charities, schools, colleges and universities, sports teams, businesses and individuals looking for an exciting way to combine travel with volunteer work. It is an ATOL-registered company. As the name suggests, it is a travel company with a difference! Sometimes known as 'voluntourism', Different Travel is a tour operator that helps people from all over the world to combine the comfort and relaxation of a two-week holiday with great accommodation and sightseeing, with time spent volunteering in the host destination. It offers unique opportunities to work alongside local people on international development projects and to volunteer programmes in host countries in Asia, Africa and South America.

TOUR OPERATORS

Contact: Sarah Yalland
Tel: +44 2380488797
Email: info@different-travel.com
Web: www.different-travel.com
Address: Unit 2, Enterprise House, Ocean Village, Southampton, Hampshire SO14 3XB, UK

VOL
YOUTH ASSOCIATION OF ZAMBIA (YAZ)

This is not where you go if you want to sip wine under a million stars and dream of the Big Five tomorrow. This is a work and study camp organization that gives volunteers the chance to visit tourist sites during excursions. You will be working mainly on environmental outreach programmes and offering your skills to support their take-up, and you will be having an intercultural experience beyond measure. YAZ offers volunteers an orientation workshop on arrival (which you pay for) and this ensures that you receive '*a less shock, if any*' during your stay. Volunteers have the opportunity to be given a wide choice of camps in Zambia, which can be extended worldwide as YAZ is a member of many international workcamp networks.

Contact: Namatama Mulikelala
Tel: +260 977759444 • +260 955981994 • +260 977464630
Email: yazworkcamps@gmail.com
Address: PO Box 31852, Lusaka, Zambia

WORKCAMPS

We would also like to refer to the traditional 'workcamp movement' that bring about international understanding and sustainable development on a basis of community involvement, equality and exchange of volunteers.

There are workcamps (and 'medium-term' projects of three to six months) in many countries, including in Africa (Botswana, Ghana, Kenya, Lesotho, Malawi, Morocco, Mozambique, Nigeria, Tanzania, Togo, Uganda and Zambia); in Asia (India, Indonesia, Sri Lanka and Vietnam); in the Americas (Argentina, Ecuador, Mexico, Peru and the USA); and in most European countries.

Volunteers should apply through one of the sending organizations listed below. All sending and host organizations are non-profit making.

In the UK, check the websites and emails of:

- VINE (Voluntary International Network for Exchange a coordinating body): www.vine-uk.org;
- Volunteer Action for Peace: www.vap.org.uk – action@vap.org.uk;
- International Voluntary Service: www.ivsgb.org – info@ivsgb.org;
- United Nations Association (UNA) Exchange: www.unaexchange.org – info@unaexchange.org;
- Concordia: www.concordia-iye.org.uk – info@concordia-iye.org.uk;
- Exchange Scotland: www.xchangescotland.org – xchange.scotland@yahoo.com.

In Ireland, search out:

- Voluntary Service International: www.vsi.ie – vsi@iol.ie.

TOUR
OPERATORS

255

RESOURCES/ FURTHER READING

Books/articles

Clark, D. (2004) *The Rough Guide to Ethical Shopping*, Rough Guides Ltd, London
Balanced and non-prescriptive.

Duffy, R. (2002) *A Trip Too Far: Ecotourism, Politics and Exploitation*, Earthscan, London
Duffy's trenchant monograph leaves one in no doubt that abuses can sail under an eco-tourism flag of convenience and thereby remain undetected. She is very good on the impacts upon host communities.

Eber, S. (ed) (1992) *Beyond the Green Horizon: Principles for Sustainable Tourism*, WWF UK, Godalming
A discussion paper commissioned from Tourism Concern by WWF UK which may now be a little old, but which remains one of the best surveys of all the relevant issues.

Harrison, R., Newholm, T. and Shaw, D. (2005) *The Ethical Consumer*, Sage, London.
The authors investigate, and try to understand, the rise in ethical consumption.

Henson, R. (2006) *The Rough Guide to Climate Change*, Rough Guides Ltd, London
The symptoms, the science, the solutions. A book lauded by James Lovelock.

Hickman, L. (2005a) *A Good Life*, Eden Project Books in association with Guardian Books, London
A guide to ethical living.

Hickman, L. (2005b) *A Life Stripped Bare: My Year Trying to Live Ethically*, The Eden Project, London
At the request of the *Guardian* Hickman spent some months attempting to live a more ethical life – this is his diary of the struggle.

Hickman, L. (2007) *The Final Call: In Search of the True Cost of our Holidays*, Eden Project, London
The title is self-indicative. An important and serious investigative work by a top-class journalist into the impacts of tourism as experienced by people living in holiday destinations around the world. Also full of fascinating facts and an excellent chapter on global warming.

Higgins-Desbiolles, F. (2005) *Hostile Meeting Grounds: Encounters between the Wretched of the Earth and the Tourist through Tourism and Terrorism in the 21st Century, Perspectives in Tourism No 4*, ECOT China, Hong Kong SAR
This is a 'must read' for anyone concerned with the interaction between the tourist from the North with the South, although admittedly the author has an agenda as the quote from Frantz Fanon in the title testifies.

Honey, M. (2008) *Ecotourism and Sustainable Development: Who Owns Paradise?*, Island Press, Washington DC
A new edition of one of the best surveys of the issues.

Krippendorf, J. (1989) *The Holiday-Makers*, Butterworth-Heinemann, London
It has been said that if you read only one book about what drives modern tourism, then this should be it. Krippendorf makes one examine one's own lifestyle.

Luck, M. and Kirstges, T. (eds) (2003) *Global Ecotourism Policies and Case Studies: Perspectives and Constraints*, Channel View Publications (Current Themes in Tourism), Clevedon
Academic – but not excessively so – with, for example, accessible chapters on Latin American ecotourism, examining whether the Maasai can benefit from conservation, and community involvement in tourism around national parks.

Mowforth, M. and Munt, I. (2008) *Tourism and Sustainability: Development, Globalization, and New Tourism in the Third World*, 3rd edition, Routledge, London
This is an extremely good survey of all the issues.

Mowforth, M., Charlton, C. and Munt, I. (2007) *Tourism and Responsibility: Perspectives from Latin America and the Caribbean*, Routledge, London
Mowforth and his collaborators examine the relationship between tourism, responsibility, power and development.

Pattullo, P. (2005) *Last Resorts: The Cost of Tourism in the Caribbean*, 2nd edition, Latin America Bureau, London
Pattullo analyses the image of the Caribbean as tropical paradise and reveals the real impact of tourism upon the people and the landscape. She witnesses to the seamy underbelly of a corrupted society and a culture that has become a pitiful parody of its true self. A quote which forms part of one her chapter titles is chillingly accurate: 'Like an alien in we own land'.

Smirth, M. and Duffy, R. (2003) *The Ethics of Tourism Development*, Routledge (Contemporary Geographies of Leisure, Tourism and Mobility), London
Rights, sustainability, ethics of travelling, codes of conduct, host–guest relations – it's all here.

Spenceley, A. (ed) (2008) *Responsible Tourism: Critical Issues for Conservation and Development*, Earthscan, London
Perhaps rather academic, but a very useful collection of essays on the interface between tourism and development.

Tearfund (2002) *Worlds Apart: A Call to Responsible Global Tourism*, Tearfund, Teddington
'Tourism is like fire. You can cook your supper with it, but it can also burn your house down' – this anonymous aphorism emanating from someone in Asia conveys the philosophy of the report.

Weaver, D. B. (1998) *Ecotourism in the Less Developed World*, CAB International, Wallingford
Academic, but very susceptible to useful 'dipping'. Many countries are represented in this book.

Magazines

Libraries sometimes call these 'journals' or 'serials' – but 'magazines' will serve our turn.

Contours
Published quarterly by the Ecumenical Coalition on Third World Tourism and reflecting the aims of both Ecumenical Coalition on Tourism (ECOT) and Ecumenical Coalition on Third World Tourism (ECTWT); see the entry on ECOT in the section on 'Organizations and websites' below.

Ethical Consumer
Published in Manchester, this is the UK's only alternative consumer organization looking at the social and environmental records of the companies behind the brand names. The website address is www.ethicalconsumer.org.

In Focus
Published by Tourism Concern in London, this appeared as an academic quarterly for many years. It was relaunched in summer 2005 with a new format and is aimed at the tourist and traveller who share the aspirations of Tourism Concern.

Reports and articles

Eco and Ethical Tourism (2003) Mintel International Group Ltd, London
Among other topics, Mintel's report researches the growth of the ethical consumer movement, the increasing choice of ethical holidays, and the future of responsible tourism.

Ethical Holidays (2005) Mintel International Group Ltd, London
This report offers the user a way of fully understanding the UK ethical holidays market. Mintel estimates that in 2005 the UK ecotourism market adds up to about 450,000 holidays a year.

Weeden, C. (2004) 'Ethical tourism: An exploration of the concept and its meaning for ethical and responsible tourists', paper presented at the University of Strathclyde, June 2004

Holiday Lifestyles: Responsible Tourism (2007) Mintel International Group Ltd, London
A more recent survey with a self-descriptive title.

Plane Truths: Do the Economic Arguments for Aviation Really Fly? (2008) World Development Movement/New Economics Foundation, London
International tourism is more of a risk than a benefit to developing nations.

Goodwin, H. and Francis, J. (2003) 'Ethical and responsible tourism: Consumer trends in the UK', *Journal of Vacation Marketing*, vol 9, no 3, pp271–284
Examines the growth in the numbers of people prepared to pay a little more for an ethical holiday and the evidence for increasing demand for responsible tourism.

Kalisch, A. (2001) *Tourism as Fair Trade: NGO Perspectives*, Tourism Concern, London
Without fair and ethical trade practice, it is not possible to achieve sustainable tourism – host communities must have a fair return on their investments in order to be able to reinvest in the social and environmental regeneration of their communities.

Tourism Concern (2005) *Behind the Smile: The Tsunami of Tourism* (2005) Tourism Concern, London
A booklet that accompanied the photo exhibition of the same title and which was part of the Tourism Concern campaign Sun, Sand, Sea and Sweatshops, which revealed the poverty trap in which so many hotel workers around the world are caught by reason of their poor working conditions.

Statistics

The principal statistics published in the tourism field emanate, not surprisingly, from the United Nations World Tourism Organization (UNWTO) in Geneva. Chief among them is the *Yearbook of Annual Statistics*. Like all such yearbooks, its 'fault' is the timelag in publication.

UNWTO also publishes a statistical series entitled *Tourism Market Trends*, within which data are published for the following areas of the world: Africa, Americas, Asia, East Asia and the Pacific, Europe, Middle East, and South Asia. The caveat about publication timelag applies also to these publications.

Health matters

Beeching, D. and Lorie, J. (eds) (2000) *The Traveller's Healthbook: The Pocket Guide to Worldwide Health*, 2nd edition, WEXAS International, London
All the nasties are here; but to quote the first words of the introduction, 'don't panic' because so are the ways to avoid them.

Jones, N. (2004) *The Rough Guide to Travel Health*, Rough Guides Ltd (A Rough Guide special), London
Written and researched by Dr Nick Jones and others, this covers all the bases – as do all their publications.

WHO (World Health Organization) (2005) *International Travel and Health* (2005) WHO Press, Geneva
'... intended to give guidance on the full range of significant health issues associated with travel'. A printed edition appears every second year, but an internet version allows ongoing updating and has links to other information on, for example, disease outbreaks (www.who.int/ith).

Wilson-Howarth, J. (1999) *Bugs, Bites and Bowels*, Cadogan Guides, London
Written with humour but an efficient survey of the field.

Finally, do not forget that the *Form E111* has been replaced by the European Health Insurance Card. Further information is available from any Branch Post Office. The URL for information, which incorporates the facility to apply online, is www.dh.gov.uk/PolicyAndGuidance/HealthAdviceForTravellers/fs/en.

Guides

The Green Guide
This extremely useful guide is published separately for England, Scotland and Wales. There are frequent revisions. There is a very good website at www.greenguide.co.uk.

Khaneka, P. (2004) *Do the Right Things! A Practical Guide to Ethical Living*, New Internationalist Publications Ltd, Oxford
This is committed campaigning material – but put together with style and humour.

If you should feel impelled, for some reason, to investigate the published literature of tourism, you will need a *vade mecum* or, if you prefer, a 'how to find out in tourism' book. In which, case seek out the following:
Scarrott, M. (1999) *Sport, Leisure and Tourism Information Sources: A Guide for Researchers*, Butterworth Heinemann, Oxford
This may be 'getting on' in years, but is still the best print resource of its type. It may be aimed primarily at the university researcher; but anyone digging around in the tourism literature should be aware of it.

Organizations and websites

Notwithstanding the daily miracles worked by search engines such as Google, some websites merit a place in even such a brief survey as this.

AITO www.aito.co.uk/
The Association of Independent Tour Operators (AITO) has over 150 members and is the first tourism industry association to incorporate a commitment to responsible tourism in its business charter. Its five key objectives are to protect the environment; respect local cultures; benefit local communities; conserve natural resources; and minimize pollution.

Foreign and Commonwealth Office (FCO)
www.fco.gov.uk/en/travelling-and-living-overseas/
Know before You Go from the Foreign and Commonwealth Office (FCO) is an ongoing travel safety campaign that encourages British nationals to be better prepared for their overseas trips.

Bluewater Network http://bluewaternetwork.org/campaign_ss_cruises.shtml
Bluewater works to move the cruise industry to protect the oceans and to take responsibility for the pollution and waste created by cruise liners. It has also led an environmental coalition in campaigning for new regulations to monitor cruise-ship waste.

EcoTravel.com www.ecotravel.com
This is a searchable directory of travel organizations with information about their eco-philosophy and practices. Its mission is to build a community of 'eco-travellers' wedded to responsible tourism.

EchoWay www.echoway.org
This French organization promotes tourism that respects both the environment and people. The website informs fully about projects which it has embraced and which conform to its criteria of ethical, ecological and fairly traded tourism. It publicizes examples of good tourism practice on a worldwide basis. Note: the language of the site is French.

ECOT www.ecotonline.org

ECOT (Ecumenical Coalition on Tourism) is a Thailand-based coalition seeking to unite people around efforts to negate the undesirable effects of modern tourism by putting in its place socially responsible and ethically oriented tourism. It believes that justice and sustainability for host communities are paramount and it campaigns for the human rights of women, children, indigenous peoples and workers in the tourist trade. ECOT also opposes tourism projects that create environmental devastation. It produces a campaigning magazine, *Contours*.

ECPAT www.ecpat.org.uk

ECPAT is an international network of organizations and individuals bent on eliminating the commercial sexual exploitation of children, including within tourism. The acronym stands for End Child Prostitution, Child Pornography and Trafficking of Children for Sexual Purposes.

Equations www.equitabletourism.org

Equations is an Indian non-profit organization established for research, training and awareness-raising. It questions the real benefits of tourism to host communities as well as the socio-cultural economic impacts. Its vision is of tourism that fits within a world structure where wealth and benefits are distributed more equitably between North and South, and where tourism is just one more way to work towards a more just world.

North South Travel www.northsouthtravel.co.uk

North South Travel is a travel agency offering worldwide discounted fares; but unlike others the profits are all channelled to projects in Africa, Asia and Latin America through its charity, the NST Development Trust.

Planeta www.planeta.com

Planeta is a 'global journal of practical ecotourism' and Planeta.com is a virtual library that archives thousands of pages about ecotourism and conservation. It looks at the whole world of practical ecotourism. The mantra is: think smart; travel slow. It is the first website to have focused on ecotourism, conservation and conscientious travel around the globe.

Responsible Travel.com www.responsibletravel.com

Responsible Travel is a tour operator marketing holidays that care passionately about the environment and local people.

Stuff Your Rucksack www.stuffyourrucksack.com

A quite new site founded by BBC reporter Kate Humble: if you'd known what to take to help a school when you set out …

Third World Network (TWN) www.twnside.org.sg/

TWN is an independent non-profit international network involved in matters relating to development, the developing world and North–South issues.

Tourism Investigation and Monitoring Team (tim-team)

An independent research and monitoring initiative founded in 1994 to próvide information for public use and to campaign for social and ecological justice in tourism and development. Tourism is treated in a developmental and environmental context. It publishes the newsletter *New Frontiers*, which highlights issues of tourism, development and the environment in the Southeast Asia Mekong sub-region. Email tim-team@access.inet.co.th

The Travel Foundation www.thetravelfoundation.org.uk/

The Travel Foundation is a UK charity that aims to help the tourism industry arrive at a happy marriage of profitability and sustainability. It hopes to safeguard both the environment and the well-being of host communities.

About Tourism Concern

Tourism Concern is an independent NGO campaigning against exploitation and human rights abuses in the world's largest industry: tourism. Founded in 1989, Tourism Concern began life as an informal network of passionate and dedicated individuals who wanted to do something constructive about the exploitation of people and places by the rapidly expanding global tourism industry. This network linked people in the UK with similar organizations elsewhere in the world at a time when the impacts of tourism were barely on the radar of the industry and the travelling public.

Two decades on, with a diverse membership, Tourism Concern remains the only organization in Europe actively campaigning against tourism's exploitative practices. It continues to work tirelessly to expose, challenge and raise awareness around these issues, nurturing a vision of tourism in which relationships between industry, tourists and host communities are based on mutual trust and respect. Tourism Concern plays a crucial role in promoting forms of tourism that provide meaningful benefits to people in destination countries. Through its collaborative efforts with campaigning groups, the tourism industry, governments and international bodies, Tourism Concern pioneers solutions to the challenges posed by the global tourism industry, particularly those centring on fair trade and sustainability. This Ethical Travel Guide is one of the tools developed by the organization, providing a vital means for small-scale community-based tourism initiatives in destination countries to market themselves to a wider audience.

Tourism Concern fulfils a unique role by responding to requests for help from individuals, communities and groups from all over the world, particularly in the global South, who are challenging threats to their human rights posed by the development of tourism. Tourism Concern collaborates with local groups in over 20 destination countries, working to ensure that otherwise marginalized voices and concerns are heard in the UK and beyond, bringing international pressure to bear on issues that would, in many cases, go unnoticed by the international community. It provides capacity-building and campaigning support to its partners, and develops longer-term campaigns around the issues raised. Labour conditions, displacement from ancestral lands, loss of access to natural resources, water rights, restrictions on freedom of movement, and the objectification of indigenous communities have all been taken up by Tourism Concern over the last 20 years. This involves sustained lobbying of governments, industry and international trade and tourism bodies. Tourism Concern also raises awareness amongst holiday-makers of tourism-related issues, encouraging tourists to 'avoid guilt trips' by challenging their perceptions about the cultures that they visit and the impacts of their holiday upon local communities and environments.

Tourism Concern's efforts have been the catalysts for much positive change. For example, following its ground-breaking campaign Trekking Wrongs: Porter's Rights, over half of trekking tour operators in the UK subscribed to Tourism Concern's code of conduct for improved working conditions for mountain porters. The UK's leading tour operators adopted policies on labour conditions for hotels included in their holiday packages as a result of Tourism Concern's Sun, Sand, Sea and Sweatshops campaign. The UK's Foreign and Commonwealth Office, prompted by lobbying from Tourism Concern, established a permanent multi-stakeholder panel to ensure that destinations are not adversely affected by unnecessarily prolonged or geographically far-reaching travel advisories warning tourists not to visit. At destination level, plans for a massive tourism development in the Nungwi Peninsula in Zanzibar, which threatened to displace 20,000 people, were scrapped as a result of Tourism Concern's campaigning efforts.

With the continued exponential growth of tourism and the myriad of new challenges arising around climate change, the economic slowdown and widespread 'greenwashing' within the tourism industry, the role of Tourism Concern as watchdog, whistleblower and pathfinder is more vital than ever. Its goal of building a global movement representing fairly traded sustainable tourism is gathering pace. For further information and to become a part of this movement, visit www.tourismconcern.org.uk.

INDEX

Without your support, Tourism Concern's work would not be possible!

Please support us! www.tourismconcern.org.uk

Please fill in your details here:

I would like to make a donation: £ _____

I would like to become a Tourism Concern member:

☐ UK waged £24   ☐ UK unwaged £15

☐ I would like to find out more about Tourism Concern's campaigns

Name   _____

Address   _____

Post code   _____

Telephone   _____

Email   _____

Occupation/course   _____

How did you hear about Tourism Concern? _____

☐ I enclose a cheque/postal order made payable to Tourism Concern or

☐ Please debit my: Visa /MasterCard/other_____

Card no   _____

Expiry date   _____

Cardholder's name   _____

Or to pay by standing order, please complete this form (UK ONLY):
You can cancel a standing order at any time by notifying us and your bank.

Bank name   _____

Bank address   _____

Post code   _____

Sort code   _____

Account no   _____

Account name   _____

Signature   _____

Date   _____

Please pay Tourism Concern (tick chosen amount)

Waged: Monthly ☐ £2 (minimum) Annually ☐ £24

Unwaged: Monthly ☐ £2 (minimum) Annually ☐ £15

Other amount: ☐ £_____ per month/year

To start on_____/_____/_____ until further notice.

Please allow 1 month from signature date.

Signature   _____

Instruction to your bank: Please pay the above amount to

Co-operative Bank, PO Box 250, Delf House Southway,
Skelmersdale WN8 6WT, UK

Sort code: 08-92-99; Account no: 65130397

Please return to Tourism Concern, Stapleton House, 277-281 Holloway Rd,
London N7 8BR

Gift Aid makes your donation worth more.

For every £1.00 you give, we can claim 25p from the Inland Revenue. I am a UK
taxpayer – please claim Gift Aid on my donation and any I may make in the
future until I notify you otherwise.

Signature   _____   Date   _____